PatrICK
mCGOOHan

DANGER MAN OR PRISONER?

Roger Langley

First published in 2007 by
Tomahawk Press
PO Box 1236
Sheffield S11 7XU
England

www.tomahawkpress.com

© Roger Langley 2007

ISBN-10: 0-9531926-4-4
ISBN-13: 978-0-9531926-4-9

Edited by Bruce Sachs
Designed by Steve Kirkham – Tree Frog Communication 01245 445377

Printed in the EU by Gutenberg Press Limited on environmentally friendly paper.

Picture Credits

A catalogue record for this book is available from the British Library.

Disclaimer
The best information and sources have been relied upon in respect of events and records from several decades ago. If any error exists, the publishers would welcome notification, for correction in any later edition or an addendum.

For Karen, who took me prisoner

Foreword
by Peter Falk

I realize this is a book on Pat McGoohan. However, we're friends and I'm sure Pat wouldn't mind my using this space to plug a book about me that I wrote about myself. There's a quote in that book – it goes likes this:

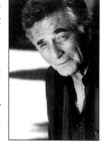

>   I sent the script of "Agenda for Murder" to a man who I considered the most underrated, under-appreciated talent on the face of the globe.
>   The first two times that he appeared on **Columbo**, he won Emmys for "Best Performance by a Guest Star in a TV series." No character in the history of television has had that honor.
>   His name is Pat McGoohan. He starred in, directed, and wrote for the show. The **Columbo** franchise, myself, Universal Studios, and the NBC Network are indebted to Pat McGoohan for his huge contribution to the show's success.
>   Incidentally, in all my years I have never played a scene with another actor who commanded my attention the way Pat did.

PETER FALK
Hollywood

Just One More Thing: Stories From My Life, Peter Falk, 2006, published by Carroll & Graf, USA.

Introduction

For more than fifty years, Patrick McGoohan's screen and personal image has been that of a tough guy, a reputation heightened by his straight talking and strong scruples. His numerous stage and cinema roles have bestowed on him that rare 'star quality' status, a rating he would detest. To say that he has played many parts applies as much to his career as it does to the several different chapters of his life. This biography of the actor – the first to appear and long overdue – covers all of his films, television appearances and theatre engagements. These are presented across twelve chapters: "Six of one, half a dozen of the other," to use a catchphrase from his famous *Prisoner* television series.[i]

McGoohan is regarded by many as being among the greatest British actors of all time. Despite his Irish parentage and dual American passport – he having been born in New York – it is the actor's many years on the British stage and screen which place him in a 'top ten' – allowing for some latitude with nationalities – of his peers: Richard Burton, Albert Finney, John Gielgud, Alec Guinness, Richard Harris, Anthony Hopkins, Laurence Olivier, Peter O' Toole and Ralph Richardson, listed alphabetically. McGoohan would often adopt a semi-American accent, enabling him to appear in drama and adventure films, or television series, for consumption in both the United Kingdom and United States. Although usually termed a British actor, the past three decades have seen McGoohan residing in the United States and the actor has described himself to journalists as "an American." However, his origins – important to himself of course – matter less to those who greatly appreciate his work; his appeal has spread throughout Europe and North America, to the Far East, Australia and New Zealand.

From a humble start, doing odd jobs at a Sheffield, England repertory theatre, McGoohan progressed to leading stage roles and moved into London's West End. The movie industry beckoned and before long Hollywood was knocking at his door. However, some sources claim that the actor's 1967 cult television series *The Prisoner* gave its star acclaim, but an anvil to bear. Although McGoohan's classic show extended the traditional TV action-adventure format into undreamed of social, political and

---

[i] Heard in the episodes *Arrival* and *Free for All*.

psychological realms, *The Prisoner* did not turn out to be a career springboard for the actor at the end of the sixties.

In conversation with this writer, McGoohan has expressed views that, over the years, too many people have said too much about *The Prisoner*. Such pronouncements have been to his annoyance, as only he knows the full facts behind the series and, additionally, some people have taken credit for contributions which were not due. In particular, the actor stressed that the use of Portmeirion for *The Prisoner* was his choice and his alone. Admittedly, he has at times been less than forthcoming with his comments about the series. Accordingly, in the absence of the star being an available source, other people have been questioned, possibly being seen by him as purporting to know things which they did not. Some have said that they injected ideas, or wrote a particular scene, or chose a location. McGoohan has been irritated by certain claims, although, understandably, reminiscences and 'inside stories' are expected from actors or crew members when being interviewed and recounting production stories.

On occasions, McGoohan has sensed being unable to escape from his cult TV series, feeling 'imprisoned' by an undue amount of claustrophobic fan attention. While the actor's acceptance of all forms of genuine appreciation of his work is not in doubt, his wish to shy away from a more concentrated circling of fans is certain. In these respects and in many others, McGoohan is a true enigma – the very reason he remains a source of fascination and continuing discussion. Now, for the first time, the actor's views – on claims by others as to their contribution, their *Prisoner* interpretations, or even declarations as to the 'meaning' or 'message' of the series – appear in this book.

This biography contains chapters dedicated to *The Prisoner* phenomenon, but there are places in subsequent chapters where the series will once more raise its head. Frequently, fellow actors and other celebrities have continued to provide opinions in later years and so these sometimes appear at a time contemporary with other events going on in McGoohan's career and life. Also included at some points are comments from *Prisoner* fans and organisers of the appreciation society for the series, Six of One. The North Wales resort of Portmeirion and the society have together caused the profile of the cult series to remain high, during the past three decades and the views of *Prisoner* enthusiasts are as vital as those of any critic, or commentator.

There are many periods between 1960 and 1970 when McGoohan was either filming episodes of *Danger Man*, or *The Prisoner*, or was promoting one of these series. As both shows were screened at different times in the UK, USA and around the world, there was a fair degree of overlap in press reports. Sometimes, a newspaper or magazine would be reviewing an episode, or heralding the new series, while another interviewer would be talking to McGoohan while he was on set, or on location filming. With a few other cinema and TV items also occurring during this period, it would often be the case that a conversation with the actor covered a number of different screen topics. Equally, some interviews regarding *Danger Man* (called *Secret Agent* in the USA and *Destination Danger* in France) would appear after a recent feature on the latest series *The Prisoner* had already been published. However, the aim of this biography has been to maintain a chronological order, as far as possible.

Often, the influence of McGoohan is reflected through the comments of others. Accordingly this book has three primary sources of content: interviews with the actor across the years; the opinions and experiences of others who saw or worked with him; this writer's own contact and dealings with him and other actors, or production team members, over twenty five years. In the seventies, McGoohan and his family took up permanent residence in the USA. Fortunately, for this writer,[ii] he kept in contact with his fans back in Britain. Firstly, he became Honorary President of the *Prisoner* appreciation society and secondly, he sent letters, faxes and cards at various intervals. He also telephoned this writer over the years, including communications during his occasional visits to England.

As will be seen later, during McGoohan's most concentrated period of stage, cinema and television work, he was receiving high praise and honours, directed at his acting prowess. Words like "definitive" were used in respect of his performances and by the time the sixties decade was well established, the actor had become a household name. The Rank Organisation-groomed star, whose face stared back from many a photo portrait, was the highest-paid actor on television. Unusually, for a major player, McGoohan projected the contrasting image of a clean-living family man and could seemingly do no wrong. It appeared that he wanted to discover every aspect of his craft, from directing to writing, acting to producing, or even taking on other projects, either collaborating, or co-financing. Did this therefore indicate that McGoohan needed constant and demanding substitutes for the high life, which he had always refused to live and perhaps to some extent had missed? His outspoken condemnation of liberalism often set him apart from the evolving free-living and free-loving society within each new generation.

This book is in praise of the actor and his many achievements. In accordance with his frequently expressed wishes, there are no incursions into unpublicised areas of his personal life. A long and happy marriage – of more than fifty years' duration and of the non-show business type – and McGoohan's dismissal of the celebrity lifestyle have often left the actor out of the spotlight, which is undoubtedly where he prefers to be. And yet there have been occasions when dramatic stories about the star have emerged, probably because there was so little opportunity over the years to present him as a hell-raiser.

Whether McGoohan is remembered as a great actor, or the sum of his idiosyncratic parts, he will always rightly command respect in screen and stage history, as much as he has compelled attention over half a century. He is sometimes tritely labelled as "the man who turned down James Bond." However, it is only when one looks back over his many years in the public eye that it becomes clear how much he achieved. Fellows and colleagues would say that he was unstoppable and would be up at 4.30 a.m. ready to work and would go on pushing himself into the night, while others gave up, exhausted, around him.

The actor also displayed strong religious convictions and an almost crusading attitude towards the industry in which he worked, plus public morals. On screen, after some early film parts, he would not enter into an embrace – certainly not a bedroom scene with a leading lady – as he was a faithful, married man. He chose not be involved in portrayals of violence, nor would he fire a gun in a gratuitous act of killing, a style which was becoming prominent in mid-twentieth century 'hard' movies and 'Spaghetti' westerns. The actor has always ruthlessly protected his family from media attention. Domestic photographs of him, his wife and three daughters are thin on the ground, outside of the McGoohan household. However, a selection of candid photographs and a number of documents are reproduced as illustrations in this book.

---

ii See Appendix Six for information about the writer

At the time of this book, the actor is nearing his eightieth birthday. This biography reveals his extensive life and work, exploring the enigma that is McGoohan. By the end of the story it might seem that he has lived several different lives in succession, with possibly none of them being the one which he would have designed for himself. Ultimately, the question must be asked "What is Patrick McGoohan most remembered for?" The answers will emerge as the chapters ahead take a look at the different stages of his career. To sum up the actor's tough image on and off screen, it is apt to use a metaphor relating to his school days, when he acquired his boxing skills: McGoohan has always punched above his weight.

ROGER LANGLEY
Autumn, 2007

The appendices to this biography contain all of McGoohan's screen productions and theatrical work (with a separate section of incorrect and unconfirmed entries). There are synopses of his cinema films, made-for-television movies and TV series, so that less action and plot details are needed in the main text. Media review extracts are used at various points in the book, to provide brief details of a film, with the appendices offering a fuller, chronological reference source. Sometimes shooting was done a year or more before the cinema release date. The writer has endeavoured to use the most reliable reference sources available, and has provided details which are verified to the best of his knowledge. However, as this is the first biography of the actor, if an error or omission is found, it would be appreciated if the publishers could be informed and any revisions which are used in a later edition will be credited. Finally, many pictures of McGoohan have been seen in books and magazine articles during the past half century, but this book presents ones which have not been published before, or have not appeared often. The quality of some images reflects their age and condition, or that the source material could not be improved upon.

CHAPTER ONE
New York's Finest

"Grandeur is not an illusion, it is a birthright."
Hysteria (1998)

Patrick Joseph McGoohan was the first child and only son born to his Irish parents, Thomas (Tommy) McGoohan and Rose Patricia, née Fitzpatrick, who both came from County Leitrim.[i] Thomas, one of a family of thirteen, lived and worked at the McGoohan farm, passed down to him by his father and grandfather before him, in the small townland of Mullaghmore.[ii] Along a cart track stood the holding of forty mixed acres, with its single storey cottage, yard and sloping garden. Rose, a dressmaker and tailor, hailed from nearby Drumshanbo North and, despite being in a family of sixteen, was the one who was always laughing and being the centre of attention.

In the Leitrim Census of 1901, there is no primary listing for any McGoohans at their family farm.[iii] The head of the household is shown as Thomas Roarke, aged eighty seven. His wife Kate, aged fifty nine, is listed, along with nephew Patrick McGoohan, aged forty two – the grandfather of the subject of this biography – and his wife, also called Kate, aged thirty eight. The other members of the McGoohan family are given as Matthew aged twenty, John, sixteen, Ellen, thirteen, Kate eleven, Anne, eight, Maggie, six, Bridget, four and lastly, Thomas, aged two.[iv]

Turning to the Fitzpatricks, the family is shown in the Census of 1901 as living in the Townland of Drumshanbo North,[v] about three miles, as the crow flies, south west of the McGoohan farm. The head of the household is listed as James Fitzpatrick, aged thirty nine,

---

[i] Four daughters would also be born to them: Patricia, Kathleen, Marie and Annette.
[ii] McGoohan, the actor, in later interviews would refer to the family home as "Mullhehmore," or what he said was incorrectly reported. He also would describe how his ancestors had farmed there for four centuries.
[iii] In the Townland of Mullaghmore, Parish of Killarga, in the Barony of Carigallen.
[iv] Son of Patrick and future father of his actor son of the same name. Some biographical writings and Internet sources incorrectly refer to a different Thomas McGoohan.
[v] In the Parish of Cloone, Barony of Mohill. The place is also sometimes referred to as Drumshambo.

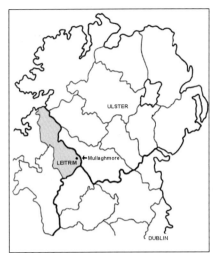

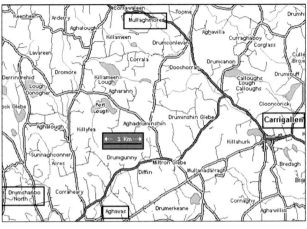

Northern Ireland and the county of Leitrim, below the Irish border

a farmer, along with his wife Rose, aged twenty eight.[vi] The other named occupants are given as Charles, aged three, Michael, two, Maggie, six months and grandmother, Margaret, aged eighty six.

In the twenties, the young Thomas McGoohan and Rose Fitzpatrick first met, although they did not immediately start courting. This was subsequently put to rights at a local dance – despite Rose being partnered by another Leitrim lad – where her future husband was playing fiddle in the band. When the musicians struck up the jig 'Haste to the Wedding', Thomas decided that he was not going to play it, but was instead going to act upon it. He put down his instrument and whisked his intended away from the rival.[1] Rose was described years later by her son as "the blue-eyed russet-haired pride of Drumshanbo and Thomas the equally blue-eyed blade who won her."[2]

The couple were married on Monday 8th June, 1925, at the Roman Catholic Church of Aughavas – sometimes referred to as Aghavas – in the adjoining district of Carrigallen. After less than four months since their wedding, the McGoohans made the difficult decision to leave farming behind and to search for better-paid work in America.[vii] They sailed on the White Star Line's steam ship Adriatic,[viii] from Liverpool to New York, on Saturday, 26th September. Thomas was recorded on the passenger list as a farmer and Rose a housewife, aged twenty six and twenty two. Their parents were noted as Thomas McGoohan, Mullaghmore, Leitrim and James Fitzpatrick, Drumshambo, Cloone, Leitrim. Both Tommy and Rose were classed as "read" and coming from the Irish Free State.

The young emigrants travelled steerage, a low cost option which enabled 'third class' passengers to make transatlantic crossings. The voyage was endured on one of the lowest decks, offering cramped facilities, little privacy and basic food. After ten days at sea, the

---

[vi] Their daughter, who would also be given the name Rose and marry Thomas McGoohan, had not yet been born.

[vii] To note a contemporary event, as the couple's departure from their native country was occurring, across the Irish sea an architect was acquiring a private peninsula of land, in North Wales, which would twice become used by McGoohan as a filming location in later years, for his TV series Danger Man and The Prisoner. This overgrown piece of coastline was transformed by its owner, Clough Williams-Ellis (later knighted) into the fantasy 'village' of Portmeirion, taking several decades to complete.

[viii] Her maiden voyage was from Liverpool to New York on 8 May, 1907 and she remained in service until 1934. In 1919 her passenger accommodation was changed to 400 first class, 465 second class and 1,320 steerage.

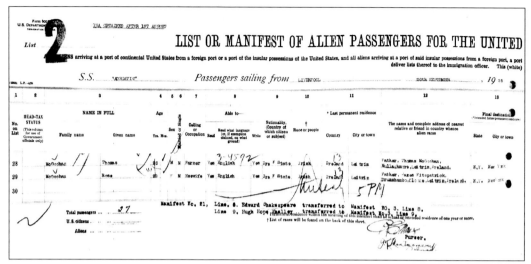

Above: Ship's passenger list, 1925.
Right: White Star Line Steam Ship Adriatic

McGoohans disembarked onto American soil[ix] on Monday, 5th October, taking up residence in the New York borough of Astoria, in the borough of Queens.[x] Thomas was soon at work, digging ditches, having found well-paid employment with the Edison Electric Light Company.[xi] Meanwhile, Rose gained work as a seamstress, in the dressmaking department of Macy's department store.[xii] Five of her brothers were already New York policemen and as many McGoohans had also previously emigrated from Ireland to the city.

Thomas and Rose were saving as much of their earnings as possible, although they were becoming resigned to the belief that they were not going to be blessed with children. However, good fortune was to visit them and by the middle of 1927 they were at last expecting their first child. At the end of her pregnancy, Rose went into St. John's Hospital, on Jackson Avenue and 12th Street, Astoria. In the early hours of Monday, 19th March, 1928, Patrick Joseph was born there, his blue eyes inherited from both parents, along with his mother's temperament. The presence of a child and the consequent lessening of working opportunities meant that when Patrick was six months old, his parents decided that they should return to Ireland. The money which had been accumulated by them in the United States proved useful back in their home country, supporting a new attempt at making the

[ix] Arriving through Ellis Island – situated at the mouth of the Hudson River – being at that time the immigration station for foreign persons entering the United States.
[x] By the 1920s, Irish immigrants founded many Catholic parishes in Astoria. Rose's aunt Mary lived on 19th Street, near Astoria Park and possibly Thomas and Rose stayed with her when they first arrived in the district.
[xi] The Edison company was founded in New York in 1878 and later employed thousands of people into the early twentieth century. An incorrect account has appeared: "(McGoohan said) that his father had worked for Brooklyn Union Gas for 45 years, and when he died the company treated his family very well." New York Press, 8-14th November. 2006, Jim Knipfel.
[xii] Macy's was founded in 1851 and transferred to New York in 1858. When the company later moved to Broadway, their enormous store occupied an entire block and was the largest in the world.

Mullaghmore farm successful, along with the hope of raising more children.

New York Astoria borough of Queens, also showing Edison Power Plant nearby

For the next eight years Thomas tended the soil – while Rose continued to do dressmaking work – taking his produce by pony and trap to Carigallen, or livestock, by horse and cart, to the larger markets of Carrick-on-Shannon and Mohill. Patrick's early years in Ireland were "rich in the simplicity and disciplines of country life."[3] He later expressed nostalgia for the family farm, its tall hay barn, stout white cottage homestead, with thatched roof and fat, rambling roses which covered the garden wall. He recalled how, during summer "their scent used to filter indoors, where it mingled with all the other smells part of childhood, peat fires, oatmeal cooking, animals and new-mown hay."[4] The Roman Catholic faith came before everything in the family. Patrick – always called Patrick Joseph by his mother – at a future time would recall, "(Rose) wanted me to be a priest. I was a late arrival by Irish standards – they'd been married several years – and I think she made a sort of bargain that she would give me to God. I didn't complete it and she was disappointed, but never minded my becoming an actor."[5] Of his father, Patrick revealed, "(He) had ten shillings in one pocket and a change of collar in the other."[6] On another occasion he would reflect: "My father couldn't read or write, but he played the violin like an angel and had total recall."[7]

Despite the best efforts by Thomas to make a decent living from the farm, he was forced to accept that the holding offered no real future for the family. The bold decision was made by him to leave Ireland once more, this time for the north of England, to take up employment in the building trade. Sheffield, Yorkshire, in 1938, was to offer a new start for the McGoohans, albeit a modest one.[xiii] The city – one of the eight largest ones in Britain, with a population of half a million – was renowned for its production of steel and silver plating. The McGoohans' first home there was a modest terraced house, located in Fulwood, a suburb two miles from the city centre. Here, the family experienced the general hardship which came with poverty. At the age of nine, Patrick had to help make his own clothes, as did his younger sisters. However, close family ties and strong Catholic values ensured that the McGoohans managed to overcome their difficult start in Britain. When Patrick began attending Sheffield's St. Vincent's Roman Catholic School[xiv] in Solly Street,[xv] he at last shared his mother's ambition for him to become a priest. The boy would stand proudly on a chair and deliver his sermons to a captive congregation, in the form of his sisters and parents.

"Growing up in Sheffield was one of the greatest experiences of my life," McGoohan later acknowledged.[8] "It was a town of steel works, but it had a truly artistic life. In fact, it was a tremendous place to grow up in."[9] The move from Ireland was recalled by him: "We went to a narrow terraced house in Sheffield, where my father had found work with a building contractor. For me, there began what I chose to regard as the monotonous penance of school days, coupled with several years of illness. I developed acute bronchial asthma. All I can

---

[xiii] The journey began from Dublin, continuing by sea to Holyhead, where a ferry transported the family to the mainland.

[xiv] Patrick reportedly had an earlier spell at St. Marie's school, on the Fulwood Road.

[xv] The church next door also ran the youth club, where Patrick's introduction to acting occurred.

Top Left: Thomas and Rose
McGoohan. Top Right: Rose
McGoohan with son Patrick, shortly
after returning to Ireland in 1928.
Left: Patrick, aged ten, with his sisters
in Sheffield, Annette (in white coat),
Patricia (in school hat) and Marie
(All pictures © Drummond
Enterprises Ltd. and Odhams Press,
1965)

remember is a stream of different doctors coming to my small bedroom, the smell of camphorated oil, inhalants and a perpetual cough. The War began when I was eleven and as a result, I, my mother and my sisters were evacuated to different homes in Loughborough, Leicestershire, leaving my father in Sheffield."[xvi] [10]

Despite having endured four years of illness and missed school terms, Patrick's natural aptitude for figures led to his being selected for a free place at the Catholic Public School, Ratcliffe College,[xvii] in Leicestershire. To his parents, the scholarship, the first in the family, was worth all their hard work and frugality. For the next five years, their eldest would live in an imposing red-walled building, up a long drive, with a few hundred other boys. Although he despised lessons and games, fortunately he was able to pick up maths quickly.[11]

At least the antiseptic fresh air was a curative environment for Patrick's asthma and there was an added dimension: "By the time I was twelve and ready to go to Ratcliffe, my sense of vocation for the priesthood was the dominating influence in my life. I was about as inflexible, arrogant and stubborn as any twelve year old boy could be – a really awkward little cuss. I refused to conform or participate in any way and this went on for two years. At home I would sulk, refusing to speak. The general discomfort this caused in our cheerful, talkative

xvi Thomas McGoohan became gardener and caretaker at the Convent of Notre Dame, on the outskirts of Sheffield.
xvii Some sources say that McGoohan went to the De La Salle school in Sheffield, but the organisation told this writer that they have no such record. Also, the age of McGoohan in Ratcliffe's records would contradict reports that he was at De La Salle as a teenager.

home was known to my sisters as 'One of Pat's Days.' Sometimes they endured as many as three or four of 'Pat's Days' in a row."[12] The sullen scholar spent the war years at Ratcliffe College. The establishment was founded mid-nineteenth century, having its own resident community of boarders, priests and gardeners, even with its own graveyard. In due course, Patrick joined the school boxing team and later became its captain, entitling him to sport a blazer with added piping. Straw boaters were worn by sixth formers and the boating team.[xviii]

At Ratcliffe, Patrick's grasp of mathematics increased, but his health excluded him from taking part in more energetic pursuits. He did not excel in general academic subjects, but showed signs of promise. While tutors struggled to develop the few nascent skills they deemed Patrick to possess, their unwilling charge grew isolated and became withdrawn. The task of drawing out the young man's introverted character fell upon another pupil, Jacques Whittington.[xix] He too had been a 'loner' and together the adolescent pair lifted each other's spirits. Patrick found a genuine interest in his school colleague and at last started to participate more in what Ratcliffe had to offer, as well as making greater effort in college pursuits. He began to grow in confidence and his self-indulgent silences disappeared. Patrick and Jacques went to each other's homes in the holidays. They made a pact that if Jacques ever married, Patrick would perform the ceremony. However, by the age of fifteen, Patrick had lost his calling, believing that he would not make a very good priest.

Prayer and Mass took up a good part of the Ratcliffe day, but some of the other activities apart from boxing and boating already mentioned, included cricket, athletics, swimming and rugby, plus societies, for example literary and musical ones. For entertainment, films were presented regularly and the Saturday programme was usually excellent, with screen features such as *The Marx Brothers at the Circus*, *The Wizard of Oz*, *Goodbye, Mr. Chips*, or *Dodge City*, together with the usual assortment of Ministry of Information films. Many plays were also performed, including musicals.

There were three houses at Ratcliffe during Patrick's time there: his, Lockhart, De Lisle and Arundel. An entry from the 1941 edition of "The Ratcliffian," within the boxing section reads: "Under 6st 7; P. McGoohan was not (well) matched and (this) gave a walk-over to Lockhart." In the 1942 edition, Patrick fared less well: "P. McGoohan (Lockhart) versus P. Mower (de Lisle); Under 8 stone; Superior attack won this fight for de Lisle. Mower was at home in fierce onslaughts that included some use of both hands in quick succession. McGoohan was unable to keep cool in such circumstances and failed to do himself justice." However, another year on saw the young boxer reaching his peak, evidenced by this simple statement: "1943; Under 11st; McGoohan secured a walk-over."[13]

Also in 1943, Patrick joined the Air Training Corps (ATC), as notes of the time recorded: "The strength of the Flight was raised to 36 by the enrolment of 13 recruits including P. McGoohan. The main activities during the term were routine classes and Drill parades." In his final year at Ratcliffe, Patrick took his "School Certificates" and secured passes in English Language, Scripture, English Literature, History, Geography, French, Elementary Mathematics, Physics and Chemistry.

Father Tony Baxter, a former teacher and headmaster at Ratcliffe, recalls: "I have only a vague memory of Patrick McGoohan. I arrived to teach in January 1944 and Patrick left in

[xviii] In McGoohan's 1967 TV series *The Prisoner* he adopted an autobiographical approach, by including many of the elements – even the boaters and blazers – of his days at Ratcliffe, as discussed later in this book, see page 160.
[xix] His mother was Belgian, hence the spelling of his first name. Jacques was tragically killed in a road accident in December, 1946.

the September, after the School Certificates. He was a quiet unobtrusive boy, being one of four lads who came from Sheffield during the war for safety. Norman St John Stevas and Ian Bannen were contemporaries and both were very active on the Ratcliffe stage."[14]

Old Ratcliffian Philip Hebbert (1939-44) describes Patrick as "a rather lonely soul" and remembers that although he did not take part in any of the College plays, he was involved in stage carpentry. He remembers Patrick's friend Jacques, who also had a quiet personality and was a self sufficient sort of boy.[15]

Ratcliffe College, Leicester, where Patrick gained a scholarship

Some Old Ratcliffians have offered their World War II reminiscences at Ratcliffe. David Thistlethwaite (1943-1950) reflects: "Ratcliffe was not exactly a prime target for the Luftwaffe, but Lower School field overlooked the airfield and the dark blue uniformed ferry pilots used it as a sort of 'pit stop,' so we saw numbers of war planes." Thistlethwaite continues: "We had Italian and German prisoners of war working in the school grounds. To celebrate VE Day a huge bonfire was built on the tarmac just outside the main entrance door at the top of the front drive and an effigy of Hitler was burnt on the top."

Peter Lambert (1938-44) remembers: "We had for one week an inch cube of butter. This was put on a small piece of bread so that we could savour the taste. On nights of intense enemy activity, we had to get up and take our mattresses downstairs and sleep in the corridors, or the masters' common room if you were lucky. You probably fell asleep with a small bag of sweets in your hand, which you found in the morning had been shared with the vermin. On the night of the big air raid in Coventry, we moved into the underground tanks in front of the school. I presume they are still there. Boys being boys we needed to relieve ourselves very regularly, so that we could go outside to see the fires and of course, hear the bombs as the raid was progressing, but Ratcliffe was relatively peaceful."[16]

Michael Sykes (1940-1946) has similar recollections: "Early in the war, the fear of bombing was considerable. The first time the sirens sounded to warn of the danger of an air raid, everyone felt very nervous and we were all taken to the shelter. This was close to the top of the front drive. It was cold, clammy, only dimly lit by oil lamps and very uncomfortable. It soon came to be accepted that it wasn't very likely that there would be (bombs), so after that first uncomfortable night the shelter was abandoned and subsequently when the sirens sounded the air raid warning we had to sleep on mattresses in the cloisters." One of Sykes' memories relates to the nearby airfield: "We were lucky that the school was next to an aerodrome. There were civilian pilots, many of them women, whose job was to ferry aircraft between factory and operational station. Quite often, new aircraft would land at Ratcliffe for some reason before being delivered, so we would be some of the first to see the latest types."[17]

John Attley (1940-46) has memories of McGoohan: "I started at Ratcliffe in September 1940. One or two notable boys who did well in the theatrical world were in the same class as me for most of the time I was there, being Ian Bannen and Patrick McGoohan. The winter of 1940 was extremely cold. I remember sitting in the Study, up against the heating pipes, to warm up before we went to bed, at 8.45 p.m. We were wakened, I think, at 6.45 a.m. – it

St. Vincent's Hall, Solly Street, Sheffield. from the book *St. Vincent's: History of a Parish*, 2003, published by St. Vincent's Parish Council

seemed like the middle of the night – and went to Mass. The Chapel was completely dark except for the candles, because of the blackout. Breakfast was at 8.15 a.m. and there was always bread, plus something else such as dried egg, with some sort of 'sausage' meat. We had sweet coupons[xx] which we could spend at the Tuck Shop. There was also an abundance of carbonated "Dandelion and Burdock" in big bottles, which was presumably prepared from harvesting the ingredients from the local fields and ditches, so was readily available.

We used to have 'The Committee of Privileges,' which was comprised of Prefects. If you had (perpetrated) some minor infraction you had to go before this committee.[xxi] This particular night they were in session and I was then in the fifth form and had got hold of a Thunderflash, which the Home Guard used for training. I went into the sixth form room, which was next to the Prefects' room, threw the Thunderflash outside their window and rejoined the queue outside in the corridor. The Head Prefect rushed out and down the cloister, followed by the others, but they never did find the culprit (until now)."[18]

Leaving Ratcliffe in 1944, at the age of sixteen, McGoohan had no idea of a career path to follow, his childhood ambitions for a religious calling having fallen by the wayside. Before he even left his teens, the death of his friend Jacques meant that Patrick also had to recover from the loss of his young soul mate. In later years he would affirm that he secured examination passes sufficient to support his entry into Oxford, but that it was his own decision not to pursue a university place. Therefore, although academic prizes were not to be his, McGoohan would insist that being self-educated, taking ideas and concepts from life and experience, created a solid base: "The right sort of education enables one to think original thoughts. There are people who know something about every subject under the sun. But they

---

[xx] Sweet coupons appear in *The Prisoner* episode *It's Your Funeral*.
[xxi] McGoohan's Number Six character has to appear before "The Committee" in *The Prisoner* episode *A Change of Mind*.

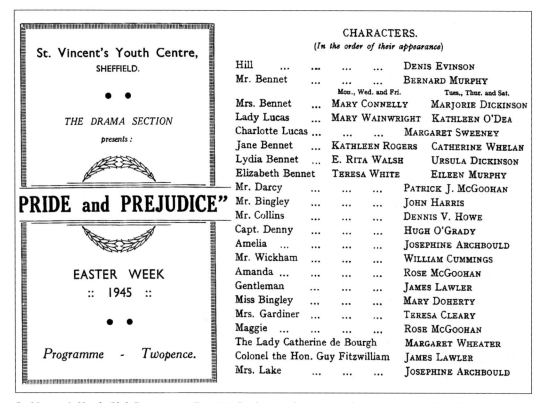

St. Vincent's Youth Club Programme (Rose McGoohan in the cast may be a sister or unrelated).

are just a reference library. Knowing too much stuff, that is closing up your mind. You will find that all the great inventors – Edison, Bell – I can't think of one who was highly educated. The exploration of their mind wasn't surrounded by too much education. The mind was set free. The innate power of creation was there."[19] Curiously, McGoohan would be equally dismissive about travel, something he would in future years experience frequently: "I don't agree that travel broadens the mind. You have to find out where you live now. How much did Shakespeare travel? Did he miss out on Broadway? Times Square? The broadening of the mind is here (tapping his head)."[20]

The first of McGoohan's meagre employments was in the steel wire mills of the British Rope Company, in Sheffield. The job involved more dirt than pay, with the young man working on the factory floor. When interviewed in later years, McGoohan offered a scenario of life at the wire rope factory, presenting his time there as if a film director's vision: "Grey, bleak, miserably oppressive atmosphere...redolent of the 'dark, satanic mills' of the 19th century. Overall the sickly metallic smell of iron filings. Enter through tall, dark gates, into blacksmith's shop...huge furnace, men wearing leather aprons and clogs. Across pitted yard to spindle factory where great bales of wire are rolled down. Youngsters being taught the knack of handling these bales without tearing their hands to ribbons." McGoohan recalled, "the factory was owned by (James Lodge) the father of a school friend. When I decided not to go to university he took me on. I was one of those youngsters, earning twenty shillings a week."[xxii][21]

[xxii] There were twenty shillings to the pound and established labourers in Britain were earning about twenty pence an hour, giving a weekly wage of around three pounds.

Above: St. Vincent's Youth Club production of *A Hundred Years Old* (1947). McGoohan is seated to the right of the fireplace.

Left: St. Vincent's Youth Club production of *Pride and Prejudice* (1945)

It was little surprise that the youth, having ambition and untapped ability, needed an outlet for his more creative energies. The highlight of the week soon became his Saturday evening visits to the local youth club, in Solly Street, operated by the St. Vincent's Roman Catholic Church. Visitors had to climb three steps, pass through the main doors and go into a lobby. On the left was an area where sandwiches were provided, along with tea and soft drinks. Over on the right side, tickets could be bought for the latest dance and coats could be left. McGoohan described in future interviews how the club offered innocuous activities like table tennis, but suddenly presented a new horror for him, as a club dance was looming:

"Sixteen, six feet two, just out of boarding school, big, clumsy, with no idea of how you went up to a strange girl and asked her to dance and even less idea of what you did with your feet if she said yes. The whole thing was impossible and I wanted to do it."[22] McGoohan revealed that he only felt secure if he was able to wear his raincoat into the dance hall: "In a mac[xxiii] you were one of the crowd, looking exactly like everybody else. On the first Saturday, I read every notice on the board five times and left. On the second Saturday a woman asked for my coat as I purchased a ticket. I replied, 'Oh, I'm waiting for somebody for a minute.' I read the notice board ten times and then left. The third Saturday I bought the ticket, handed over my mac and gave the swing doors a bold push. As a gust of music, laughter and chatter swept out and hit me full in the face, I whipped around smartly, wasted another three pence on two glasses of lemonade I didn't want, retrieved my mac and vanished."[23]

When McGoohan finally summoned the courage to go into the dance, his entrance was further delayed. Father McDonagh waylaid him and told the lad that his employer, James Lodge, who also happened to organise the youth club's theatrical group, wanted some help

---

[xxiii] This is the popular term for a raincoat, named after Charles Macintosh, Scots inventor of the garment, waterproofed with rubber.

with a forthcoming play. On a handshake, Lodge selected McGoohan for a part in *The Thread of Scarlet*. The young recruit was told: "We want someone fairly big and strong, who can look like a man, not a boy. All you have to do is cart a couple of buckets of coal across the stage."[24] The acting debut lasted under a minute, but the youth's proud family – both parents and four sisters – all turned out to witness the triumphant performance. Lodge, an amateur thespian, gave his time voluntarily at the youth club. His standards were higher than those of some professionals and he taught McGoohan the much needed disciplines of the theatre. So impressed with Lodge was the young protégé that he would later assert that his best work was done while he was being directed by the gentleman. "He could make a stone act. He made me. Soon I was in all his plays."[25]

The next challenge for McGoohan was to master dancing. In the youth club, a patient woman[xxiv] volunteered to teach him some steps. In the lessons he met a bunch of other "Crimson-faced, ungainly characters with outsized hands and feet. We were known to my sisters as 'the wallflowers' delights,' since the general method of picking partners was to make a bee-line for any girl who looked too scared and timid either to refuse, or to complain if we trod on them."[26] McGoohan was told that the tuition was needed for yet another performance, which gave the actor a new terror: "I suspect I was lulled by the knowledge that it would be performed on a stage, behind my new-found safety barrier of the footlights. Neither the fact that I had to be conspicuous in white cricket flannels and shirt, nor that I put my foot right through the hem of my partner's dress, daunted me on the night. Even looking out at the faceless blur of the audience was all right. But looking at the girl with whom I was dancing was something I never managed. To this day I don't know whether she was fair, dark or redheaded. But I swear, if I ever met them again, I'd know her feet anywhere!"[xxv][27]

Performing in public had ignited a new thirst within McGoohan for the theatre. He began to see his factory work as hardly providing a suitable destiny for his talent. To obtain a better position, it seemed that endless departments would have to be worked through and the slow pace of promotion and pay enhancement would be unbearable. Therefore, in 1945, with his maths acumen to fall back upon, the apprentice left behind the Rope Company,[xxvi] at the age of seventeen, in favour of the National Provincial Bank.[xxvii] Here, he worked in a big general room behind the public counters. "I was allotted a place at the long table to address and lick envelopes and to balance the accounts – of the stamp box.[xxviii] It was a life of careful initialling, signing and accurate arithmetic, which began at 8.30 a.m. and ended, if you were lucky, at 4 p.m. If you were unlucky, you could be there till past midnight."[28] McGoohan did not anticipate being in the job for long – earning the magnificent salary of thirty six shillings a week – as the war was still on and he expected to be called up.[xxix] However, by the time the bank clerk was nineteen and a half, he was earning three pounds ten shillings

---

[xxiv] Sources say that she was Eileen Lodge, wife of James.

[xxv] Curiously, when McGoohan had a scene waltzing with a female partner in an early episode of *The Prisoner*, he played the sequence almost in the way in which he had described his dancing debut. His eyes and arms barely made contact with actress Annette Carrell. Another actress from the same series, Annette Andre, recalled how playing a scene with McGoohan was a strange experience, as the actor's eyes never met hers.

[xxvi] Leaving the steel mill was put down to quarrelling with other employees, according to McGoohan at a later date.

[xxvii] Resigning from work would become a further aspect of McGoohan's life to feature in his future *Prisoner* TV series.

[xxviii] In *The Prisoner* episode *Once upon a Time*, there would be direct reference to this employment.

[xxix] The war ended in 1945, the year before McGoohan's eighteenth birthday. He was not old enough to enlist and was not later 'called up' to do National Service – the system of post-war military training in Britain which ran from 1945 to 1963 – possibly on health grounds, or even nationality.

Early photo portrait of McGoohan

a week, cycling out daily to the sub branch at Tinsley.[xxx] He was even handling the account of the factory, where he had started his working life as a labourer and was now, according to his own description, "sub-sub-sub assistant manager."[29] Before long, McGoohan became actual assistant manager and stayed with the bank for three years.

A new opportunity to earn more money was eagerly seized when McGoohan took up a position running a chicken farm in the nearby town of Chesterfield. He had bought the *Sheffield Telegraph and Star* and looked down the situations vacant columns. The advertisement he saw was: "Wanted: Energetic young man with some experience to re-manage and organise chicken farm. £5 per week." McGoohan cycled the twelve miles to Chesterfield, told the advertiser and his wife that he had lived on a farm all his life and successfully obtained the job. His mother put his bank suit and stiff white collars into mothballs, while he packed two pairs of old trousers, some sweaters and shirts and went off to manage five thousand hens and a herd of pigs, on thirteen acres of land.[xxxi]

The farm owners, Mr. and Mrs. Brown, were in their fifties and, being childless, were missing their own wartime evacuee, who had been like a son to them. Consequently, they welcomed the young McGoohan and he returned their affection. The factor which had led him to quit the bank was explained by him in an odd way: "I couldn't stand seeing all that money about, knowing that none of it was mine, or ever likely to be. I decided that as I couldn't get rich, I'd better get out of sight of all those bills. The temptation might be too much. So I packed up and went to work as a chicken farmer. The first time I saw a tiny chicken pecking its way out of its egg I thought this is the way life starts, this is beginning of it all. It all sounds corny but that little yellow powder puff gave me a reverence for the miracle of birth. I was happier than I had ever been. My idea of the good life was a bucket full of chicken meal and couple of dozen broody hens clucking contentedly. I'd become almost like one of them. I was cock of the walk, ruling my little roost."[xxxii] [30]

During his time looking after poultry and livestock, McGoohan lodged in the bungalow of Mr. and Mrs. Brown, opposite the farm. He enjoyed his duties immensely: "After the inactivity of the bank I went almost berserk with the sheer luxury of physical hard work."[31] Mrs. Brown was a wonderful cook, serving enormous and marvellous meals. In the evening, McGoohan would play chess[xxxiii] with Mr. Brown, a railway track maintenance man. The

---

[xxx] Sheffield people who have spoken to this writer say that McGoohan also worked in the more central George Street branch. Also, see later the remarks of Elizabeth Ewing who says that she worked at George Street, while McGoohan was at the High Street branch – page 26.
[xxxi] Information around this time is sketchy, as some accounts claim that between the bank and the farm McGoohan undertook jobs for short periods as a butcher, a gardener, a truck driver and even a miner, all of which seems most unlikely.
[xxxii] See also page 215, as to McGoohan resuming chicken farming in about 1980.
[xxxiii] Chess featured strongly in the later *Prisoner* series.

lodger was also performing household odd jobs, or outdoor tasks, such as trimming the hedge. Life would have been idyllic, with hard work and mutual affection between him and his temporary 'parents,' plus an increased wage of five pounds per week. However, a sudden allergy to chicken feathers brought about a severe resurgence of McGoohan's childhood bronchial asthma. This caused him to have to return to his parents' Sheffield home and also to lose his latest employment. So severe was the young man's affliction, he had to endure strict bed rest for six months.

Once back on his feet, McGoohan had a series of temporary office jobs, although nearing the end of his convalescence he resumed taking acting parts and further developed his talent. The restless youth now yearned for the weekends, having become associated with several local drama groups. He was able to spend a great deal of time, both acting and assisting in various ways with a number of productions, mainly at the St. Vincent's Youth Centre. Known to all there as "Paddy," the future star of stage and screen always remembered his humble acting beginnings.[xxxiv]

Another amateur group, St. Thomas', called upon McGoohan at short notice, when their leading man fell ill the day before their opening night of *The Duke in Darkness*.[xxxv] The stand-in inherited a lengthy speaking part and his sisters took it in turns to sit through the night with him, helping him memorise the lines and cues. When he went on stage he was word perfect. After this, three other groups invited him to join them and he was soon a member of five different dramatic societies, rehearsing, or acting, on an amateur stage nearly every night. McGoohan lived for the evenings: he took the lead in the youth club play *A Hundred Years Old* and had to age throughout the performance, applying his own make-up to create the ageing effect. The opening night occurred during a severe fall of snow, although the story being presented was set in sunny Spain. The actor experienced a feeling of wonder, between himself, all of the players on stage and the audience. He felt that although he was only in his teens, he really had turned into the centenarian he was portraying.

Several Sheffield past acquaintances of the younger McGoohan still remember fondly their years of knowing the young man and budding actor, watching his progress through school, youth club and amateur dramatic circles. This writer has obtained their recollections, which are now conveniently presented. In Chapter Two, the story continues, with McGoohan joining his final amateur group, The Curtain Club, before moving on to the world of repertory theatre, at the Sheffield Playhouse. A few of the following stories from local people do make brief mention of the Playhouse and so in the interests of space and continuity, these memories have been combined with the earlier amateur dramatic stories:

VINCENT MAHER

I used to attend St. Vincent's Roman Catholic School. It was run by the Brothers and the church and school were together, with a hall next door. I was in Patrick McGoohan's class and we called him Paddy. I was a tall lad as was Paddy, and I was already at the school when he came. After his arrival, the other boys used to push me into him and tell me to fight him. I didn't want to, but I did have a few fights with him. If I see Paddy on TV I say to my family, "That's my old friend from school. I used to box his ears years ago."

[xxxiv] So deep was McGoohan's affection for his former amateur acting days, that he returned to St Vincent's two decades later for a reunion. A subsequent event was also held, on 23rd September, 1989, but McGoohan – now living in the US – was unable to attend.

[xxxv] McGoohan would also appear in a later version of the play, at a different venue, see page 27.

TERESA LODGE

James Lodge, who taught Patrick McGoohan at the youth club amateur dramatic society, was my husband's cousin. I also acted in the productions and I played opposite Patrick a few times. My favourite was *Pride and Prejudice* when he was Mr. Darcy and I was Miss Elizabeth. I knew Patrick when he was in the amateur club from when he was about sixteen, until he left and went to the Curtain Club. I remember him doing various things like learning to dance and we were in several plays together. In one production he played a hundred year old man and I was his daughter. He was really good as the old man. In make-up he was putting little lines on his hands for veins.

AUDREY HAYDEN

I used to be a secretary at Cole Brothers' department store in Sheffield. It was several storeys high and our office was on the third floor. Patrick McGoohan was in his early days of working at the Playhouse theatre. He used to come to our store to borrow props as an errand boy. He was very shy. He used to tell us which items were wanted and he had to get a book signed for them in our office. He did not really communicate and if ever he passed us in the street he would just nod. In return for loaning props, our store would be mentioned in the play programmes at the theatre and we also used to get free tickets for performances. I recall how Patrick always used to wear a tweed jacket and had auburn hair, plus freckles.

JAMES BLAKE

I knew Patrick McGoohan at St. Vincent's youth club and at that time he had started working at the Playhouse. I used to box at St. Vincent's and I remember one night when I was fifteen, we had a ring in the hall and Paddy came in with several young ladies. He was wearing a Sherlock Holmes outfit and looked flamboyant, with a deerstalker and cape.[xxxvi] While the boxing was going on he was making comments from the side, as if to entertain his female party. He was therefore challenged to show us how it should be done and he climbed into my ring. He was a beanpole, taller than me and I was five feet nine inches. He got into the ring and seemed more interested in amusing the ladies and so I set about him. The referee jumped in and dragged me off him. I was told that Paddy had to appear in the theatre later that night.

ANN DALE

I didn't know Patrick McGoohan but I observed him when I was younger. My aunt worked at St. Vincent's youth club and she used to cook for the players between performances. I was about eleven at the time and I would watch them rehearse. Patrick stood out from the rest as he was so professional. I remember him in a play when he was a hundred year old man. He was about eighteen and was incredible. His make up was excellent. He would get annoyed if the others didn't know their lines, as he knew his perfectly. His sisters went to Notre Dame School where I attended. I remember going to a girl's birthday party and Patrick was there. I thought it was great that they could invite someone like him, as I was in awe of him. He said he was always grateful for what James Lodge taught him about acting, at the youth club.

[xxxvi] McGoohan later appeared dressed as Sherlock Holmes in *The Prisoner* episode *The Girl Who Was Death*, in a scene which takes place in a boxing ring.

CHRISTINE SMITH

I met Patrick McGoohan at the Playhouse. I wanted to be an actress and I went to help out, with sweeping and making tea. Although he was just one of the jobbing actors when I knew him, he was very striking and had a presence. He was polite and always thanked me for a cup of tea if I made one for him. He responded as though you'd given him the world, even if it was just a cup of tea. He had good manners.

TED WAINWRIGHT

When I was at St. Vincent's school with Patrick there used to be regular functions for the Children of Mary. At one party, Patrick played an Irish medley on the fiddle and I accompanied him on the piano. He was a good friend of our family, but was a bit of a character. At school he would say things and we would believe him. He told us that there was an aeroplane in his back garden. My school friends and I went to check later in the day. Naturally the aeroplane was missing and so was Patrick. He was later in a play, as a man aged a hundred and was absolutely fantastic. In those days, the Playhouse at Sheffield used to assist the St. Vincent's drama group.

MARY FLEMING

I am Ted Wainwright's older sister. I was sixteen when I was at St. Vincent's youth club, in 1942. I used to sing solo there and I still have some programmes from the plays performed. I recall Patrick in the play *A Hundred Years Old*. Nobody has ever forgotten it, as he was absolutely marvellous. Jimmy Lodge, who had a factory near to the youth club, took us for drama. He used to invite the manager of the Playhouse to our productions. I was the drama club secretary and used to do typing and send out invitations and letters. There was also an old boy's dance on Saturday nights and Patrick used to go to them. He would make us laugh by behaving as if he was drunk. He was only acting but he was very good at it.

VINCENT HALE

I was sixteen when Paddy was in plays at the St. Vincent's youth centre. My first play was in fact his last, called *Viceroy Sarah*. I previously sat in on prompts with Paddy and after evening performances we used to walk up the road together. When Paddy first wanted to go to the youth club he was standing outside, as he was too shy to go in and so Father McDonagh took hold of him and ushered him inside. We used to put on displays at the club, such as ballroom dancing, boxing, or first aid. For one dancing display there were four couples, myself and Mary Whelan, Paddy and Ursula Dickinson, Jack Harris (Paddy's friend) and Margaret Sweeney, Frank Lee Ward and Kitty Whelan, the sister of my partner.

KATHLEEN PAGE

I knew Paddy as I was friends with his sisters. His parents had a cottage at Notre Dame Convent, where his father was gardener and caretaker. We used to roll the carpet back and do Irish dancing there, with Paddy playing the fiddle. I saw him act at the St. Vincent's Youth Club, when he was in the play *The Duke in Darkness*. He also was in the play *A Hundred Years Old* and was wonderful.

BRYAN DUNSTAN

I remember when I was about eight years old; I and some of my mates would go to our local youth club in Sheffield. Early evening, every Friday, while we were on our way to the club, we walked past the Playhouse theatre in Townhead Street. As we reached the secondary door, which was at pavement level, we would give it a great big kick and run off. This was done, regular as clockwork, at six o'clock each Friday. On one particular evening Patrick McGoohan must have been waiting for us. We kicked the door and like lightning he shot out and ran after us. He grabbed me by the collar and dragged me back into the Playhouse. There was another balding man present, with glasses, and Patrick McGoohan said "I've got him. He was the one." He clipped me round the ear and said, "If you ever do that again, you'll get a bigger clip." The day he grabbed me and pulled me inside was the only time I went into the theatre and it is a moment I will never forget.

BILL CUMMINGS

I knew Patrick McGoohan from the St. Vincent's Youth Club. The drama centre there opened on Easter Sunday in 1942. After Patrick had been to Ratcliffe College he came back to Sheffield and was in his first production at the drama centre, in 1945 I believe, *The Thread of Scarlet*. Jimmy Lodge, the producer and director, was a wonderful man. The youth centre put on displays of gymnastics, drama and dancing. In *The Thread of Scarlet*, in which I also played a part, at the age of nineteen, Pat was cast in the role of a landlord. He had one line to speak as he called, "Time, gentlemen please." At the time, there was a youth drama competition and even his one spoken line impressed the judges greatly.

He was then in his second drama, aged sixteen, playing the part of a man who ages through three generations to become a centenarian. The play was called *A Hundred Years Old* and I was also in the production. The ageing process could have been a difficult task for a teenager, but Pat tackled it magnificently, owing to his talent. In one scene the whole cast was on stage except for Pat as he was still in make-up and there was a pause in the talking. I went to do my exit from stage right just as Pat came on, having descended down two flights of rickety stairs, his whiskers flowing in the breeze. He put in a wonderful performance and at the end of the play his character dies, which I recall, left the audience in tears. The next production in which he and I both appeared was the St. Vincent's presentation of *Pride and Prejudice*. Pat was at his magnificent best and the image stays with me today as his greatest performance there.

In 1959 I went to see Pat in *Brand*, in London. I recall *Brand* being broadcast on TV and it was a great honour for Pat to be given the television actor of the year award. It was wonderful to see him again after several years and following the play we went back to my hotel, the Regent Palace, in London's Piccadilly. We talked at length about our earlier days and I was proud to see that Pat had achieved so much. Eventually he had to leave and jumped into his red sports car which he had parked outside and drove off. He told me that he was going to meet television bosses to discuss the part of *Danger Man*.

GEOFF HESPE

I knew Pat McGoohan when we were both working at the National Provincial Bank in George Street, Sheffield. I met him there when I was sixteen and he was about two years older. Pat was employed as a 'senior junior' and I was a 'junior junior.' He also occasionally worked on the front counter. We became good friends and used to do a fair amount of overtime, checking all the envelopes which had to go out, including late overseas ones and putting postage stamps on each one. We were earning good money doing overtime and we used to spend a fair amount of time playing table tennis together in the staff room.

Sometimes Pat would visit our home and once we even stayed in a tent in our back garden. Pat also stood in for my older brother Dick in a play at St. Thomas' dramatic society. Dick had fractured his elbow and so Pat took over his part. Subsequently I joined the army and lost contact with Pat.

One day, years later, after I had finished my army service, I was in London's Oxford Street. I felt a tap on my shoulder and it was Pat. We were pleased to meet up again after so many years and we chatted. I went to see his agent[xxxvii] with him and then I stayed at his Mill Hill home. Joan, his wife, was appearing in *The Mousetrap* and so I did not see much of her. She went off to the theatre on her Lambretta scooter. Pat was also busy at the time, filming *The Gypsy and the Gentleman* at Pinewood. He took me to the studio and I was able to see some of the production taking place. After this I again lost contact with Pat and have not seen him since.

KITTY WARD

I was Catherine "Kitty" Whelan when I first knew Patrick McGoohan in Sheffield. I later married his friend Frank Ward and we always called Patrick "Paddy Mac." We stayed good friends in the days of St. Vincent's Youth Club. We were about eighteen at the time and in the early days, when Paddy would take me home sometimes; I didn't know that he had an interest in me. One evening after play rehearsals he said to me, in a determined way, "You are going to make your mind up between Frank and myself." I was not expecting this and so it came as a surprise to me. Everyone else called me Kitty, but Paddy insisted upon calling me Catherine. We were in *Pride and Prejudice* together at the youth centre and we also did some dancing there.

SHELAGH TURNER

I went to school with Patrick's sister Rose, at St. Vincent's. I left there in 1944 but Rose went on to Notre Dame Convent. I met Patrick in St. Vincent's Youth Centre. He was three years older than me. I particularly remember him as being the principal actor in the play *A Hundred Years Old*. Later, he was sought after by the Playhouse theatre, in Sheffield. The organisers had received word that Patrick was very good and they came over to see him.

At the St. Vincent's dances, there would always be the "Paul Jones." In this dance the boys would go round one way and the girls the other way. When the music stopped you would dance with the partner opposite. One night the music stopped and I was opposite Patrick. I did not normally speak to him because he was a senior and I was only a junior at school. However, on this evening he said to me "Hello beautiful" and it made my night. I danced with him and I'll never forget it."

Finally, two Sheffield ladies have recently provided their memories. Barbara Bowles recalls: "I knew Pat McGoohan when he worked with us (at the National Provincial) bank. When he went to the Playhouse he had to go as assistant stage manager and the fact that he was a good actor had nothing to do with it. He started at the bottom and learnt the trade

---

[xxxvii] McGoohan has had a number of different agents, over the years, in the UK and the US.

until he started taking the leading parts and then got to London. He was in television series for ages. But he never changed, when I saw him in Sheffield he was 'Hi Babs' you know. He was really one of those people who never change."[32] Elizabeth Ewing remembers how, "(McGoohan) worked at the High Street branch and I worked at George Street (branch). We used to have to meet up each day at the local clearing house to do our cheques and he used to help me, the little junior, do my sums."[33] The years ahead would see McGoohan – already well known in his own city – becoming popular with countless more theatre and television audiences, as well as cinema-goers.

[1] Joan Reeder, Woman magazine, 4 issues between 9th and 30th October, 1965
[2] Ibid
[3] Ibid
[4] Ibid
[5] You Magazine, The Mail on Sunday, March, 1983, Mike Bygrave
[6] Joan Reeder, Woman magazine, 4 issues between 9th and 30th October, 1965
[7] You Magazine, The Mail on Sunday, March, 1983, Mike Bygrave
[8] TV Week, 21st October, 1995, Jane Oddy
[9] Premiere Magazine, October 1995, Jean Yves Katelan (translations Rosemary Camilleri and Jane Rawson)
[10] Joan Reeder, Woman magazine, 4 issues between 9th and 30th October, 1965
[11] Ibid
[12] Ibid
[13] Ratcliffe College books, 1940-44, kindly provided by Sian Truszkowska
[14] Ibid
[15] Ibid
[16] Ibid
[17] Ibid
[18] Ibid
[19] Video Magazine, July, 1985, Tom Soter
[20] Top Secret magazine, December, 1985, Tom Soter
[21] Joan Reeder, Woman magazine, 4 issues between 9th and 30th October, 1965
[22] Ibid
[23] Ibid
[24] Ibid
[25] Ibid
[26] Ibid
[27] Ibid
[28] Ibid
[29] Ibid
[30] TV Radio Mirror, August, 1966, Dave Hanington
[31] Ibid
[32] Interview with Alan Lane, British Library Age Concern Drama Appreciation Group, 2004
[33] Interview with Kate Dorney

CHAPTER TWO
The Curtain Rises

"Such wind as scatters young men through the world,
to seek their fortunes farther than at home."
The Taming of the Shrew (Act I, Scene 2)

McGoohan continued to appear in dramatic productions with the St. Vincent's Youth Club, as well as with other amateur groups, but in 1945 he joined the Sheffield Curtain Club, founded in 1938. Plays were performed firstly at the Unity Hall and subsequently at the Walkley Ebenezer Church Hall in Greenhow Street. *House Lights*, the newsletter of the Curtain Club, from February 1943, described the later venue in these glowing terms: "Situated at the corner of South Road and Greenhow Street the Walkley Ebenezer Church Hall is in many ways easier of access than Unity Hall. It is a three-halfpenny ride from the city on the Walkley Tram...We believe we will find Walkley Ebenezer a most satisfactory substitute for Unity and we trust our patrons will endorse this view."[1]

A dissenting correspondent, who clearly did not intend his words for publication, observed: "The first view of Ebenezer Hall is enough to chill the warmest heart. There is no doubt that these uncompromising surroundings greatly increase the difficulty of building up the (dramatic) illusion." For good measure, the writer summed up the church hall as "Methodist squalor."[2] It seems that the Curtain Club had survived wartime hostilities, including blackouts and various shortages, but perhaps suffered more privations in the form of the austere premises in which its performances took place.

The first play which involved McGoohan was *The Duke in Darkness*, by Patrick Hamilton, staged at the new venue early in March, 1946. The production, in which the young actor had appeared once before, in earlier youth club days, concerned a duke, in sixteenth century France, captured and kept in confinement for fifteen years by a nobleman. Feigning blindness, the captive is preparing for his escape and is assisted by a conspirator, Voulain (McGoohan), who manages to become his gaoler. In the all-male cast of ten actors,

The Sheffield Playhouse repertory theatre. Picture is 1945, taken from the book *The Sheffield Repertory Theatre: A History*, 1959, by T. Alec Seed

McGoohan was singled out as being "spirited and expressive as the bogus gaoler,"[3] and in the *Sheffield Star* the actor was described as "a virile Voulain."[4] After the play, a critique concerning McGoohan's performance appeared in a letter to the Curtain Club: "I have never seen an amateur show better cast, as each character seemed to fit well into his part ... I liked Patrick J. McGoohan's stage presence, and his voice is good, but he must avoid speaking too quickly in dramatic passages, and thus making his end of words indistinct. Apart from his haste, his voice carried well. He should too guard against fidgeting whilst speaking."[5]

Similarly, one H. Talbot Leak wrote: "Patrick J. McGoohan's 'Voulain' was a clean cut piece of work. Mr. McGoohan has a most pleasing stage presence, excellent repose, knows how to wear costume (how many amateurs fall at this hurdle! And some 'pros'), has a good voice and should go a long way – if he pays due attention to his diction. This was really a very pleasing piece of work, but it was marred and valuable lines swallowed on account of periodic 'speed wobbles.' Go as fast as you like, by all means, but *never* lose control of the vehicle of the voice."[6]

The next Curtain Club presentation of the year was *Rookery Nook*, a play by Ben Travers, in which McGoohan played Gerald Popkiss. More praise was bestowed upon the fledgling actor: "Chief honours went to Patrick J. McGoohan who despite slight awkwardness due to youthful inexperience, set and maintained a good pace in his delightful portrayal of the 'silly ass' Gerald Popkiss – a grand performance."[7] One H.J. Elliott, in his letter to the Curtain Club of 18th May, felt that: "Pat McGoohan as Gerald was quite the best performance of the show. His lines not too easy to learn were prompt and clear throughout the show. I was particularly pleased with his nonsensical, jumbled speeches, which would have done credit to Oliver Wakefield[i] and his facial expressions were admirable."[8] Reta Wild felt: "Pat McGoohan has ability and enthusiasm and although he is inclined to swallow words at the end of sentences he gave an enjoyable performance."[9]

A summer play was staged on the Curtain Club Night in the Club Room situated over 155/157 St. Phillips Road, Sheffield. The entertainment for the evening was *Curtains for Two* by Hewson H. Wagstaff, a stalwart club member. McGoohan took the

Early repertory photograph of McGoohan

role of First Man, the play's writer appearing alongside him as Second Man. Additionally, a spoof of the 1946 season's plays was presented, under the title of *My Lady in Darkness at Rookery Nook*, written by Jack Walsh, the action being staged in "a tower room of the Quayside Inn at Chumpton On Sea."[10]

The first Walkley Ebenezer production of 1947 was *Rope*, written by Patrick Hamilton, author of the club's earlier presentation of *The Duke in Darkness*. He had also written *Gaslight*, which was made into a number of film versions. In *Rope*, two university students murder a fellow undergraduate for sadistic pleasure. The killing occurs before the curtain rises and the audience is faced with finding out who did it and whether the criminal will be brought to justice. In this unusual and diverting play, McGoohan was described in the *Sheffield Telegraph* as the "the chilling genius of the crime, as confident in small talk as he is wretched in detection."[11] The actor's role as Wyndham Brandon was said to be a difficult part, which he carried with ease. The *Sheffield Star* was less complimentary, with critic Albert Meakin writing: "Patrick J. McGoohan did not descend the character's full range from strained nonchalance to gibbering terror, but acted and spoke well."[12]

One of the club's writers, Hewson Wagstaff, was not enamoured with the church hall: "Top coated and gloved, I managed to keep up a moderate circulation at the cost of physical exertion during the intervals and frantic note taking all over my programme in the darkness." As for McGoohan's performance, Wagstaff opined, "Brandon very well done indeed by a member who improves with every part he takes (and he was good in his first). I noticed

---

[i] Oliver Wakefield, an actor who was also seen in a few films, was described as, "An English comedian with an American sense of humour. A master of droll, unfinished sentences and pithy remarks."

ST.   JAMES'S   THEATRE
KING STREET, S.W.I
Licensed by the Lord Chamberlain to PRINCE LITTLER

BRITISH THEATRE GROUP

Director: BASIL DEAN

In association with the Arts Council of Great Britain
THE SHEFFIELD REPERTORY COMPANY
in

THE BRONTES
by
ALFRED SANGSTER
Produced by GEOFFREY OST

Right: *The Brontes* (1948) at St. James's Theatre,
London.
Above: The cast of the play visit Haworth, home of
the Brontes (McGoohan is at the back on the left in
the door)

particularly a very praiseworthy control of speed and exuberance. He should I think look to
the habit of turning every time to the person being addressed."[13]

Audience members who had fought through the driving snow of February, 1947 – the
coldest winter of the twentieth century – to attend the Walkley performance of *Rope*, now
turned up for the next Curtain Club production, at the newly opened Library Theatre,
beneath the Sheffield Central Library in Tudor Place. The latest production was *Problem in
Porcelain*, in the spring of 1947. The up-to-date little theatre was conveniently situated for
playgoers and was comfortably furnished. The new presentation was an original work by Jack
Walsh, a club member and prominent player, who also wrote the *Amateur Stage* column in
the *Sheffield Star*. The highest number of tickets so far was sold for the play, being seven
hundred, but the membership was still seeking to increase attendance figures to a thousand,
to guarantee commercial viability.

Problem in Porcelain found McGoohan playing the part of Julian Force. The action was set
in England in the early forties. In a country house on the outskirts of London, two brothers
and their two sisters argue over a trust clause in their late father's will, concerning a valuable
Chinese vase. According to Albert Meakin, writing in the *Sheffield Star*, "Patrick J.
McGoohan...made a superb first entrance, and lifted the action every time he appeared. Full
marks to...his playing of Julian...selfish and affected B.B.C. intellectual."[14] The club's internal

correspondence began with a letter from one E. Jowett who wrote: "Patrick J. McGoohan has a good sense of comedy and timing. Excellent first entry and final curtain. Occasionally, sacrificed clarity for pace."[15] Rosamond Williams' assessment was: "Patrick J. McGoohan's work is always good to watch, but here his facial grinnations were occasionally overdone. His sense of timing is excellent. Perhaps he was a little over explosive even for such a character as Julian."[16] Finally, Jack R.C. Sharman concluded: "The honours of the evening undoubtedly went to Pat McGoohan. He was certain of his words and quick on his cues. It was noticeable that whenever he was on stage the pace was faster. He definitely had the best lines in the play, and always delivered them to the best advantage."[17]

Later in the year, August's high summer revelries centred around A Club Night Playlet, by Prescription Competition: "The club organisers, having delved into the murky depths of the club room, emerged triumphant bearing:

a) One telephone of the old fashioned type.
b) One property hurricane lamp.
c) One piece of black velvet, approximately 3' by 4.'

You are asked to write a short playlet, lasting not less than four minutes, but not more than six minutes, in which each of these objects is mentioned, one of them forming the focal point of the play. The cast should not exceed four persons.

Each member is asked, if possible to portray some well known character, with the use of such simple props as may be necessary and a few sentences from the play concerned. At some point in the proceedings members will be asked to guess both the name of the plays and characters portrayed. As prizes will be offered it is suggested that members keep their contributions a dark secret until the crucial moment."[18]

It was not recorded which character McGoohan chose to portray, in what must have been a lively variation on the game of charades. In addition to these festivities, according to the Club Night programme, the assembly could look forward to a mysterious "Unknown Offering which will be perpetrated by Patrick J. McGoohan." Later that evening, the young actor was back on stage as A Visitor in Devon and Earth Horatio, by Jack Walsh. This was one of possibly three playlets written to prescription and performed that night. McGoohan also played a curious hybrid character Julian Brandon in one of Walsh's traditional Club Night spoofs of that season's Curtain Club offerings. Entitled The Arrow of Rope Problem, the surreal action was revealed to take place in "The sun lounge on the first floor of a house in Seville." The closing wording on that Club Night programme expressed that: "The hour is late: the time is right to wish the Curtain Club 'goodnight'!"[19] The statement was apt, as McGoohan would soon be leaving the club, as a result of obtaining full-time work with the Sheffield Playhouse repertory theatre.

His last performance with the Curtain Club was in February, 1948, in the opening presentation of the year, The Taming of the Shrew, in which he played Petruchio. The drama critic of the Sheffield Telegraph announced: "Brenda Olivant and Patrick McGoohan both played capitally and with abundant energy and humour."[20] Jack Walsh wrote in his Amateur Stage column: "Patrick J. McGoohan delighted; all the swagger, bluff and braggadocio, added to an engaging personality fitted him ideally."[21] In the same issue of the Star, the drama critic wrote: "Dominating (as he should) the whole play, striding, swashbuckling, cursing roundly, flinging dishes at the servants and clothes at the tailor and taming his wife with simulated anger, and with irony, yet with a touch of tenderness withal, was a really

Left: Caricatures used in Sheffield Playhouse repertory productions reviews c. 1951 Right: John Tanner, *Man and Superman*, 1951

excellent Petruchio (Patrick J. McGoohan)."[22] In another South Yorkshire paper, McGoohan's performance was applauded: "Towering above all was Patrick McGoohan's prodigious Petruchio. Mr. McGoohan plunged headlong into the part and rightly abandoned himself to its sound and fury."[23]

One final review was provided by a writer under the intriguing pen name of Bon Pomerance: "Patrick J. McGoohan as Petruchio was excellent. I was unfortunate in seeing an understudy to Trevor Howard with the Old Vic and I have no hesitation in saying your Petruchio left him standing. This actor has personality, a pleasing voice and an excellent sense of comic timing. His appearance too is an asset. I am not certain whether that slight Raymond Massey mannerism of lip curling might not in time tend to irritate slightly. In this play at any rate it was pleasing. He is a sufficiently good actor to take heed of an exhortation to avoid mannerisms."[24]

McGoohan's acting aspirations were given a boost by his next employment, although he would not initially be performing on stage. His newly obtained job was at the Sheffield Playhouse, a repertory theatre which he had only visited once before, when he was in the audience for the play *Ten Little N*gg*rs*. He had also cycled many times past the Townhead Street building,[ii] but, providentially, on a day when the young actor happened to walk past the theatre, he saw an advertisement: "Carpenter Wanted." On impulse, he went inside and marched straight up to the stage, where director Geoffrey Ost,[iii] was supervising a rehearsal. The young applicant asked, "Can I have a job?" and Ost's answer was, "Yes, if you don't want any money."[25] Ost was a quiet, fair man; bespectacled, he was the consummate professional, looking and sounding more like the architect he once had trained to be.

[ii] The theatre moved to Townhead Street in 1927.
[iii] Geoffrey M. Ost was artistic director of the Sheffield Playhouse, from 1938 to 1964.

Left: Petruchio in *The Taming of the Shrew*, 1952. Right: Another shot from *The Taming of the Shrew* 1952

Soon, McGoohan became a trainee stage manager, but for only two pounds a week. This was not only a drop in salary compared to earnings from his recent employments, but was also an amount a thousand times less than the one he would be receiving for seven days' work, a decade and a half later. For now, he was busy making sets in the basement of the seven hundred and fifty seater.[iv] The young apprentice also assisted with scene building, backdrop painting and light rigging. Other tasks, such as sweeping the boards, helping with props and wardrobe, or even prompting, were all duties which he enthusiastically undertook and, in due course, McGoohan would end his spell as an assistant and become stage manager. For now, the acceptance of the young man as a theatrical "student" was recorded in the Sheffield Repertory Theatre Executive Committee minutes of 9th March, 1948. It was noted that it was not Geoffrey Ost's policy to take on students, but that the new applicant would be an exception to the rule. Some sources have mentioned that McGoohan was in fact, having to pay the theatre for his studentship, rather than the other way round. Either way, the spell at the Playhouse – stretching eventually to around four years – would become a life-changing experience and a proving ground for the trainee. He declared, "I was a member of different dramatic societies all through my banking days, but it had never occurred to me that such an enjoyable occupation could also be a job."[26]

After several months, McGoohan's Playhouse studentship ended and he was accepted as one of the theatre's regular players, in October, 1948. In July of the following year, he became a full professional member of the company. In order to secure this elevated acting status, the Ost protégé had boldly threatened his mentor with his own departure: "I'm not coming back till you make me an actor." Without pausing, the Playhouse director replied: "Welcome

---

[iv] The Playhouse was regarded as one of the leading producing units in the country, with its large seating capacity and being entirely self-supporting.

Ham, *Noah*, 1949

back."[27] The Playhouse's fortnightly turnover of plays saw McGoohan embracing a routine of performing in one role in the evening and rehearsing another during the day. Casting for forthcoming plays was posted on bulletin boards on Saturday afternoons and was eagerly awaited by all the players. Also on display was a printed edict, which McGoohan always remembered: "The only reason for being late is death, or some better excuse."[28]

His parents praised their son as he progressed – the young man's salary had been raised to four pounds ten shillings a week – and soon they would frequently be coming to the theatre to watch him on the boards. This change in fortunes arose when another player was struck down with appendicitis.[v] Now, unexpectedly, McGoohan was set to enjoy his Playhouse stage debut, on 31st May, 1948, in *The Brontes*. "So they shoved me on. It felt good. But nerve-wracking. Scary. I'm always scared. You have to be nervous. I don't want to be placid about my work."[29] As a result, the actor was able to take the role of Rev William Weightman in a production, written by Alfred Sangster and directed by Geoffrey Ost. To promote the run, the players and repertory company officials visited the home of the Brontës, at Haworth, West Yorkshire and were photographed as a group.[vi] The production even transferred the following month to the St. James Theatre, London, bringing for the young actor a prestigious, first appearance in the capital.[vii] From July onwards, his name was regularly appearing in the casts of Sheffield plays, performed during the rest of the year and beyond, bringing an instant increase in remuneration, to six pounds per week.

Actor Paul Eddington[viii] was friends with McGoohan, when the young men were both players in the Sheffield Repertory Company. "I first met him when he was a teenager. Patrick is an utterly honest and straightforward person and I admire him very much. We both share a reverence for our artistic mentor Geoffrey Ost, director of the Playhouse. The first thing that struck one in those days was that Patrick had got tremendous strength and integrity. Although he was only just beginning his career, he knew exactly what he was doing. He wouldn't compromise and he still has got this extraordinary resolution. You could offer him £500,000 to play a role and if he didn't like it he would reject it out of hand. I suppose I know him as well as any man, but I cannot claim that I really (knew) him, because he is such a difficult person to get to know. He is so very reserved and genuinely shy."[30]

It was Eddington who in fact introduced McGoohan to the woman he would later marry. The name Joan Drummond[ix] had newly appeared on the theatre's bulletin board. Joan, aged eighteen and born in Liverpool, was a sophisticated Londoner, the daughter of a divorce

---

[v] This was the second occasion that a part had fortuitously been obtained through another person's unfortunate indisposition, the first instance having occurred during youth club days.
[vi] See picture and caption on page 30. The picture appears in the book *The Sheffield Repertory Theatre: A History* by T. Alec Seed, 1959
[vii] Sources say that excerpts from Playhouse productions were broadcast on radio, as *Saturday Night Theatre* presentations and that McGoohan's voice was heard.
[viii] See footnotes on pages 34, 169 and 204.
[ix] A 'stage' surname, Joan's full maiden name being Effie Joan Maureen Stein.

lawyer[x] in the capital. Straight from the Royal Academy of Dramatic Art (RADA) via the West Riding Repertory Company, Joan was a vivacious mixture of her Viennese mother and Scottish father. Her husband-to-be described her as, "A glowing sunburst-to-mahogany girl with black hair and dark eyes. I found her overwhelming and fascinating."[31] The stricken McGoohan admitted that when he had first spoken to Joan he was shaking and this condition continued for a few days. However, although he was clearly in love with the new arrival, he was already seeing another young woman. Therefore, very correctly he informed his present girlfriend that their doomed friendship had to end.

The actor's sisters told their brother that every young man in town was after Joan. Fortunately, McGoohan's opportunity to win her heart came during rehearsals for the play *Noah*.[xi] The young Miss Drummond turned up with a puppy, explaining that she had bought the pet because she felt homesick. The creature produced so many impromptu 'floods' of its own, that it was christened "Noah." Miss Drummond was actually not permitted to keep a pet in her digs and clearly the puppy was far from trained. Therefore, she asked McGoohan to take care of him, a request which he could hardly refuse. This gave the couple a daily excuse for conversation. "How's Noah?" Joan would ask, with the keeper replying, "All right, considering the way he's been brought up." Sparks would then fly and Joan would toss back her black hair and march off. Years later, McGoohan would comment, "Asking her out was, for me, like going back to that youth club dance. The whole idea was impossible and I wanted to do it."[32] The *Sheffield Star* revealed that the couple's romance started when they appeared as newly-weds in *The Browning Version*, in November, 1949.

During their years together in Sheffield,[xii] the actors would cycle into the countryside, on Sundays, for a picnic. In the evenings, they would go to shows and afterwards walk home, eating fish and chips. Mrs. Wood, the wife of one of the directors of the Playhouse, gave an annual Christmas party for the company at her house in Fulwood and at one point Joan was dancing with another man. McGoohan recalled, "As Joan danced by I reached out and pulled her down on the seat beside me." Soon they were "rattling back on the tram to Sheffield."[33] On arriving at Joan's lodgings, Patrick asked her to marry him, but his request was declined as Joan felt she was too young, being aged only nineteen.

A few months later, Patrick popped the question again, but his intended bride wanted him formally to ask her parents for her hand in marriage. This presented a problem, as the Drummonds had not yet met the man of their daughter's dreams. The first glimpse of their prospective son-in-law – a year after the courting of Joan had started – was of him portraying an idiot character in a play. McGoohan was, as he subsequently put it, "playing a sinister loon and an axe wielder, with Joan in the part of a young nurse as my next target.[xiii] As I chased her round the stage she had to scream out her terror that I would lay my filthy paws on her." Mr. Drummond's audible reaction from the stalls was, "Oh my God!" The subject of his concern said he knew exactly where Joan's father's seat was located, as he had booked it himself, with great care.

McGoohan reflected years later how he would have felt, in the position of Joan's father:

"London lawyer, specialising in divorce, parent of one attractive impulsive daughter, who after only seven months in provincial repertory now wants to marry a twenty two year old

[x] Walter Oscar Stein.
[xi] Performed at the Playhouse, from 17th October, 1949.
[xii] Joan was at the Playhouse for about two and a half years.
[xiii] *Bonaventure* (20th November, 1950), in which McGoohan played Willy Pentridge, with Joan Drummond in the role of Nurse Phillips.

actor earning the same salary as she does, eight pounds a week. I was wearing heavy make-up to produce the repellent characteristics of a half-demented simpleton. But, behind the dressing room door, hung my best dark suit, out of mothballs for the first time since my job as a bank clerk. My plan was contrast."[34]

The courtship lasted for eighteen months, as Joan's father wanted to slow down the pace of the relationship. Finally, McGoohan successfully proposed to Joan in 1950, while the couple were standing on a manhole cover[xiv] in a Sheffield street.[xv] The *Sheffield Star* reported that romantic history had been made for the local repertory company, by the engagement of the twenty two year old actor to twenty year old actress Joan Drummond. It was stated that the couple hoped to be married in Sheffield within the year[35] and the prophecy was fulfilled on Saturday, nineteenth May, 1951. The ceremony took place at St. William's Catholic Church,[xvi] Ecclesall, Sheffield.[xvii] At the time, both husband and wife were appearing in *The Rivals*, firstly at the Sheffield Playhouse and at the end of the month at the Theatre Royal, Bath.[xviii]

Meanwhile, good critical notices continued. Of *Man and Superman*, the *Sheffield Star* enthused: "Taken at a tempestuous pace, with Patrick McGoohan brilliantly leading the hue and cry, Mr. Geoffrey Ost's production took (the) audience by storm and deservedly received one of the warmest possible ovations. Mr. McGoohan it must be recorded, has definitely arrived. His performance in this play marks him as an actor of profound and mature capabilities."[36] A similarly glowing review in the *Sheffield Telegraph* in 1951 concerning the presentation of *The Princess and the Swineherd*, offered critical praise: "Although...moments when the vision of the dramatist seems to melt away all traces of reality, are rare, it is by their presence that one ultimately judges the true worth of a production."[37] The report enthused that the Geoffrey Ost production of the adapted Hans Andersen story created "real magic" in the audience: "Such a production demands style and it was abundant in the performances of Patrick McGoohan as the Prince who turns Swineherd...Add to these the deliciously petulant Princess of Joan Drummond, the play possessed potent powers."[38]

More enthusiastic reviews were carried in other provincial papers and the Playhouse's male lead was receiving high praise: "Patrick McGoohan is excellent as the Prince who became a Swineherd to win a lady, a neat mixture of quiet humour and dignity, but he is run very close for honours by Joan Drummond as the temperamental Princess."[39] In *The Stage*, a compliment was paid: "There are now Patrick McGoohan, who is nicely developing his natural gift of characterisation...and Joan Drummond, who has a fascinating restraint in sympathetic portrayals."[40] Press reports of the actress showed that she was highly regarded: "Hers is a name you are going to hear a lot of on the radio.[xix] Three plays in eight days – good going for a first send-off on the air. She married actor Patrick McGoohan whom she met when they were in the same play at Sheffield."[41] There soon followed a report that Joan was expecting their first child and her consequent departure from the Sheffield company was described as "one of their greatest losses for many years."[42] Now, a move to London for the McGoohans beckoned.

[xiv] Between Leopold Street and Pinstone Street.
[xv] McGoohan would return his wife to the same spot in future years, to relive the magic of the original moment – see page 200.
[xvi] Joan reportedly converted to the Roman Catholic faith at that time.
[xvii] Patrick, just turned twenty three, was residing at 373 Fulwood Road, Sheffield and Joan, aged twenty, was at nearby 402.
[xviii] Part of the 1951 "Festival of Britain" celebrations.
[xix] There were few television sets in Britain at that time. It would be the 1953 coronation of Queen Elizabeth that would cause many thousands of people to go out and buy a TV, in order to watch the pageantry. By 1954 there were three million TV sets in Britain and the theatre world had growing concerns that those in the acting profession could be out of work in the months ahead.

[1] The Curtain Club Cuttings, January 1943 – December 1946; Local Studies Library; Sheffield Central Library
[2] Ibid
[3] Drama Critic, The Sheffield Telegraph, 18th March, 1946
[4] The Sheffield Star, 8th March, 1946
[5] Letter to The Curtain Club, 11th March, 1946
[6] The Curtain Club Cuttings, May, 1946
[7] Ibid
[8] Letter to The Curtain Club, 18th May, 1946
[9] Letter to The Curtain Club, May, 1946
[10] The Curtain Club Cuttings, January 1943 – December 1946; Local Studies Library; Sheffield Central Library
[11] The Sheffield Telegraph, 21st February, 1947
[12] Albert Meakin, Amateur Stage in the Sheffield Star, 26th February, 1947
[13] Letter to The Curtain Club, 22nd February, 1947
[14] The Sheffield Star, 3rd April,1947
[15] Letter to The Curtain Club, 27th April, 1947
[16] Letter to The Curtain Club
[17] Ibid
[18] The Curtain Club Cuttings; Local Studies Library; Sheffield Central Library
[19] Ibid
[20] The Sheffield Telegraph, c. February, 1948
[21] Amateur Stage in the Sheffield Star, 27th February, 1948
[22] Drama Critic in the Sheffield Star, 27th February, 1948
[23] South Yorkshire paper, January, 1952, review by S.C.H., details unknown
[24] The Curtain Club Cuttings; Local Studies Library; Sheffield Central Library
[25] The Sheffield Telegraph, 10th February, 1956
[26] Joan Reeder, Woman magazine, 4 issues between 9th and 30th October, 1965
[27] Ibid
[28] TV Guide, 17th September, 1977, Arnold Hano
[29] TV Guide, 1977, US
[30] Letter to Six of One, The Prisoner Appreciation Society, 12th May, 1977
[31] Joan Reeder, Woman magazine, 4 issues between 9th and 30th October, 1965
[32] Ibid
[33] Ibid
[34] Ibid
[35] Sheffield Star, 1950, details unknown
[36] Sheffield Star, 12th October, 1951
[37] Sheffield Telegraph, 1951, details unknown
[38] Ibid
[39] Source not verified
[40] The Stage, c. 1951, details unknown
[41] Weekly News, 1952
[42] The Stage, c. 1951, details unknown

McGoohan as Jess in *The Gypsy and The Gentleman* (1957)

CHAPTER THREE
All or Nothing!

"Forward! Forward! Victory lies ahead."
Brand (Act 5)

In the early months of their marriage, Patrick and Joan McGoohan's joint earnings in Sheffield totalled eighteen pounds a week and they felt "immensely rich."[1] However, when they knew that they were starting a family, Patrick decided that the time had come for him to earn a higher level of pay than repertory work could offer. "That meant London,"[2] he later recalled. The actor had been in Liverpool, from 21st April, with the play *Cupid and Psyche* and at the end of the month a London presentation was planned, although this did not happen. Joan, being only a few weeks away from her confinement, went to stay with her parents in Hampstead. Patrick, now "resting," had to make his next port of call the Labour Exchange. He was given work in an ice cream factory, which entailed standing at a conveyor belt, wrapping choc ices by the thousand; the disaffected worker quit after three nights. He next gained temporary employment in a Fleet Street all night café, from 7 p.m. to 6 a.m., including waiting on tables. The job paid him thirteen pounds per week and the hours meant that he could still try out for parts in theatrical productions, later in the day. "Hard on the feet, it was easier on the eyes," he commented, "and I had enough black coffee to keep me awake for rehearsals."[3]

Soon the expected happy event occurred, on Saturday, 31st May, 1952, Patrick being present when Joan gave birth to their first child, Catherine. In the following month he landed his first West End engagement,[i] as Albert Prosser,[ii] in *Hobson's Choice*,[iii] at London's Arts Theatre Club. The production was scheduled for a month,[iv] but ended unexpectedly

---

[i] As mentioned in the previous chapter, there had been a touring visit to London with *The Brontes*, in 1948.
[ii] Not the leading role, but this would be remedied in 1955, with *Serious Charge* – see page 45.
[iii] McGoohan was also in the earlier Sheffield production, in 1949 and a later Midlands presentation.
[iv] Described as an early career break for McGoohan, with actors Donald Pleasance and Beryl Bainbridge.

Programme for *Cupid and Psyche*, Liverpool, 1952

during the second week, leaving Patrick unemployed once more.[v] Fortunately, he was successfully interviewed by the Midland Theatre Company, allowing the new parents to move out of the expensive capital. With baby Catherine, they took an attic room in Coventry, where a spread of work for Patrick lasted for several months. Midland plays were funded by the Arts Council, to perform in towns where there was no established theatre. Touring[vi] occurred with four week runs, plays being presented for several days at a time at four regular locations: College Theatre, Coventry, where the company was based, the Co-operative Hall, Nuneaton, The Arts Centre, Netherton and Stanford Hall, Loughborough. During a performance of *The Cocktail Party*, by T. S. Eliot, the theatre lights failed and a party of miners, who were conveniently in the audience, moved to the front of the house and turned on their helmet lamps. These were sufficient to illuminate the stage and the actor described that night as "magic."[4]

Actor Earl Cameron[vii] appeared with McGoohan in the Midlands Theatre Group's production of *Deep Are the Roots*, set in the United States Deep South in 1945. McGoohan played Sheriff Serkin and in one scene he had to hit Cameron on the head with his revolver. The audience usually heard the gun butt connecting with a concealed sandbag, but in one performance McGoohan accidentally struck Cameron's head. The former was extremely apologetic and the show continued with the latter only slightly the worse for wear.

Cameron recalled, "I don't think anybody ever gets to know Patrick McGoohan too well. He's a very private person, a man with great principles, but he's a very lone person. He's a hard worker, a man who knows his craft very well. A kind of power emanated from him. He was just that little bit aloof from the rest of the company."[5]

Early in 1953, McGoohan ended his time with the Midland establishment and enjoyed more appearances with the Windsor Repertory Company, at the Theatre Royal, Windsor.[viii] He performed in five plays there, during a two year period: *A Priest in the Family* (1952), *Wishing Well* (1953), *Spring Model* (1953), *The River Line* (1954) and *The Male Animal* (1954). However, a greater move occurred later that year, when the actor joined the Bristol Old Vic Company, whose productions usually ran for three weeks at a time. On 23rd June, he was opening in *Henry V*, at the Theatre Royal, King Street, Bristol, taking three roles in the play: Chorus, Montjoy and MacMorris. The production drew mixed comments from local critic Dennis Bushell, of the *Bristol Evening World*. The report's headline was "Commons Outshine Royalty," implying that Bushell preferred McGoohan's performance to that of the lead actor: "(John) Neville moves with a stark dignity, but for all his zest and thrust, he does not dominate the play. It is upon our imaginations that we must work, through the Chorus of Patrick McGoohan, who exhorts us to do this ... with an astonishing savagery. Instead of coaxing these imaginary forces, Mr. McGoohan would bludgeon us into submission as he

[v] McGoohan reportedly took another role at the Arts Theatre, paying ten pounds a week, although no details of the assignment have been verified.
[vi] Touring ceased in 1957.
[vii] Earl Cameron later appeared with McGoohan in *Danger Man* and *The Prisoner*.
[viii] About twenty five miles west of London.

bludgeons the rich, sinewy verse at his disposal."[6]

The production transferred to London – courtesy of the 'parent' Old Vic – for a two week presentation. The actor received good notices in the capital also: "... Patrick McGoohan, shedding the robe of a somewhat forensic Chorus, gave a vitality to the brief sketch of MacMorris."[7] The troupe was even invited to present *Henry V* in Switzerland: "The company took their Coronation[ix] production... and flew from London airport to Zurich. It was 5 days of packed excitement for the youngsters – some of them had never been out of England before[x], and the reception of *Henry V* was rapturous. The Press was most cordial and appreciative."[8]

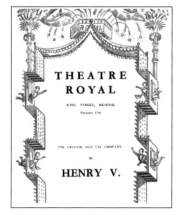

THEATRE
ROYAL

KING STREET, BRISTOL

THE BRISTOL OLD VIC COMPANY

in

HENRY V.

Programme for *Henry V*, Bristol, 1953

McGoohan would spend much of 1953 on the Bristol stage,[xi] staying in lodgings. Plays included *The Castiglioni Brothers* and *The Cherry Orchard*, in September, with *Antony and Cleopatra* being performed in October. That month, Joan returned to acting, becoming Chief Wife of the King's four spouses in the hit musical *The King and I*,[xii] at the Theatre Royal, Drury Lane. The couple's theatrical commitments meant week-long separations being forced upon them. They were only reunited on Sundays, having to part on Monday mornings. However, McGoohan's last Bristol play, *Old Bailey*, was performed in November and he was on his way back to town. In the following year, after two February productions at Windsor, mentioned earlier, he became part-manager of the Q Theatre, situated at Kew – hence the name "Q" – in London.[xiii] During several months there,[xiv] the actor took roles in three productions in as many months: in May, as Jack Connolly,[xv] in *Burning Bright*, in June as Roy Mawson,[xvi] in *Spring Model*[xvii] and in July as Leonard White, in *Time on Their Hands*.[xviii]

Actor George Baker[xix] was also considered for the role of Leonard White. He recalled "The rivalry was for real. Both of us were up for the male lead in *Time on Their Hands* at the Q Theatre and we were both anxious to get the job. The final choice lay between us and Pat got the part." Baker continued, "I am not sure whether Pat had a season as a director at (the) Q, or whether it was a one-off play, but he did offer me a part in a play he was directing at that time. I met him on occasions throughout our careers and I would just like to add what a generous actor he is."[9]

Significantly, from 1954 onwards, McGoohan moved into cinema and television. His initial engagement was with the BBC, then the only TV channel in Britain. The actor

---

[ix] Referring to Queen Elizabeth's accession to the throne that year.

[x] McGoohan had been in Britain continuously, since being brought there as a child.

[xi] McGoohan spent at least two seasons at Bristol, although one source states that he spent three seasons there.

[xii] Valerie Hobson and Herbert Lom took the leads.

[xiii] The Q became one of the most important of London's small theatres - seating four hundred and ninety people – staging many plays which would go on to become West End hits. In the nineteen fifties the theatre fell on hard times, mainly due to the spread of television. The Q closed in 1956.

[xiv] During the Q theatre's 1954 summer season, McGoohan was producer and director of *Grace and Favour*, the play running throughout July.

[xv] Listed elsewhere as Jock Connelly.

[xvi] "...a delightful performance by Patrick McGoohan which almost made the whole thing worthwhile..." was how his part was described in *Theatre World*.

[xvii] *Spring Model* was also performed in 1953 with the Windsor Repertory Company – see list at end of this book.

[xviii] The play was later revised as *Ring for Catty*, when McGoohan reprised his Leonard White role at the Lyric Theatre, London, in 1956.

[xix] George Baker appeared with McGoohan in *Arrival*, the opening episode of *The Prisoner*.

Above: A bearded McGoohan in *The Fall of Parnell* (1954). Right: McGoohan as Seaman McIsaacs in *Passage Home* (1955)

appeared on 13th June, 1954,[xx] in a half hour episode of the BBC series *You Are There*, in which veteran newsman Walter Cronkite hosted and narrated re-enactments of historical events. In the episode *The Fall of Parnell*, McGoohan played the scandal-hit Irish politician Charles Stewart Parnell.[xxi] The actor next worked on *The Vise* – an Americanisation of the English word for a vice clamp – a drama TV series, made in Britain by The Danziger brothers for the US market.[xxii] An introductory voice-over – that of Australian host Ron Randell – revealed: "The story we are going to tell is about people caught in the jaws of a vice, in a dilemma of their own making." The internationally slanted tales gave opportunities to British newcomers, including McGoohan. The plot line for his first episode, *A Gift from Heaven*,[xxiii] involved a witness to an airplane crash removing some diamonds from the wreckage. The thief wants to sell them illegally and approaches a private detective, Tony Mason (McGoohan) to find a 'fence' for the jewels. In a subsequent episode, *Blood in the Sky*,[xxiv] McGoohan was cast as Tom Vance, the plot involving another air disaster. The lead detective character, Mark Saber, investigates a mid-air explosion and scrutinises various suspects, one of them being a possible saboteur. Some sources refer to a possible third McGoohan episode, apparently directed by Pat Jackson.[xxv]

[xx] A different source says 6th September, 1954.

[xxi] Some sources refer to the part being taken by Lorne Greene, but McGoohan did play Parnell.

[xxii] The series originated in the US in 1951. After a few years it ended and British stories were then produced, with McGoohan being involved. After these, the central detective character Mark Saber (played by Tom Conway and later Donald Gray) from the US shows returned to replace *The Vise*. McGoohan did not participate and both *Mark Saber* and *Saber of London* lasted for some time. *The Vise* and later series were also known in the UK and US by other names: *(Mark Saber) Mystery Theater*, *(Inspector Mark Saber) Homicide Squad*, *Detective's Diary*, *Tension*, *The Pendulum*, *The Crooked Path* and *Uncovered*, as well as *The Vise: Mark Saber*. Some episodes were shown in British cinemas as 'shorts,' or as longer combined stories 'features.' TV airings in certain UK regions ran at various times until 1963 (in the US till 1961).

[xxiii] The episode was directed by Ernest (Ernie) Morris, who later was assistant director on *The Prisoner* episode *Many Happy Returns*. Some sources list only *Gift from Heaven* as the episode title. The broadcast, on 9th December, 1955, is referred variously by sources as being in the UK or the US.

[xxiv] Also directed by Ernest (Ernie) Morris, produced 1956 and shown on 6th May, 1958, the series then being called *Mark Saber*.

[xxv] See page 52 regarding Pat Jackson screen testing McGoohan at Pinewood studios, plus the footnote to that page and also page 59 as to the TV series *Rendezvous*, in which McGoohan appeared, under Jackson's direction, as well as later chapters about *Danger Man* and *The Prisoner*, Jackson having directed episodes of those series as well.

There followed another BBC appearance in May, 1955, when the actor took a part in *Terminus*.[xxvi] This was the umbrella title for a series of six half hour plays, presented on Saturday nights. The short stories always started off inside a railway terminus and in *Margin for Error* – starring Andre Morrell, Ursula Howells and Raymond Francis – McGoohan played James Hartley.[xxvii] In November, the actor secured the part of Colin Brown in *Aren't People Wonderful*, at the Embassy Theatre, London, a play about a group of lodgers in a boarding house. Wife Joan would soon be appearing at the same theatre, although in a different production. Meanwhile, she had been performing from the previous month with a repertory group, at the Strand Theatre, London, in the play *The Adventures of Peregrine Pickle*.

Importantly, McGoohan was about to make his cinema debut, in the films *The Dam Busters* (1954) and *Passage Home* (1955). In the first of these McGoohan had a speaking role, although his part was not credited. This classic British war movie,[xxviii] directed by Michael Anderson, told the story of Dr. Barnes Wallis, whose creation was the 'bouncing bomb,' designed to penetrate the defences of Germany's Ruhr dams and paralyse the enemy's industrial nerve centre. Wallace fought persistent scepticism that such a scheme was possible. Eventually, through the skill, determination and courage of RAF Wing Commander Guy Gibson and his squadron, the mission succeeded. Thrilling action and riveting suspense were combined in the true life drama heightened with actual newsreel of the legendary raid.

The Dam Busters' locations were shot in the Peak District, in the north of England and at RAF Hemswell, Lincolnshire. McGoohan appears in two short sequences, as the squadron receives final orders. His part is that of a grim-looking Military Policeman, guarding the door to the briefing room. Director Anderson cuts to him twice, the first to establish the scene and the second time to show the arrival of Gibson's black Labrador. The actor, affecting a Cockney accent, sends the dog away with a pat on its head, saying "Sorry old boy, it's secret. You can't go in, now hop it!"[xxix]

Variety review: "As a record of a British operational triumph during the last war, *The Dam Busters* is a small slice of history, told with painstaking attention to detail and overflowing with the British quality of understatement. This is the story of the successful raid on the Ruhr dams, when a small fleet of British bombers, using a new type of explosive, successfully breached the water supplies, which fed the Ruhr factories and caused desolation and havoc to the German war machine. For more than 90 minutes, the film is devoted to the planning and preparation, and very absorbing material this proves to be. The reconstruction of the raid and the pounding of the dams is done with graphic realism. The aerial photography is one of the major technical credits."

The second movie, *Passage Home*, was an intense drama – set in 1931 on a merchant ship – McGoohan having a small, credited role, as seaman McIsaacs. His main dialogue is delivered when he and his crew mates are seated around a table in the galley. As their

---

[xxvi] Some listings refer to *Terminus Number One* – albeit with the year as 1959 – but this is probably a misreporting of the play being 'number one' in the series of six plays. Another source describes the play as one for the BBC , while another says that it was not a BBC production. The drama should not be confused with a 1961 documentary *Terminus*, with a jazz soundtrack by Ron Grainer, who later composed *The Prisoner* main theme.

[xxvii] There are unconfirmed entries relating to a BBC presentation *The Whiteoak Chronicles* (1954). Some sources refer to McGoohan's involvement, but his name does not appear in any case details, although he could have appeared briefly and been uncredited.

[xxviii] The movie won an Oscar for Best Effects and a BAFTA for Best British Film.

[xxix] Shelagh Turner, whose reminiscences appear earlier – see page 25 – knew McGoohan from Sheffield. She told this writer that when *The Dam Busters* came out, she and a local crowd went to the Scala cinema in the city to see him: "He was only on screen for a minute or so, but we all cheered when he appeared."

spokesman, he threatens mutiny over the condition of the food stocks, mainly "the spuds" (potatoes). New York Times review: "Set in 1931, the film takes place aboard a merchant ship, briefly harbored in South America. A young woman boards the ship as a passenger, resulting in disharmony among the superstitious crew members. Virtuous seaman Anthony Steel protects the girl from the lecherous advances of captain Peter Finch. The film's predictable highlight is an outsized sea storm, during which a besotted Finch struggles to stay sober long enough to keep everyone from falling overboard." (Hal Erickson, All Movie Guide)

Other smallish film parts soon came along. In *I Am a Camera* (1955), forerunner to the musical *Cabaret*, McGoohan played a Swedish masseur. Bursting in on a party, he demands two baths, one to be filled with hot water and the other with cold. He is a 'water therapist' and his part becomes more of a pantomime one. Variety review: "A young author gets himself involved, innocently, with a crackpot girl in pre-World War II Berlin. In transferring the play to the screen ... the effect is always more that of a filmed stage play than a motion picture. The top players, and others, are competent in answering the rather light demands of story and direction. The filming was done in London and lacks the production polish accomplished on practically all domestic features."

McGoohan next appeared as Sir Oswald, uncredited, in the historical drama *The Dark Avenger* (1955; US title *The Warriors*). With location shooting taking place in the county of Hertfordshire and on MGM's back lot there,[xxx] the production gave McGoohan a couple of days' work.[xxxi] The film was Errol Flynn's final swashbuckler and made extensive use of the castle originally constructed for the MGM movie *Ivanhoe* (1952). Flynn starred as Prince Edward, the 'Black Prince,' ordered to stay behind in France after the Hundred Years' War to safeguard the estates conquered by his father, Edward III (Michael Hordern). Rebel French landowners led by the evil Count de Ville (Peter Finch) spend most of the film trying to murder Flynn while he attempts to rescue his fair lady (Joanne Dru). McGoohan appears as a member of Prince Edward's retinue. He would later recall that he had only two lines of dialogue, while John Welsh, playing Gurd, the leader of the French peasants, had a much larger role in the film: "He was there every day, but because he was a peasant and I was the titled nobleman, when it came to lunchtime...there were two tents; one for the peasants and the crowd actors and a smaller tent for the producer and director, Errol and some of the leading actors. The first day I was there, when we broke for lunch, this black limousine pulled up. I asked John 'Why is that car here?' As it turns out they were sent to pick up someone called Sir Oswald! It was me! Because I was called Sir Oswald, a car was sent to take me to their tent and dear old John who was playing this huge role, was with the peasants. Fiction had become reality."[10]

New York Times review: "Shot on location in Hertfordshire, England, the film stars Flynn as Edward, the 'Black Prince' of England. At the end of the Hundred Years' war, Edward remains in France to guard the lands taken by his predecessor-father. He is opposed in this by Count DeVille (Peter Finch). The story comes to a rousing conclusion as Edward and his followers defend their castle against DeVille's minions." (Hal Erickson, All Movie Guide).

[xxx] Film studios were set up in the small town of Boreham Wood in the 1920s and 1930s. The area became known as Elstree – the name being taken from nearby Elstree, larger than Borehamwood, although the sizes have since been reversed – and was even termed the "British Hollywood." The MGM studios' address later became the single word "Borehamwood."

[xxxi] He would return there at the end of the decade to film the first *Danger Man* episodes and in the sixties for *The Prisoner*.

McGoohan as Rev. Howard Phillips in *Serious Charge*, Garrick Theatre, London, 17th February, 1955

Although the assortment of small film roles both elevated McGoohan on the career ladder and supplemented his theatrical earnings, he still regarded himself principally as a stage actor. In February, 1955, he was receiving excellent notices for his impressive portrayal of Reverend Howard Phillips, in *Serious Charge* at the Garrick Theatre. This production was McGoohan's West End debut in a leading role. Produced by Martin Landau, the drama focuses on accusations by a young boy that Phillips made homosexual advances towards him.

McGoohan's stage performance was reviewed in *Plays and Players*: "Patrick McGoohan skilfully makes the priest an upright man of high Christian ideals, without once making him appear priggish. He exploits the moments of comedy to the full with his excellent timing." The critic observed that McGoohan learned the hard way in provincial repertory and "never studied at any of our drama schools." More in the form of a backhanded compliment the write-up continued: "The practical way in which he has learned his job is reflected both in his acting and in his general outlook on the theatre. He has been too busy acting to have time to become pretentious about it. Reverend Howard Phillips, as a character, might not have great depth, but the role demands an actor with a wide range, capable of bringing out many facets of the character."[11] Another critic found McGoohan's performance in *Serious Charge* "compelling and convincing,"[12] while a different writer reported that "Patrick McGoohan may be accounted unlucky insomuch as the vicar, when he loses his head, also changes his character, but he tackles both halves of the part with resource and address."[13] Peter Sallis,[xxxii] one of McGoohan's fellow players, from their Sheffield repertory days, revealed: "I think that Patrick's attitude was that if he could not get a good part, it didn't have to be a lead, but as long as it was a worthwhile part, he wasn't going to accept anything less. Consequently, he went on for instance to do *Moby Dick* with Orson Welles, where he played Starbuck the mate, and rather sneakily pinched many of the acting notices from under Orson's well made up nose."[14]

Before turning to *Moby Dick*, a few lines need to be devoted to the theatrical and cinematic legend that was Orson Welles (1915-1985). His infamous 1938 Halloween

---

[xxxii] Peter Sallis also appeared with McGoohan in *Moby Dick*. The title became *Moby Dick – Rehearsed* when the play was later published by Samuel French, but on the Duke of York's theatre programme, the title omits the word Rehearsed. In 1959, Sallis again appeared with McGoohan, in the play *Brand*, as well as becoming a player in the "59 Theatre Company," of which McGoohan was a part owner; see later in this chapter regarding *Moby Dick, Brand* and the "59" company.

MOBY DICK

Cast in order of their appearance:

A YOUNG ACTOR (afterwards "Ishmael")   GORDON JACKSON

A YOUNG ACTRESS (afterwards "Pip") ... ...   JOAN PLOWRIGHT

A STAGE MANAGER (afterwards "Flask") ... ...   PETER SALLIS

AN ASSISTANT STAGE MANAGER (afterwards "Bo'sun") ... JOHN GRAY

A SECOND ASSISTANT STAGE MANAGER
    (afterwards "Tashtego" & "Captain of the Rachel") JOHN BOYD-BRENT

A STAGE HAND WITH AN HARMONICA
    (afterwards "Portuguese Sailor" and "Dagoo"... JOSEPH CHELTON

OTHER STAGE HANDS   ...   .   PHILIPPE PERROTET
                                     HARRY CORDWELL
                                       DAVID SAIRE

A MIDDLE-AGED ACTOR (afterwards "Stubb") ...WENSLEY PITHEY

AN EXPERIENCED ACTOR
    (afterwards "Peleg" and "Old Cornish Sailor") JEFFERSON CLIFFORD

A SERIOUS ACTOR (afterwards "Starbuck") ... PATRICK McGOOHAN

A VERY SERIOUS ACTOR (afterwards "Elijah"
"Ship's Carpenter" "Old Bedford Sailor" and others) KENNETH WILLIAMS

AN ACTOR MANAGER
    (afterwards "Father Mapple" and "Ahab") ... ... ORSON WELLES

The action of the play takes place in a provincial American theatre towards the end of the last century

The play will be presented in two parts with one interval of 15 minutes

GENERAL MANAGER			MICHAEL THOMPSON
PRODUCTION ASSISTANT ...	For		JOAN RICHARDSON
Stage Director	OSCAR		Peter Banks
Stage Manager	LEWENSTEIN		...David Booth
Assistant Stage Manager	PRODUCTIONS		Susan Newall
Wardrobe Mistress	LIMITED		Margot Martin
Press Representative			George Fearon
			(Ger. 2169)

It is intended that this play, now presented for a limited season of four weeks, shall form part of a programme of repertory to be presented by Mr. Welles in the forthcoming season.

Costumes by Messrs. B. J. Simmons Ltd. Lighting Equipment by Strand Electrical and Engineering Co. Ltd. Sound by Bishop Sound. Virginia Cigarettes by Abdulla.

The Management reserve the right to refuse admission, also to make any alteration in the cast which may be rendered necessary by illness or other unavoidable causes.

SMOKING IS NOT PERMITTED IN THE AUDITORIUM

Programme for *Moby Dick* (1955)

broadcast of *The War of the Worlds* terrified thousands of American listeners. Three years later, aged only twenty six, Welles was given complete control over his first film *Citizen Kane* (1941). His dedication towards freedom of artistic expression underpinned his standing as a maverick artist, combining the disciplines of performer, writer, producer and director. During their short time together, Welles had a profound and lasting effect upon McGoohan, taking on the role of mentor and demonstrating to the younger artist how being an idiosyncratic performer could go hand in hand with taking charge of a production. McGoohan revealed, "It was talking to him that was so great! I remember one of the conversations we had. He said: 'What do you think is the most dangerous thing on Earth?' I knew it wasn't the Bomb. Welles said: 'Television.' That's what he thought was the most dangerous thing on Earth."[15] McGoohan also reflected, "I got to know (Orson) pretty well. He felt (*Moby Dick*) was the best thing that he had done since his early years. But it is true that Orson was never completely satisfied with his own performance."[16]

However, the actor's relationship with Welles did not begin well. When McGoohan auditioned for his part in the play *Moby Dick*, he was given no more than a nod to start. Welles, gripping a large cigar in his mouth, was preoccupied with a heated discussion over finances. As McGoohan described it, "I came in to audition. All the stage lights were on. The rest of the theatre was a black abyss with Welles out there, listening. I started to read and then I heard two voices, Welles and somebody next to him, discussing production costs. So I stopped and Welles immediately boomed out: 'Why did you stop?' I said: 'I thought you might want to listen to me.' Welles snapped: 'I can listen and talk at the same time. Keep reading.' I started in again, and again he began talking and again I stopped and Welles said: 'I told you to keep reading.' When I continued, Welles and his unseen partner began muttering and this time I took the script and threw it down and said, 'Mr. Welles, you can stuff Moby Dick' and I began storming out. To my surprise, Welles called out, 'Mr. McGoohan? Will you play Starbuck?' The three and a half week run was one of the most exciting times in my career."[17]

Starbuck was the biggest role in the play, after Welles' own Captain Ahab. McGoohan's appointment demonstrated Welles' faith in his new protégé. Throughout rehearsals the director positioned himself at a microphone in the dark stalls, speaking his lines and shouting instructions to the other players. Welles regarded *Moby Dick* as "the best thing I ever did in *any* form – and I seriously think if I ever did anything really good, that was it."[18] Welles also commended McGoohan's performance: "I was enormously impressed by the actor who was playing Starbuck and I kept thinking how good he would be in the part of Ahab."[19]

However, the production was not without its difficulties. McGoohan recalled that Welles had "A dozen different, creative ideas a minute."[20] At one point the actors and stage crew were approaching mutiny, when Welles kept the cast in the theatre until 5 a.m. repeating the same three lines of dialogue, over and over again until he was satisfied.[21] The play cost nearly two thousand pounds to put on and Welles was to receive a third of the net profits of the production. The original plan was for a run of several weeks, followed by a provincial tour. However, Welles decided to limit the play to one venue, for only a month, although even this would become shortened. Owing to a prior booking of the theatre for another production, the play was only able to chalk up twenty five performances.[xxxiii]

Moby Dick opened on sixteenth June, 1955, at the Duke of York's Theatre, in London. The audacity of adapting the epic novel by Herman Melville confounded the critics who claimed that it would be impossible to have a full-sized whale, or a ship, on stage. Instead, Welles' ingenuity saw the production going ahead without any elaborate sets or special effects. Cleverly, the adaptation involved a travelling company of actors in nineteenth century New England, who are gathered to perform *King Lear,* but instead choose to rehearse their own version of *Moby Dick.* Rather than presenting the audience with a sweeping, nautical set, Welles introduced the device of a play-within-a-play, creating an intimate, old-fashioned theatrical setting. The sea and the ship *Pequod* were suggested with minimal props and staging. Welles could even get away with such tricks as having a giant cardboard whale flapped about, with actors standing aslant and swaying in unison, to suggest the movement of the waves.[xxxiv] Welles paid remarkable attention to production details. The actor wrote notes as to how the players should be dressed; his own costume and those of McGoohan, Peter Sallis,[xxxv] Gordon Jackson, Wensley Pithey and Kenneth Williams were covered in this way.

Welles later confided in film director Peter Bogdanovich: "The idea was to conjure up some of that empty-theatre magic. We had to do it with an audience out front, of course; it was a sort of magic trick. In London, anyway, I think it worked. That show was the last pure joy I've had in the theatre. Great cast – most of them are stars now. Kenneth Williams, Joan Plowright – it was her first important role; she was extraordinary in it as Little Pip. And Patrick McGoohan, who'd now be, I think, one of the big actors of his generation if TV hadn't grabbed him. Well, he was tremendous as Starbuck." Welles added that McGoohan,

---

[xxxiii] There is a listing of the play as a telecast by NBC in 1955, but the lack of mentions by other source suggests that this is something else, possibly an adaptation of the original Herman Melville book. In 1962, the play opened on Broadway, with Rod Steiger as Ahab. Owing to unfavourable reviews, there were only ten performances.

[xxxiv] Welles, as Ahab, also played Father Mapple later in the play and took the same part in John Huston's film version of *Moby Dick* (1956).

[xxxv] Sallis, like McGoohan had also been with the Sheffield Playhouse, as well as being in the play Brand with him and acting with the "59 Theatre Company," covered in this chapter.

"had the required attributes: looks, intensity, unquestionable acting ability and a twinkle in his eye suggesting self-deferential humor."[22]

Moby Dick received universal acclaim. The critics revelled in Welles' constant ad-libbing and way he the reinterpreted his part each night. McGoohan was more than able to keep up with the on-stage inventiveness and his own performance was said to be inspired. Peter Sallis, who played "A Stage Manager," afterwards "Flask,"[xxxvi] recalled, "You were very lucky to be there as an actor, as well as in the audience."[23] Kenneth Tynan echoed these sentiments in *The Sunday Observer*: "British audiences have been unemployed for far too long. If they wish to exert themselves, to have their minds set whirling at sheer theatrical virtuosity, *Moby Dick* is their opportunity. With it, the theatre becomes once more a house of magic. McGoohan's is the best performance of the evening." *Moby Dick*, Tynan enthused, was: "Pure theatrical megalomania. A sustained assault on the senses which dwarfs anything London has ever seen since, perhaps, the Great Fire."[24] Another notice gave forth: "There is a fine portrayal of Starbuck, the mate who fights against Ahab's fanaticism, by Patrick McGoohan. He is a first-rate actor who, while the star's performance remains a work-in-progress, is giving the ablest characterisation of the evening."[25]

Peter Noble's 1956 biography[26] of Welles quoted Paul Holt from the *Daily Herald*, "The stage effects are quite brilliant," and John Barber from the *Daily Express*, "The discerning will thrill to its lofty courage and seize from the storm-wracked moments of the biggest theatrical thunder in years...the evocation of a ship at sea is quite astonishingly impressive." Noble's own view was that Welles "brought red blood into the theatre, and his production – the storm-tossed ocean, the crazily swinging lamps, the broken masts, the mounting obsession of Ahab, the muttering sailors, the tragic inevitability of the sea saga – made magic and mystery of the Duke of York's stage. He had set his play on the bare stage of an actual theatre, where a group of actors were rehearsing a play of Moby Dick, thus circumventing the difficulties involved in providing extensive scenery and props, not forgetting a full-sized white whale."[27] Noble reported how the play "romped home as a triple success for Orson, as actor, director and dramatist."

Welles even commissioned his own sixteen millimetre film of *Moby Dick*,[xxxvii] using the original London cast. He decided that he would produce his play on stage for a limited season and then create a telefilm of it, running for an hour, to be suitable for showing on TV.[xxxviii] Accordingly, he filmed *Moby Dick* being performed with no audience, at the Hackney Empire and also the Scala theatre, in London. Welles shot about seventy five minutes, or three spools, using cameraman Ted Lloyd and editor Bill Morton. Hilton Craig, who acted as lighting cameraman, told Peter Noble that "Orson had worked on a complete screen adaptation of his play and that it was by no means merely a photographed stage-play. On the contrary, it was shot largely in close-ups and looked very impressive on near-completion."[xxxix] However, Noble described problems with the film version, as the stage lighting was too dark to be satisfactory on small TV screens.

Peter Sallis was involved with Welles' filming of the play. "Orson...did come back in three or four weeks...at the Hackney Empire. I think it was a variety hall when it was first built, but

[xxxvi] Some sources refer to actor Christopher Lee as taking these roles, but the printed Duke of York's Theatre programme makes no mention of Lee and shows Peter Sallis. Lee did however participate in an attempted film adaptation – see page 50.
[xxxvii] See earlier footnote on page 47 regarding a claimed 1955 television broadcast of the play, or presentation of the film.
[xxxviii] Welles planned to sell the film for showing in the US television series *Omnibus*. However, according to the chronology of his career in the Joseph Rosenbaum book *This is Orson Welles*, the great man stopped filming when he was dissatisfied with the results.

we were going to use it to film *Moby Dick*. Orson had raised some money...and...we were going to film it, presumably for television in black and white and it would probably have made a fine movie. We went on filming and I would think we had done perhaps a couple of weeks, when the word filtered through that Orson had used up all (the) money. Well...the filming came to an end and we went home and that was that."[28]

Problems with lighting and finance apart, Welles' plans were also being compromised by an approaching big screen version of *Moby Dick*, being directed by John Huston. Ironically, Welles was given a part in the cinema production[xl] and his earnings at least helped

The Makepeace Story (1956)

provide some funding for his own film. However, Welles later asserted that the project was abandoned: "We shot for three days (in London) and it was obvious it wasn't going to be any good, so we stopped. There was no film (completed). We only did one and a half scenes."[29] However, Welles did arrange for some additional shooting to occur at the Turin film studios,[xli] with Henry Margolis as producer and Hilton Craig the cinematographer.

McGoohan was informed by Welles that he would be required for filming of the play in Italy. The actor disclosed: "We were filming (in London) everything but our parts (Ahab and Starbuck). I went up to (Orson) one day and said: 'When are we going to film our stuff?' He said: 'Not here, Italy.' We...still hadn't filmed our stuff, apart from the crowd scenes, which involved the other people. I said, 'Orson when?' 'I'll call you,' he said. Eventually I got a call: 'Still standing by?' 'Yes'. 'Well stand by a little longer.' I hung around for another five weeks and eventually got a telegram to come to Milan.[xlii] I spent three weeks with him in Milan shooting our stuff." Peter Sallis recounted how McGoohan had received his call to go to Turin, Welles instructing him to bring not only himself, but also certain items of equipment. "He told (McGoohan) to check into this hotel, he gave him the name and (said): 'Don't come to the studio until I send for you.'" Of Welles, Sallis was respectful, but claimed that McGoohan "had his measure."

While in Italy, McGoohan accidentally saw some of the *Moby Dick* film coverage: "I crept into the back of (Welles') screening room, and there were rushes! Of the shots we had filmed.

[xxxix] It is not clear how much of the stage sets from the Duke of York's was transferred to the Empire or the Scala, but any lack of stage dressing could explain the need to film the action as close ups.

[xl] See footnote on page 47.

[xli] Turin was among the first cities in the world to have a film studio. At the time of Welles' planned project, the city boasted one of the world's busiest movie-making scenes.

[xlii] Turin can be reached in an hour by train from Milan, being about 70 miles apart.

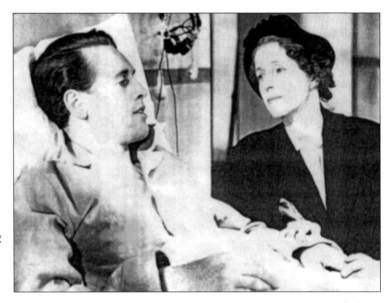

Above: Poster for *Ring for Catty* (1956). Right: McGoohan bedridden in *Ring for Catty* (1956)

I stayed there when the lights went down and saw about forty five minutes of them. And when they were done and the lights came on, he turned around and saw me and went berserk, *berserk*! 'What are you doing here? I don't want *anyone* to see this!' I said, 'But Orson it's fantastic, *fantastic*!' He said, 'It's not done yet.'[30] I saw some scenes, they were marvellous."[31]   Director Peter Graham Scott[xliii] – who had seen the stage version[xliv] – continues the story: "Associated Rediffusion[xlv] bought (Welles' film) and said to me that I must go and pick it up from Italy, but I said no. The company had bought the film which Welles had made of his play, but they found that there were no close-ups of the star as Captain Ahab. They wanted me to go out directing in Italy, where Welles was at the time and I said that directing him was where I draw the line. The guy that went out in my place stayed for a week until the Friday and was kept waiting until finally Welles was ready to do the close-ups one evening."[32]

Actor Christopher Lee said that he appeared with McGoohan in Welles' filmed TV adaptation of his 1955 *Moby Dick* – he was not in the stage play – but that it was never shown.[xlvi] The production, according to Lee, "...was mostly done in mime, drinking from non-existent cups, throwing non-existent harpoons. The notion was that of a play within a play, where the actors step in and out of their roles." The actor added, "In one scene, I had to say to Patrick McGoohan, 'There's bad news from that ship,' when the Pequod is approaching the Rachel. And suddenly, Orson's voice came booming from behind the camera, 'There's bad news from that ship – mark my words.' Well, I looked at Patrick, and Patrick looked at me, because we didn't quite know what was going on – why he was repeating our lines." Lee had seen the original play in London and recalled the hunt for the whale, "... in which the cast kneeled, sat, and stood on each others shoulders, faced the audience at

---

[xliii] In the sixties, Graham Scott directed *Danger Man* and *Prisoner* episodes, mentioned later in this book, as well as McGoohan's TV film *Jamaica Inn* (1982).
[xliv] His view of the play was "...a disaster, a mess of a thing. It was a silly pompous thing by Orson," he told this writer in 2006.
[xlv] See page 53.
[xlvi] A check with the BBC TV listing archive, through Radio Times magazine, revealed only a 1955 showing of *Orson Welles' Sketch Book*, which did not include any footage from *Moby Dick*.

Left: McGoohan receiving a bed bath in *Ring for Catty* (1956). Right: McGoohan with Terence Alexander and William Hartnell in *Ring for Catty* (1956)

centre stage, swaying from side to side, as if in a whaling boat. At the end, after the bows, to a shouting, standing ovation, Welles walked out on stage to praise the players."[33]

The solution to the mystery of whether the post-production was ever completed – and the whereabouts of the film, if any – is knowledge which Welles took with him to the grave. There are three possibilities. First, the film could have continued being made in Italy, as McGoohan recalls, and may have just vanished in the mists of time. Second, the finished film could have remained stored at Welles' Spanish villa and been destroyed in a fire there, which occurred in 1970. Finally, there is the assertion from various quarters that the cans of film did indeed come back to Great Britain. It is claimed that they were placed in bond by Customs, owing to non-payment of duties. Perhaps they remain there still, in viewable condition, or as dust. Jim People, who worked for Associated Rediffusion in 1955, as a film editor and director, recalled many cans of *Moby Dick* footage being delivered to the company at its Television House, in Kingsway, London, in the late 1960s, with a customs demand for duty. He believed that the cans were returned to customs because the company wouldn't pay the duty.[xlvii][34]

To close the whole story, mention of a second Welles production at that time is needed, being one which possibly diverted the director from his planned *Moby Dick* film. While McGoohan was in Italy, he found Welles busily engaged upon filming a television travel series.[xlviii] The younger actor unwittingly walked in on his 'employer': "I went down to the studio one day... looking for Orson, and I found him on the stage (the stage we were rehearsing on the day before) and heard him carrying on a conversation with someone. I peeked around the corner to see. I see two chairs, an empty table, and a huge placard from a bullfight.[xlix] And there's Orson talking to an empty chair; having a conversation with it. And the cameras are going. And I watched this for a moment...That turned out to be his part of a conversation with Kenneth Tynan, the critic, who was not there. They filmed the other half

[xlvii] According to one source, Welles abandoned his first attempt at filming *Moby Dick* in July of 1955 with seventy five minutes of footage shot. Welles seemed to undertake little subsequent work on the film and may have lost a little artistic interest, although he did revisit the project years later (see footnote a few paragraphs on).
[xlviii] The series was called *Around the World with Orson Welles* (1955) – now released on DVD – made for Associated Rediffusion.
[xlix] A prop from *Around the World with Orson Welles* (1955).

Above: Cannes Film Festival (1957)
Right: McGoohan as G. "Red" Redman in
Hell Drivers (1957)

in England, with Tynan, who didn't know he was going to be in it! That's Orson! He would go off and shoot these things, these reels of film...miles of film, that no-one has ever seen. Amazing man."[35] On another occasion in Italy, McGoohan said that he had caught Welles alone, weeping, adding "He was a very lonely man."[36]

At last McGoohan was able to put Italy and the *Moby Dick* saga behind him[l] and return to Britain. In the autumn of 1955, he appeared in a BBC television mini-series, *The Makepeace Story*. Presented under the banner of *Sunday Night Theatre*, four live plays told the saga of a Lancashire textiles firm and its family owners, from 1774 to 1955. In the opening segment, *Ruthless Destiny*, McGoohan played the stubborn founder, Seth Makepeace.[li] The BBC had also required the actor's services on 11th August, 1955, for a radio recording of *Farewell Companions*, a ballad opera on the life of the Irish rebel Robert Emmet, broadcast on 23rd March, 1956.[37] McGoohan contributed as an actor, but was reportedly so unhappy with the radio medium that he refused to do radio plays ever again and instructed his agent never to secure any such work for him.

The latter half of the decade was something of a watershed for McGoohan's stage career, as the greater financial rewards of the cinema could not be ignored. His chance for a big screen break-through came in the mid-fifties, when the actor visited the Rank Organisation's film studios at Pinewood. Reports differ as to his being there to seek an odd day's work, or trying out as a stand-in for Dirk Bogarde, or simply playing opposite a young actress who herself was being screen tested. However, director Pat Jackson[lii] firmly recalled selecting McGoohan and inviting him to be screen tested: "I saw him in *Moby Dick*,[liii] with Orson Welles. I was struck by him and I got in touch with his agent. He was a wonderful actor (and) the result was first-class. Patrick was perfect for the heroic role I had in mind."[38]

---

[l] Welles shot another *Moby Dick* film in 1971, playing all the parts himself, in close-up. The footage was never edited, but in 1999 Filmmuseum München edited the rushes. McGoohan was not involved. See also later in this book regarding a 2007 version – page 271.

[li] The production was scripted by Frank and Vincent Tilsley, the latter of whom would write for *The Prisoner*.

[lii] Pat Jackson also worked on the TV series *The Vise* - see page 42 - and *Rendezvous* - see page 59 - in which McGoohan appeared and later he would work with the actor on *Danger Man* and *The Prisoner*.

Jackson remembered his own involvement: "I was assigned to direct *High Tide at Noon*,[liv] a Woman's Own type of story about an island off the coast of Maine." He described his 'claim to fame', as he put it: "I brought Pat McGoohan to the screen. (I) wanted him to play the hero in *High Tide at Noon*. Apart from a couple of bits, he'd barely done any film. Then new to the screen, (he) was to play the lead. I arranged a test for him, he was extremely nervous, but he did it beautifully and got the contract. Eddie Carrick, one of our great art directors, and I went location hunting. I came back to Pinewood to discover that the film had been cancelled. I demanded to see John Davis[lv] (who told) me that he had cancelled the film (because he) had lost faith in the subject. Shortly after ... Phil Leacock was told that he was to make *High Tide at Noon* in the studio: a sea picture about lobster fishermen. He did and many months later, the film having cost a fortune, it emptied the Rank circuit so fast that it had to be withdrawn. I took my full fee for *High Tide At Noon* and was never forgiven. In the ensuing debacle that *High Tide at Noon* became, McGoohan didn't in fact play the hero, he played the villain, and from then on the poor man was always cast as villains."[39]

Whatever may have led to McGoohan's Rank try-out, when the casting office saw the rushes, it was the quality of the actor's work and his screen presence which resulted in the offer of a five year signing,[lvi] plus an impressive commencing salary of four thousand pounds a year. With his new film contract secured, in February, 1956 McGoohan was meanwhile, back on the boards, this time at the Lyric Theatre, Shaftesbury Avenue, London, for the comedy *Ring for Catty*.[lvii] Reprising his role of Leonard White, McGoohan was delighted to be able to appear on stage with wife Joan, who was playing his girlfriend, Madge Williams.[lviii] One critic declared, "There is some pleasant realistic acting. Mr. Patrick McGoohan is the sick man who suddenly gives up the will to live after a gallantly cheerful struggle. Miss Joan Drummond[lix] is his girl who at last falls in love with someone else."[40] Another review read: "Mr. Patrick McGoohan and Mr. William Hartnell, immobilised in beds, give impressive demonstrations of horizontal acting."[41]

In the recent past McGoohan had enjoyed roles in BBC television dramas, but now a second TV channel was setting up.[lx] ITV, standing for "Independent Television," was soon to spread across the UK,[lxi] potentially doubling work opportunities for actors. In Britain, the monopoly of the BBC having been lost, the new commercial station was able to attract audiences away from its rival channel. The expanding organisation, with its regional outlets, offered a popular staple diet of filmed action-adventure series, usually of a half hour's duration. Historical figures frequently formed the subject matter, with each local ITV

[liii] *Moby Dick* ran from mid-June, to early July, 1955.
[liv] The film's eventual release was in 1957, covered later in this chapter.
[lv] John Davis became managing director of Rank's companies and was largely responsible for moving the whole of their productions to Pinewood.
[lvi] However, see later in this chapter as to Rank spotting McGoohan in the movie *Zarak* and being impressed with his performance.
[lvii] The production was revised from the original play, *Time on Their Hands*, in which McGoohan appeared at the Q Theatre and was later adapted as the film *Carry on Nurse* (1959).
[lviii] Also in the cast was William Hartnell, who would appear alongside McGoohan, the following year, in the film *Hell Drivers*. *Ring for Catty* was co-written by actor Patrick Cargill, who would later be seen in two episodes of *The Prisoner*.
[lix] Joan Drummond also appeared as Miss Casewell, in the long-running production of *The Mousetrap* at the Ambassadors Theatre, London, in 1956/7, 1957/8 and 1958/9 seasons.
[lx] Rediffusion became the first ITV company in Britain. Broadcasting from September, 1955, mainly for the London area, the station was still not an alternative to the national BBC organisation. However, other regional ITV companies would spread coverage across the country by the end of the decade.
[lxi] See page 269 as to ITV's fiftieth anniversary.

company often producing its own original programmes. Costume dramas came to fill screens in homes up and down the country, as television regions in Britain gradually gained more of ITV's commercial coverage. In the autumn of 1956, McGoohan made his ITV debut in *The Adventures of Aggie*.[lxii] A vehicle for Joan Shawlee, Aggie – full name Asgaard Agnete Anderson – was a London fashion expert, criss-crossing the world, selling exotic creations. Her travels bring incidents, accidents and events – ranging from dangerous to humorous – involving spies, smugglers and murderers. McGoohan featured in two *Aggie* episodes, playing Migual in *Spanish Sauce* and Jocko in *Cock and Bull*.[lxiii] Another ITV series in which McGoohan was involved at that time was *The Adventures of Sir Lancelot*, starring William Russell, a Sapphire Films production for distributors ITC. The episode *The Outcast*,[lxiv] saw McGoohan playing Sir Glavin, in a story in which Lancelot's squire is accused of stealing the Queen's ring.

So far, the cinema had not provided the actor with major opportunities and his next movie appearance was still a limited one, although he received good reviews. In *Zarak* (1956), a military tale set in India, McGoohan was cast[lxv] amongst such big screen names as Victor Mature and Anita Ekberg. Film journalist, Margaret Hinxman, singled out McGoohan for special praise. Perhaps recognising that his part had not been a principal one, the actor responded by telling Ms. Hinxman that she was "mad."[42] However, another report heaped praise on the actor: "In the fantastic hodge-podge of *Zarak*, there's only one acting performance worth of the name – from Patrick McGoohan. He plays that invariably thankless role of the doom-predicting second-in-command to the British Army hero (Michael Wilding). Yet McGoohan – an Irish-American newcomer to the British screen – gives his stupid character a stature and strength. In a half-way decent role, McGoohan will be really SOMETHING!"[43]

New York Times review: "In this desert adventure, a bandit chieftain roams the northwest deserts of India. Wherever he goes, he leaves a trail of ruin. A British major is assigned to capture the bandit and his gang. He succeeds, but soon the bandit, with the assistance of a sadistic nomad, escapes. The raiders then head for a British garrison where more bloodshed ensues as they begin slaughtering the hapless soldiers. The nomad captures the colonel and begins torturing him. The bandit, who has grown to respect his British adversary, sacrifices his own life to stop him." (Sandra Brennan, All Movie Guide)

McGoohan's glowing mentions in the press as an impressive newcomer in *Zarak* led to Rank deciding that he was ideal for substantial parts in their coming motion pictures, *High Tide at Noon* (1957), soon followed by *Hell Drivers* (1957), *The Gypsy and the Gentleman* (1957) and *Nor the Moon by Night* (1958). *High Tide at Noon* was shot on location in Canada and at Pinewood, starring McGoohan as an aggressive character, Simon Brett, in a story set in a secluded fishing village.[lxvi] The movie also showed the actor's first screen kiss. A journalist's report commented on the newcomer, describing his performance as being, "as twitchy as that of James Dean in *Giant* (1956)."[44]

New York Times review: "A rugged, isolated island off the coast of Nova Scotia provides

[lxii] The series – sometimes just Aggie – aired in the UK between September, 1956 and March, 1957 and was also shown that year in the US.
[lxiii] *Cock and Bull* was not screened until 1958.
[lxiv] The episode was broadcast on 6th October, 1956 by ATV and 22nd October, 1956 by NBC. Internet sources wrongly refer to an episode of that name in McGoohan's later *Rafferty* series. There was a story so named in the *Assignment Foreign Legion* series, although he was not in the episode of that title, but was in another, *The Coward*, see page 57.
[lxv] He played Indian Army Adjutant Moor Larkin.
[lxvi] The movie was helmed by Philip Leacock, who would later direct the 1984 McGoohan TV film *Three Sovereigns for Sarah*.

the setting for this drama. Much of the island is owned by one person, the other inhabitants, primarily lobster fishermen, rent from him. One of the lobster men begins romancing the wealthy owner's daughter and marries her. After the wedding, the bride is disturbed to learn that her hubby is a compulsive gambler who quickly squanders their small savings. The impoverished couple has no choice but to leave the island and live on the mainland." (Sandra Brennan, All Movie Guide)

McGoohan attended the 1957 Cannes Film Festival, to promote *High Tide at Noon* and to participate in Rank's "Parade of Stars." Also present was wife Joan, looking on as her husband was expected to pose for publicity shots, with glamorous starlets. Being on the Rank payroll certainly brought financial security, but there were disadvantages. The actor was required to conform to the studio system and support its publicity machine. McGoohan, aged twenty nine and being groomed by Rank's famous "Charm School," now had the opportunity to become one of a number of bankable young faces. However, he later made no secret of the fact that he found promotional work unpalatable, degrading and superficial: "Getting me to take part in the Parade of Stars at Cannes Films Festival, or to cultivate a smooth line in cocktail party talk, was an unrewarding task. They must have felt that in me they'd netted an oyster with more sand than pearl. They compensated for this by projecting a public image of me as a 'rebel.'" The actor felt a growing dislike of the "phoney nonsense" and what the Rank studio called "glamour."[45]

McGoohan's fervent wish to remain loyal as the private, family man, together with his moral and religious beliefs, turned him away from a more exciting life in show business and the many networking opportunities it offered. A publicity feature presented him as a "rebel with a cause."[46] "I hope to be a constructive rebel," the actor responded: "I believe that compromise is dangerous – whether in acting, politics, or anything else." Clearly, he remembered the advice of his mentor Orson Welles, adding: "The ideal set-up is one man in control – one man who knows exactly what he wants. Integrity and honesty are the highest goals an actor can set himself."[47]

The rising star's next film for Rank was *Hell Drivers* (1957), which would become an early screen showcase for one of his most memorable performances.[lxvii] With shooting taking place at Pinewood studios – the release would occur in July that year – the actor was cast as the dynamic G. "Red" Redman. The role of a violent haulage trucker placed him amongst famous faces such as Stanley Baker, Herbert Lom, Sidney James, William Hartnell and Gordon Jackson. He was becoming established faster with the public than fellow newcomers in *Hell Drivers*, Sean Connery and David McCallum. "At every opportunity, McGoohan rolls his eyes, snarls, gibbers and attempts to eat the scenery – sometimes simultaneously." The actor's violent exit at the end of the movie drew the comment, "... the sight of the (cigarette) falling from McGoohan's panic-stricken lips is one the evocative sights in post-war crime films."[48]

Variety review: "Hell Drivers is a slab of unabashed melodrama. The story has to do with the rivalries of a gang of haulage truck drivers, operating between gravel pits and a construction site. Stanley Baker is an ex convict who gets a job as one of these drivers and immediately falls foul of Patrick McGoohan, the firm's ace driver. Baker discovers that McGoohan and William Hartnell, the manager, are running a racket. The drama comes to

---

[lxvii] Many years later, McGoohan would rue the day he did *Hell Drivers*, perceiving that this gave him an unwanted, early reputation as a villain – see page 276.

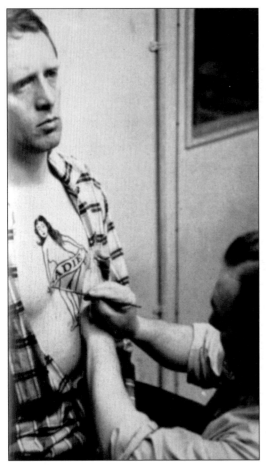

The Greatest Man in the World (1958), in which McGoohan has his chest tattooed with "Sadie"

an uneasy head when Baker's lorry is doctored. Endfield's direction is straightforward and conventional, but some of the speed sequences provide some tingling thrills. Acting is adequate, but uninspired. Baker gives a forceful performance of restrained strength and Herbert Lom has some neat moments as his Italian buddy. Patrick McGoohan gives an exaggerated study as the villain. Peggy Cummins, as a village vamp, fails to spark a tepid love interest."

New York Times review: "In this efficient British crime drama, Tom Yately (Stanley Baker) is an ex-con looking for honest work. He thinks he's found it when he takes a job as a truck driver, but he soon discovers that the trucking firm he's signed on with is not playing by the rules. Red (Patrick McGoohan), the company's best driver, and Cartley (William Hartnell), the manager, have created five fictional drivers who have been added to the payroll. The other staff drivers are given the shifts that the phony drivers are supposed to be working, while Red and Cartley divide their pay packets. When Tom attempts to expose the corruption at the trucking firm, he soon discovers that he's taken his life in his hands in the process." (Mark Deming, All Movie Guide)

Despite *Hell Drivers'* exciting action, *Picturegoer* magazine put the brakes on, suggesting that McGoohan was being presented as a major personality too quickly. Columnist Elizabeth Forrest observed that his was just a supporting role – although his face figured largely in advertisements and posters for the film – "a sure indication of how a studio rates an artist." She felt that in McGoohan's own best interests his progress should be curbed a little: "There's a real danger of the actor being pushed too far, too fast." Despite her reservations, Forrest predicted that along with the current screen idol Michael Craig,[lxviii] McGoohan would become one of the two most striking young male personalities of the future. Clearly the writer felt that directors were so bewitched by McGoohan's talent that they could not bear to restrain it. What the actor needed just then, she stated, was a director to control and discipline him. In trying to unravel the McGoohan mystery, Forrest described him as: "A strange and unusual recruit to British films. He has a quiet integrity that blazes into burning enthusiasm when he talks about the things that matter. And those are acting, his ambition to direct and produce films and his practical admiration for Orson

[lxviii] With whom McGoohan would appear in the 1958 film *Nor the Moon by Night*, called *Elephant Gun* in the USA, and in the 1962 movie *Life for Ruth*.

McGoohan giving a drink to the local wildlife, on *Nor the Moon by Night* (1958) location

Welles. He'll be big – make no mistake. But growth takes time. And in the early stages, you just can't rush it!"[lxix] [49]

Also in 1957, McGoohan appeared in a short-lived series, *Assignment Foreign Legion*. He took the role of Captain Valadon in the episode *The Coward*,[lxx] broadcast in February, 1957. These half hour stories featured Merle Oberon as hostess, occasionally starring as a foreign correspondent telling the stories of men in the Legion. The series was partly filmed on location and in British studios. McGoohan's episode involved an attempt to stop slave trading in French Equatorial Africa, organised by a sultan, ruling from within his impenetrable fortress.[lxxi] In 1958, a series of five television plays followed for McGoohan. The experience of live broadcasts excited him, as the productions were not too dissimilar

[lxix] Pinewood celebrated its twenty first birthday on 30th September, 1957. Five hundred guests sat at sixty seven tables in a big marquee erected in the studios' gardens. McGoohan joined a host of well-known actors, including Dirk Bogarde, Stanley Baker, Diana Dors, Peter Finch, Anne Heywood, Glynis Johns, Margaret Lockwood, Virginia McKenna, Donald Sinden and Kenneth More.
[lxx] Internet sources wrongly refer to an episode of that name in McGoohan's later *Rafferty* series. There was a story so named in the earlier *Adventures of Sir Lancelot* series, in which the actor appeared – see page 54.
[lxxi] Around this time, McGoohan's television appearances are often listed as including two plays *The Third Miracle* and *The Little World*. These BBC dramas were part of a cycle of four plays broadcast between 27th October and 17th November 1957. They were an adaptation of *The English Family Robinson*, by Iain MacCormic: 1. *Night of the Tigers*; 2. *The Little World*; 3. *The Third Miracle*; 4. *Free Passage Home*. The BBC Archive kindly provided to this writer broadcast details which do not show any mention of McGoohan being in the cast. However, the two plays frequently are listed amongst his work in other written and Internet sources. The BBC archive showed very full production details and it seems more likely that McGoohan was not involved.

to his time in repertory: "They were exciting for the same reason the Sheffield plays were...you had to work so hard. They were good plays and the days of live drama were exciting. When you were in the studio and it said 'Vision On,' you knew if you did anything wrong people might see it. No second takes, no rushes. And what that does to the adrenaline is just fantastic! And the performance is done on a level of nervous energy that you don't get when you are working on film and can do scenes over. The tapes of these plays don't exist anymore."[lxxii] [50]

On 14th May 1958, the ITV *Play of the Week* presentation from Granada TV was *All My Sons*, directed by Clifford Owen. McGoohan appeared as Chris Keller, the son of an aircraft manufacturer who, during the war, allegedly sent out a batch of aircraft parts knowing them to be faulty. As a consequence, many pilots reportedly died and Keller's partner was apparently wrongfully convicted. With time, son Chris discovered the truth about his father. According to one review, "this was television drama at its finest."[51] McGoohan was clearly being selected for highly dramatic roles at this time and a collection of outstanding TV plays was soon under his belt. On 4th June, 1958 he appeared in another ITV *Play of the Week*, Hugh Forbes' *Disturbance*. McGoohan played Flint, a convict who captures three prison officers. They are used as hostages and six fellow prisoners act as judge, clerk, prosecutor and witnesses.[lxxiii] The drama unravels the secret passions of Flint and fellow prisoner Jenks (Jack Watling). Flint's demand to the governor is to be left in peace while awaiting a retrial on his original charge. His cross examination of Jenks results in the interrogator being consumed by his own jealous rage.

On 1st July, 1958, on BBC TV, McGoohan starred in a *Television Playwright* production, *This Day in Fear*, a drama set in the aftermath of the Irish Revolution in the nineteen twenties. He played a pacifist architect James Coogan, believed to be responsible for the death of a rebel leader. The actor co-starred with Billie Whitelaw,[lxxiv] who even received a screen peck[lxxv] on the cheek from her male lead. McGoohan next appeared on ITV, on 12th September, 1958, alongside Richard Harris,[lxxvi] in the *Television Playhouse* production *Rest in Violence*, once more directed by Clifford Owen. The play's theme was one of violent conflict and its effect upon two Irish brothers. The script was apparently created within a fortnight or so, between Harris, McGoohan and Owen, although it was reported that tempers flew during rehearsals. McGoohan took the role of Matthew "Mat" Galvin, a farmer who boasts strength and purpose, while Harris played his passionate brother, Dan, an overzealous IRA recruit. Mat, a person who loathes violence, is driven to extremes when he discovers what seems to be an affair between his wife and his brother. McGoohan commented, "My father is a farmer and...I understand Matthew in this play because I wanted to become a farmer and for a time ran a chicken farm."[52]

On 9th November, 1958, McGoohan was in the *Armchair Theatre* production of a new

---

[lxxii] The one major performance later to be captured on film would be when McGoohan took to the stage in *Brand*. For many years the actor was saddened by the thought that even this classic piece of film might have not survived. Fortunately, the BBC film of the stage play was preserved and a DVD of this was released in 2003. McGoohan expressed a wish long ago that his children and grandchildren should see his *Brand* performance, the one which he regarded as the greatest of his career.

[lxxiii] McGoohan would be seen in a similar hostage setting in the movie *Kings and Desperate Men* (1981).

[lxxiv] She would also later appear with McGoohan in *Jamaica Inn* (1982).

[lxxv] Apart from this and screen kisses in three Rank films, mentioned in this chapter, the actor was also kissed by Jane Merrow in *Danger Man* – see footnote to page 83 – and received an unexpected smacker from another actress in that series – see page 82 These half dozen smooches contradict the widely reported claim that McGoohan would never kiss another woman on screen.

[lxxvi] Richard Harris is also listed in some sources as having been in McGoohan's earlier play *All My Sons*.

Lyric Opera House
Hammersmith

Lessees: Associated Theatre
Seasons Ltd.
Licensee: J. Baxter Somerville
Box Office Riv 4432 & 6000

59 THEATRE COMPANY

under the direction of

JAMES H. LAWRIE and CASPER WREDE

presents

DANTON'S DEATH

by **GEORG BUECHNER**

translated and adapted by **JAMES MAXWELL**

Directed by **CASPER WREDE**

Designed by **MALCOLM PRIDE**

Lighting by **RICHARD PILBROW**

First performance at this theatre Tuesday, January 27th, 1959

CHARACTERS:

Deputies of The National Convention

Danton	**PATRICK WYMARK**
Camille Desmoulins (a poet)	**JAMES MAXWELL**
Herault-Sechelles	**JOHN TURNER**
Lacroix	**FULTON MacKAY**
Philippeau	**DONALD BRADLEY**
Legendre	**LEE FOX**

Members of the Committee of Public Safety

Robespierre	**HAROLD LANG**
St. Just	**PATRICK McGOOHAN**
Barere	**PETER SALLIS**
Collot d'Herbois	**ROBERT BERNAL**
Billaud-Varennes	**ROBERT POINTON**
Fouquier-Tinville (the Public Prosecutor)	**MARC SHELDON**
Tom Paine (an English philosopher)	**LEE FOX**
Simon (a theatrical prompter)	**PETER SALLIS**
A Deputy from Lyons	**MAXWELL SHAW**
A Young Gentleman	**HARALD JENSEN**
Julie (Danton's wife)	**DILYS HAMLETT**
Lucille (Camille's wife)	**AVRIL ELGAR**

Prostitutes

Marion	**PENELOPE HORNER**
Rosalie	**ANITA GIORGI**
Aurore	**JUNE BAILEY**

The Action of the Play, which is in two parts with one interval of fifteen minutes, takes place in Paris during March and April 1794.

Programme for *Danton's Death* (1959)

comedy, *The Greatest Man in the World*, with Donald Pleasance. Based on a short story by humourist James Thurber, McGoohan starred as American citizen, Jack "Pal" Smurch. The action was set in the near future of 1961, when the president of the United States hears that Smurch, using a secret, privately funded rocket trip, has landed on the moon. A hero's welcome is arranged, but subsequent events hold some surprises, which embarrass the government's publicity machine. McGoohan was awarded the Television Guild Award for "Best Television Actor of the Year" for his performance.

McGoohan also took parts in the popular British television series, *Rendezvous*, a collection of stories running for several seasons, from 1957 to 1961. Actor Charles Drake played John Burden, introducing segments in which he also occasionally took a role as a different character. Pat Jackson – prevented from casting McGoohan at their first professional meeting[lxxvii] – now successfully selected him for *Rendezvous*. The director recalled, "Eddie Knopf[lxxviii] came over to produce an anthology of short stories for television, *Rendezvous*. I directed about half of the series and got Pat McGoohan in three or four of them."[53] Jackson added, "Patrick was required to play a Catholic priest in the story *The Hanging of Alfred*

[lxxvii] See page 52 as to Jackson screen testing McGoohan at Pinewood and also footnotes there.
[lxxviii] Edwin H. Knopf, producer of *Rendezvous*.

Lyric Opera House
Hammersmith

Lessees: Associated Theatre
Seasons Ltd.
Licensee: J. Baxter Somerville
Box Office Riv 4432 & 6000

59 THEATRE COMPANY

under the direction of

JAMES H. LAWRIE and CASPER WREDE

presents

BRAND

by HENRIK IBSEN

Translated by MICHAEL MEYER

Directed by MICHAEL ELLIOTT

Designed by RICHARD NEGRI

Lighting by RICHARD PILBROW

First performance at this theatre Wednesday, April 8th, 1959

CHARACTERS: (in order of appearance)

Brand	PATRICK McGOOHAN
A Guide	ROBERT BERNAL
Guide's Son	WILLIAM McLAUGHLIN
Agnes	DILYS HAMLETT
Ejnar	HAROLD LANG
Gerd	OLIVE McFARLAND
Mayor	PATRICK WYMARK
Woman from the Headland	JUNE BAILEY
A Villager	FULTON MacKAY
Brand's mother	ENID LORIMER
Doctor	PETER SALLIS
Sexton	ROBERT BERNAL
Schoolmaster	FRANK WINDSOR
Provost	PETER SALLIS
Gypsy Woman	ANITA GIORGI
Villagers	JUNE BAILEY
	HOWARD BAKER
	ANITA GIORGI
	RONALD HARWOOD
	HARALD JENSEN
	PATRICK KAVANAGH
	WILLIAM McLAUGHLIN
	HELEN MONTAGUE
	JOCELYN PAGE
	ROY SPENCE
	JOHN STERLAND
	FRANK WINDSOR

Programme for *Brand* (1959)

Wadham. Such was his success that I gave him parts in two further episodes."[lxxix] [54] The second story Jackson directed[lxxx] was entitled *The Executioner,*[lxxxi] in which McGoohan played a character called Gil Stoner, who finds his friend murdered, in Paris. On the body is pinned a note bearing a clover leaf sign, being the mark used by a French resistance organisation, during the war.

McGoohan would also see two more of his films for Rank being released in 1958. The first of these was *The Gypsy and the Gentleman*, in which his spirited role as Jess the gypsy required some untypical romantic sequences, including some more screen kissing. One report praised the actor, considering him as part of the British scene: "I regard (McGoohan) as the most important picture discovery since Kirk Douglas. McGoohan is destined to be a giant cinema personality. Held here and properly produced, he will make more dollars for Britain than Guinness, canned or bottled. He's almost all wrong. He has a mouthful of crooked, blue-white teeth. Hollywood, notorious for directed dentistry, would give them up at a glance – rightly. They are part of his charm, like his

---

[lxxix] A possible third episode has not been verified.
[lxxx] He directed several more *Rendezvous* episodes, in which McGoohan did not appear.
[lxxxi] The episode was broadcast on 1st December, 1961.

Above: Publicity photo used for the
Brand programme
Left: Another scene from *Brand*

too flat nose for such a craggy face, his wry, sensitive mouth, his blazing blue eyes, at war with his Irish red hair. He is playing Melina Mercouri's lover in *The Gypsy and the Gentleman*. Physically, he is (Charlton) Heston, (Kirk) Douglas and (Burt) Lancaster rolled into one. Women picturegoers, I believe, will find him terrifying – and irresistible. Properly produced, he will be BIG Box Office."[55] A much later reviewer, writing retrospectively, admired "the sight of McGoohan in his full russet-haired glory." The writer continued: "With full beard he bounds through his scenes with the carefree abandon of a man completing a contractual request. His bullying and abusive treatment of Melina Mercouri also forms a neat contradiction to his gallant *Danger Man* persona of a few years later. She is craven when dealing with the ruthless McGoohan. He meanwhile, is a physical coward when confronted. This high quality colour epic has given a snapshot of McGoohan to be treasured."[56]

New York Times review: "Greek actress Melina Mercouri made her English-language film debut in this film. She plays tempestuous gypsy girl Belle, while the 'gentleman' is Sir Paul Deverill (Keith Michell). Escaping an arranged marriage, Sir Paul weds the bewitching Belle, who intends to take him for every penny he's got, then move on to other lovers. Imagine her disappointment when she discovers that her prize catch is flat broke. All sorts of bizarre complications ensue, including the kidnapping of an heiress (June Laverick) by Belle's gypsy compadres. (Hal Erickson, All Movie Guide)

While working on *Gypsy*, McGoohan gave an interview, which appeared under the title "Meet Mr. Menace," in a "Man of the Month" movie magazine feature.[57] The actor revealed, "I'm not a tough guy and I'm not a beast. I'm soft-hearted, gentle and understanding. I don't even beat my wife." According to the assigned journalist, McGoohan had been branded "the Brute of Pinewood," after such films as *High Tide at Noon* and *Hell Drivers*. The actor rubbed his bearded chin – grown for his current movie *The Gypsy and the Gentleman* – and admitted, "Those films were not good. I was not good. The love scenes in *Hell Drivers* were done the same as the truck scenes. And no-one is going to pretend that *The Gypsy and the Gentleman* is a classical piece of work." The reporter observed that McGoohan appeared to be "a little peeved about the whole business." The actor admitted, "I only have to make two pictures a year. When this is over I'm finished for a while." The journalist concluded that there was "a lot to like and admire about McGoohan. He is a character. He had ambition and enthusiasm. His main fault, it seems, is that he wants everything to go his way." Meanwhile, McGoohan told his listener of some forthcoming big plans. The actor was intending to hire a West End theatre to present five plays, spending hours hunting for material and even writing a play himself, the latter being a farce, taking place in a caravan.

McGoohan's fourth film for Rank, *Nor the Moon by Night* (1958),[lxxxii] turned out in fact to be his final one for the studio. The movie was shot in South Africa, during a three month assignment, at the Kruger National Park. The actor played a game reserve warden, with the role bringing yet more on screen kissing. Director Ken Annakin recalled a particular scene from the film and some inherent difficulties with the production. "Anna Gaylor, in the storyline, was devastated and McGoohan was unable to resist comforting her with a kiss." Annakin remembered McGoohan having resolved to remain faithful to his wife Joan back home. However, being a true actor, recounted the director, he performed as required. The experience, claimed Annakin, caused McGoohan to seek an excessive amount of liquid comfort, leading to his driving his car so crazily that he had a bad vehicle crash.[58] The official version of the incident was that McGoohan had been motoring alone on a South African road when his axle broke. The mechanical failure led to the car leaving the deserted road and the actor being stranded there, with severe head and facial injuries. Several hours passed before he was discovered by another motorist, bleeding and unconscious. He was not fit to resume work on the film for a further three weeks.

The actor also had a scene where he was being stalked round a room by a ferocious lioness. For the sake of realism – a McGoohan trademark even in those days – he decided to do the whole scene himself in one long tracking shot. No cutting or camera tricks involved: "Unknown to me," he recalled "on the day of the shot the trainer had starved the animal for 24 hours. I had to hold a piece of liver on a stick by my side hidden from the camera. The only precaution was a white hunter up in the gallery with an elephant gun and several people about with revolvers. But if the lioness *had* jumped on me, they'd have had to shoot through my head, so I felt pretty unsafe. I was backing away and its claws were flashing within inches of my face as it tried to grab the liver. I was really terrified because I knew there was no such thing as a completely tamed lion. But we did get the shot! In the end, I just dropped the liver and took off! Years later, I heard the lion *had* turned on his trainer and he'd been forced to

---

[lxxxii] The only one for the studio not in a villainous role.

give it to a zoo, so my fears were well-founded."[59]

New York Times review: "In this romantic comedy, a young woman spends all her time caring for her ailing mother. The one bright spot in her life is her African pen pal. Her mother finally dies, and the woman immediately sets off for Africa to meet the pen pal. There she finds that he is too busy chasing elephants to notice her. Instead she ends up falling for his brother. The two brothers find themselves entangled in various adventures involving African wildlife." (Sandra Brennan, All Movie Guide)

A portrait photo of the actor

McGoohan's split with Rank occurred when he became less than enthralled with the studio publicity machine. There were growing signs that the restrictions upon him outweighed any glamour arising from his contract. Conflicting descriptions of the actor appeared in publications during August, 1958. In the first, the actor's disillusionment with Rank was highlighted: "My name has been made far more important by the three TV plays I've done, than by any of the films I've made at Pinewood. They said I was an awkward customer so, to prove I wasn't, I accepted two roles without even reading the scripts. Their names, *The Gypsy and the Gentleman* and *Nor the Moon by Night*. Draw your own conclusions. *Nor the Moon by Night* should be released this month. I'm not defending myself on that one; it's just that I'm ashamed of it. You'd have thought they'd have cashed in on me because I'm told that my plays *All My Sons*, *Disturbance* and *This Day in Fear* were very popular.[lxxxiii] But – nothing."[60] It was reported that McGoohan and the Rank bosses "rarely saw eye to eye and by mutual consent the five year contract was terminated early."[lxxxiv] [61] The actor later declared: "I would rather do twenty TV series than go through what I went through under that Rank contract... for which I blame no one but myself."[62] McGoohan also reflected, "I got so terribly bored and depressed while I was with Rank mainly, I think, because of the inactivity. I did some terrible films."[63]

On 30th December, 1958,[lxxxv] the actor ended the year by starring in the ITV *Play of the Week*, being a ninety minute presentation of *The Big Knife*,[lxxxvi] by Clifford Odets. The play provided a gritty insight into Hollywood corruption. McGoohan played 'Tinseltown' star, Charles Castle,[lxxxvii] who opts for the trappings of a show business life. Castle's wife is pressuring him to end his contract, but the film studio has a hold over her husband and some delving into his past gives rise to a sensational ending. *Variety* was effusive in its praise: "The presentation can hardly be faulted on any count and may be ranked as one of the gems of British tele-drama. Acting was maintained at a high standard by the entire cast, but special mention must be made of the performances of Patrick McGoohan as Charles Castle, the movie star with a load of problems, and Louise Albritton as his wife."[64] One reviewer

---

[lxxxiii] See page 58.

[lxxxiv] However, McGoohan's films in the sixties sometimes involved Rank Studios or their affiliates.

[lxxxv] Some sources incorrectly list 1959.

[lxxxvi] There was no award for the role, although some sources incorrectly state this. However, McGoohan's appearance was seen by TV mogul Lew Grade, who chose the actor to play the lead role of John Drake, in the new TV series *Danger Man*; see page 67 and Chapter Four.

[lxxxvii] Jack Palance played the part in the 1955 film version.

observed. "(McGoohan's) mannerisms, movements and voice were always those of a mature actor. Even in his earliest work he moved as an actor much older than his actual years."[65] A further critic claimed that Patrick McGoohan had been a 'method actor' long before the likes of James Dean made the term popular.[66]

The actor's TV roles had recently been plentiful, but he did not ignore the theatre. In 1959, he joined the 59 Theatre Company,[lxxxviii] at the Lyric Opera House,[lxxxix] King Street, Hammersmith. The premises had been leased for twenty four weeks, from the February, in order to present a series of classical plays.[xc] A group of theatrical individuals started the venture: Finnish director Casper Wrede, director Michael Elliott, actor James Maxwell and other designers, musicians and playwrights, with financial backing from James H. Lawrie. McGoohan appeared in the company's production of *Danton's Death*, from 27th January,[xci] a play by George Buechner about the French Revolution and Robespierre's trial and execution. The actor was cast as the revolutionary leader's right hand man. "The St. Just of Patrick McGoohan was grimly sinister at all times."[67] Dilys Hamlett, an actress in the company and wife of Casper Wrede, opined: "He played St. Just, marvellously, although I always had the suspicion that he wanted to play Robespierre." She also recalled that Trevor Howard was at one time interested in joining the company and it was the prospect of working with Howard which initially attracted McGoohan. Hamlett said that he "admired (Howard) tremendously as an actor. He talked of him with reverential awe."[xcii] [68]

During March, McGoohan was busy with a pair of television productions. Firstly, he took the leading role of Frederick S. Dyson, in the *Play of the Week* production of *A Dead Secret*,[xciii] shown on 3rd March. Set in a gas-lit London villa, in 1911, the residence is that of Dyson's family, with some lodgers, one of whom, Miss Lummus, is murdered. The drama was a fascinating study of whether Dyson had motive to kill the unfortunate woman. Later in the month, McGoohan appeared in *The Iron Harp*, a one hour play for CBC, transmitted in Canada on 17th March. The play was set during the 1920 Irish rebellion, when the British Army was sent to crush the IRA.

The next production to be considered by the 59 Theatre Company was *Brand*. Michael Elliott, formerly a director with BBC television, suggested performing the play, which was a mammoth proposal. The original 1866 play, by Norwegian Henrik Ibsen (1828-1906), was written as a poetic drama, composed in rhymed octosyllabics, solely for the reading public and not to be produced for the theatre. A stage performance of *Brand* had only taken place once before, in 1912, at the Royal Court Theatre, in London. To perform the whole work would take an estimated five hours.[xciv] The new, intended version, adapted by Michael Meyer, would reduce *Brand* to a reasonable playing time, of less than three hours. Meyer's adaptation removed long topical discussions, such as land reform and the encroaching perils of the industrial revolution, and sought to tighten the narrative. The central character –

[lxxxviii] Formed that year, hence the name.

[lxxxix] Operatic productions had first been performed there towards the end of the previous century.

[xc] These also included *Creditors*, by Strindberg and *The Cheats of Scapin*, by Thomas Otway.

[xci] There was a hope that some of the plays would be broadcast by BBC television, although no such transmissions involving McGoohan have been verified. *Danton's Death* was later broadcast by the BBC in the World Theatre series, but after the actor had left the cast.

[xcii] Trevor Howard unfortunately did not join the group. Also, Howard was put forward for a part in the 1967 *Prisoner* TV series, although in the end he was not involved. However, McGoohan would later appear in the same production as Howard, in the form of the movie *Mary, Queen of Scots* (1971)

[xciii] Some sources list this as *Dead Secret*.

[xciv] Michael Elliott made what were referred to as "judicious cuts."

discontented priest, Pastor Brand – was based by Ibsen partly on his good friend Christopher Bruun.[xcv] The playwright also drew inspiration for the character from his childhood memories of a priest, called Lammers.[xcvi] However, Ibsen said that the occupation of priest was only secondary to the message of the play, that a powerful faith in God must be tempered with love and tolerance and that he could easily have made him a sculptor, or politician.

Initially, a contractual dispute over the rights to perform *Brand* reportedly halted production plans. Later, when the company finally secured the rights to perform *Brand*, McGoohan had apparently cooled over the project. Michael Meyer said "I think the problem was that Patrick saw a bad translation of the play."[69] "It was an off and on situation" observed Dilys Hamlett "and he kept his director Michael Elliott hanging on a string for quite a long time."[70] The lead role of Pastor Brand was offered instead to Ian Bannen[xcvii] and John Neville, but both actors declined. Actor Peter Sallis[xcviii] – whose main character in the play was "Provost" – recalled how McGoohan was chosen to be part of the company, "principally to do *Brand*."[71] "They had, in Patrick McGoohan, probably the only man in the country who could have played that part. Single-minded, physically of the right strength – I'm tempted to say when he was on full throttle; he was the best actor we had."[72]

McGoohan finally agreed to play the lead part after a visit to Elliott's flat. While the director was in another room, the actor leafed through Meyer's new translation of *Brand*. Impressed by the power of the material, McGoohan announced that he would take the principal role. "The money I got for doing 'Brand' was peanuts, but then I didn't do 'Brand' just for the money."[73]

Michael Meyer commented: "Patrick McGoohan wasn't good at acting relationships. He was very much like Laurence Olivier in that respect; he couldn't act convincingly a son, a husband or a father. But what Pat was good at was acting loners or people who can't make contact." Peter Sallis explained the lead actor's immense undertaking: "*Brand* is probably the most single-minded character ever written in any form of literature. In Patrick McGoohan they had got the man who could...make the character compelling in every sense of the word, instead of entertaining. There is no softness in *Brand* at all."[74]

With McGoohan's March television appearances, mentioned earlier, behind him, there was now little remaining time to complete rehearsals of *Brand* – for an April opening – and the cast found the work exhausting. McGoohan revealed, "The play was bigger than me. I found it to be bigger than *Lear*. People talk about *Lear* as being a most exhausting part...the thing I found most exhausting was the hanging around so much! 'When can I get on and do my part?' But in *Brand* you start strong in the beginning and keep going *up*! On stage the whole time!"[xcix] [75] Peter Sallis echoed McGoohan's description of his approach to the role of Pastor Brand: "If you said an acting performance was from between A-Z. Patrick started at Z. He never went back. It was Z plus, Z plus, plus. But the astonishing concentration the total absorption in the character was there... to see... for any of us that were on the stage."[76] According to Sallis, the instruction from director Michael Elliott was: "'I know what you're

---

[xcv] A Norwegian theologian who refused Holy Orders because he felt life and the teachings of the State Church were fundamentally incompatible.

[xcvi] Lammers organised a fundamentalist Christian movement, in Skein, Norway.

[xcvii] Ian Bannen had been at Ratcliffe College in the early 1940s with Patrick McGoohan

[xcviii] Peter Sallis, as mentioned earlier in this book, was a fellow player with McGoohan in Sheffield repertory, as well as in *Moby Dick*, 1955.

[xcix] In the play, Brand sacrifices his only child. His wife is driven to madness through her grief and when she dies he rebuilds the village church into a cathedral, dedicating everything he possesses to his unforgiving God.

going to do, Patrick, you're going to start at the top,' – meaning at the top of his performance – 'you're going to sustain it throughout the whole play and then the audience will tell you when to go into overdrive and you'll go into overdrive and you will wring their withers.' And so he did, night after night, although the first night had, of course, something very special about it."[77]

In fact, believing that nothing was working as it should, Michael Meyer was tempted to warn off the critics from attending the first night. The play's opening, on 8th April, 1959, was a nail-biting premiere. However, as Peter Sallis recalled, the occasion was supremely rewarding: "As far as we could see from the stage, the whole audience stood up at the end. It was the most exciting first night that I have ever had anything to do with. I used to stand in the wings every night, because I thought I'm never going to see better acting than this as long as I live."[78] Sallis added, "(Patrick) was terrifying on stage to be with. I mean you saw the look of God going right through you. And he sustained it. The audience admired the production, the lighting, the acting, but it was McGoohan's evening and it went on to be that through the full length of the run."[c][79]

Sallis also savoured the play's first night, how the audience "stood and cheered and Patrick's career and his life were transformed." He remarked, "I couldn't help thinking, even though he was a mate of mine, this is a real privilege. I am working with somebody now who is actually giving as near to a great performance as you can possibly get. His eyes – you couldn't take your eyes off him and they really did drill right through you. Very, very moving and very, very satisfying as an actor to be in that sort of presence. I don't think it happens very often."[80] Sallis concluded, "Patrick has the inability to compromise over anything."[81] Actress Rosalind Knight, widow of director Michael Elliott, was part of that first night audience: "(McGoohan) doesn't let up for one single second till the end of the play. And the audience was totally overtaken and stood up and yelled and clapped. They had never seen anything like it as a theatrical experience for years."[82]

In his commentary upon Brand, Michael Meyer observed that seldom in recent years had any performance of a foreign classic received such praise as was bestowed upon this production. There was cheering every night and many other press comments were highly enthusiastic.[ci] Harold Hobson of The Sunday Times described Brand as "A revelation,"[83] while the summer issue of Drama reported, "This dwarfs everything else in the recent London theatre."[84] Critic Kenneth Tynan wrote in The Observer, "Patrick McGoohan in the name part is on the brink of an admirable performance and comes at times so near to the Brand one dreams of that I could well wish he were less enamoured of the seemingly fashionable Morse-code delivery of speech. Why he does it – in order to thrust forward the image of the Spartan Calvinist – is completely understandable, but a richer and more trumpet-tongued delivery, a more nervous tempo, a greater authority of bearing would serve him better."[85]

J.C. Trewin celebrated the actor's performance in The Illustrated London News: "(The) 59 Theatre (Company), which has had the courage to stage Brand, so long neglected in Britain, has found miraculously the right actor in Patrick McGoohan. Here he has made one of the most exciting personal successes for a very long time. The word Brand can mean both sword and fire. We have both in Mister McGoohan. He is tall, governing of mien, craggily

---

[c] The successful run was extended to 30th May.
[ci] Michael Meyer said that Brand was very successful in the April, but in the May, during a heat wave, the public stayed away as nobody wanted to be in a hot theatre and so the play lost as much as it had made in the preceding month.

handsome. Throughout the play the thunder sounds in his voice and in his eyes we see the lightning. There can be no compromise. He too must cry, 'All or nothing!' and Mister McGoohan's performance is an extraordinary reply to scholars who have claimed that the part is un-actable. Nothing written by a great dramatist is un-actable whatever it may appear in the study."[86]

McGoohan has always regarded *Brand* as his finest work. Although several members of the cast enjoyed excellent notices,[cii] it was his tour-de-force performance which gained special comment. A *Times* critic stated, "Patrick McGoohan is magnificent throughout, in a part which is pitched on a single note."[87] For his performance in *Brand*, McGoohan received the London Drama Critics' Award for "Best Theatre Actor of the Year." *Brand* not only attracted high praise, but the production was also filmed by the BBC. McGoohan's performance could be seen as a transmitted recording, on 11th August, 1959, as part of the *Television World Theatre* series. Even on small televisions, his portrayal of Pastor Brand was a commanding one, the actor striding across the stage, straight backed, wide eyed and pouting. It has been said that McGoohan's unique way of speaking was acquired from his repertory days, with each syllable being made to sound as if it had "leapt off the sharp edge of a razorblade."[88] However, Michael Meyer observed, "Patrick's performance was a bit too big for television. He wasn't yet a skilful film actor – knowing that you had to do rather little and that the camera would do the rest. And this enormously powerful performance he had given was a bit too explosive for the small screen."[89]

The glowing reports of McGoohan's *Brand* were enough for the actor to treat the play as his theatrical swansong, the performance for which he wished to be remembered: "All of the plays I did, all of the training, really came together in *(Brand)* And that's one of the reasons I didn't do any more plays.[ciii] I thought 'That one, for the time being, is what I want to have on the boards, that piece of work is such an extraordinary piece of work. The crying out to be 'All or Nothing!' people are scared of it. It's hard."[90] The actor was asked whether there was some of Pastor Brand in him, eliciting the reply: "The parallel is there certainly, the 'All or Nothing' business."

1959 was clearly a superlative year for McGoohan, he having moved at an impressive pace between several major productions. Therefore, with so many critics seeing him as the next big theatrical star and with the actor's mentor, Orson Welles' outspoken disapproval of the medium of television, it is perhaps surprising that McGoohan stepped so smartly into a new and long-running television series, *Danger Man*.[civ] Television impresario Lew Grade had already seen the actor in the ITV play *The Big Knife*, mentioned earlier in this chapter and had begun talks with him about *Danger Man*. According to McGoohan, Grade wanted to see *Brand* and so tickets for a performance were arranged by the actor, who recalled: "(*Brand* is) a huge, classic sort of King Lear type play. I said to Lew (Grade) would you like to come and see the play and (he) wanted good seats. So I got him tickets for the front row. And he'd seen me in this other thing which was very different.[cv] And then he came to see this thing which was thunder and storm and huge drama. And I remember seeing him in the front row there when we were taking the curtain call with his eyes popping out of his head thinking, 'Jesus Christ, what have I got myself into? I've signed this guy up and look at the crap he's doing.'"[91]

---

cii The cast also included Patrick Wymark and Frank Windsor.
ciii McGoohan appeared just once more on the stage, twenty five years later in the Broadway play *Pack of Lies*, see page 237.
civ The new series went into production at the end of 1959, covered next chapter.
cv *The Big Knife* – see page 63.

[1] Joan Reeder, Woman magazine, 4 issues between 9th and 30th October, 1965

[2] Joan Reeder, Woman magazine, 4 issues between 9th and 30th October, 1965

[3] Joan Reeder, Woman magazine, 4 issues between 9th and 30th October, 1965

[4] You – The Mail on Sunday Magazine, March,1983, Mike Bygrave

[5] Six of One Prisoner twenty fifth and thirtieth anniversary events, 1993 and 1997, London

[6] Bristol Evening World, June, 1953, Dennis Bushell

[7] Theatre World, 1953

[8] Bristol Old Vic first ten years' records

[9] ITC press book, 1967 and letter to the writer 2006

[10] Joan Reeder, Woman magazine, 4 issues between 9th and 30th October, 1965

[11] Plays and Players, May, 1955

[12] The Evening Standard, February, 1965

[13] The Times, 18th February,1955, Philip King

[14] A Ribbon of Dreams: The Cinema of Orson Welles, Peter Cowie, A. S. Barnes & Co., 1973

[15] A Ribbon of Dreams: The Cinema of Orson Welles, Peter Cowie, A. S. Barnes & Co., 1973

[16] A Ribbon of Dreams: The Cinema of Orson Welles, Peter Cowie, A. S. Barnes & Co., 1973

[17] A Ribbon of Dreams: The Cinema of Orson Welles, Peter Cowie, A. S. Barnes & Co., 1973

[18] Orson Welles: A Biography, Barbara Leaming; Weidenfeld & Nicolson, 1985

[19] Orson Welles: A Biography, Barbara Leaming; Weidenfeld & Nicolson, 1985

[20] A Ribbon of Dreams: The Cinema of Orson Welles, Peter Cowie, A. S. Barnes & Co., 1973

[21] Joan Reeder, Woman magazine, 4 issues between 9th and 30th October, 1965

[22] This is Orson Welles, by Orson Welles, Peter Bogdanovich, Jonathan Rosenbaum, 1992; HarperCollins

[23] A Ribbon of Dreams: The Cinema of Orson Welles, Peter Cowie, A. S. Barnes & Co., 1973

[24] Sunday Observer, 19th June, 1955, Kenneth Tynan

[25] New York Post, 1955, details unknown

[26] The Fabulous Orson Welles, Hutchinson, 1965, Peter Noble

[27] The Fabulous Orson Welles, Hutchinson, 1965, Peter Noble

[28] Fading into the Limelight, 2006, Orion, Peter Sallis

[29] Orson Welles: A Biography, Barbara Leaming; Weidenfeld & Nicolson, 1985

[30] Classic Images Magazine, 1987, Barbara Pruett

[31] Premiere Magazine, October 1995, Jean Yves Katelan (translations Rosemary Camilleri and Jane Rawson)

[32] Interview with the writer, 2006

[33] Information from Andre Perkowski and Glenn Anders and from Christopher Lee's autobiography

[34] What Ever Happened to Orson Welles? 2006, University Press of Kentucky, Joseph McBride

[35] Classic Images Magazine, 1987, Barbara Pruett

[36] Rosebud, David Thomson; Alfred A. Knopf Inc., 1996

[37] BBC online programme catalogue

[38] Interview with the writer, 2006

[39] Film Dope, July 1983, interview By Bob Baker And Markku Salmi

[40] The Times, 15th February, 1956

[41] Theatre World, February, 1956

[42] Picturegoer Magazine, 27th. April, 1957, Elizabeth Forrest

[43] Picturegoer magazine, 12th January, 1957

[44] Picturegoer, 27th April, 1957, Elizabeth Forrest

[45] Joan Reeder, Woman magazine, 4 issues between 9th and 30th October, 1965

[46] British article, 1957, details unknown

[47] British article, 1957, details unknown

[48] Classic and Vintage Commercials, January, 2007, Andrew Roberts

[49] Picturegoer, 27th April, 1957, Elizabeth Forrest

[50] Classic Images Magazine, 1987, Barbara Pruett

[51] Daily Mail All Channels TV Book for 1958

[52] TV Times, 12th September,1958, Cecilie Leslie

[53] Film Dope, July 1983, interview By Bob Baker and Markku Salmi

[54] Interview with the writer, 2006

[55] Picturegoer, 27th July, 1957, Donovan Pedelty

[56] Internet Movie DataBase

[57] Photoplay, November, 1967, Peter Tipthorp

[58] Written response to Bruce Sachs, Tomahawk Press, 2006

[59] Motion Picture, June, 1966

[60] August, 1958, Tom Hutchinson, British, details unknown

[61] Source not verified

[62] Photoplay, April, 1961

[63] Photoplay, April, 1961

[64] Variety, 1959, details unknown

[65] Variety, 1959, details unknown

[66] Variety, 1959, details unknown
[67] Theatre World, 1959
[68] Brand DVD, Network, 2003
[69] Brand DVD, Network, 2003
[70] Brand DVD, Network, 2003
[71] Brand DVD, Network, 2003
[72] *Fading into the Limelight*, 2006, Orion, Peter Sallis
[73] Photoplay, April, 1961
[74] Brand DVD, Network, 2003
[75] Brand DVD, Network, 2003
[76] Brand DVD, Network, 2003
[77] *Fading into the Limelight*, 2006, Orion, Peter Sallis
[78] Brand DVD, Network, 2003
[79] Brand DVD, Network, 2003
[80] Fading into the Limelight, 2006, Orion, Peter Sallis
[81] Brand DVD, Network, 2003
[82] Brand DVD, Network, 2003
[83] The Sunday Times, 1959, Harold Hobson, date unknown
[84] Drama Magazine, summer, 1959, details unknown
[85] The Observer, 1959, Kenneth Tynan, date unknown
[86] The Illustrated London News, 1959, J.C. Trewin, date unknown
[87] The Times, 1959, details unknown
[88] TV Radio Mirror, August 1966
[89] Brand DVD, Network, 2003
[90] Classic Images Magazine, 1987, Barbara Pruett
[91] Lew Grade: The Greatest of them All, 24th and 25th December, 2006, BBC Radio 2.

McGoohan in a dramatic scene from *Life for Ruth* (1962)

CHAPTER FOUR
Danger Man

"My name is Drake, John Drake."
First series opening sequence (1960-61)

In 1959, McGoohan was poised to become a famous face and a household name. As covered in the previous chapter, entrepreneur Lew Grade had recently seen him in action on stage and the small screen. Grade was exploring new opportunities to create TV programmes from within his company, ATV – Associated Television – which could be exported to the United States, through linked distribution company, ITC. Initial successes such as *The Adventures of Robin Hood* (1955-9), *The Buccaneers* (1956) and *The Adventures of Sir Lancelot* (1956), had paved the way for more ambitious or unusual dramas, such as *The Invisible Man* (1958) or *Interpol Calling* (1959). In addition, Grade's close business association with the Television Corporation of America meant he was able to sell directly to the lucrative North American market.

One of the TV shows for which Grade had high hopes was the new half hour spy series *Danger Man.*[i] This was the creation of former film director and screenwriter Ralph Smart, being the first of its kind to popularise the secret agent drama on the small screen. Grade explained his choice of McGoohan for the lead role: "It was the way he moved, like a panther, firm and decisive."[1] The actor was duly cast as the new screen hero, John Drake. He revealed the attraction of appearing in a regular television series as being a fast track to achieving financial security for his family and to help him fund future projects. "I'd have been quite happy at Sheffield if I'd been able to make enough of a living to bring up my children. But the series came along and I wanted things for my children, so I thought I'd go where the money was. It had nothing to do with ambition at all. I've never had any ambition or drive. I thought, if things go right, I might get a little pension out of this. And

---

[i] Later hour-long episodes were known as *Secret Agent* in the US and *Destination Danger* in France. In Germany, episodes were called *Geheimauftrag für John Drake* (Secret Assignment for John Drake).

Promotional shot of McGoohan drumming for *All Night Long* (1961)

then I can go do what I want. After having got the pension, then I'm free to be off; that was the idea. A very, very stupid way to think. Because then I got locked into a mould."[2]

McGoohan reflected upon his exit from the unfulfilling Rank contract, no doubt hoping that the new medium of a television series would rekindle his interest in screen work. One critic remarked, "Patrick McGoohan is a rebel. They know that in the film world. They also know it in the theatre. NOW they're finding it out in television. He had a two-year contract with the Rank Organisation. The parting was without even sweet sorrow – and McGoohan made no secret of what he thought about his treatment. In the theatre, he has gone into plays which few other actors would have dared try – and won critical plaudits for his courage. He is as forthright in his views on television series as he is about any other form of entertainment. Which makes it all the more surprising that an actor of his integrity should step into (*Danger Man*) which, on the surface, sounds as though it was tailored for the late Errol Flynn. It could be that McGoohan will go down in television history as the man who combined intelligence with excitement and put an adventure series onto an adult level."[3]

Britain was about to meet John Drake, when the first episode of *Danger Man* was broadcast on Sunday, 11th September, 1960. Starting with a strident jazz theme, the opening titles blazed across British screens with the legend, "Introducing Patrick McGoohan." The star was seen running out of Drake's international headquarters building and leaping into his waiting open-topped Aston Martin sports car. His clipped, transatlantic accent announced: "Every government has its Secret Service branch. America, it's CIA, France Deuxième Bureau, England MI5. A messy job. Well, that's when they usually call on me, or someone like me." Tagged on the end was the classic line: "Oh yes, my name is Drake, John Drake." This preceded the hallmark catchphrase of 007, "My name is Bond, James Bond," famously uttered two years later by Sean Connery, in *Dr. No* (1962).

The ATV Star Book proclaimed, "A tall, athletic figure emerges from a federal building in Washington D.C., quickly crosses a brightly lit main thoroughfare, gets into a sleek, low-slung sports car and roars away. On this note, each episode of the *Danger Man* series is introduced, bringing to the screens the latest adventure-packed stories of a lone wolf in a word of international tension and intrigue. The hero is John Drake, special security agent free to go wherever duty calls, working only at top government level, taking calculated risks in the cause of world peace."[4]

Book and comic covers from *Danger Man*, also known as *Secret Agent*

McGoohan as Warder Thomas Crimmin in *The Quare Fellow* (1962)

Around the time of *Danger Man's* premiere McGoohan formed Everyman Films Limited[ii] with David Tomblin,[iii] the series' assistant director. There was nothing particularly distinctive about the company's stated aims; its Memorandum of Association previously existed for Keystone Films Limited and was simply overwritten in hand with the new name. However, the company would later produce *The Prisoner* and Tomblin would become that series' producer and part-director. He and McGoohan were also directors of another company, called Drummond Enterprises Limited; this was used on occasions to channel publicity and photographs through the media, being named after Patrick's wife Joan.

Danger Man was produced at the MGM[iv] studios, at Borehamwood, in Hertfordshire. The first series comprised thirty nine black and white episodes.[v] These half hour filmed segments appeared on British TV screens between 1960 and 1962.[vi] In publicity for the show, producer Ralph Smart announced: "It is our intention to present pictorial and interesting backgrounds, as well as fast-moving, exciting shows. We intend to scour the world for our settings."[5] Accordingly, McGoohan appeared in a new, far-flung 'location' each week, ranging from South Africa to the Far East. In contrast to well-dressed studio sets, sometimes appropriate British locations were used, to create exteriors with 'local realism,' standing in for the real place. The production became popular across the Atlantic: "The series ... is one of Britain's most successful exports ..., having received widespread acclaim when shown on America's C.B.S. coast-to-coast network. Its earnings from the dollar area, including Canada and South America, were estimated to be about $2,000,000 at the end of 1961.[6]

It was during the first such *Danger Man* location shoot that Portmeirion, in North Wales, doubled for Italy, in the story *View from the Villa*. A screen credit appeared: "Locations with the kind co-operation of Mr. Clough Williams-Ellis, Portmeirion." The

[ii] The organisation was wound up finally in 1974, after McGoohan had taken up permanent residence in the USA.

[iii] In future years David Tomblin worked on such major movies as *Raiders of the Lost Ark* (1981), *Star Wars: Return of the Jedi* (1983) and Sean Connery's James Bond *Thunderball* remake, *Never Say Never Again* (1983) as well as working once more with McGoohan on *Braveheart* (1995).

[iv] The studios were built in the thirties and were owned by MGM from the late forties. There were ten soundstages and over a hundred acres of lot. Closure came in 1970, but the buildings and famous MGM clock tower were not demolished until the mid-eighties. Today a residential development stands on the site, with streets named after the studio and its stars.

[v] The same title was used for North American screenings, although later one hour stories were called *Secret Agent* there.

[vi] Recent online sources refer to a 1960 TV series *Tales of the Vikings*, filmed in Europe. One episode listing, *The Barbarian*, has McGoohan shown as its guest star. The series was also known as *The Vikings*, having thirty nine black and white thirty minute episodes. Whilst it is possible that the actor had a guest role, he was busy with *Danger Man* at the time and no mention of any *Vikings* involvement has appeared in the past.

Left: On set in the first series of *Danger Man* (1959/60) Above: A script session for an early *Danger Man* episode

resort, set on the North Wales Cardigan Bay coast, was created over many years by Williams-Ellis, an architect who acquired the private peninsula in 1925. The unusual place remained in McGoohan's mind and was later chosen by him as the ideal setting for "The Village," in his cult TV series *The Prisoner*, covered in the next chapter.

Danger Man's exotic settings and attractive female co-stars made the series highly popular, even generating tie-in merchandise such as theme music records, a novelisation, TV annuals, bubblegum cards and a board game. However, McGoohan did not initially regard the series' scripts as being very good. "When the first *Danger Man* script arrived there was stuff in there that I didn't particularly care for, you know, because I mean they were trying to do a secret agent series rather like a pale version of Bond. There were women and there were implications of romance and … the guy carried a gun and he shot people. Well those two things I wanted out right away. So they re-wrote the script and that's the way the scripts stayed from then on."[7] The actor was being sent many ideas for television programmes at the time and he saw the new spy show offer as "just one more." However, he decided to accept the role of John Drake and would eventually star in eighty six episodes.[vii] McGoohan recalled: "It was a completely different series when we started. I remember reading the first script. It was all about this John Drake character and he was after a secret document in a safe behind a picture that was over a bed. He's lying on the bed with a girl and in order to move the picture to get to the safe, he has to roll over the girl. Sort of 'excuse me sweetheart,' and then roll back. That was the first script. And he also shot three people. Of course that was all changed and we didn't do any of it."[8] The actor also explained his moral objections to the original make-up of the lead character: "I didn't like the way Drake came over when I started to read the scripts. He was painted as a rough, tough, sexy guy, who hit below the belt in his fights, was always using a gun and making passes at pretty girls. I wanted to change him and I had a fight in getting my own way."[9]

Danger Man producer Sidney Cole said, "I'd seen Pat McGoohan in the theatre at the Lyric, Hammersmith. He was extremely good in *Brand* and *Danton's Death*. I admired McGoohan as an actor and I found him very interesting to work with on *Danger Man*. He

---

[vii] Some sources incorrectly list a total of eighty eight episodes, as do some people whose comments are reproduced in this book. However, the remarks were made by them and so have not been changed. See also Appendix Two for full *Danger Man* episode guides.

was a very fervent Roman Catholic which meant he had a fervent sense of sin. He always refused to kiss a woman, even if they were supposed to be in a scene which implied some degree of intimacy between them. I asked him once why this was so and he said he didn't want his children asking their mother, 'why is daddy kissing that strange woman?' As a result of this I used to take a certain amount of pleasure in casting the most attractive actresses opposite Pat. I cast Adrienne Corri in one episode[viii] and I mentioned this little foible of Pat's to her. Pat had reacted when I said I was casting Adrienne. He disapproved because Adrienne announced to the press that she was the proud mother of two children, although she didn't happen to be married. I told Adrienne that Pat seemed to disapprove of that. Apparently, the first morning she was on call she came out of her dressing room the same time as McGoohan and called down the corridor, 'Hey McGoohan.' He turned round and she said, 'I understand you disapprove of me. Well f**k you for a start.' After which they became quite good friends."[10] Adrienne Corri herself generously recalled, "He knows a lot of very funny stories, but once he is on the set he is the utter professional – terribly serious. I think I must have been one of the few women who have worked with him who have ever made him laugh on the set, but it was a rare occasion."[11]

Selecting McGoohan, with his edgy screen presence and unpredictable nature, undoubtedly had a profound effect upon the development of the series. For the budding star, "Drake was an agent who never carried a gun, never shot anyone. He used his wits instead. He didn't go around knocking people off and he didn't go to bed with a different girl in each of thirty nine episodes. My theory was very simple. I felt that television was a guest in one's home and should behave like a guest. So therefore, for young people watching *Danger Man* I'd rather they'd seen a hero than an anti-hero. That's what I tried to go for. In *Danger Man* there is a lot of action, but never gratuitous violence. If a man dies, it is not just another cherry falling off the tree. When Drake fights, it is a clean fight. He has a horror of bloodbaths and although he carries a revolver he only uses it in cases of absolute necessity. He does not shoot to kill."[12] The star's views on his character were clear: "Patrick McGoohan sees John Drake as a man who has done a lot of jobs in his time. 'He doesn't come from a well-off family, and has had to struggle for an education. He worked his way through university, studying science and its effect on world affairs. He has seen a lot of the world and has studied people. He is also an athlete. He has reached the staging of wanting to do something exciting, something that will do good. When he comes into contact with international politics, he finds himself embarking on this new career.'"[13]

Drake would nowadays be regarded as an old fashioned style of hero; with right on his side, able to defeat enemies with his fists, his brain and an array of gadgets. His female companions, attracted by his honesty and honourable characteristics, respect Drake as a clean-cut man of action. American actress Beverly Garland said of McGoohan, "He's one of the best looking men I've ever played opposite."[ix] [14] British actress Barbara Murray said, "(Pat's) main appeal is his strength. He is like a rock. You get the feeling that you could always depend on him, whatever happened and whatever the situation."[x] [15] One of the other female leads in the *Danger Man* first series was Barbara Shelley,[xi] who revealed: "I

[viii] Corri appeared in 1965 in two episodes: *The Ubiquitous Mr. Lovegrove*, as Elaine and *Whatever Happened to George Foster?* as Pauline.
[ix] Garland appeared in the *Danger Man* episode *Bury the Dead*, 1961.
[x] Murray was in the *Danger Man* episode *The Sisters*, 1961
[xi] See also page 186.

Filming on location and at rest in the studio with *Danger Man*

worked with Patrick and always found him a wonderful man to work with, but self-contained. He was always one hundred per cent professional and I appreciated that. He would come into the studio make-up room each day and say 'Good morning' and deliver the script dialogue changes. I didn't mind because the changes were always much better. Also, where it is someone else's series and you are just the guest star, you accept it. He could be a little distant at times, but we got on and did the job."

Ms. Shelley continued, "I did two *Danger Man* episodes with him in the first series. I was in the opening episode *View from the Villa*. The *Danger Man* character John Drake was supposed to speak every language. I played an Italian lady but with an English accent. I had to dub the Italian later and I do speak the language fluently, but it was extremely difficult. I must have been to their liking because I was called back to do a second episode. This was *The Traitors* and I played the wife of a man who suddenly leaves his important post and John Drake has to pursue us.

"Patrick was very business-like and yet on the second day we were sitting, between scenes, and he just threw his head back and recited a very funny and risqué Irish poem. This was not at all the man I had seen during the first story. He had relaxed a little. I know it is hard to be sociable when you have the weight of the production on your shoulders and the responsibility. I believe that he knew that he could trust me and so it was his way of saying that things were OK. I almost laughed during the actual filming, because I couldn't stop thinking of the secret agent John Drake reciting that poem. I said to Patrick, 'You shouldn't have done that.' After thirty years in the business I've worked with a lot of people and although I didn't know Patrick well, he stood out, as he was an interesting person. He was a man of great integrity. I know there were other great actors, but Patrick impressed me. When the red light came on he was a hundred per cent actor, working with you and not just by himself in front of the camera. I thought that when he read out that Irish poem to me, it was very endearing. I know that he must have impressed me because I still remember him and think about my time with him on *Danger Man* after all these years."[16]

Hollywood star Hazel Court also recalled working with McGoohan. She appeared in a pair of the early *Danger Man* stories, *The Contessa* and *The Lonely Chair* and had clear memories of the assignments. "In *The Contessa*, I wore a black wig over my red hair and was heavily made up. He said to me, 'What have you got all that make-up on for? With your features you don't need all that stuff.' He was very outspoken. His attitude made him seem a little abrupt, although he was friendly towards me. It was not always easy working with him, but he was usually right and I really did appreciate his knowledge of acting. We were around at TV's golden time."[17] Lisa Daniely, who appeared in The *Danger Man* episode *Not So Jolly Roger*, added: "(Patrick McGoohan) was rather taciturn and had this touch-me-not quality. He didn't have a sense of humour at all and... kept himself enclosed in this very fierce exterior."[18]

At this time, McGoohan and wife Joan were arranging to purchase a new home. The chosen abode for the family was a former gardener's cottage, on the outskirts of London, in the Mill Hill district. Tramps had been sleeping in the property, which was now almost derelict, but the views it offered over Totteridge Common were magnificent. Despite their needing to rebuild from scratch, the couple knew it was the place for them. The conversion work was speedily undertaken, as their second child, Anne, was due early in January, 1960. Mill Hill's close proximity to London made it popular as a 'country retreat'

More studio shots and a location run during *Danger Man*

Top: Mid-1960s portrait photo
Bottom: A bespectacled McGoohan, mid-1960s

from the capital. Distinctive large houses, and quaint cottages were a feature of the area, locally referred to as "The Village" and being set along The Ridgway, an ancient byroad. The family's new three bedroomed home was an ideal base for McGoohan to visit Elstree, Borehamwood and other Home Counties studios, being situated not far from the M1 motorway, which had just opened.

Danger Man director Peter Graham Scott[xii] gave an intriguing description of the McGoohan residence: "Patrick's home was very nicely furnished with mainly antique furniture. But it had this cellar, which was decorated and furnished, like a drawing room, which had a bathroom attached. This room was effectively Patrick's nuclear shelter, which presumably he intended to use when the bomb was dropped and he would have holed himself up. He was quite serious about this."[19] Another *Danger Man* director, Clive Donner, divulged, "(McGoohan) was Roman Catholic and held strong beliefs. He was also a strange man. I heard he bought a house near the studios and had some young daughters, so surrounded the place with barbed wire. I think it was just to protect the children, but there was a certain sense of paranoia." The basement of McGoohan's house was reported by one writer to be a virtual shelter where he and his family could live if there was an atomic explosion. The writer concluded, "*Danger Man* changed everything, becoming the blueprint for practically every future ITC show. In the person of Patrick McGoohan, TV also had its first big star, but an eccentric one who insisted that his spy never carry a gun or indulges in promiscuous sex."[20]

There was also a real-life feature in *TV Week*, involving the star at his Mill Hill home. The interview was described as taking place in a room which was furnished comfortably, but elegantly: "Book-cases cover most of two walls, well-filled with an assortment of books – leather-bound sets and paper-backs – obviously there more for use than for show. It is a library that gives a sense of being lived with. Pictures of his wife and children are dotted around. In a corner stands a reasonably well stocked drinks table. It is a family room, a pleasant room – not too coldly tidy, but clean and welcoming. McGoohan is at ease. He sits relaxed without sprawling. He exudes a healthy well-being. His wife Joan, dark-haired, attractive, complements him. He enjoys making films with his family. He writes special scripts for his daughters and shoots them on 8mm film[xiii] as

---

[xii] Graham Scott directed several *Danger Man* episodes and a later *Prisoner* one.
[xiii] See page 98.

Left: Jimmy Millar in centre of family snap, probably taken by McGoohan. Right: On the set of *Dr. Syn* (1963)
- photo by Jimmy Millar

professionally as possible. And he enjoys taking his wife for an occasional extravagant night out, giving her what he calls 'Un-Birthday presents.' McGoohan's romantic view of life ties in with what he sees as a fault in himself: a habit of putting off decisions and then taking a whole lot at once."[21]

The McGoohans stayed at their Mill Hill residence for several years. Their third daughter, Frances, was born when Anne was one year old.[xiv] The new home provided some of the family's happiest times and gave Patrick much pleasure: "In summer I like to spend the first hour walking round the garden, making plans for all the landscaping I've never yet had time to do. There should have been a swimming pool for our youngest daughter to enjoy, when she arrived. Instead, the only sign of that pool is a twenty foot muddy hole I began to dig when she was six months old and still haven't finished."[22] McGoohan also described how his two young daughters would accompany him in their dressing gowns with their corgi, "Honey," for walks in the garden early in the morning, before the studio car would come to take the actor to MGM, to film a *Danger Man* scene.[23] However, owing to busy shooting schedules and family commitments, he and Joan could not find time for a holiday. They invested in a "caravette"[xv] to use for long weekends. Camping proved to be a disaster and the vehicle was sold. The McGoohans next bought a half share in a twenty-five foot sailing yacht, upon which they experienced only one trip, this being on the stormiest day of the year.[24]

McGoohan stressed the importance of his family in a magazine interview: "If I were offered a million pounds to make the greatest film in the world and I couldn't take my family with me, I'd turn it down. Ambition obscures everything else. You can see the ambitious everywhere, surrounded by broken marriages and alimonies."[25] It has always been to the actor's credit that he has placed his near and dear ones first, having at least wife Joan present with him on location filming in other countries. "I have two guiding lights every day. The first is my daughters. The second, my religion. Every hero since Jesus Christ has been moral. He wasn't a coward. Like John Drake He fought His battles fiercely but honourably. I hope it won't sound blasphemous when I say that I think He might have enjoyed a program like *Secret Agent*."[26]

[xiv] When Frances arrived, the family outgrew their gardener's cottage and built a larger house nearby.
[xv] A motorised caravan, sometimes called a camper van, or caravanette.

Left: ITC's promotional brochure for *Danger Man*. Right: McGoohan on the cover of the Catholic magazine *Annunciation* (1966)

McGoohan also provided some insight into his private life by obligingly completing and returning a fan's four page 'personal questionnaire.'[xvi] The actor described himself as being six feet two inches tall, thirteen stone seven pounds in weight and a "British subject." He confirmed that he had appeared in "about 200 plays" and when asked if he could dance, he replied, with tongue in cheek, "yes, Cossack." Asked who had been his greatest influence, McGoohan disclosed, "Jesus Christ." He gave his favourite occupation as "writing," listing also chess as a pastime, adding that he played the violin. Regarding his acting career he recalled that the hardest challenge had been an early play, in which he had "only one line." McGoohan's greatest thrill was recorded as "living," while his biggest disappointment was revealed as "living with myself." The actor modestly confirmed that he had begun his career as a "tea boy in a repertory company," while most of his remaining responses were jocular or dismissive.

Another magazine article carried the title "Leave My Family Out of This!" The piece started in a fiery manner with a tale of McGoohan filming a *Secret Agent* scene. It was stated that the actor was delivering some lines of dialogue when a "shapely brunette threw her arms around McGoohan's neck and gave a romantic sigh." The article continued, "Amorously, she drew her co-star close to her and planted a far-from-platonic kiss on his lips. In an instant, the calm, detached demeanour of Patrick McGoohan erupted into raging fury." The story revealed that the star yelled "Cut" to the camera man and faced the girl, shouting "That wasn't in the script! Nobody gets in a clinch with John Drake –

[xvi] See Appendix Five .

nobody!" The columnist observed that McGoohan seized the film and set fire to it. Later in the studio bar the actor had mellowed and said calmly, "Sorry about that" to all present. The article yielded a revealing interview with McGoohan. He confided, "I just can't go around necking with women. I'm a happily married man. Whatever would Joan think if she heard I'd been making love to another woman!" The article's conclusion was clear: "He will not answer searching questions about his family, will not permit a newspaper or magazine photographer to cross his doorstep. A writer

McGoohan gets a taste of directing on *Danger Man*

who travelled all the way from Los Angeles to England was rewarded with a four-word exclusive interview: 'Mind your own business.' The gentleman in question had been unwise enough to ask Pat if he planned to have any more children."

McGoohan at least lowered his guard on some topics. "To me a kiss is something magic and meaningful – not just an action to satisfy the whim of a scriptwriter or TV director. On *Secret Agent* I allowed myself to be kissed just once, by actress Jane Merrow. It was a kiss of friendship, fitting in with the story."[xvii] It was revealed that McGoohan was a regular church goer, often helping out at charity bazaars. "I know people think I'm a prig and a prude. I don't give a damn what they say. I act the way I do for one very simple reason – my daughters. I am trying to protect them in the only way I know how; by setting a good example. How do you think they would feel if they saw me in a torrid love scene with a total stranger? It would do them incalculable harm if a schoolmate came up and said, 'That was a nice bit of fluff I saw your old man necking with on TV last night.'" McGoohan disclosed, "I am strict with the younger ones. They have to look at the papers and tick what shows they want to watch. After a program is over they switch off and we have a sensible discussion on what they've seen. In that way TV helps them to think, instead of giving them brains like vacuum cleaners, to suck every scrap of muck and dirt that's going."[27]

Amidst the long-running *Danger Man* series, McGoohan revealed how he kept Sundays free, as they were precious. On the Sabbath he would unwind, play with his children and also write. Journalists noticed that he had steadfastly refused to employ a publicity agent. They also frequently observed that he dodged personal questions "as adroitly as Drake side-steps a smart right hook."[28] Although *Danger Man* elevated McGoohan to become a major personality on TV screens at the time, his decision to turn down the role of James Bond pushed his career onto a branch track, rather than a main line leading to blockbuster exposure. The actor declined the Bond role in the emergent "007" movies on moral grounds. He was not hesitant in explaining why, as a Catholic-raised boy, he grew up with definite opinions about the big and small screens: "I'd hate to offend children or anyone else by portraying a hero like Bond. My refusal to portray him was my way of rebelling against

---

[xvii] Jane Merrow kisses John Drake as he arrives at an airport, in the story *A Room in the Basement*. She would later have a close relationship with McGoohan's Prisoner character, in the story *The Schizoid Man*, although only a telepathic one, with no physical contact.

Learning lines for a *Danger Man* episode

what was expected of me as an actor." However, at a later time, McGoohan dismissed claims about his having turned down of the role of 007. "That story has been greatly exaggerated. It was Broccoli's partner (Harry Saltzman) who offered me the role of Bond, at the end of the first year of *Danger Man*. I read the script, which was not very good at that stage, although it improved thereafter. The real reason I refused was that there was a certain person on the technical team with whom I did not want to work again."[29]

Interestingly, the actor confessed that he had read all the Ian Fleming James Bond novels, and found 007's character fascinating.[xviii] In many future interviews, the actor would explain his reasons for turning down an offer to play Bond – a character he described as his bête noire – in the movies. "I didn't think it was a very good script," McGoohan disclosed, "and I thought 'This has got nothing to do with James Bond.' The *real* James Bond...The

xviii In 1959 *Goldfinger* was published and the Fleming novels were then half way through the fourteen hardbacks eventually to appear.

Left: Going through the script on *Danger Man*. Right: A casual studio shot during *Danger Man*

character in the books … had some interesting concepts about him; none of that was in the script. It was just the girls and the guns and the villains…and the stunts…The James Bond thing became what it was, not by design but by accident. When that film *Dr. No* was first made, they weren't quite sure what to do with it. They didn't think it was that great and then when it 'hit'…it doesn't matter who's in it because (the audience) will buy a ticket for the sake of seeing pretty girls, great sex, exotic locations, and great action sequences. It's just pure entertainment. It's great!"[30]

In another interview, McGoohan described James Bond as "immoral. A different woman every night." The actor even confirmed that he had insisted upon anti-sex and anti-violence clauses being written into his contract for *Danger Man*. McGoohan recalled the reaction of one TV executive – "A celibate spy? Why don't we go the whole way and hire a monk?"[31]

Despite these opinions, McGoohan scoffed at the idea that he was against accepting roles which involved sex. "I would have jumped at the chance of playing Larry Harvey's role in *Room at the Top*. I don't mind if sex and violence are an essential part of the character. But I hate to see them dragged in as a gimmick."[32] This was an unexpected comment from the actor, he having claimed that kissing another woman, not his wife, on screen was unacceptable. Certainly, there had been some pressing of lips in three of his films from the fifties, but the practice was not allowed to recur: "I'm a family man. I wouldn't want my children to see me slopping around with sexy pieces like James Bond does, or beating up people, or being beaten up. But surely that doesn't make me a prude."[33]

According to reports, McGoohan also declined the part of Leslie Charteris' suave anti-hero, Simon Templar, in the long-running TV series *The Saint*. It can be imagined how, in such a role, McGoohan would have been able to develop more of his ability to play comedy, a talent which came to the fore at later points during his career. The actor's explanation

A scene from *Danger Man*

was: "I refused *The Saint* because I thought – and still think – that the character's a rogue, a rat. And he's a wicked influence on anyone who tries to live decently."[34] McGoohan maintained that he had a responsibility to children other than his own. On a lighter note, one eight year old boy apparently wrote to him stating, "My dad and I have a bet. I say you dive through the window every morning on your way to work." McGoohan, realising he had to let the youngster down lightly, wrote back, "Only when I'm late. Actually," he reflected, "the insurance company won't let me dive through windows."[35]

There is no doubt that McGoohan found his time, whilst engaged upon the first series of *Danger Man,* stimulating. The actor declared, "I have never enjoyed myself so much since I was in rep. I think of the series as a kind of fortnightly rep. The cast and the story change every fourteen days." This particular interviewer was told that during lunch breaks

McGoohan had a secretary come to the studio to work on his other business activities. "If I can make somebody forget about the tax man and the mortgage for an hour, then I think I'm doing some little public service."[36] Therefore, although the actor had initially regarded the episode scripts as not being particularly good, he later relented and admitted that: "Once into (*Danger Man*) I got interested in it."[37] Director Peter Graham Scott disclosed, "I found Patrick McGoohan a demanding leading man to work with, frequently challenging my visual concept of a scene, though often allowing himself to be convinced (by me). Patrick would sometimes arrive on a Monday morning to confront us with a completely rewritten script. But it was usually much better."[38]

The star himself said that working on the series gave him "a great insight into the technicalities of film production" and he even took the helm on one episode: "I was allowed to direct … *The Vacation* which I personally think had the best story of the lot, not because I directed it but because it *was* a good story."[39] The actor added, "In fact, soon I am going to direct and produce my first feature film." However, in contrast, McGoohan found that working on production of a fast-paced television series stretched him to the limit at times. "I did get terribly depressed on one occasion. If you have ever been a boxer you'll know how I felt. It was like getting up on the count of nine and all around you is a haze of blurred faces and the ceiling is going round."[40]

As the early sixties' new, faster TV style began to wake up Britain, McGoohan's face was to be seen more than ever. Having studied the views of his subject towards the character of John Drake, one journalist announced, "He wends his knightly way across the globe, seeking out villainy, his fists as virtuous as his cause. Those who fall before him are clobbered with a fairness which could make the Queensbury Rules look almost criminal. A look at McGoohan's broad frame suggests that any risk in the series would be taken by those he opposes. This perfection, this relentless demand for reality, extends to the tender moments of the series. And in these, though he carefully avoids entanglements, McGoohan takes the same line as with moments involving thugs. He is fair. He is considerate. He is a gentleman. But McGoohan insists that he is not a star. He says: 'A star is a personality whose name is enough to draw people to a cinema, or theatre, or to the television screen. My name will not do this.'"[41] The star admitted to one reporter having a variety of interests and yet modest aspirations: "(McGoohan) enjoys writing and making his own 16mm. films. In spasms, he goes in for squash, climbing, carpentry, interior modern architecture, theology and 'sorting out the mess on my desk when it won't hold any more.' His principle ambition: 'to keep that desk straight from day to day.'"[42]

Eventually, production on the first *Danger Man* series came to an end,[xix] although McGoohan would resume the role of John Drake a couple of years later. Meanwhile, as a break from the show, the actor's first movie in the sixties was a Swedish one, *Two Living, One Dead* (1961), filmed in Stockholm. McGoohan was now playing a downbeat role of a post office clerk who avoids becoming a casualty during a robbery. In the story he is criticised for not risking his life to prevent the money from being stolen. *Two Living, One Dead* explores the mental strain upon the post office clerk and his family, as his confidence in his actions is shaken. The film gave McGoohan an opportunity to play a part with more depth than in previous movie scripts. He called the director, Anthony Asquith, one of the best with whom he had ever worked.

[xix] A BFI listing for 1960 has McGoohan as the narrator for *The Flying Carpet*, although no other entries verify this.

Left: Preparing for a scene in *Danger Man*
Above: Time for a smoke break during *Danger Man*

New York Times review: "The film examines the pitfalls of hero worship, and the culpability of the media in fostering misguided adulation. A robbery and murder is committed in a British pub, during which Bill Travers, a friend of the dead man, apparently acts with rare courage. His companion Patrick McGoohan, also apparently, did not lift a finger to help during the holdup. Travers is lauded publicly as a hero, while McGoohan is condemned as a coward. When the truth comes out, Travers is exposed not only for his feet of clay but for his intimate involvement in the fatal incident. The film is an undeservedly obscure work from a major British director." (Hal Erickson, All Movie Guide)

The actor's experimentation with film roles continued, with *All Night Long* (1961), based loosely upon *Othello*. McGoohan had reportedly performed the Shakespearean play in rep[xx] and would be due to direct an musical interpretation of it, *Catch My Soul*, a decade later. For now, the jazz-based version saw the actor playing Johnny Cousin, a dishonest and manipulative drummer. The broad American-type accent perhaps did him few favours, although his drumming was impressive. McGoohan once more showed his trademark commitment to a part by spending several weeks learning how to beat the skins. He commented later, "In *All Night Long* I actually played the drums in the film. I learned three pieces for that. It took me four months. Almost drove my family crazy! I had a set of drums in the garage and practised relentlessly."[43]

New York Times review: "This British film is Othello to a jazz beat. Paul Harris is the Othello counterpart, a bandleader happily married to 'Desdemona' Marti Stevens. Patrick McGoohan plays the film's funky Iago character, who covets Harris' job. He hopes to unnerve Harris by spreading rumors that Stevens has been unfaithful." (Hal Erickson, All Movie Guide)

[xx] There are references to McGoohan having acted in *Othello* in 1949, but no such performance appears in the Sheffield Playhouse history, which lists *Othello* as being produced there only in 1932 and 1955. Similarly, he was said to have appeared in *King Lear*, although no such listing has been found.

More TV work was also being offered to McGoohan. In the ABC *Armchair Theatre* production *The Man out There*, broadcast on 12th March, 1961, he was given top billing as 'The Man', Nicholai Soloviov, a Soviet space pilot. In these relatively early days of television, often productions were no more than a visual version of a radio play. McGoohan played a Russian astronaut,[xxi] trapped in space, with only a few hours to live. He makes freak radio contact with the wife of a trapper, stranded during a blizzard, in a remote Canadian outpost. The woman's child is dying, but the Russian is able to use his medical knowledge to help her perform a life saving operation. In return, the mother writes down the astronaut's final message before he becomes inaudible and is lost to the emptiness of space. McGoohan was strapped alone in the space capsule prop during the entire action of the play, maintaining dramatic tension by his strong performance.[xxii]

In 1961 and 1962 came two ITV *Play of the Week* productions: *Serjeant Musgrave's Dance* and *Shadow of a Pale Horse*. In the former, a bearded McGoohan played a Victorian soldier, fighting with a rifle in one hand and a Bible in the other. Interviewed about the production, McGoohan commented, "You do what turns up, from *Lear* to *Danger Man*, as long as it's interesting."[44] The second play was described in an article: "…in an Australian setting…a boy has been killed and a young man, found drunk near the body, stands accused: a lynching is just averted… The trial scene…effectively exploited the…exchange of position between accuser and defender. Mr. Patrick McGoohan gave a powerful, if mannered, performance as the prosecutor."[45]

Another returning theme for McGoohan was the exploration of religious beliefs and connected conflicts.[xxiii] In the film *Life for Ruth* (1962; released in the USA as *Walk in the Shadow*) the actor played Dr. James Brown. The movie, shot on location in the north of England, involved the parents of a young girl who would not allow the doctor to administer a medical aid to their daughter. The plot moved into the area of legal proceedings while the family's issues were publicly exposed. The highly rated film explored the conflict between the right to practice individual religious faiths and the legal responsibilities of society, as well as the beliefs of other individuals. McGoohan played a physician faced with seeing a child die because the parents' religion forbade a blood transfusion.[xxiv] "Craig and McGoohan both give towering performances as ideological opposites…"[46]

Variety review: "First problem that confronts an honest working man (Michael Craig) occurs when his eight-year-old daughter and her next door playmate are involved in a boating accident. His daughter is clinging to the boat and is not in such immediate danger as the drowning boy. Which should he try first to save? He rescues both, but by then his daughter is gravely ill. Only a blood transfusion can save her. Because of his strict religious principles he adamantly refuses, and the child dies. That was his second distressing problem. The doctor who urged the transfusion is so irate that he gets the father tried for manslaughter. This is good telling stuff for drama and it brings up issues about religion, the law, conscience, marital relationship – all posed with intelligence and conviction. Thesping is crisp all around, with Craig surmounting a gloomy type of role as the dogged religionist,

---

[xxi] This was McGoohan's second TV role as a cosmonaut, having played a similar part in *The Greatest Man in The World* (1958)

[xxii] The Russian general at HQ was played by Clifford Evans who became a Number Two character in the episode of *The Prisoner* called *Do Not Forsake Me Oh My Darling*.

[xxiii] In the 1959 play *Brand*, the child of McGoohan's lead character dies, in circumstances of religious inflexibility.

[xxiv] Fifteen years later, McGoohan would take the leading role in the US television series *Rafferty*, in which he played a hospital doctor, whose principles place him at odds with the medical establishment.

An excited card-playing McGoohan in *Danger Man*

and Janet Munro as his baffled dismayed young wife. Patrick McGoohan is excellent in a tricky role – the doctor – which is not so clearly defined as the other top jobs."

New York Times review: "Religion and medical ethics clash in this provocative drama that tells the story of a man prosecuted by the system because he refused to grant his dying daughter badly needed blood transfusions because he had faith that God would miraculously heal her. Unfortunately, the girl dies and now, in addition to dealing with the courts, angry doctors and an embittered wife (who had finally caved-in and signed the papers too late), he must also wrestle with his own conflicting feelings." (Tana Hobart, All Movie Guide)

An equally demanding role was McGoohan's part as Prison Warder Thomas Crimmin in the film adaptation of Brendan Behan's *The Quare Fellow* (1962), shot in County Wicklow, Ireland. Here, as a new recruit, McGoohan had to mind a prisoner awaiting the execution of a death sentence. The plot investigated the rights or wrongs of capital punishment and the effect of such a tense situation on the characters' moral and religious beliefs. Shot on location in Ireland, the film's dark and brooding screenplay made for a bleak production. However, the film won the British Producers' Association Award for the best film of 1962.

Variety review: "Patrick McGoohan is a young man from the Irish backwoods who takes up his first appointment as a jail warder with lofty ideals. Criminals must be punished for the sake of society is his inflexible theory and that also embraces capital punishment. But when he arrives he is shaken by the prison atmosphere. Two men are awaiting the noose. One is reprieved but hangs himself. That shakes McGoohan. He meets the young wife (Sylvia Syms) of the other murderer and his convictions totter still more when he hears precisely what caused her

Los Angeles Herald Examiner, mid-1960s

husband to murder his brother. Mostly, though, he is influenced by a veteran warder (Walter Macken) who believes that capital punishment is often a worse crime than the original offence. The film, a mixture of grim humor and cynical starkness, brings out the clamminess and misery of prison life."

New York Times review: "Brendan Behan, the quixotic, eternally sloshed Irish poet/playwright, peppered his play The Quare Fellow with plenty of 'gallows humor.' The film version dispenses with most the play's morbid jests, leaving us with a grim, straightforward account of a Dublin death-row prison guard (Patrick McGoohan) and his growing empathy with two condemned prisoners. One could understand the removal of the play's comic elements had the film been made in timorous Hollywood. But since the film was financed and produced in Ireland, it seems an inappropriately glum tribute to one of the country's boldest and most brilliant talents." (Hal Erickson, All Movie Guide)

Another intense performance by McGoohan was witnessed on television in 1963. The BBC's presentation of *The Prisoner*, from the 1954 play, by Bridget Boland,[xxv] depicted the conflict between the prisoner of the title and his questioner. The former is a cardinal (Alan Badel) – allegedly inspired by real-life Hungarian Cardinal Mindszenty[xxvi] – who is a national hero, but a thorn in the side of the New People's Democracy. The Interrogator (McGoohan) is intent upon obtaining the cardinal's signature to a written confession, recanting his spiritual convictions. The questioning is subtle, but persistent, in order to entrap the religious figure, by breaking down both his will and his faith.

Some light relief was waiting round the corner for McGoohan. The influential Walt Disney Studios had chosen him for their new major feature, *The Three Lives of Thomasina* (1964).[xxvii] The story, shot in Scotland and at Pinewood, concerned a vet, played by McGoohan, who is required to deal with a little girl's sick pet. As expected the movie veered from heartbreak and momentary sadness to a happy-ever-after ending. During

[xxv] The broadcast was on 24th February. There was also a 1955 film version, with Alec Guinness as the Cardinal.
[xxvi] See also later reference to McGoohan wishing to make a film about the cardinal, with Kenneth Griffith, on page 191.
[xxvii] Directed by Don Chaffey, who would later helm several episodes of *The Prisoner*.

9.0
THE
SUNDAY-NIGHT PLAY
starring
PATRICK   ALAN
McGOOHAN   BADEL
as   as
The Interrogator The Prisoner
in
The Prisoner
by BRIDGET BOLAND
Adapted for televison
by Ian Kennedy Martin
with
Warren Mitchell
as The Cell Warder
Directed by Alan Cooke
The Secretary.................GARY HOPE
The Doctor.................REX ROBINSON
A warder.................BILL CORNELIUS
Music by NORMAN KAY
Designer, Roy Oxley

Radio Times magazine from 24th February 1963

THE PRISONER

Tonight's play stars
Alan Badel
(Above left)
Patrick McGoohan

Two men who once fought together in the Resistance now face each other as enemies—in a battle of wills. On one side, the prisoner: a cardinal who is a national hero and a thorn in the side of the New People's Democracy. On the other, his interrogator, bent on obtaining the cardinal's signature to a confession 'that will dispel the black magic of your name.' It is an interrogation without threats or violence: a subtle contest between a man of science employing his knowledge of the human mind, and a man of God 'difficult to trap, impossible to persuade, even more impossible to appeal to.'

Alan Badel appears as the cardinal—a part created by Alec Guinness in the stage and film versions of this most absorbing play—with Patrick McGoohan as the interrogator.

filming of *Thomasina*, co-actor Susan Hampshire[xxviii] said, "(McGoohan) will talk quite intensely about all kinds of things. Everything, in fact, except about himself. At the end of the film I still didn't know much more about him than when we started. I think he's shy. He bought me a beautiful bunch of flowers, but was too shy to give them to me himself and sent a porter round with them. He doesn't like being photographed. He's rather strict about it."[47] At least one reporter concluded that McGoohan could not be blamed for wanting his wife and family to lead a normal existence, outside the glare of publicity.[48] Certainly, the actor had so far achieved this and would carry on doing so throughout the rest of his career.

New York Times review: "This is an imaginative tale of a resourceful cat. Thomasina is the pet of the daughter of a taciturn Scottish veterinarian (Patrick McGoohan). When Thomasina falls ill, McGoohan coldly diagnoses the cat as suffering from tetanus and declares that the pet must be put out of its misery. As Dotrice and her friends sadly prepare to bury the 'dead' Thomasina, backwoods girl Susan Hampshire, who is said to be a witch, shows up and runs off with the kitty corpse. Using equal doses of intuition and love, Hampshire revives Thomasina, who of course wasn't dead at all. While in limbo, Thomasina ascends to Cat Heaven, where her case is heard by the Cat Goddess (this is a wonderful piece of special-effects wizardry, even if you don't like cats). Returned to life, Thomasina has no memory of her previous existence. Thus, the cat runs off in terror when Dotrice sees her again during a torrential downpour. Now it is Dotrice who becomes seriously ill, necessitating a collaboration between the cold, cut-and-dried ministrations of her father and the tender loving care of the 'bewitched' Hampshire. As it turns out, Thomasina is the catalyst for both Dotrice's recovery and the film's happy ending." (Hal Erickson, All Movie Guide)

The actor enjoyed a second Disney role at this time with *Dr. Syn, Alias the Scarecrow*, again filmed in Britain in 1963. The production was screened on US television as a Disney

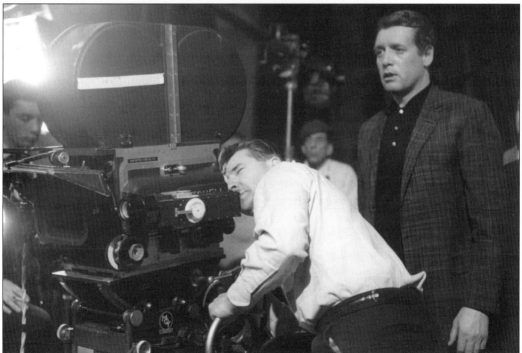

Top: McGoohan under the glare of the camera in *Danger Man*. Bottom: McGoohan sizing up a scene in *Danger Man*

presentation, in three parts, during February, 1964.[xxix] However, as the film also had a theatrical release, it is included in this book as a movie, not a TV show. McGoohan played Reverend Dr. Christopher Syn, a mild-mannered vicar during the day, whilst by night roaming Romney Marsh as a costumed smuggler. His Robin Hood motives saw him dealing in contraband, to avoid duties, in order to assist his impoverished congregation. *Photoplay* magazine met up with the actor during work on *Dr. Syn*. The assigned journalist commented: "I've met (McGoohan) on several occasions and I've learned if you can survive the first fifteen minutes you'll be all right. But those first fifteen minutes usually turn out tricky, to say the least." The actor was quoted as saying: "What makes me angry is when I see trash on the screen. I've never seen any of my films, only bits of them, because I don't think I've ever made a really good film. I've always liked Disney's films – good, clean family entertainment. That's why I'm making *Dr. Syn* – I think everyone will enjoy it."[49]

New York Times review: "This Disney drama, originally broadcast as a three part TV show, tells the story of a vicar's double life. Outwardly he is the model of upstanding citizenship and loyalty to an oppressive British government. But he is also a notorious smuggler who uses his ill-gotten gains to benefit his impoverished village." (Sandra Brennan, All Movie Guide)

After his two productions with Disney, McGoohan was wooed back into the role of John Drake, in 1964. ITC produced a seventeen page information booklet on a second season of *Danger Man* episodes, now one hour in length, allowing for commercial breaks: "The new programmes are on a more spectacular scale than before, once more with world-wide settings, with big name stars in support of Patrick McGoohan, and made by Britain's top directors." The description of the main character, John Drake, had changed. "He is four years older, but his idealism remains undimmed. He now works for a special department in London." McGoohan's comment was that "Drake now finds himself more emotionally involved with the other characters. Maturity has given him a greater depth of understanding. He rebels against some of his assignments. He doesn't really want to do them, because he sympathises with the under-dog."

The actor himself described Drake's view of marriage: "He realises that he is getting older and is not yet married. Basically, he would like the security of home, marriage and family, and he is beginning to feel that the time is approaching when he must consider this before it is too late. He intends, however, to give up his job before he takes this step. This development is making him change his attitude towards women. They are no longer deliberately out of his reach, potentially dangerous to his own happiness and way of life. He regards them with more personal interest and understanding, because one of them might be the woman who appeals to him strongly enough to make him break away from his job at last and settle down to a more secure way of living." McGoohan was asked about coming back to the production: "An odd feeling, to return to a character after such a long break," he admitted, "I'm feeling quite nervous." However, there was one aspect of the series which appealed to him: "I find it as stimulating as playing in repertory, with something fresh to tackle in every new (story)."[50]

ITC's publicity material stated that McGoohan currently received: "An enormous shoal of fan mail letters every day, from fans throughout the world. They come to him written in almost every language under the sun, many addressed simply to 'The Danger Man,

---

[xxix] The title was *The Scarecrow of Romney Marsh*.

Falling to the floor for an action scene in *Danger Man*

McGoohan behind the camera in *Danger Man*

Music soundtrack from *Danger Man*

London.'" One of McGoohan's fans, living locally to him, was Karen Howell. She had begun collecting cuttings and photographs of the actor when she was a schoolgirl and could spot the star's Mill Hill home, by virtue of the gypsy caravan parked in his back garden.[xxx] Her father occasionally met McGoohan in the nearby Old Bull and Bush pub and the two men would chat about cultivating roses. The actor was described as always charming and courteous, even providing an autograph for Ms Howell to add to her collection.

The second *Danger Man* season was again filmed at the MGM Studios in Borehamwood, apart from the last half dozen stories. Thirty two episodes were made over a twelve month period, between 1964 and 1965. At the end of the second season, a third one went into production, yielding thirteen more episodes, this time using the Shepperton studios, in Surrey.[xxxi] Finally, again at Shepperton, a pair of one hour stories was filmed, mid-1966, for the first time in colour.[xxxii] The initial series of *Danger Man* was syndicated by CBS, mid-1961. Now with the series re-titled *Secret Agent* for the US market, in 1964 the show became the first non-American TV imported production to be given a nationwide network screening. A delighted Lew Grade – having sold the series once more in a seven figure deal – said to McGoohan, "My boy, they want to meet you out there. Go over and talk to them for a couple of weeks." Accompanied by Joan, Patrick enjoyed a stateside family get-together with seventy-five aunts, uncles, first and second and third cousins, all but two of whom he had never met before.[51]

John Drake's exploits were eventually sold to sixty-one countries: in the US, *Secret Agent* was shown in 1965 and 1966. Lew Grade had a simple explanation as to why *Danger Man* was so successful. "Mainly because of the personality of Patrick McGoohan."[52] During the decade, McGoohan would become the highest paid actor in British television, although he claimed that his quoted salary of two thousand pounds a week per week was an exaggerated figure: "I give most of it away to the Inland Revenue anyway."[53]

Although most actors would wish to be accommodating in media interviews, McGoohan did not shrink from expressing his disapproval of journalists who wanted to know too much: "I'm against any kind of invasion of my privacy. Most people want to talk about one's own personal and private life. They want to strip you of all your little secrets – find out the real you, as they say. Well I understand they have a job to do, but I don't see why I should fall 'victim' to their inquisitive questions when they don't relate to my professional work. Anyone who wants to talk about me as an actor, I'm only too happy to

[xxx] A prop acquired by the actor from the Disney studios after the caravan was used in the movie *The Three Lives of Thomasina*.
[xxxi] Nowadays the studio has become merged with Pinewood. It was at the famous Buckinghamshire studio (home to the James Bond movies) that McGoohan worked on some of his Rank movies.
[xxxii] *Koroshi* and *Shinda Shima* – see page 100.

oblige."[54] With the second series of one hour *Danger Man* episodes well into production, McGoohan confided, "There have been the odd episodes that haven't been too good and I squirm when I watch them." He liked the idea of Drake being "a man of ideals, with a passionate belief in the dignity of mankind, risking his life in the cause of international peace and understanding." Clearly, McGoohan held a sincerely stated view of the role of Drake: "A man who has seen a lot of the world, who has studied people and has reached the stage of wanting to do something exciting, but also something that will do good."[55]

The star continued to keep Drake pure during the coming years in which the series flourished. Even at the end of its run, he was commenting, "TV is like another parent. It has an insidious and powerful influence on children. Would you like your son to grow up like James Bond?"[56] Perhaps in order to meet the challenge presented by 007 movies, the role of John Drake metamorphosed into that of international agent, ridding the world of any menace which might threaten global stability. Drake was now based in London, with a regular "M" style boss. Again, in an attempt to match Bond's weapons, Drake was kitted out with many ingenious gadgets. Hidden cameras and tape recorders helped him with spying and collection of evidence, although as this was television, the more lethal type of weaponry was excluded.

In the sixties, 'Swinging London' was hailed as the fashion and pop music capital of the world. The zeitgeist was rubbing off even on TV shows like *Danger Man*. For the USA, a completely different opening sequence was devised, with American artist Johnny Rivers performing "Secret Agent Man,"[xxxiii] the opening lyrics of which are:

There's a man who lives a life of danger.
To everyone he meets he stays a stranger.
With every move he makes,
another chance he takes.
Odds are he won't live to see tomorrow.
(Chorus) Secret Agent man,
Secret Agent man.
They've given you a number and taken away your name.

Along with all this, McGoohan's popularity peak was maintained. However, although the *New York Times* described the spy production as, "crisp and smooth, with the hero being ruggedly droll," the newspaper insisted this was "at the expense of storyline values."[57] Another critic suggested that McGoohan was too "sang-froid," rating his performance as "barely passable."[58] Meanwhile, back in England, McGoohan was being observed by a show business writer: "His appeal comes from his wild romantic Celtic charm, mixed with the stiff upper lip traditions of his adopted home, Britain." The actor explained, "At the very top you have to get a million dollars a picture to pay the tax on the last million." Prophetically, McGoohan was claiming, "I fear by AD 2000, we'll all have numbers, no names. By then, workmen will be able to operate their lathes by push-button from their beds. How are we going to educate people for an abundance of leisure like that?" So as not to repel admiring female viewers, Mr. Sproat added in his article, "John Drake is surrounded by beautiful women, but he is always the gentleman. An actress who played opposite McGoohan in the series said 'He's a man's man, who appeals to women.'"[59]

At this time, an American writer recalled how the actor had first appeared to US audiences as "a brawny hulk of Irish muscle."[60] Pointing out that McGoohan insisted that

---

xxxiii The song, written by and © S. Barri and P. F. Sloan, became a massive hit single and still receives airplay today.

public performers have a right to private lives, it was noted that the actor rarely saw journalists and usually limited members of the British press to fifteen minutes per interview. It was recalled how a fellow reporter had once suggested, bravely or stupidly, that McGoohan should change his name. "(This) brought the savage retort that it would be an insult to his father." Presently, the thirty eight year old performer was described as being even better looking than on screen, with "cold blue eyes under hooded lids, a crinkle of lines in the corners." The reporter revealed that travel was one of McGoohan's hobbies, but always with his wife. "He rarely visits the bright lights of London. He prefers to drink, mainly beer, at an ordinary pub. There was a stampede when the word first reached the secretaries that McGoohan had come to film at Shepperton. The biggest stars have played at Shepperton, but you wouldn't have believed it from the stir his arrival caused. Pretty heads spun his way. Red lips smiled in his direction. McGoohan, the family man, paid them no attention."[61] Another writer shared a fair amount of McGoohan's time during the middle of the latest *Danger Man* production. Amidst all the usual interview angles: family background, reluctance to be interviewed, forbidding access to his private life and so on, McGoohan showed his interviewer a framed photograph of President Kennedy, his personal hero. The actor's perspective on his career so far was, "I enjoy working. I like being totally absorbed. I am scared of drifting, of having nothing to do."[62]

A feature on McGoohan in *TV Star Parade*, from the summer of 1965, asked "How many affairs should a married man have?" Despite the title, the article looked instead at the actor's "understanding wife," named as "Mrs. Patrick McGoohan." It was noted that her husband was often forced to spend many weeks away from his family, surrounded by the most beautiful women in the world, on film sets. The writer inventively stated, "In each of the countries he's visited, he's left a lady with a wistful smile and dreams of what might have been." There were no direct quotes from the actor's wife and the reader could be forgiven for wondering whether Joan McGoohan had been interviewed at all. Using reported speech, the piece concluded that "she knows Pat's love scenes are strictly make-believe on the set. The real love affair centres around his family."[63]

When *Secret Agent* was airing on the CBS Television Network at the end of 1965, a press release declared: "Patrick McGoohan enjoys his busman's holidays." The notes stated that the actor was a home movie enthusiast. "He is currently involved in one of his most ambitious vocational undertakings, the making of a full-length film that involves writing, filming and editing the production." McGoohan's quote in the release was that "The film, as yet untitled, is one that no member of the public will ever see. It is being made along strictly professional lines as an exercise for Catherine, my teen-aged daughter. Her ambition is to become a film director. It's not just a passing phase on her part. She has had the ambition for a long time now and there is no sign of its wearing off. So we are making this picture just as if it was a real feature with a complete script, story break-downs, schedules, call-sheets, music cue-sheets and the lot. It's a deliberate effort to let her learn for herself what lies behind making a motion picture."[64]

According to CBS, the movie had involved wife Joan, daughter Catherine, plus both her sisters, with McGoohan appearing in the production as a villain. Curiously, the actor gave lengthy advice through the press release on his approach to filmmaking: "I always draft out a script, even while on a holiday trip," the actor enthused. As an example, he cited a journey, which he and his wife had recently taken to France and

Italy. He had cast himself as a "lady's man," stalking Joan's character. The spooky script eventually brought the 'players' back to England, finally depicting McGoohan following Joan right into their own home, with the twist-ending that the characters were really man and wife.[65]

McGoohan described to a US interviewer in 1966 his reprised TV role:" Drake is a moral fellow … ladies might show an interest … but he doesn't reciprocate. Drake is basically good, is unarmed, never kills and never has promiscuous relationships. On our show, good guys are really good and villains are really villains. Drake's private life is his own. It's important not to tell too much about him. I like the idea of Drake being the mysterious stranger." The interviewer could not resist comparing the actor to his screen character: "Patrick McGoohan is a bit of the mysterious stranger. In contrast to the reams of material published about the personal lives of (other actors and spy guys) he's practically anonymous."[66] In June the same year, *TV Motion Picture* magazine announced that "(McGoohan) likes a night out with the lads occasionally too, and sometimes he can be found playing darts in the public bar of old London pubs." The reporter referred to the actor having been "… convicted,[xxxiv] after pleading guilty to driving under the influence of alcohol, and banned from driving for a year. It was an extraordinary and highly unlikely thing to happen to a man like McGoohan, who drinks sparingly and takes good care of himself. But Patrick disdained the help of studio cars after his sentence, and as if almost to punish himself for his temporary slip-up, he bought a bike and rode all the way from his home to the studios at Elstree, some five miles away, every working day. In the studio parking lot, the space allocated to the car of Patrick McGoohan, star of *Secret Agent,* was occupied by his bike!"[67]

Another 1966 article appeared under the banner "Behind the Image of Danger Man." The ensuing feature commended the series and its hard working star: "The weekly adventures of super agent John Drake … have acquired for Patrick McGoohan a huge following. Drake has captured the world with his exciting, daredevil exploits. For Patrick McGoohan, the man behind the image of Drake, the series has meant hard work, long hours in the role, and a life which he himself adores. 'I love hard work,' he says. 'I want to be completely absorbed. I would hate not having anything to do.' The article described his day starting at 5.30 a.m., followed by a quick breakfast and a drive to the film studios. The next nine hours are spent in the role of John Drake: "He will be word-perfect in his lines; he will have discarded his own personality … though he states that he and Drake do have many things in common. They both loathe violence." The actor was described as a man who does not mince his words. "He speaks his mind and doesn't stand any nonsense. He is not, however, easily angered. On the contrary, he is a pleasant, amiable man, a wonderful conversationalist with a keen sense of humour. He once said that if he ever feels like losing his temper he will walk into a corner and bang his head against the wall!" McGoohan's shyness was highlighted: "I am self-conscious, trip over my own feet and so on. In company, I tend to hide." Despite his being the highest paid actor on television, he was said to have his feet firmly on the ground. McGoohan even admitted to being a little worried about taking on the Drake role: "It is very difficult on a TV series to maintain a high standard of production. But I am sure we have done so. Each story is filmed in fourteen days. The pressures are great but we've survived!"[68]

[xxxiv] May 1964, at South Western Court, London, according to the article.

Such survival was short-lived and 1966 saw the end of the third *Danger Man* series. Only a final pair of 'stand alone' colour episodes[xxxv] were produced, *Koroshi* and *Shinda Shima*. These embraced the growing popularity of screen martial arts, with karate featuring in the oriental screenplay.[xxxvi] While the episodes could have been intended to represent some kind of a finale – the storyline of one continues into the next – there is no suggestion that they were to be a double 'season opener' of a fourth series.[xxxvii] Another possibility is that the opportunity was seen to combine them into a colour, feature-length TV movie. This is precisely what was done and the singly named ninety minute[xxxviii] *Koroshi* was marketed around the globe, being shown as a cinema presentation in countries such as Germany and Pakistan.[xxxix]

However, a mystery still arises at this point, which has not been – and probably never will be – satisfactorily resolved.[xl] It is not known whether McGoohan already had an idea to create his next series *The Prisoner*, wanting therefore to leave *Danger Man*, or whether his desire to quit the long running spy show led to the new production. The latter is often claimed as being the reason for McGoohan's departure from *Danger Man* and for his having alluded to this in the opening episode of *The Prisoner*. However, there were not many weeks between the end of the John Drake stories and the new project, which started shooting in the summer of 1966. Therefore, this writer thinks that McGoohan had been hatching his plan for the 'sequel,' with input provided by story editor George Markstein and producer-director David Tomblin. They had all worked on *Danger Man* and would be involved with *The Prisoner* from the outset. The creation of the new cult TV series is covered in the next chapter, but before leaving *Danger Man*, this is a convenient point to consider the spy genre itself. Mention has already been made of McGoohan's views on James Bond. However, the world of spies had a great effect on McGoohan's *Danger Man* TV show and his later series, *The Prisoner*. The sixties decade being awash with secret agent movies and TV adventures, clearly many productions were being born out of the realms of espionage. Apart from the James Bond novels, from Ian Fleming, there were also the writings of Len Deighton, who introduced his own cool spy character Harry Palmer, as well as other popular fictional 'undercover' offerings at that time.

In *The Ipcress File*, made into a movie in 1965, Palmer[xli] (Michael Caine) escapes from what he thinks is a Russian prison, only to find that he is somewhere much closer to home. A like plot device would be used for the *Prisoner* episodes *The Chimes of Big Ben* and *Many Happy Returns*. Similarly, in the James Bond *Thunderball* movie of the same year, enemy agents have numbers instead of names – as in *The Prisoner* – and the person in control is "Number One." The character James Bond did more to popularise the secret agent in films than any other. Fleming saw in Bond the strong and ruthless character he – and other men – dreamed of being. And yet, it was the immoral and indulgent side of Bond to which McGoohan took exception. However, the actor spoke about Bond in so many interviews that it is essential to look briefly at the Fleming phenomenon.

[xxxv] Shown in Britain, in monochrome, between February 1967 and January 1968, in various ITV regions.

[xxxvi] The plot involved a secret Japanese death cult, with John Drake infiltrating the organisation's headquarters.

[xxxvii] Four of the actors would go on to appear in *The Prisoner*, along with a dozen members of the production team

[xxxviii] Various different running times were advertised, up to two hours.

[xxxix] The screening in Pakistan was retitled *Danger Man in Tokyo*. The 'movie' was screened on US TV and was also released on video there and in France, but not in the UK. However, it did surface twice in Britain, being provided with a *Prisoner* magazine part work, in 2004 and 2005.

[xl] There seem to be as many questions about how *The Prisoner* started – and why it ended – as those which relate to what the series is about.

[xli] His boss is played by Guy Doleman, who McGoohan's character faces as the Village leader, in the opening *Prisoner* story, *Arrival*.

The author was born in 1908, in England and was educated at Eton College and Sandhurst military academy. After working for the Reuters news agency, Fleming was recruited to Royal Naval Intelligence during World War II. He took charge of numerous missions, travelling the world as part of his covert undertakings. Upon visiting Jamaica he fell in love with the place and when the war ended he purchased a holiday home, *Goldeneye*, there. Fleming was forty three when he left Naval Intelligence to begin his writing career. Before he started writing Bond novels at his West Indies winter retreat, he started an affair with Lady Anne Rothermere. She became divorced following the discovery that she was pregnant with Fleming's child, after which she and her lover married. Fleming was by now working for the foreign sections of various newspapers and still travelling widely. With summer in London and the Caribbean in winter, Fleming behaved like an adventurer, also indulging in excessive drinking and heavy cigarette smoking.

The force of the first Bond novel, *Casino Royale*, in 1953,[xlii] was recognised by Jonathan Cape, who agreed a publishing deal. By 1961, after writing several more 'Bonds,' Fleming agreed to Albert "Cubby" Broccoli and Harry Saltzman producing the first 007 movie *Dr. No* (1962), based on the 1958 novel. The film made a star out of lead actor Sean Connery overnight and gave Fleming immense fame. More Bond novels were soon made into movies, but the writer would only live to see one more completed, *From Russia With Love* (1963). Fleming was at least aware of the third screen outing for Bond, *Goldfinger* (1964), being put into in production, although he died later that year, aged only fifty six.

Naturally, the spy genre could never transfer to television as successfully as it did for cinema audiences. In the sixties, features about spies became a craze, with numerous films and TV shows being churned out, ranging from cold to comical in their approach. Consider the following list of espionage movies, both serious and spoof ones:

The Spy Who Came in from the Cold (1965); Richard Burton as Alec Leamas
Licensed to Kill (1965); Tom Adams as Charles Vine
Where the Bullets Fly (1966); Tom Adams as Charles Vine
The Liquidator (1965); Rod Taylor as 'Boysie' Oakes
The Quiller Memorandum (1966); George Segal as Quiller
The Silencers (1966); Dean Martin as Matt Helm
Where the Spies Are (1965); David Niven as Dr. Jason Love
Modesty Blaise (1966); Monica Vitti as Modesty Blaise
Our Man Flint (1966); James Coburn as Derek Flint
In Like Flint (1967); James Coburn as Derek Flint
Billion Dollar Brain (1967); Michael Caine as Harry Palmer
Funeral in Berlin (1966); Michael Caine as Harry Palmer
The Ipcress File (1965); Michael Caine as Harry Palmer
Additionally, there were the TV spies, agents and operatives:
Callan (1967 onwards); Edward Woodward as David Callan
The Man from U.N.C.L.E. (1964, TV and movies); an ensemble cast
The Avengers (1961 onwards); with cast changes, but Patrick Macnee as John Steed
I Spy (1965, TV) Robert Culp and Bill Cosby as a pair of undercover agents
Get Smart (1965); Don Adams as Maxwell Smart, with an ensemble cast

---

[xlii] The novel was finally made into a movie in 2006, after a spoof version in 1967, which also saw several of the *Prisoner* MGM Borehamwood studio sets being used.

Some of the spy-orientated dialogue which would soon be heard in *Prisoner* episodes – the central character being referred to only as "Number Six" – embraces the spy genre:

Villiers: "What is your name?"

Number Six: "Code, or real?"

Villiers: "Code."

Number Six: "In France, Duvall. In Germany, Schmidt. You would know me best as ZM73. And your code number is PR12."

(*Do Not Forsake Me Oh My Darling*)

Col J: "Where is this village?"

Number Six: "Lithuania, on the Baltic, thirty miles from the Polish border."

Col J: "How did you find out?"

Number Six: "Nadia told me."

Col J: "How did she know?"

Number Six: "She used to work for their government. She came across a secret file."

Col J: "On how to catch a spy in six lessons?"

(*The Chimes of Big Ben*)

Number Two: "I know who you are!"

Number Six: "I'm Number Six."

Number Two: "No! D Six!"

Number Six: "D Six?"

Number Two: "Yes, sent here by our masters to spy on me!"

(*Hammer Into Anvil*)

So much for spies and stardom; McGoohan had experienced a rise towards star status, through repertory theatre, West End productions, television plays, adventure series and cinema films. As will be seen, during the sixties, McGoohan worked on *Danger Man* and *The Prisoner*, almost to the exclusion of other work in the second half of the decade.[xliii] The question to be posed later by this book is if McGoohan became consumed by these productions, or whether these shows began to type-cast him. In retrospect, the time when the star hit the ground running with *The Prisoner* can be seen as his creative peak. Financial stability, fame and the energy to pursue fresh ventures all made for a solid foundation, from which he might have never looked back.

However, McGoohan's new series *The Prisoner* was destined to become, in many ways, as much of a curse as it was a blessing. As will be seen in the next chapter, the series would not only become a huge task for its star, but would also challenge TV viewers like nothing else on television had ever done before – many say since – with media writers still commenting on this, forty years on: "When it was originally screened on TV in 1967, *The Prisoner* baffled the critics but intrigued the viewing public who watched in their millions. Part science fiction fantasy, part spy thriller, and partly a morality tale for modern times, there had never been anything like it before, and there has never been anything like it since. Often complex, confusing and contrarily perverse in equal measure – perhaps too much so for some people's tastes – *The Prisoner* nevertheless retains an enigmatic quality that bears repeated viewing."[69]

[xliii] A break in filming *The Prisoner*, in 1967, allowed McGoohan to appear in the movie *Ice Station Zebra*, see page 178.

EVERYMAN FILMS

M-G-M Studios,
Boreham Wood,
Herts,
England.

Dear

Thank you for your generous letter;   I am
grateful for a good run of the show and value
the support of our many followers.

Currently, I am engaged in preparation for a
new Series entitled " THE PRISONER " which
we hope will be with you some time in September
'67.   If you care for prior information on this
please write me at the above address and I shall
be delighted to oblige.

Kind regards.

Cordially,

Patrick McGoohan

As *Danger Man* ends, the new *Prisoner* project begins

[1] Classic Images Magazine, 1987, Barbara Pruett
[2] Classic Images Magazine, 1987, Barbara Pruett
[3] Picturegoer, 5th December 1959, John K. Newnham
[4] ATV Star Book, 1961
[5] Top Secret magazine, August, 1985, Dave Rogers
[6] ATV Star Book, 1961
[7] Lew Grade: The Greatest of them All, 24th and 25th December, 2006, BBC Radio 2.
[8] Classic Images Magazine, 1987, Barbara Pruett
[9] Television Starbook, year unknown, 1960s
[10] Broadcasting Entertainment Cinematograph and Theatre Union Interview by Alan Lawson, 1987
[11] Photoplay, May, 1965
[12] Top Secret magazine, August, 1985, Dave Rogers
[13] ATV Star Book, 1961
[14] TV Star Parade, August, 1965
[15] TV Star Parade, August, 1965
[16] Interview with the writer, 2006
[17] Interview with the writer, 2006
[18] Cult TV The Golden Age of ITC, 2006, Plexus, Robert Sellers
[19] Number Six Magazine, Six of One, The Prisoner Appreciation Society, January, 1993, Mathew Lock
[20] The Independent Online, 30th November, 2006, Robert Sellers
[21] TV Week, 7th May, 1966, Iain Sproat
[22] Joan Reeder, Woman magazine, 4 issues between 9th and 30th October, 1965
[23] Joan Reeder, Woman magazine, 4 issues between 9th and 30th October, 1965
[24] Joan Reeder, Woman magazine, 4 issues between 9th and 30th October, 1965
[25] Woman's Mirror, 22nd May, 1965
[26] TV Radio Mirror, August 1966
[27] TV Radio Mirror, August, 1966, Dave Hanington
[28] Woman's Mirror, 22nd May, 1965
[29] Premiere Magazine, October 1995, Jean Yves Katelan (translations Rosemary Camilleri and Jane Rawson)
[30] Classic Images Magazine, 1987, Barbara Pruett
[31] TV Radio Mirror, August, 1966, Dave Hanington
[32] Showtime, 1965, Dick Richards
[33] Showtime, 1965, Dick Richards
[34] TV Radio Mirror, August, 1966, Dave Hanington
[35] Photoplay, November, 1965, K.G.
[36] Photoplay, November, 1965, K.G.
[37] Classic Images Magazine, 1987, Barbara Pruett
[38] British Television: An Insider's History, Peter Graham Scott; McFarland, 1999
[39] Photoplay, April, 1961
[40] Photoplay, April, 1961
[41] Source not verified
[42] ATV Star Book, 1961
[43] Classic Images Magazine, 1987, Barbara Pruett
[44] TV review page 11, details unknown
[45] The Times, 5th August, 1959
[46] Moviemail, DVD release, 2007
[47] Photoplay, May, 1965
[48] Source not verified
[49] Photoplay, August, 1963, Ken Ferguson
[50] ITC press book, 1964
[51] Joan Reeder, Woman magazine, 4 issues between 9th and 30th October, 1965
[52] Six into One: The Prisoner File, Channel 4, 1983
[53] TV Week, 19th February,1966
[54] Television Star Book, 1964
[55] Television Starbook, year unknown, 1960s
[56] New York Times, c.1965, details unknown
[57] New York Times, 1966, Jack Gould, date unknown
[58] 1966, source not verified
[59] TV Week, 19th and 26th February, 1966, Iain Sproat
[60] Source not verified
[61] TV Guide, 14th – 20th May, 1966, Robert Musel
[62] UK newspaper article, c. 1965, by Ann Leslie, details unknown
[63] TV Star Parade, 6th August, 1965
[64] CBS Television Feature, 17th November, 1965

[65] CBS Television Feature, 17th November, 1965
[66] Spies, Spoofs & Super Guys, Dell, 1966
[67] TV Motion Picture, June, 1966
[68] Television Stars, Purnell, 1966
[69] Best of British magazine, February 2007, Lin Bensley

Top: Break for a cigarette during filming a scene in the *Prisoner* episode *Free for All*
Bottom: Queuing outside the Salutation Restaurant in Portmeirion

CHAPTER FIVE
The Prisoner: Arrival

"You know, it's so crazy it might work."
Lew Grade (1966)

Danger Man's John Drake had left the studio building and the publicity machine for McGoohan's next venture was presently silent. As the months passed and the autumn of 1966 was reached, a few news stories filtered through, telling of mysterious goings-on in North Wales. Occasionally, a press hound would manage to track down McGoohan and be briefed – brief being the operative word – on the actor's new production, *The Prisoner*. The series was to be about an unnamed man held in isolation, in a secret community; he would not know where he was, why he was being held, or who was detaining him. The actor's advance revelations had to be taken on trust; his past success and star status, earned with the long running *Danger Man* series, surely meant that he was going to turn up with something even bigger and better. However, when the first few episodes of the new series were screened a year later, reaction from the media and public would initially turn out to be lukewarm. The show's cult status was not to be achieved until a decade later.

But for now – even on the other side of the world – exciting reports were being given to TV audiences: "After 88 episodes (sic) of *Danger Man*, Patrick McGoohan bows out to create a new TV programme. The series is being made in colour and it is suggested in some quarters that Lew Grade, the financial mastermind behind the production company, Associated Television (ATV), will hold its release in England in the hopes of getting colour television introduced on the independent channel as early as possible ... then *The Prisoner* may be shown as his ace programme. Pat McGoohan is not a great man for publicity, and with a total involvement in making the new series (writing, acting, directing cameras and lighting) there is not much time for speaking with outsiders. He makes do with only three hours sleep a night. With *The Prisoner* there is an even greater need for a smokescreen against publicity – McGoohan's basic idea may be stolen by another company before the

EVERYMAN FILMS

M-G-M Studios,
Boreham Wood,
Hertfordshire.

Dear

Thank you for your letter and enquiry regarding the
new Series "The Prisoner"

I have pleasure in sending you an outline format and
hope you will find it of interest.

Cordially,

Patrick McGoohan

Reply to an enquirer, from Everyman Films

series gets on to the screen. Patrick plays in the new series a character who seems to resemble 'John Drake' after he has left active service and gone into retirement. But the retirement is not the traditional one of comfort – he is held prisoner by some of his former enemies. In every episode he manages to escape by some means or other but is recaptured at the end ... ready for his next escape in the next episode. – A sort of *The Fugitive* (an American programme about a prisoner who is constantly evading capture) in reverse."[1]

Discussing *The Prisoner* and its making naturally forms a large part of any study concerning McGoohan. In this book, the task has been approached with a trio of chapters. Firstly, this initial one provides the story behind the series' idea and the months of production, with comments – from interviews given in person, screened or published – made by the people involved. Some of the scriptwriters became irritated when McGoohan would require many changes to storylines. Experienced editors were frustrated when he would demand that sequences should be re-cut. Actors would find that they had to please two masters: the designated director and the show's star. All of these tales can be conveniently housed in the present chapter, bearing in mind that during 1967, there was a hiatus in the series' production. This occurred when McGoohan went to Hollywood, to film the movie *Ice Station Zebra* (1968)[i] and some accounts refer to this.

Secondly, the next chapter offers analysis of the series, its concepts and interpretations, with McGoohan's own views, particularly the autobiographical element he embedded. Finally, the third chapter covers the series' finale – the phenomenon that was *Fall Out* – in 1968. This was when screenings around Britain ceased and McGoohan subsequently left for Switzerland. Some interviews with cast and technicians necessarily refer to later times, but those of the same speaker are kept together where this allows, the aim also being to retain a loosely chronological order. Accounts of cast members, directors, writers, editors and stunt actors are grouped, except where one person's story better follows on from the account of another. The pair of *Prisoner* 'sandwiching' chapters, plus their middle 'filling' one, ensure an integral approach to the many and wide-ranging strands of the series' story.

McGoohan claimed that *The Prisoner* was going to be "posing questions." Through the storylines he would be challenging: "Has one the right to tell a man what to think, how to behave, to coerce others? Has one the right to be an individual? I (want) to make (viewers) ask questions, argue and think. The function of any art is to speak ahead of the times, to herald warnings that are not obvious but which are there."[2] The actor was not only setting himself quite a task, but was also employing a high risk strategy, by experimenting through the medium of commercial, primetime television. One can only imagine how the television executives and viewing public would have reacted, in advance of the series' screen

[i] See mainly Chapter Seven.

appearance, if they had seen the type of summing up which would be applied in the future: "*The Prisoner*, TV's most cultish series, owes its form and content to a number of dissonant factors. The story – a spy, the nameless Number 6, resigns for an undisclosed reason and is abducted to a mystery village for debriefing – has its roots in Cold War paranoia, hippy counter-culture ideology and growing concerns about the involvement of the state in the daily lives of its citizens. It might also have been influenced by the experiences of its star and co-creator, Patrick McGoohan, who had unexpectedly resigned from his previous series, *Danger Man*, because he felt trapped by the role of NATO agent John Drake."[3] Another future verdict revealed the series to be something which was never envisaged originally: "Primarily concerned with what it means to be an individual in a conformist, regimented society, (*The Prisoner*) took satirical potshots at various elements of English society. Many found the series' surreal conclusion unsatisfying, but its very obscurity served to guarantee its continuing cult status."[4]

Signed photo of McGoohan for an enquirer

However, in the early days, there was no indication – and probably no plan on the part of the star or his team – to create as popular television material something as cryptic as *The Prisoner*. The series was to be made by McGoohan's own production company, Everyman Films Limited[ii] and its name[iii] appeared in the end credits of each episode. Elizabeth Feely, wife of one of the series' scriptwriters, commented, "The name of the company – Everyman – is a clue to the identity of Number Six.[iv] He's 'Every Man,' in the Kafka sense: we all live behind bars, which we make ourselves."[5] The company itself did not boast enough working capital to finance the production and so, once again, Lew Grade, of ATV, stepped up to provide funding. The TV impresario regarded McGoohan as a prize property, a bankable figure with a wealth of 'hands-on' production experience. Grade was sure that the actor would provide ATV with another critical and commercial success. McGoohan related how he visited the mogul's office early one morning with a prepared *Prisoner* proposal: "I pulled out this script I had written, and (Grade) said, 'You know I can't read, tell me about it.' So I talked about it, and he paced up and down in his office smoking his cigar and paused and said, 'You know, it's so crazy it might work.' He would later say to me, 'Still don't understand a word of it.'"[6] Grade always confirmed that the deal was done simply on a handshake and that he had no more than a gentleman's agreement with McGoohan. There was genuine trust on the part of the TV grandee towards his protégé, as the ATV boss would joke, "I have no problems with (McGoohan). I just give in to all his requests."[v7] As for David

---

ii See previous chapter, page 74.

iii An Everyman is an ordinary human being, an individual with whom an audience, or reader, is able to identify. Such a figure – the name deriving from an English mediaeval morality play – is often placed in adventure stories, the character being idealistic, highly intelligent, or even having many talents. The beholder can place himself in the same situation and experience the action, vicariously. It is likely that McGoohan chose the name, given his theatrical background.

iv The main character's numeral was chosen to be one which would not be too high in the Village hierarchy, but still small enough to indicate some importance. Accordingly, the number seven was omitted from all Village displays and badges etc.

v Grade repeated the tale in a later TV documentary about him, see page 252.

Tomblin – McGoohan's company co-director – he recalled how he was told by McGoohan that they had a go-project: "I've seen Lew, we've got the money; we've got the series." "I said, 'Great, what series is that?'"[8]

Although the story is known as to how and when the new project was greenlit, it is not clear who came up with the initial idea for the series. There has been much debate about who first dreamed up *The Prisoner* and upon what the original concept was based. Some people have credited George Markstein, the series' script editor, with the early framework.[vi] He did indeed create a basic outline, describing the nature of the programme, the geography of the place where the main character would be imprisoned and what the regime was all about. Markstein was careful not to reveal which country, or side, was holding the unnamed man captive. He insisted that he came up with the concept of *The Prisoner* at 6.21 one evening, while travelling on a London train – between Waterloo station and Shepperton studio – and that he put together the first synopsis. The script editor disclosed, "Without any warning McGoohan decided he didn't want to do any more *Danger Man*. So I came up with the idea of *The Prisoner*, which although a blend of espionage and sci-fi fantasy, had its roots set in hard fact. The action was based on a secret wartime internment camp in Scotland,[vii] which housed suspect refugees from the continent and our own agents, who knew too much to be allowed to roam free. McGoohan was a secret agent who had walked out on his bosses. I decided to call him No. 6 because it's high enough to make him important and low enough for him to get pushed around. McGoohan was soon obsessed by the series. He became its executive producer, writer, actor, casting director and composer."[9]

McGoohan and Markstein would later part company, the writer quitting the production mid-1967, leaving the star to run an almost one-man show during completion of the remaining episodes.[viii] At the time of the script editor's departure from the production, reasons for his exit were not disclosed. However, years afterwards Markstein would reveal that he resigned in protest, saying, "I think McGoohan would like to be God. *The Prisoner* is a tragedy because McGoohan became a prisoner of the series."[10] In support of the script editor's assertion, actor Derren Nesbitt, who had appeared in several *Danger Man* stories and also was to play a major part in the *Prisoner* episode *It's Your Funeral* said at a future point: "I'd known George Markstein for a long time. We were brought up together and he always grumbled about the way he had been treated over *The Prisoner*. His original idea was about what happens to spies when they are not needed, or they retire."[11] Some other directors also claimed to have heard Markstein talking about basing the action upon the wartime secret establishment he knew of, where inmates were kept in comfort, but not allowed to leave the holding facility. According to Lewis Greifer,[ix] "It was George who came up with his own pet idea, *The Prisoner*."[12]

Notwithstanding claims by McGoohan, or Markstein, the seeds for *The Prisoner* had probably been sown in the later episodes of *Danger Man*. Stories like *The Ubiquitous Mr. Lovegrove* and *Colony Three* had seen John Drake in strange and surreal circumstances, or

---

[vi] For more discussion as to how the series came into being, see page 127.

[vii] Invelair Lodge, Inverness, a sixteen bedroom hunting lodge, where 'guests' were held in wartime. Markstein based his novel *The Cooler* – written shortly after *The Prisoner* ended – on this establishment.

[viii] Seventeen episodes in all were completed and screened. The first thirteen might have represented a first 'season,' but this is not certain, as McGoohan then went to Hollywood, to film *Ice Station Zebra* (1967). After his return, production on *The Prisoner* resumed, but for some new reason – discussed later in this book – only four more episodes were made.

[ix] Writer of the episode *The General*, under the pen name Joshua Adam, using the names of his two sons.

surroundings.[x] One writer commented: "McGoohan didn't entirely abandon (*Danger Man*). His next project, *The Prisoner* was partly inspired by the *Danger Man* episode Colony Three which featured a mysterious village behind the Iron Curtain from which no one returns. Whether the nameless British agent banished to a mystery location in *The Prisoner* is meant to be John Drake is not clear. McGoohan denied it, perhaps to avoid having to pay (Ralph) Smart a royalty for his character, but in the public's mind the link between the two shows was compelling."[13] One of the *Prisoner* directors, Peter Graham Scott, told this writer that he believed the true origin of the series to have been a simple progression of *Danger Man* into the later format.

Another *Prisoner* director, Pat Jackson,[xi] who helmed several episodes, recounted a different story as to what was behind the idea for McGoohan's new series: "A Home Office official, perhaps a little the worse for drink, had intimated that such places as the Village existed. Patrick was inspired and commissioned script writers, directors and ideas. He approached me and the scripts I was offered were worth doing. They were interesting, new and original."[14] *Prisoner* production manager Bernard Williams had a slightly different account of the Jackson story. He said that McGoohan had told him about a big party, held after production of *Danger Man* ended: "There were some members of parliament there and presumably some people from some kind of secret service in England. Patrick posed the question 'what happens to agents who want to retire? What do you do with them?' They said, 'Well, we have places to send them, to stop them from going across the border to other countries.' So that's how the idea started. Pat did a lot of writing. It was a very complicated idea because it was, I guess, intellectual. It was over and above the general standard of writing at that time."[15]

Doubtless the truth about the origin of *The Prisoner* is 'somewhere in the middle' and all of the influences came to work together in the minds of McGoohan and his colleagues. Whether the star's possible mid-life crisis, a realisation that there was a crossroads in his career mid-decade or whether the actor harboured a wish to be experimental – like his mentor, Orson Welles – might never be known. The time was the sixties and with everything going on around McGoohan and youthful revolutions occurring in all areas, the very spirit of the age was a strong influence upon the actor. Questions as to who devised the new series, or whether the star simply wanted to quit the long-running *Danger Man* series as he felt trapped, will remain subjects for debate. Whatever the background, the new production was now in progress and an ad hoc team of writers was asked to provide storylines, with various directors being signed up to shoot episodes. Overseeing everything was McGoohan, as lead actor, executive producer, part-writer, part-editor, occasional director and even publicity spokesman. The involvement of David Tomblin[xii] and George Markstein meant that from the outset McGoohan had a power base, an inner core, from which he and his two close colleagues could instruct their writers, crew and actors as to how *The Prisoner* was going to be produced. Tomblin commented, "With *The Prisoner* you didn't have a format, you just had an idea and you could (take) fantasies in any direction you liked."[16] With more

---

[x] Stories with an 'it was all a dream' premise caused a similar theory to be advanced about *The Prisoner*. In the opening sequence, McGoohan is rendered unconscious and wakes up in an unknown setting. It has been asserted that the action seen in episodes is 'all in the mind,' until Number Six becomes free – or wakes up – in the final story, *Fall Out*.

[xi] As mentioned earlier in this book, Pat Jackson had worked with McGoohan on other TV series, including *Danger Man*.

[xii] David Tomblin never revealed from where the series' original premise had come.

Left: MGM studios at Borehamwood, Hertfordshire.
Right: MGM backlot, where the 'other' *Prisoner*
village was located and the Western town.

than a little bravado, the star and his team took the visual image of the former hero John Drake and returned him to Portmeirion, the place where viewers had first seen the agent in the opening *Danger Man* episode, fifteen years earlier. Those with a long memory of the location screen credit[xiii] at that time, could have deduced that the follow-on series was being filmed at the same spot.[xiv] Whilst it is not known who chose the resort as the filming location for *Danger Man*, there is no doubt as to who selected it for "The Village." McGoohan emphatically told this writer that he and he alone chose Portmeirion for *The Prisoner*.

Whether the new figure was Drake or not, the recognisable face and familiar McGoohan mannerisms treated viewers not only to a fresh series, but also one with an added dimension on top of the normal adventure-fantasy format. There have been off-the-record admissions that using the name John Drake would have involved paying heavy copyright fees and royalties to Ralph Smart, producer of the earlier series and to whomever else held rights. How impish then it was of McGoohan to have, in one of the last *Prisoner* episodes, *The Girl Who Was Death*, an actor with the true stage name of John Drake, which would appear prominently in the screen credits.[xv] Also, how risky it was for the makers of the series to chance using photos[xvi] and placards of the old Drake face throughout the episodes, calling the man simply "Number Six." With no name, this even left open the possibility that he *was* Drake. Of course, McGoohan and his fellows constantly asserted that there was no connection with *Danger Man* at all, whereas George Markstein, years later, freely claimed that it was always John Drake.

Such revelations were certainly not made at the outset. In fact, the new show was shrouded in mystery, with publicity from ITC – the TV distribution company – teasing the public's appetite with their style of announcement. The main character would have no name but he would appear to be the former John Drake, having been abducted and taken to a strange, exotic place called 'The Village'. This could be run by any of the foreign countries which the agent had visited in earlier years. Thus, still fresh from his Drake persona, the star was saying that the new part of Number Six involved a character who could be "anything at all." Most people have always regarded him as some kind of spy, or secret agent, but McGoohan insisted that he could be a government official, or even a

---

[xiii] A location acknowledgment appeared at the end of the Portmeirion-based *Danger Man* episode, *View from the Villa*.
[xiv] At the end of the final *Prisoner* episode, a location screen credit appeared: "In the grounds of The Hotel Portmeirion, Penrhyndeudraeth, North Wales, by courtesy of Mr. Clough Williams-Ellis."
[xv] McGoohan even resurrected a character from the earlier *Danger Man* series, Potter, played by the same actor, Christopher Benjamin.
[xvi] Photos of other actors from the casting directory *Spotlight* were used for their faces on Village newspapers or posters.

McGoohan on location in Portmeirion, filming *The Prisoner*, 1966

nuclear scientist.[xvii] Announcements from ITC about the new series, played up the left-field angle: "The Irish in Patrick McGoohan surges to the surface when asked about his new television series *The Prisoner*. A leprechaunish smile creeps over his face as he admits that he is the only person in the world who knows the answers to all the questions that are going to be fired at him when the programme is shown. He has conceived the idea himself and originality is the key-note of the most off-beat stories ever filmed for television."[17] Clearly, nobody at ITC knew any details about the episodes being made. In fact, many of the actors and crew members would later reveal that they were never told what was going on.

With almost a blank canvas, the team started filming: first, the *Prisoner*'s London-based opening sequence was shot.[xviii] There was now no turning back and for the next year, work would be non-stop, as a UK autumn 1967 premiere was scheduled and also the series was being sold to North America. For a month, from the first week of September, 1966, McGoohan took his Everyman Films main and second film units to the North Wales private village resort of Portmeirion,[xix] where location shooting began.[xx] While filming there, the actor stayed in the resort's most 'remote' cottage, White Horses, with his family present at times.[xxi]

The opening episode *Arrival* and the early *Free for All* story – both featuring much outdoor filming – were the first to be shot.[xxii] A sudden casualty was a prototype mechanical robot 'guardian.' The contraption had been designed over a go-kart type chassis, with 'hovercraft' propulsion and a blue flashing light on top. McGoohan's recollection was, "It could do anything, but the engineers, mechanics and scientific geniuses hadn't quite completed it to perfection. On the first day of shooting, Rover[xxiii] was supposed to go down the beach, into the water, do a couple of signals and a couple of wheel spins and come back. But it went down into the water and stayed down, permanently."[18] The machine's sudden demise necessitated the urgent acquisition of a replacement 'entity.' This was realised in the form of a meteorological balloon, which provided an unplanned, but highly effective, substitute.[xxiv] The makeshift arrangement ironically led to the creation of one of TV's most memorable monsters. The actor recalled that moment: "So we're standing there, my production manager, Bernard Williams, wonderful fellow, beside me and he says, 'What are we gonna do?' And he looked up and there was this balloon in the sky. And he says 'What's that?' and I said 'I dunno, what it is?' He says, 'I think it's a meteorological balloon.' I said, 'How many can ya get within two hours?' He took an ambulance so that he could get to the meteorological station and get back fast because it was quite a ways. He came back with

[xvii] At a later time, McGoohan referred to a scientist with "space secrets" – see page 149.
[xviii] For the unnamed man's home, 1 Buckingham Place, SW1, was used, along with shots of Westminster Bridge, Parliament, Buckingham Palace and the Mall. An airfield at Elstree, Radlett or possibly even Hatfield, was used for the sportscar on the deserted runway opening shot.
[xix] See pages 74 and 260.
[xx] The production team was blessed with four weeks of sunny weather. If the unpredictable North Wales climate had produced heavy and frequent rain, the location filming would have been severely blighted. As it was, being away from internal studio security and disciplines, plus the open-air 'holiday' setting, undoubtedly created a unique atmosphere as well as a free approach – allowing many improvisations – which was taken back to MGM after the month on location.
[xxi] In the following spring there followed some further Portmeirion shooting on *Many Happy Returns* and *Hammer Into Anvil*, completing the main North Wales location work for McGoohan and bringing to an end his third and final time there, including the earlier Danger Man visit. The *Many Happy Returns* raft escape filming was done off the Abersoch shore, about twenty miles away.
[xxii] See also Appendix Four as to the order of production of *Prisoner* episodes.
[xxiii] From McGoohan's comment it seems that the name might have been applied to the prototype, as well as the later spherical substitute.
[xxiv] However, assistant art director Ken Ryan recalled how the balloons were "expendable and expensive," with up to ten a day being needed for filming.

them and there were these funny balloons, all sizes, and that's how Rover[xxv] came to be. And sometimes we filled them with a little water, sometimes with oxygen, sometimes with helium, depending on what we wanted it to do. In the end we could make Rover do anything: lie down, beg, anything. We used about six thousand of them."[xxvi] [19]

As for Portmeirion, the resort's exclusive clientele was replaced by technicians and actors, while curious day visitors looked on. Indoor dramatic scenes would have to wait until the crew returned to their MGM studio base in Borehamwood, Hertfordshire. In the meantime the 'invasion' presented a colourful spectacle: actors and extras were attired in straw boaters, capes, or even undertakers' frock coats, with top hats and many period costumes on display for carnival scenes. The quaint, olde-world setting of Portmeirion now took on a 'holiday camp' appearance. Pretty signs appeared, a fancy telephone kiosk, along with open-topped buggies and canopied bicycles. Central areas were decked out with sunshades, while candy-striped screens were used to mask any parked cars belonging to hotel customers or staff. Local extras, from office staff to teachers, were recruited to play the incarcerated citizens of the Village. People came from as far as two hundred miles away to be extras in crowd scenes: retired businessmen, quarrymen, labourers, telephone operators, retired seafarers and local hotel staff. One old sea captain who lived on a boat arranged for a friend ashore to signal him by flashing lights, should he be required for filming each day. A massive production budget for the time – equating to some seventy five thousand pounds per episode – had been allocated. The extras received ten shillings[xxvii] for a day's filming, while the actors were paid fifty pounds and upwards a day.

There was extensive use of Portmeirion and its grounds during the initial month of filming. Shots of and from an overhead helicopter, plus filming on the beach, in the woods and along all streets and paths, helped create a feeling of disorientation, with the unusual architectural styles presenting a striking backdrop. Trick photography and strange editing sequences – which even made buildings appear in the wrong place – all added flavour to *The Prisoner*. The makers of the series used as much imagination in crafting the early episodes, as did Clough Williams-Ellis in creating Portmeirion. The production team was fortunate to have such a large and distinctive 'set'. The resort was largely free of moving vehicles – the odd one can occasionally be spotted on screen – and there were not too many members of the general public, the time being past the main holiday season. Later, back at the studio, the look of the stories would be maintained through careful use of sets, matching up the visual look of Portmeirion. McGoohan and his associates made sure that the place[xxviii] of filming and the details of the series were kept as secret as possible, until work back at the studios could be completed. Not until the final episode, *Fall Out*, was the name of the location transmitted.[xxix] However, for a select few, a late evening[xxx] screening of recent filming 'rushes' took place. A small bus would take personnel to the Coliseum cinema in the nearby town of Porthmadog, as well as ferrying them back to Portmeirion after the 'show'.

[xxv] The white sphere – used to replace the 'missing in action' mechanical robot guardian – was called "Rover" in just one *Prisoner* episode, *The Schizoid Man*.

[xxvi] Despite McGoohan's story, the balloons were actually specified on props lists and, as recalled by certain crew members, were dispatched from Paddington station, in London, to the shooting location in Wales.

[xxvii] Another report mentioned fifty shillings a day, see page 116.

[xxviii] By this time, the production had long since left Portmeirion.

[xxix] The resort's intake of visitors increased dramatically

[xxx] The cinema's own programme had to end first and patrons needed to have vacated the premises.

An early 'scoop' report appeared under the heading of "Hush – He's in Danger Again," the article tantalising readers with a few pieces of information about filming in North Wales: "No-one really wants you to know, but '*Danger Man*' Patrick McGoohan is shooting a television film. Says the TV company: 'The owner of the location is only allowing us to use it on condition that no publicity is given out.' But, of course, everybody around the holiday village where the film is being made knows about it. Visitors on five shilling day tickets are lining up with the camera men to take their own image of McGoohan. A small army of technicians has been imported with their equipment. The script calls for a helicopter, power boats, water skiers, scooters and bicycles with striped canopies – hardly things which can appear in a quiet part of Wales without comment." The article ended by revealing that "a busload of extras had to be hired from Portmadoc to dress in everything from straw hats and track suits to undertakers' frock coats and toppers. Local pensioners were in demand for 50 shillings-a-day walk-on parts."[20]

One of the local people used in several filmed scenes was Heulwen Vaughan-Hatcher. In one scene, she had to wear a bikini and walk past McGoohan by the hotel swimming pool. In order to be prepared for this type of shot, Heulwen would receive a call at the local telephone exchange where she worked in the evenings: "They would say, 'Tomorrow, bikini girls please.' So we would come down with our bikinis the next morning. Sometimes we would meet Mr. McGoohan coming up the hill and he would say, 'Oh, you are the bikini girls. Well forget it, I've been up all night and we are doing something else today.' That happened a lot. However, he was a real gentleman. We did not always know what we were doing, but he was always smiling, always nice to us."[21] The swimwear costumes helped publicity, with one magazine providing a shot of several skimpily clad girls and the caption: "Beaches, bikinis and villas … but a helicopter flies overhead to show the inhabitants that they are all prisoners – and escape is futile."[22]

With stories being shot in colour on thirty five millimetre cine film, the production resembled more of a movie set-up than a regular TV assignment. Famous names from the big screen and theatre would be guesting each week and the look of the episodes was one of high quality. Portmeirion would soon be closing for the winter and production schedules were tight, so that Sundays were also worked.[xxxi] Weather permitting, filming continued to get the exterior scenes 'in the can'. A unique combination of Portmeirion's beach at low tide and bay at high tide allowed scenes on foot, or in vehicles, as well as with power boats. *The Prisoner* became a massive undertaking, requiring months of development during 1967.

When the main studio work commenced at MGM Borehamwood, vast sets were constructed, to meet the enormous task of 'replacing' Portmeirion. The studio's ten massive sound stages covered nearly a hundred thousand square feet, with an equally large backlot. Stages one and two had a removable dividing wall, allowing the creation of a huge production platform. The finale of *The Prisoner* – set in a giant subterranean cavern – was shot there, while, appropriately, the series' main interiors were shot on stage six. As well as attracting top stars and producing blockbuster movies, MGM also boasted a small army of in-house carpenters, painters, hairdressers and make-up staff, with extensive workshops and a huge scene dock. The series' editors, of which there were several, had the task of matching location and studio footage, bringing many a technical, or continuity, problem.

[xxxi] In those days Sundays meant that some of North Wales was, by law, 'dry,' prohibiting the sale of alcohol. See page 143 for a story by McGoohan's stunt double, Frank Maher, about a drinking session just over the border.

Art director Jack Shampan built up a magical world in a large tank below some of the sets. His 'engine room' featured much equipment, with substantial power on hand. At the press of a button, scenery could be made to move and effects could be created. The art director declared: "I had the whole of *The Prisoner* unit in my grasp. I could have blown the whole place, and everyone there, sky-high!"[23] Shampan also designed the surreal and futuristic *Prisoner* sets. He recalled being engaged as art director for the series: "I was just going on holiday. They gave me five incomplete scripts to work from, so I took them with me and that was

Summer 1966, filming the *Prisoner* opening sequence in London

my holiday. Everyone else was out sunbathing, and I was sitting in the hotel sketching out ideas for *The Prisoner*." The penny farthing bicycle logo[xxxii] – seen throughout the Village and on inmates' numbered badges – was one of Shampan's original designs: "It was an heraldic symbol representing the Establishment, with their Victorian, die-hard, biased methods of coping with current affairs."[24] The art director constructed three permanent sets: Number Six's cottage, Number Two's official quarters and the Village control room. For the banks of metal cabinets seen at the start of *Prisoner* episodes – into one of which McGoohan's character's expired identity card is cast – Shampan devised a forced perspective. He used cabinets of decreasing size, to create an illusion of an immense room receding into the distance. The set took much time and money to complete, although it is on screen for only three seconds.

Eventually, the art director experienced rising pressures, as studio production reached its peak and with the series already pre-sold to the USA. "The Americans were clamouring for us to deliver more episodes, but it became impossible for Pat to keep going, doing so many different jobs. He was wearing himself out."[25] When the time came for the final episode had to be shot. Shampan's view was to have a different looking set for *Fall Out*: "We'd seen inside the Village, throughout the series, so it seemed logical to go below (it) to find out just what was underneath." Looking back with pride on what he and his studio team produced, Shampan felt that *The Prisoner* was ahead of its time, with its own philosophy. He reflected, "In the end we are all of us prisoners, setting our own limits on the kind of lives that we lead."[26]

Although George Markstein had invited his known base of writers to submit stories, from the beginning it was McGoohan who injected much of his personal philosophy into the screenplays and even his own biographical details. When the first episode *Arrival* would be screened in the Autumn of 1967, the new main character would only be introduced with the title of "Number Six," given to him by the leader of "The Village," the unknown place where the man was being held. His scripted angry retort was, "I am not a number. I am a person!" The line would change to, "I am a free man!" for the opening sequence of following

---

[xxxii] The image was used for a distinctive Christmas greeting, sent to members of the production team at the end of 1966. The card featured a cut-out eye, through which could be seen the bicycle and McGoohan's printed signature.

episodes. In the initial story, the dialogue required the Number Six character to yell, defiantly, "I will not be pushed, filed, stamped, indexed, briefed, debriefed, or numbered!" Tagged onto the end of this line – a play on the much older dictate: "Do Not Fold, Bend, Mutilate or Spindle."[xxxiii] – would be McGoohan's his own date of birth: "Four thirty-one a.m., nineteenth of March, nineteen twenty-eight. I've nothing to say."[xxxiv]

The action in *Arrival* included a file of photographs, on display in the residence of the Village leader, "Number Two." These would soon be showing the actor's early life and apparently his *Danger Man* John Drake persona. Later in the series, more autobiographical details would be included, making reference to the prisoner's acumen with figures, his woodwork ability and proficiency at boxing. Lines liberally quoted from Shakespeare were harking back to McGoohan's acting days in repertory. As each month of production passed, throughout 1967, the actor was developing a free and often experimental style with *The Prisoner*.

After several stories had been created, George Markstein left the production and the final four episodes seemed to be deliberately crafted by McGoohan to tantalise his audience. In the concluding episode, *Fall Out*[xxxv] – the star then solely at the helm – there would be no obvious plot, with even religious themes being woven in. Although the finale is discussed later in this book, *Fall Out* reveals the sea change which came about in the latter days of the series. The unnamed character, at last being called merely "Sir," would be seen to leave the Village, his place of perpetual torment. The idea, as yet not formulated, would see the man freed from both mental and physical imprisonment, cleansed and able once more to go out into the world, having 'found himself'. This sort of symbolism, being wrapped up as the finale of a prime-time television drama series, was unprecedented. When the constant changes of direction in *The Prisoner* eventually led to the series' financial backing being reined in, an ending had to be devised. With the funding tap about to be turned off, McGoohan had to provide a conclusion within the space of one fifty minute episode and he decided to go all out: *Fall Out* became a piece of sixties TV mayhem with few equals.

McGoohan talked freely to a journalist: "Computers have everything worked out for us. And we're constantly being numeralised. The other day I went through the number of units that an ordinary citizen is subject to, including license plate numbers and all the rest and it added up to some 340 separate digits. I used the secret-agent thing as a launching pad and the numeralisation thing as a progression. Now I just hope that there are a couple of things in *The Prisoner* that relate to the things that are going on around us, to our situation at the moment." On the subject of prisons, McGoohan added, "I've always been obsessed with the idea of prisons in a liberal, democratic society. I believe in democracy, but the inherent danger is that with an excess of freedom in all directions we will eventually destroy ourselves."[27]

It can be seen how difficult it was to describe *The Prisoner* and how widespread would become the interpretations. Cleverly being stirred into the mix were drugs, religion, politics, coercion, brainwashing and power abuse. Viewers would be seeing almost the same set and backdrop each week, but with constantly changing characters and different events,

---

[xxxiii] The phrase later became a protest slogan: "Human being: do not fold, tear or mutilate."

[xxxiv] In the story *Many Happy Returns*, McGoohan's birth date is used again. After a short spell of freedom his character arrives back in The Village on his birthday, Sunday, 19th March. In 1967, when the episode was being made – directed by the star himself – the date did actually fall on a Sunday.

[xxxv] *Fall Out* was first screened in the UK at the beginning of February, 1968, in some ITV regions and in one other area on 1st March.

guaranteed to raise questions as to why a current episode was so unlike a previous one. The stories had a slight science fiction slant, with a strong element of fantasy. The opening episode *Arrival*, threw in some 'mysterioso' moments, with characters like maids or gardeners disappearing, re-appearing, or popping up in a different place; all very 'Alice in Wonderland', with the landscape, as the series progressed, morphing more into a McGoohan mindscape.

The star claimed that he never set out to do anything surrealistic, insisting that the series was not an action-adventure show, but an allegory, with a concealed message, allowing enormous latitude. However, injection of the actor's autobiographical subject matter exposed the series' raison d'être as two-fold: McGoohan commenting and warning about society and the planet, while adding his personal school of thought and background. The star's own reasoning behind his groundbreaking series was revealed in an interview: "I've always been concerned with – one could say compulsively fascinated by – the individual in isolation wishing to be understood. *The Prisoner* is an allegory. The individual being broken – or the attempt to break him – because of his refusal to conform is really what it's about. It's not on any political level at all; it's not even on a social level. I'm wary of defining it too much, because I think an allegory should be left to be interpreted by the beholder in his or her way. I rarely come across two people who agree on what *The Prisoner* was about, which was my intention. They know it's somebody up against somethin,' that's for sure, whether it's symbolized by a white balloon, or the oppression of bureaucracy."[28]

At this time, McGoohan was engaged on his own real-life battle with bureaucracy. In his Mill Hill home he felt his privacy had been compromised. He complained of being "goggled at," a local planning inquiry was told. The grounds of the house sloped away from the road and the actor claimed that fans were gathering in groups to peer into his home. They were staring at his wife Joan and three daughters Catherine, aged sixteen, Anne aged seven and six year old Frances, when they were using the family swimming pool – completed at last – and were even taking pictures with telescopic lenses. Joan had been photographed washing dishes in the kitchen and the family members were watched over by every passing double-decker bus. Mrs. McGoohan, in later years, recalled the events, bemoaning the fact that, "When Patrick was doing *Danger Man* and *The Prisoner* he was the number one and they wouldn't leave us alone. The British press were awful. Everybody knew we lived there, that was the spot. There was nowhere for us to hide." To avoid this unwanted attention, McGoohan erected a six foot high fence. However, other local residents complained that he had blocked out a fine view over the contiguous Totteridge valley.

Barnet Council ruled that he had not obtained the necessary planning permission and ordered him to demolish the fence. The actor subsequently appealed against the Council's order and his submissions were considered at Hendon Town Hall. McGoohan wrote, "As I have become increasingly well known as a TV and film actor, my family has become increasingly subject to sightseers gathering to watch our activities. While I accept this as an occupational hazard, I think my wife and children are entitled to some privacy."[29] Unfortunately, the letter was not sympathetically received and the inquiry upheld the earlier decision that the fence had to be removed and the view restored, McGoohans and all.[xxxvi]

[xxxvi] This incident would be referred to at a future point, when McGoohan gave reasons for leaving the country and moving to Switzerland; see later in this book.

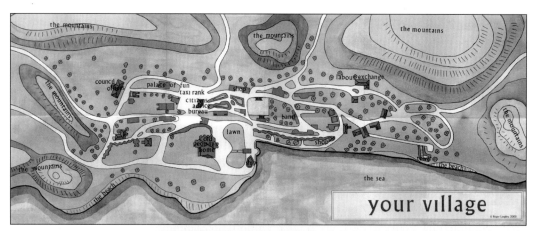

Above: Map of The Village in *The Prisoner* (produced by the author)

Right: Portmeirion, which was transformed into "The Village"

Other countries were still screening *Danger Man* and as the long running series was also still fresh in British viewers' minds, press articles would refer to both the old series and the new. One of the first to mention the latest project – along with a scooped pair of Portmeirion location filming photos – was a TV annual,[xxxvii] which devoted two pages to McGoohan and *The Prisoner*. The actor pointed out that his new character should not be confused with John Drake: "I'm not a tough guy. I'm an actor who plays at being tough. I loathe violence. I abhor it. I go out of my way to avoid trouble." McGoohan would not allow the term 'star' to be used in describing him: "The word makes the back hair of my neck curl up. The word is misused in our profession. Of course, it is nice to know that what you are doing is appreciated and that people care about what you do. I hate insincerity. I am frank. I speak my mind and say what ought to be said. I expect the same from everyone else." Describing McGoohan as a "dedicated professional who knows what show business is all about," the summing up was that success and adulation had not changed him. The actor confirmed, "It's nice to know what you are doing is appreciated and that people really care about what you do. After all, it is our business to please. We are in the acting profession to entertain. I've never forgotten that."[30]

[xxxvii] Popular in Britain for decades were books which came out at the end of each year, designed as Christmas gifts for the young. Pop stars, comic characters, plus film and TV actors would be celebrated annually in these publications, often published by ATV.

When the series' screening date was not far away, to maximise press attention McGoohan held a publicity event, at MGM Borehamwood. There was a private screening of the first two episodes, *Arrival* and *The Chimes of Big Ben*, as a preview for the assembled journalists. Slightly unfairly, the two episodes were shown to the visitors in colour, as cine film on a large screen, while the production team knew that on Britain's small TV sets the monochrome presentation would look very different. After viewing the episodes, the pressmen were led into no normal conference room and they were not gathered, as would usually happen, in front of a spokesperson at a lectern microphone. Instead, they found themselves in a studio, decorated with Village props and paintings. Dominating the layout of the room was the cage from the episode *Once Upon A Time*, taking up the length of one wall. A well-stocked bar was set up inside the cage, with bottles of beer and wine. Centre stage – mirroring the layout in the residence of "Number Two" – was an iconic sixties globe chair, encircled by a curved desk upon which a buffet was laid out. This had last been seen in the Council Chamber setting, from some *Prisoner* episodes. There was a striped-canopied Mini Moke Village taxi, a huge penny farthing symbol on one wall, a real penny farthing bicycle – for those daring enough to try and ride it – as well as numerous concept paintings of *Prisoner* sets, by series art director Jack Shampan, "Lava Lamps" and arcane symbols from the series.

While the press sampled the buffet and fired questions at McGoohan, he stood behind the bars of his cage[xxxviii] shouting questions back at them, providing no answers. He put forward an image of individuality, capturing well the strange atmosphere from his latest, idiosyncratic series. The actor, by now, was so fired up with the development of the series and the part he had been playing,[xxxix] that he treated the reporters with almost the same scorn as Number Six offered each new leader of the Village, Number Two. He had just been filming the western episode *Living in Harmony* prior to the arrival of his guests and had changed from his cowboy costume to a Cossack-style "Kosho" outfit, donned during the nonsensical 'martial arts' sequence seen in two episodes. Now, an Astrakhan cap replaced the combat crash helmet worn on screen and the actor's crimson, belted robe and boxer's laced boots contrasted sharply with the daywear of the gathered journalists. Other actors and members of the production team were present and the admittance of 'outsiders' was quite a departure from the usual tight procedures, when the studio was normally banned to visitors.

One review of the conference appeared under the heading: "Don't expect a follow-up to 'Danger Man' – you could be disappointed!" The reporter tantalised readers by revealing that *The Prisoner* would be shown in full colour to American TV audiences. On the press day McGoohan was described as being "behind the bars of a prison set on one of the sound stages. His fellow actors (all in bizarre costume) handed out drinks between the bars of the cell, flashlights popped and questions flew – mostly parried (by) McGoohan ..." The actor was said to have admitted that he did not know how the series would progress and disclosed that the last episode had not yet been written. Although the journalist confidently picked the new show as a "winner," he made it clear that some of the other critics present were "not so sure and (had) suspended judgement until they had seen more episodes." It was

---

[xxxviii] Perhaps 'acting' and preferring there to be a threshold between him and his 'audience,' as had been the case on stage, with footlights at that time forming an 'invisible barrier' according to the actor.

[xxxix] It should be remembered that at the time of the press conference, the last few episodes had still not been completed and filming was still in progress, with the final episode *Fall Out* not even having been written.

Left: Smiling for the camera, in Portmeirion
Above: Saluting a snapper in Portmeirion

acknowledged that the new series was unlikely to appeal to as wide an audience as *Danger Man* did. "Those who like to doze before the goggle box and let the show flow over them will be annoyed by the unresolved puzzles provided by *The Prisoner*." It was clear that the star ruled the roost. "Soundstages have been banned to visitors since filming began. McGoohan wanted to break into completely new territory ... The idea is his own and he is executive producer, star and also director of many sequences. He worked on every script, no matter who originally wrote it and edited the film himself ..." According to the article, the actor had even gone into a new partnership with John Sturges[xl] "to co-produce, sometimes direct, but mostly act in movies."[xli] Describing McGoohan as "a millionaire film tycoon", it was confirmed that no decision had yet been made whether to close *The Prisoner* at the end of the first series "with all the mysteries explained," or to leave things open for a second series. Summing up the actor, it was said that he was "the only man to fight against sex and sadism on television ... Having established that a television thriller series can have integrity, (his) aim with *Prisoner* is to demonstrate that it can also provide food for thought." Sensibly, the writer closed his piece by pondering "whether or not the world will find this notion to be digestible as well as entertaining."[31]

One other reporter did not go away empty-handed. He told McGoohan that he thought the action in the Village was great. "I'm glad you liked that," returned McGoohan, "for I found the Village. I've loved the place for years. In fact, it was seeing the Village which really sparked off the basic idea for *The Prisoner*. It's a real place, a sort of architectural showpiece." The star enlightened the reporter as to how involved he was in *The Prisoner*, as star, executive producer and even director. Working closely on writing scripts, he had created what the reporter felt could be called "The Pat McGoohan Show."[32] Journalist Anthony Davis described McGoohan as "dynamic, unpredictable, restless and intense," adding that here was "a remarkable man and reputedly the highest-paid actor on TV." Davis promised that the series would become more bizarre as it progressed and that McGoohan

---

[xl] Director of *Ice Station Zebra* (1968)
[xli] It was said that McGoohan would be going back to Hollywood to make a Western, possibly being the reason he created a cowboy episode late in the Prisoner series.

would take the credit or shoulder the blame. Meanwhile, at the press party, Davis observed how McGoohan "emerged from his cage for further pictures. The fur hat and long robe on his 6ft. 2in. frame increased his dominance of the room."[33] The press conference presented McGoohan on top form. The studio had been his 'home' for many weeks and the setting had thereby become his professional – and perhaps even personal – 'prison'. Continuing the analogy, the press meeting was one extraordinary 'visiting day'. By toying with the journalists, behaving enigmatically and challenging everyone present to think for themselves, McGoohan demonstrated that he was utterly consumed by his work on *The Prisoner*. At least the reporters had advance warning of the coming enigma, unlike the unsuspecting waiting viewing public.

In fact, so in control was McGoohan that after the press event, he made more changes to the first two episodes, *Arrival* and *The Chimes of Big Ben*, before they were screened. This pair of pre-broadcast edits found their way to North America, by mistake, either in the sixties,[xlii] or at the time of much later repeats.[xliii] This is a convenient point to cover the 'alternative' versions – or 'alternate', as they were called in the US – before moving on to the series' television premiere in Britain. It is even possible that the press saw the original versions, while the public saw the opening episodes after hurried changes had been made. Either way, it would be another twenty years before the different *Chimes* variant was commercially released in the States,[xliv] followed by the alternative *Arrival* being similarly released in the UK, after several more years.[xlv] The story of how those two early cuts came to light – or as much as is known – can now conveniently be presented at this point.

On 10th May, 1974, *Prisoner* Appreciation Society member Christopher Campbell was about to record on audiotape the start of a repeat screening of *The Prisoner*, on station WHDH, Channel 5 in Boston, Massachusetts. When *Arrival* started, Campbell noticed immediately that the title theme music was different. Another *Prisoner* fan later video-taped what was probably the same print, off-air, in New York State. There had clearly been an error with the distribution or labelling of the sixteen millimetre film cans, causing this incorrect edit to be sent out for transmission. Bruce Clark, a US-based organiser within *The Prisoner* Society, subsequently acquired the videocassette, made a copy and contacted McGoohan about the discovery. The actor was furious that this version had been screened and wanted to know the names of "those responsible."

The obvious differences between the original and later standard versions are not numerous: the opening runway shot has a changed opening screen credit "Patrick McGoohan in" and an earlier appearance of the series' title; there are altered sound effects and a rejected, vastly different main title theme;[xlvi] McGoohan's face at his Village cottage window offers a startled 'double take' – being something which the actor probably disliked – and there are other small things to be spotted. The tale did not end here, for it was discovered that there was a different edit of the second episode as well: *The Chimes of Big Ben*. This contained a whole scene – later excised – in which Number Six builds an ancient

---

[xlii] For the debut Canadian run, see footnote on page 124.
[xliii] See also page 267.
[xliv] It was called "The Lost Episode" and was released on video, at the time of the other seventeen episodes being released in the US on individual tapes. Therefore the "alternate *Chimes*" was also referred to as the "18th episode."
[xlv] A DVD was produced at the time of the series' thirty fifth anniversary, in 2002, which included for the first time the alternative *Arrival*, see page 267. The item has still not been released in the US.
[xlvi] Early offered main title themes from composers Robert Farnon and Wilfred Josephs were rejected in favour of one from Ron Grainer.

Greek astronomical apparatus, called a triquetrum, to plot his position. Along with drawn notes and sightings, there is an unusual 'narration' by the actor. It is said that night sky 'stars' were 'borrowed' from the set of the movie *2001: A Space Odyssey*, which was in production at MGM at that time. The alternative endings for the first two episodes are different from other episodes and even from each other. *Arrival*'s closing has an animation of the world tuning into a penny farthing bicycle, while the *Chimes* ending has the Earth going "Pop!" Probably McGoohan and his production team found the sequences mentioned above to be too quirky – even for *The Prisoner* – or below standard.

According to series script editor George Markstein, *Arrival* was made as a longer pilot episode for the series, lasting up to ninety minutes, although no evidence to support this has ever been found. However, McGoohan has claimed to own a personal copy of the extended, first episode. Apart from this possible lengthier pilot, there is one more 'Holy Grail' item, which might not exist, in the form of footage from the 1967 *Prisoner* press conference. In photos taken of the event, there is a film camera on view. Whether this was a dummy, or was being used for a newspaper report, or even as a private record for McGoohan, remains unknown and no film has ever come to light.

Following the 1967 *Prisoner* press event and amidst much secrecy-turned-publicity, Britain's TV viewers were now about to see for themselves, in the autumn of that year,[xlvii] what McGoohan's latest, exciting show was all about.[xlviii] "Every (week) viewers are glued to their T.V. sets in an agony of suspense over Patrick McGoohan's latest A.T.V series '*The Prisoner*'. McGoohan knows all the answers because the idea for the series is his own! He's not only the star of the series, he is executive producer, he has directed several of the episodes, he has written some of the stories, he is closely involved in the scripting, AND he is even his own stunt man! Now he continues his television career in his most provocative role yet."[34]

The first episode, *Arrival*, began with a clap of thunder, followed by a shot of a deserted road, or the runway of an abandoned airfield. A dot on the horizon quickly became a speeding sportscar, the face of the driver, McGoohan, filling viewers' TV screens. The vehicle was instantly in London, the lone man resigning his job, before returning home to start a holiday overseas. Ominously, a funeral hearse glided to a halt outside the smart residence and a top-hatted undertaker sprayed knock-out gas through the letterbox. The occupant of the apartment fell unconscious, waking up at a later point in what seemed to be the same room. However, the view outside was that of a strange village and the man, clearly abducted and transported elsewhere, was now a prisoner. This opening sequence[xlix] was revised for following episodes, with an added exchange of dialogue between the new inmate and the leader of 'The Village':

Number Six: "Where am I?"
Number Two: "In the Village."
Number Six: "What do you want?"

[xlvii] The opening episode *Arrival* aired from the end of September, 1967, in London and other areas, while some parts of the country had to wait until late October.

[xlviii] What is not widely known is that the series' premiere in September 1967 was not in England, but in Canada. A part run began at the start of the month, while the British 'debut' was not until the end of the month. Strangely, only the first dozen or so episodes were shown in Canada and it is not known why the final ones (often regarded as the start of a 'second series' of *The Prisoner*) were not screened.

[xlix] Many believe the *Prisoner* opening sequence to be one of the finest starts to any TV series, the very essence of the series being cleverly and neatly encapsulated within a three minute collection of scenes.

A selection of shots taken during the location filming on *The Prisoner*, 1966

Number Two: "Information."
Number Six: "Whose side are you on?"
Number Two: "That would be telling. We want information. Information. Information."
Number Six: "You won't get it!"
Number Two: "By hook or by crook, we will!"
Number Six: "Who are you?"
Number Two: "The new Number Two."
Number Six: "Who is Number One?"
Number Two: "You are Number Six."
Number Six: "I am not a number. I am a free man!"
Number Two: (Loud, sarcastic laughter).

Over the ensuing weeks, with each new episode bearing little relation to the previous one, audiences became sharply divided, with some of the country hailing the brilliance and originality of the show, while others switched off in disgust. The screening of the series was regional and so ITV audiences, in various parts of the country, were seeing different episodes, sometimes a month apart. Fortunately, the weekly television listings magazines were also regional and so viewers would only be able to read details of their local episode. Ironically, the area covering Portmeirion, in North Wales, where *The Prisoner* was filmed twelve months earlier, would have to wait almost another year for a sight of the resort-turned-TV village.[l] The aftermath of the final episode – literally the 'fall out' – is covered later in this book. However, this is a convenient, if not essential, point at which to hear what the various actors and crew members from *The Prisoner* were saying about the production. As might be imagined, they were not interviewed at the time of the series. Despite the inherent secrecy surrounding the series' production (in any event in the sixties), *The Prisoner*, like other TV shows came and went. There were rarely repeats within the following few years and as there were no video releases, there was no event around which to broadcast any discussion. It would be another two decades before there were documentaries about the series, on TV, or included with commercial videotapes.

Therefore, to present the comments of those involved with the making of *The Prisoner*, the following pages feature a television documentary[li] and a pair of celebratory events which were held in London, organised by *The Prisoner* Appreciation Society[lii] for the series. In addition, comments from the same people – and some others – made on different occasions, are included. The recollections of actors, directors, producers, crew members and scriptwriters are about to be provided in this section. In the next chapter, analysis and a closer study of *The Prisoner* appear, but for the moment, interviews from those who produced the series should rightly come first. McGoohan participated in the TV documentary, the makers having visited him the US, and in fact he even made his own film, covered later, although this was not screened.[liii] Additionally, he faxed a message to this writer, for the London event.[liv] Firstly, the topic of how *The Prisoner* came into being was discussed. The actor acknowledged: "George Markstein brought scriptwriters with a particular bent of mind. I'm grateful to him." Markstein also appeared in the documentary

[l] TWW (Wales and West) and HTV (Harlech, Wales) did not screen *The Prisoner* until the summer of 1969.
[li] *Six Into One: The Prisoner File* (1983), Channel 4, screened January, 1984, the making of which is covered later, see page 230.
[lii] Six of One's celebrations were in 1993 and 1997, but they are conveniently referred to in the main text as if one event.
[liii] McGoohan's film became known as *The L.A. Tape*, see page 231.
[liv] See Chapter Eleven, page 249.

and explained, "I sat down at a typewriter and wrote two pages of script about how a secret agent had suddenly resigned, in the way that McGoohan had quit as John Drake." He recalled[lv] how he had based his Village on an establishment in Scotland, where during the War and afterwards, recalcitrant spies were held, adding "And who was more recalcitrant than McGoohan?" This suggests that Markstein gained his idea from the very event of McGoohan quitting *Danger Man*. Of course, he and McGoohan might well have previously talked about creating a new show out of the long-running one, like some phoenix rising from the ashes of *Danger Man*.

Markstein claimed that he held in his hands the ethos or spirit of the series. While for others the main character without a name was equally without an identity, for Markstein there was no doubt about the matter. "He was of course John Drake, the secret agent who quit from *Danger Man*." Markstein was similarly dismissive about the question "Who is Number One?" explaining that he was merely, "The man in charge." Markstein, having appeared in a *Prisoner* cameo role, as the boss before whom McGoohan was seen resigning his top secret post, commented that he, himself, was the Number One of the series, "visible in every episode," including opening sequences.[lvi] Lew Grade recalled that he was anxious when he had first seen a number of the finished *Prisoner* episodes. "I kept asking Pat 'What's going to happen in the end?'" He did not feel particularly comforted when McGoohan had simply replied, "Don't worry, there will be an ending." Grade continued, "Later he came to me and said he could not find an ending, as he had become too confused with the project. I thought it was very nice of him to come straight out and admit it to me. I told the networks, 'We have no ending.'" Actor Roger Moore claimed that he questioned Grade about the series' conclusion and that he received the short reply: "Don't bloody ask me. McGoohan won't tell me how it's going to end."[35] Other sources also revealed that the series' star had admitted to them that he had "no idea" regarding the ending. Producer David Tomblin said that the actor showed the script of the final episode to him, while they were in a café at separate tables. McGoohan sipped tea and Tomblin read the dialogue. The producer then looked up, smirked and said to his colleague, "I thought it might be you in the end!" Therefore, the actor's claims that he devised the ending of the series from the outset – with Number One being revealed as himself – was contradicted in some quarters.

Tomblin reflected: "We put everything into it, all our time, sixteen hours a day and tried to make every episode really one thousand per cent. Eventually, it became fairly obvious that we could not sustain this pace and quality in the time that was left, as we were running out of time and the screening dates were fast approaching." The intensity of *Prisoner* production work was revealed by David Tomblin: "When you're making a television series, you reckon to get through fifteen to twenty set-ups a day. Pat has often averaged thirty three a day and in one two-day spell achieved one hundred and four."[36] The producer reported that McGoohan carried the crew with him because they respected his tremendous enthusiasm and energy. The actor would be on set by 7 a.m. and usually worked on the scripts until 2 a.m. the following morning. He would then work on set during the new day until 5.50 p.m., before disappearing into the cutting room, where he would stay until 10 p.m. On one weekend it was observed that he had spent all day in the

---

[lv] See also earlier in this book, page 110.
[lvi] Markstein wanted to take the Number Six character out into the world, where he would find that 'The Village' still controlled him and that there was no escape.

studio, leaving on that Friday evening at 7.30 p.m., followed by a long drive to a location, working throughout Saturday, leaving the location at 9.30 in the evening and arriving back in the studio at 4 a.m.[lvii][37]

As to the number of episodes originally planned, Tomblin said," Quite a few, but it came to a point that they were so complex, so the number was eventually seventeen. If we had kept on filming we wouldn't have met the showing dates. With most TV things, you have to find a way to make shortcuts, so you do come out on time, but *The Prisoner* was such an involved, complex subject, that you couldn't really take the shortcuts, you had to see the story through."[38] Tomblin even disclosed that McGoohan contacted him after many years, to ask about his views on doing a film called *Whatever Happened to The Prisoner?* although the producer never heard from the star again.

Director Pat Jackson remembered how they tried to shoot six minutes of film a day, being twice the normal amount for a TV feature, although quality was not allowed to drop. Jackson expressed pride regarding the filming of his segments. "Pat asked me to come over to Elstree to MGM and said, 'I've got a proposition that might interest you' and he showed me location stills of Portmeirion and a rough outline of the story which wasn't absolutely clear then and said, 'Would you be interested?' and I said 'Yes, Pat, very interested indeed.' Then he sent me the script and I tore open the envelope and started to read 'The Schizoid Man.' I was absolutely thrilled. I didn't know what the hell it was all about, but I thought it was an absolutely wonderful idea, very interesting. So down to Elstree I went for the first day's shooting and there was Pat ready. You took the script, read it, analysed it, worked out your shooting plan, how the artists moved and then you got on the floor and quickly blocked in the scene and everybody was happy and comfortable and off you went. I had no brief at all, you just analysed it as a conductor would a score. Oh, I'd love to be able to say yes, I saw the significance of this series, but I didn't at all. I took it as a drama and I was thankful that one could do it with conscience and do it with pride and it was a fascinating project." Jackson concluded, "*The Prisoner*... what a tremendous achievement that was! (McGoohan) devised it single-handedly, he wrote many of the episodes, he produced it and he acted in every one. Not that I knew what it was all about, and I don't think he did really. But what a concept!"[39]

Don Chaffey[lviii] recalled how he had first met McGoohan during production of the Walt Disney film *The Three Lives of Thomasina*, which he directed. Chaffey related how he had also seen the actor at the Lyric Theatre in Hammersmith and was well aware of McGoohan's acting prowess. The Chaffeys later became good friends with the actor and his family. The director remembered initially declining McGoohan's invitation to helm *Prisoner* episodes: "I was meant to do another feature over in Ireland and Pat suddenly came along and said he'd got this idea and I said 'Great, good, take it, it's fine, do what you like with it'

[lvii] Portmeirion and the MGM studio and back lot were the prime locations, but there was also shooting at Beachy Head – for *Many Happy Returns* – at Eltisley near Cambridge for a cricket scene, as well as in a field local to the studio – for *The Girl Who Was Death* – and at Mayfield, in Sussex, for the escape by truck in *Fall Out*. More cricket footage was stock material, showing Meopham, in Kent. Several London locations were used, including 1 Buckingham Place, SW1, for the prisoner's home. The funfair sequences from *The Girl Who Was Death* were shot at the Kursaal, Southend. The amusement park was closed for the season, but opened for the film crew, who brought with them a coach load of 'extras.'

[lviii] Chaffey had also helmed several *Danger Man* episodes – including the seminal *The Ubiquitous Mr. Lovegrove* – and was the only *Prisoner* director to be on location in Portmeirion, apart from McGoohan. However, director Pat Jackson was present in March, 1967, when there was a brief return to Portmeirion, to film some fill-in shots – with stunt double Frank Maher standing in for McGoohan – and some more exteriors.

McGoohan in Portmeirion with actress Norma West

and he said 'I'd like you to direct the first episode to set a style or whatever you like.' I just refused point blank and went off over to Ireland. Pat grabbed my daughter and gave her these scripts and said, 'Get your father to read these.' My daughter finally read them herself and she said 'You've got to read these; they're going to be compulsive viewing. I reckon you'll have 11 million people loving to hate you every Sunday night if you do these. They're so intriguing.' So I started to read them and Pat came across to Ireland where I was doing a picture with Don Murray and I agreed to do them. Pat's not an easy person as you probably know to get on with, but at least he knows what he wants and I have sort of clear cut ideas too and so by sitting down, there were some bitter arguments but that's not here nor there. Out of them came what I think is one of the best television series ever made." Chaffey also recounted how his local pub would fill each Sunday evening, after drinkers had been watching the evening's *Prisoner* episode. "An almighty row would break out, with people yelling at me about all this rubbish I had been making."

Prisoner production manager Bernard Williams[lix] provided his memories: "We were a very tight team – an impregnable team in fact. We demanded a lot of ourselves and quality was one of them. We were all workaholics. We all worked six, seven days a week. We'd be up to ten, eleven, twelve, one o'clock in the morning, because once you start rolling those cameras you can't stop. The only worry we had when we made the series was that it did become one of the most expensive series in England at that time, but very prestigious. We had no idea, from episode to episode, where we were going. We just suddenly got into a western – I mean, what's that about? We didn't even know where we were going with *Fall Out*."[lx] Similarly, assistant director Gino Marotta opined, "*The Prisoner* was one of the most demanding jobs I've ever had. But it was a wonderful experience."

Asked about George Markstein's input to the series, Williams replied, "George Markstein's is zero. God rest his soul, wherever he is. I shouldn't say it was zero, but it was Patrick McGoohan who created the idea, developed the idea, rejected lots of ideas and he brought George Markstein in as story editor, who I believe got the credit, but it was undeserved, because Patrick was the guy who focused the series to where it was. He anchored it, he focused it, he remodelled it, he shaped it and he told Markstein what to do. There were a lot of hidden messages there, about control, about losing your identity and selling out – a lot of morals there. It was a mirror on life, really. Pretty intense stuff."[40]

[lix] Williams had been preceded in Portmeirion by Leslie Gilliat, a founder Prisoner producer. He left the production after only two months, citing uncertainty as to the months ahead as his reason for wanting to take a more orthodox job elsewhere. Before his departure, Gilliat – together with Bernard Williams and other production team members – went to Portmeirion, in the summer of 1966, to make a sixteen millimetre reconnaissance film. This writer has slides of the local geography, taken at the time, including nearby Minffordd cemetery, which was obviously considered for the funeral scene in *Arrival*, but was rejected, in place of Portmeirion's beach.

[lx] *The Prisoner* was apparently the only TV series upon which Williams was production manager. He started at MGM as a post boy, before moving onto the sound department and finally into production. From the end of the sixties and still continuing, Williams has worked on an impressive list of movies, also sometimes as executive producer, or producer. Based now in the USA, he stays in touch with *The Prisoner* Appreciation Society's organiser there.

Mr. Clough Williams-Ellis,   M.G.M. Studios,
Hotel Portmeirion,   Borehamwood,
Penrhyndeudraeth,   Herts.
Merionethshire,
North Wales.
                                              4th October, '66.

Dear Mr. Clough Williams-Ellis,

          Please forgive my mental and physical
fatigue of Saturday evening. Any lack of enthusiasm was
not for want of appreciation of your beautiful home. I
wish I had the privilege to wander and ponder through
the gardens. A good place to cool the mind and balm
the soul!!

          I promised to let you have an assembly
of some material this week. However, having viewed the
mass of film that was shot I feel it would be fairer to
both of us if we complete an entire episode with Interiors
and Sound so that you could get an overall impression
of what we are about. There are some splendid shots of
the village and I hope you will agree that the "charade"
does not detract from its character.

          Once again, our profound thanks for
your patience and gracious forbearance in very trying
circumstances.

          Miss Fabia Drake desires me to
convey her warmest wishes to your goodselves.

          Kind regards.

          Yours sincerely,

          Patrick McGoohan

Letter from McGoohan thanking Portmeirion for providing filming facilities

McGoohan's opinion of Williams was unequivocal: "His work on *The Prisoner* was superb and his contribution to the show far beyond his nominal status. He's the tops."[41] Finally, Williams shed more light[lxi] on what happened after *The Prisoner*: "We were contracted to do thirteen episodes. Then it became seventeen, which was an odd number, because most series are always thirteen. Patrick was offered *Ice Station Zebra*,[lxii] which he wanted to do. So after thirteen episodes we shut down the company for four months, while he went to Hollywood.[lxiii] Then the company was resurrected to finish the last four."[lxiv] [42] Ronald Liles was asked to replace Bernard Williams – who had gone to another assignment – as

[lxi] The final days of *The Prisoner* – and what followed – are covered in Chapter Seven.
[lxii] See page 178.
[lxiii] See page 178.
[lxiv] Williams moved on to the movie, *Battle of Britain* (1969).

production manager. During the making of *The Girl Who Was Death*, McGoohan had to return to Hollywood to complete some scenes for *Ice Station Zebra*. His further absence was covered by scenes being in long shot, or heavy disguises, such as a Sherlock Holmes costume, with dark sunglasses, deerstalker hat, side whiskers and moustache. McGoohan's action shots were also arranged against a back projection screen, showing sequences filmed earlier.

Another of the *Prisoner* directors, Peter Graham Scott, worked with McGoohan at three separate times.[lxv] He commented: "Television has few legends. *The Prisoner* is still remembered and even taken seriously more than (forty) years after its inception." Graham Scott opined, "Today, Patrick's concept seems banal, but it was different enough then to startle Lew Grade's complacent salesmen into blank refusal. In the end, Lew agreed to let McGoohan make seventeen episodes – but at a much reduced fee." The director admitted that his involvement in *The Prisoner* was minimal. "Patrick called me one Friday night in some distress. Halfway through the sixth episode of his new series … he needed me to start reshooting the episode (in progress) on Monday morning."[43] The director continued, "I was producing the BBC action series *The Troubleshooters*, throughout the second half of the sixties (and) the episodes must have come to Patrick's attention. He rang me and said, 'Peter, I want you to start at Elstree on Monday as I've fired the director and the script will arrive with you tomorrow.' I said to him, 'But I'm already under contract to the BBC.' He replied, 'They can spare you for two weeks.' Somehow he spoke to (them), and prised me out of the BBC." The director disclosed, "I got my agent to secure an enormous fee and my work on *The Prisoner* turned out to be just like making *Danger Man* again. Some actresses didn't understand him. Those in *Danger Man* or *The Prisoner* who say that he was unfriendly towards them were wrong. He just hated unprofessionalism. Patrick was a seriously compassionate actor and when somebody was not doing very well he would relax them and help them play the part. I was and am full of admiration for him. I really like the man and he was original and impressive. For *Danger Man* he rewrote the scripts and this is why I think *The Prisoner* started. He started to sleep in the studio every night and really live in the studio. What he did for food I don't know. I think this is how the series began as he felt like a sort of prisoner. It was a very clever idea and a very good series. The public did not respond well at first but *The Prisoner* is now a classic."[44]

Graham Scott confirmed that McGoohan carried the whole pressure of the *Prisoner* show, rewriting scripts and toiling relentlessly every day of the week. The director made light of *The Prisoner*, relating how he had used story editor George Markstein to help him unravel "the nuances of the script." Most of the old *Danger Man* crew had joined the *Prisoner* production and the episode *The General* was completed under Graham Scott's stewardship, within ten days. "I enjoyed the experience but had no sense of making a work of any significance." The director believed that it was simply McGoohan's forceful conviction which gave the episodes their power. Graham Scott revealed more of McGoohan's pivotal role in the series: "Patrick had this intensity; this is what makes him such a remarkable actor. That's what makes his acting so utterly gripping. I mean, *The Prisoner*, if you look at the stories, they are tosh. And the one I directed was tosh. Nobody ever said (it) was rubbish; it was all to do with those penetrating blue eyes telling you this is the *truth*, be sure this is *truth*."[45]

[lxv] Graham Scott directed several episodes of *Danger Man*, the *Prisoner* story *The General* and the TV movie *Jamaica Inn* (1982).

Graham Scott spoke enthusiastically about the star: "Patrick McGoohan was I think one of the most professional actors I ever worked with. My television productions included the series *The Onedin Line* and *The Troubleshooters* (also known as *Mogul* in other countries). He thought very much about detail. The trouble was, when I worked with him in the *Danger Man* days, he had not heard of me or seen what I'd done. The series' producer Ralph Smart had heard of me in my days as a film editor. Initially I had a cold reaction from Patrick, but once he had seen how I did things we worked well together."

Joan McGoohan's ability to cope with Patrick's punishing work schedule was underpinned by the pair's repertory days, when at times they had only seen one another for brief hours at the end of each week. Even her husband's long-term personal assistant and dresser, Jimmy Millar,[lxvi] divulged that he had only seen McGoohan once take a five-minute cat-nap.[46] The star himself claimed that he had worked through three nervous breakdowns and had been told initially by his doctor to take three weeks off, but was ordered the second time to make it three months off. The effects of the *Prisoner* star's methods – both on his actors and team, as well as on himself is now covered, in the following pages, from the mouths of those who worked alongside him.

All of the actors who were either in Portmeirion,[lxvii] or were filmed on set, at the MGM Borehamwood studios, were polarised in their views about the show's executive producer. McGoohan was either lionised as an Orson Welles style genius, or dismissed as arrogant, churlish and bad-tempered. All agreed that he worked himself to the limit, being up before everybody else and working long into the hours of darkness. The star was toiling for exceptionally long hours, whether he was acting, writing – and rewriting – or directing. He claimed to be supervising the overall production, rewriting scripts and overseeing editing. The pressure was enormous, but McGoohan wanted *The Prisoner* to be the best TV series ever seen. In fact the very word "television" was banned. By engendering a cinematic frame of mind, the star ensured no cutting of corners and precluded any TV-style 'fix it in the mix' methods, later down the road. In effect, the executive producer was insisting that his crew should produce something with same high quality as a major movie.

One of the few actresses who took part in the 1966 North Wales location filming was Rosalie Crutchley, who spoke warmly of the production and its star. She enjoyed major scenes with McGoohan in her episode *Checkmate*, recalling, "Every one of us who took part in *The Prisoner* remember very happy times at Portmeirion and are delighted with the series' long-standing success. (Pat) was delightful. He couldn't have been more charming. The night that I arrived in Portmeirion I got a phone call straight away to ask if I was happy and if everything was OK."[47]

Rachel Herbert – who appeared with McGoohan in the earlier *Danger Man* series – reflected upon the difference she had seen in the star, while working on *The Prisoner*. "He used to have time to sit and talk with me," she recalled. "That never happened in *The Prisoner*. Oh no."[48] As the female lead in the Village election story, *Free for All* – filmed with her in Portmeirion – she advanced, "The whole series seems to happen so much from Pat's point of view that it's almost in his head. I wouldn't have been surprised if the last episode had said that the Village wasn't really there and that (he) was lying on a bed in an asylum!"[49]

[lxvi] See also Chapter Ten for more on Jimmy Millar, page 238.
[lxvii] Guy Doleman, as the *Arrival* Number Two, was in Portmeirion, but nearly all of his appearances were from footage shot in the studio.

Mary Morris[lxviii] and Norma West also went to Portmeirion, to shoot the *Prisoner* episode *Dance of the Dead*.[lxix] They were interviewed together[50] about their production experiences of working on location and at the MGM Borehamwood studio. Morris said that during filming she found McGoohan to be very quiet. "He never seemed to speak to anyone, even when we were doing the shots. Although he was semi-directing all the time, he never suggested anything at all. Pat was terribly tired. I arrived at the studio one morning and there he was, sitting beside me in make-up and I told him he was looking terribly ill. 'I know,' he said." Norma West added: "He was a driven man in the end. He'd never chat to us in the evenings. He was in a state of exhaustion and really refusing to delegate responsibility. He was taking everything on himself, even down to composing the music. He never went home. He slept in his dressing room and hardly ate."

Signed photo from the Portmeirion shoot

In contrast, West gave her first impressions on meeting the star: "Well, I was crazy about him. He was the most extremely attractive man. And his unattainability was another thing which was incredibly attractive. He always had this distance. He'd let you think that you were getting to know him, being a friend and somehow you'd just ... go too far ... and he'd snap back immediately. If you found yourself at a bar with him, drinking, and you ... leaned forward to say something, he'd take a step back and so you'd gradually 'dance' around the bar, moving further and further away. I had worked with him before, on *Danger Man*[lxx] and we had got on very well, or as well as any woman can get on with Pat."

However, all was not smooth sailing; West remembered a "difficult area" in her episode's dancing sequence: "The scene at the fancy dress ball should have been played with the two of us very close. When we came to do it, (Pat) just wouldn't.[lxxi] (He) said, 'Nothing personal, nothing personal, Norma.'"[51] Despite the jaded jig, West still held a high opinion of her fellow: "He's marvellous. He has a very special quality and it does come from his wonderful personality. And you know that he is holding something back. You want to know what it is."[52]

Annette Andre provided her memory of the only time she worked with the *Prisoner* star. It was both simple and blunt: "I hated him!" Ms Andre, who had had a leading role in the cult British TV series *Randall and Hopkirk (Deceased)* – known in the USA as *My Partner the Ghost* – appeared in many television productions, as well as in a number of movies. However, her work on the *Prisoner* episode *It's Your Funeral* brought forth the reaction, "I

[lxviii] Morris assumed the character and costume of Peter Pan later in her episode, *Dance of the Dead*. Actor Trevor Howard was originally considered for the part and at an early point his character was proposed to be Old Father Time.
[lxix] The episode was later edited by Geoffrey Foot – who also edited three other episodes – but McGoohan did not approve of the cut. Consequently *Dance of the Dead* was shelved for many weeks, until another editor, John S. Smith – who also edited other episodes – re-edited it and received the screen credit.
[lxx] Norma West appeared in the episode *A Very Dangerous Game*.
[lxxi] See also footnote on page 19 in Chapter One regarding McGoohan's early dancing experiences and in the episode *A. B. and C.*, in which he would only dance with Annette Carrell at arms' length, barely making contact.

Left: Promotional card for *The Prisoner* with replica McGoohan signed message

Far Left: TV magazine cover, 1967, North America

hated every minute of it. I couldn't stand Patrick McGoohan. He was very nasty to me." The actress recalled how she had done one piece with McGoohan which required close contact and dialogue between them, which made for an intense scene. She found it disconcerting that the star would not look into her eyes. Although they were face to face, he was looking to the side, his vision off somewhere behind her head, as if she were not there. In another scene, the actress was involved in some action which was difficult and unusual, resulting in several takes. Eventually the director, Robert Asher, was satisfied with the last take and the players began to leave the set. As Ms. Andre went past McGoohan, he said to her, "I suppose you think that was good." This was uttered in a loud voice and a silence fell over the set, amongst the actors and crew members. McGoohan then proceeded to tell her, the actress recalled, how absolutely appalling her performance had been. The young woman was devastated, while the whole studio stood by, rigid, listening to the star berating a fellow actor. However, she was not the only one to be on the receiving end of McGoohan's ire. She also recalled how the director had halted one scene, feeling that it should be conducted differently. "Patrick McGoohan went berserk and absolutely shattered this poor young director, in front of everybody, using awful language. I just can't forgive that."[lxxii]

Andre, on being asked whether she felt that McGoohan had a problem acting with women, had no hesitation in answering affirmatively. "It was obvious. It was something to do with his being tied up with wife and family, or something, as if he felt that actresses were tarts." Ms. Andre related that McGoohan even took it upon himself to instruct her in the art of acting. She recalled how he had told her in his clipped style of tone, "You act with too much emotion. You have too much heart. You have to think the part. I do it entirely technically, which is the only way you can do it." She told the star that she did not feel able to perform in that way as her own method was the one she had developed and had always used. Not accepting this, the star then lectured her for half an hour on how the job needed to be done. Perhaps the actress' difficulty stemmed from the lack of explanation she had

---

[lxxii] McGoohan also removed Michael Truman – who directed the penultimate, colour, *Danger Man* episode *Koroshi* – from production of *Many Happy Returns* and director Roy Rossotti from *A Change of Mind*. He then directed the stories himself, under the name Joseph Serf. As well as dismissing director Robert Asher, mentioned in the text relating to this footnote – although Asher's name is retained in the screen credits – McGoohan also rejected editor Geoffrey Foot's work on *Dance of the Dead*, as mentioned earlier in this chapter.

been given as to the part she was playing. "From day one, even now, I never understood a thing that I was doing. I talked to Alexis Kanner[lxxiii] and he couldn't help. I spoke to Leo McKern[lxxiv] and he didn't know either."[53]

Derren Nesbitt[lxxv] appeared in the same episode as Annette Andre and supported some of the comments she made. "I confronted McGoohan, saying, "Bob Asher, the director, doesn't know what's going on. I don't know, nor do the others. Even you don't understand what's happening." Nesbitt confided, "Pat was having, or going to have, a nervous breakdown. He was acting really nutty – going round the bend – and that's not just my opinion – everybody thought the same."[54] However, there was only one answer for the man himself and that was to keep working. "You can't let up when you're in charge."[55]

Another actor who appeared in It's Your Funeral was Mark Eden. He recalled, "There was a bust-up on the set one day and Patrick McGoohan took over direction of the piece."[56] Chris Cook, who was employed in the Jack Shampan art department at the MGM studio, related how he once found McGoohan sitting on the studio floor: "He was so tired, he had to stop filming. It was the scene in the watchmaker's shop, from the episode It's Your Funeral. McGoohan was just so whacked. We had had to wind up all of the clocks, which were ticking and chiming, and then they all had to be stopped, before we could start shooting sound. On Sundays I sometimes met Pat in the Red Lion pub down the road, while he was still writing. He always bought me a drink and was such a kind, calm and gentle guy. He would wait for his wife to collect him and take him home, just up the road. Once I asked him how the series was going to end and he said, 'I've no idea.'"[57]

Peter Wyngarde, who co-starred in the episode Checkmate, commented on the cult series, its star and the inadvisability of trying ever to make a sequel: "I have extolled the merits of Pat's work on The Prisoner on several occasions. (If they are remaking it) I wonder if they realise, apart from taking away our fondest memories, if they can capture the impossible, originality. No matter how well made or faithful, we already know the original, which was always a conundrum and a surprise. Or is their premise (going to be) based on those who have never seen it? Should I say unbelievably those who have never seen it?! I wish Pat could have found a way to work in London and L.A., but actors can't be choosers, even at his level. He is British (sic) and not English and so his decision (to live in the US) makes sense, if all the work is there. I just felt that his talent lay in so many other directions and how it would be channelled here more appropriately than in vast often empty hills of Los Angeles, where image is more important than talent, where the Three As are paramount: Age, Agent and Arselickin'!"

Peter Howell[lxxvi] – who played a professor kept under 'house arrest, who rebels against the abuse of his innovative education system – marvelled at McGoohan's creativity: "I shall never forget the excitement of working with Patrick McGoohan on The Prisoner. His charisma and magnetism were remarkable – it was like working with Laurence Olivier."[58] Similarly, George Baker, who appeared in the series' first episode – and had worked with McGoohan in the past – applauded the star's achievement: "The astonishing thing about The Prisoner is not only Patrick's conceiving, acting and producing of the series, but the

---

[lxxiii] A fellow Prisoner actor, mentioned later in this chapter. Kanner appeared in three episodes of the series.
[lxxiv] One of the main Prisoner actors, who guest-starred in a trio of episodes.
[lxxv] Derren Nesbitt appeared in a few Danger Man episodes with McGoohan.
[lxxvi] Peter Howell co-starred in the Prisoner episode, The General.

enormous pleasure it has given to countless people over the last 40 years. Patrick could not possibly have conceived how much pleasure he was likely to give."[59] Alan White, who played a fellow prisoner in the series, remarked, "Everyone who worked on *The Prisoner* felt that it was special and Pat McGoohan was inspired – probably his best ever performance."[60]

John Castle was in the same episode as Peter Howell. He recalled, "Working on *The Prisoner* was very exciting. Patrick McGoohan is one of my favourite actors and he was a real joy to work with. In front of camera, he made it very easy for you, because he was so good. And off camera he was just as wonderful: generous and kind and full of wry humour; one of my favourite acting experiences. I'm so glad the series has given so much pleasure to many people."[61]

Actor Alexis Kanner, who appeared late in the *Prisoner* series, had already become popular with millions of viewers in Britain, as Detective Constable Matt Stone, in the 1966 BBC TV police drama series *Softly Softly Task Force*. His departure from the show, after only nine episodes, was hugely unwelcome and, extraordinarily, the matter was even raised in Parliament. The young actor took different parts in three *Prisoner* episodes: *Living in Harmony*, as a crazed cowboy gunslinger; *The Girl Who Was Death*, uncredited, as a fairground fashion photographer and unseen as a mystery voice; *Fall Out*, as a rebellious, Hippie youth, in the series' finale. He did not appear in the penultimate episode, *Once upon a Time*, because that story had been filmed many months earlier. Kanner's revealing comment about his transition from his recent, standard format TV series, to McGoohan's new show was: "It was like working in putty or plasticene and then being asked to do the ceiling of the Sistine Chapel."[62]

McGoohan was so impressed with Kanner that he placed the actor's name inside a frame on screen – no other actor received this preferential treatment – during the opening credits. The two men spent a good deal of time together – both on and off set – McGoohan seeing in the younger man much of the energy, enthusiasm and innovative approach, which were part of his own make up. Kanner also remembered McGoohan wanting him to persuade fellow *Prisoner* actor Leo McKern to join them, to be cast – after a gap of months – in *Fall Out*. Kanner's task was to convince McKern, who had apparently had personal difficulties with McGoohan earlier in the series, that the star was now a changed man, considerate and calm. "Leo asked me, 'Will you be there, with me, the whole time, same set, not a different room?'" With Kanner persuading the older actor that this was so, McKern at last agreed to participate once more. Kanner added, "There were some scenes where I really didn't need to hang around, but I stayed on set, as I had promised him, and we were all in it together. Occasionally he would look over to see if I was there. I remained there, to comfort him, just in case McGoohan might turn to him and go 'Boo!'"[63] Kanner ended his recollections by referring to McKern being discovered once, lying on his dressing room floor, in a foetal position.[lxxvii]

It is therefore perhaps not surprising to find that McKern, in his later autobiography,[lxxviii] made no mention of *The Prisoner*. This was despite his having appeared in three episodes and being one of the most memorable players from the series. At least McKern commended the artistic values of *The Prisoner*. "We are all prisoners of one kind or another, of our jobs, our careers, our ambitions, our loves and

[lxxvii] More from Alexis Kanner appears later in this chapter, as to different events, see page 144.
[lxxviii] *Just Resting* (1983); McKern later narrated a TV tribute to Lew Grade – see page 252

our hates, our environment, our government and so on ad infinitum. I don't think McGoohan himself ever bothered with details. The idea gave enormous scope and was, to my mind, a quite brilliant one."[64] McKern added, "Laws will not change the personal convictions and prejudices of anyone."[65]

On another occasion,[lxxix] McKern spoke freely about *The Prisoner* and McGoohan: "He was almost impossible to work with, a dreadful bully. Always shouting and screaming and yelling about the place and hurrying up and saving money. It was great fun, even though it

On the backlot at MGM, Borehamwood, filming the Western *Living In Harmony*

was agony to work with him. There was a dreadful sense of pressure all the time, being shouted at. I used to get very depressed. I used to lie in my dressing room in the short times we had off and worry and be depressed and very silent." Mckern went on to say: "In a bar, before we even started the series, we were drinking and McGoohan said to me, 'You're a funny little f**ker, aren't you?' He put in a boxing scene in one (episode) and took a lot of pleasure in punishing me with gloves on. Not as hard as he could, thank God, but hard enough to hurt. I can't remember if I hit him but if I did it must have given me enormous satisfaction."[66]

Experienced film editor John S. Smith – present at the same event as Annette Andre, whose experiences appeared earlier in this section – recalled how he had been brought in to work on her episode *It's Your Funeral*: "I cut the film, put the scenes together and showed it to the director. I asked (Robert Asher) what he thought. He said he didn't know and to ask Pat." Now, Ms Andre, sitting beside Smith, was to hear how McGoohan required Smith to remove much of her dialogue from the edit, instructing that the star's voice be trailed over her shots. Certainly, at the time of her work, the actress would have been even more devastated, had she known that apart from being demeaned on set by the executive producer, the lines she delivered were also later to be savaged by him.[lxxx]

However, Smith's account soon turned to praise, as he recalled how he was helped, career-wise, by McGoohan after editing work on *The Prisoner* had ended. "I was looking for work. I went to the set of the movie *Submarine X-1*, starring James Caan, and the editor asked for whom I had been working. I told him and he picked up the phone, saying 'Get me Patrick McGoohan.' As soon as he asked Pat about my work, he was told from the other end 'You've got a good man there. Hire him.' I will always be grateful to Pat for that." Smith also mentioned, in contrast to the treatment Annette Andre had received, how McGoohan had always been polite to him. "I used to get him at the end of the day, when he was exhausted, and he would put on his humble Irish accent, knock on my cutting room door and say 'Can I come in?'" Smith commented in glowing terms about McGoohan's involvement in the show: "I think the series rests upon the man's inner

[lxxix] Interview from the 2001 DVD release of *The Day the Earth Caught Fire* (1961).
[lxxx] See earlier, page 133.

Left: The *Prisoner* episode *The Girl who was Death* with Jimmy Millar behind McGoohan
Right: Close-up of Jimmy Millar as a Napoleonic soldier in *The Girl Who Was Death*

conviction. He's dynamic. His disturbance, his distress – it was almost like Orson Welles, the British equivalent."

Some of Smith's remembrances were shared by Ian Rakoff, a writer who suggested a Prisoner storyline. Initially, he had an assistant editing role towards the end of the series' production. Later, Rakoff's idea for a western was turned into *Living in Harmony*,[lxxxi] an episode set outside the Village, with a cast of cowboys, in place of the usual closed community citizens.[lxxxii] According to him, he "came in at the tail end of things," adding, "McGoohan's promise that I'd have four episodes in the next tranche of the series was perhaps not seriously meant. It was probably only a well-meaning apology for having abandoned me in order to be free to go to Hollywood." Rakoff originally chose as the title of his idea for a western Prisoner episode "Do Not Forsake Me Oh My Darling," although this was eventually used for the Vincent Tilsley story, which was devised to cover McGoohan's absence while away filming *Ice Station Zebra* (1968).

Being initially involved on the fringe of production at the MGM studios, Rakoff had not yet encountered McGoohan. In his autobiography, he related how he heard "appalling rumours" about the star as an ogre and was apprehensive when he learned that the actor would be visiting the studio editing suite. "(Editor) John S. Smith and I waited anxiously for McGoohan to appear. He was supposed to arrive at six p.m. It had gone seven. We waited and waited. Seven-thirty p.m. came and went with no sign of the actor. (Then) framed in the door's glass porthole was a smiling face. 'Can I come in?' McGoohan asked, with an exaggerated Irish accent, clutching a gin and tonic. He moved around the room, sipping his drink. John and I exchanged a glance. Where was the monster we'd been forewarned about?" Rakoff recounted how time passed with no conversation. "At the end of the first ten-minute reel, McGoohan said nothing and walked out. John leaned over and asked if I thought Pat was coming back. I pointed out that his glass had been empty. (He) returned with his refilled glass and we carried on. McGoohan pointed out that too many

---

[lxxxi] Credited in the opening titles of the *Prisoner* episode *Living in Harmony*: "from an idea by David Tomblin and Ian L. Rakoff ."
[lxxxii] In the U.S. the episode was not initially shown, possibly because it was thought to have an 'anti-war' message – at the time of Vietnam – featuring a man who would not take up a gun. Another claim is that the hallucinogenic aspects of the story were viewed as sending an undesirable drugs message. The hippie youth culture – including 'Draft' dodgers – was an influence in the decision not to screen *Living in Harmony*.

stock shots were being overused. He needed to direct more himself, he said, but finding the time was the problem. He wished us luck and said goodnight. John and I slumped onto our swivel chairs. We were both drained. The room had become suddenly much larger with Pat's absence."[67]

However, Rakoff later experienced a more traumatic meeting with McGoohan. Towards the end of the Prisoner production, he was asked to attend an appointment with the star. "I got to MGM at 10-30 a.m. It was past 1 o'clock when the door behind me swept open and Pat lurched in. He didn't notice me or so it seemed. He strode past and closed his office door behind him." After an interval, Rakoff was finally summoned into the actor's room. "For the first time, I entered McGoohan's office. It was an unusually massive room, even by studio standards. Pat paced round the room. I glanced up at the clock on the wall. I'd been in the room over 5 minutes and I was still waiting for him to start. Pat slammed a bottle of Malvern mineral water on the desk. He was banging the bottle up and down. My heart was beating so fast and my head was pounding so much, I was worried that I might pass out."

It became clear to Rakoff that the purpose of the appointment had been temporarily forgotten and that McGoohan was presently furious about Lew Grade having 'let him down.' Suddenly, mid-flow, the actor switched to an angry criticism of Rakoff's scripting. After enduring an abusive barrage, the writer felt numb. "Defeated and depleted, I scrambled up out of the chair and hoped that I could walk in a straight line. With great relief my hand gripped the door handle. 'Ian ,' Pat snapped as I drew the door open." To Rakoff's relief, McGoohan's red mist had cleared and he was now ready to embrace the notion of a western setting. In fact, Rakoff realised, the creative side of the actor's mind was already at work, visualising the cowboy story.

In the end, Rakoff valued his brief but eventful involvement with the *Prisoner* production.

"The association with McGoohan ... changed my direction. He was the role-model for me ... a thinking, caring, egalitarian. I believed in him as a valid moral force. McGoohan refused to permit the dictates of commercialism to dilute the ideas he had in mind. Steadfastly he pursued a provocative course to engage his perception of the truth." As to the series and its longevity, Rakoff concluded, "*The Prisoner* was a journey to save an individual from moral decline into the anonymity of the melting community. It was the battle of the 1960s. With the testing of time, it is *The Prisoner* which has prevailed, though continuing to intrigue with unanswerable questions. What is the ongoing appreciation of a piece of art, literature, film or television beyond the aspects of its construction? It is termed by some as a cult. Of its time, and ahead of its time, *The Prisoner* remains beyond category. Its durability has proved its potency to stay in the mind. It strikes a chord and appeals to a sense of responsibility still denied in our daily lives. It provides a clear-cut delineation between what is right and what is wrong. It's about repression but it speaks, across the years, with the voice of freedom." He summarised his evaluation of the series: "It was a leap of the imagination that I don't think was done in cinema and television in this country. The series owed almost everything to (McGoohan's) intensity."[68]

Music editor from the series, Eric Mival,[lxxxiii] remarked upon the way that McGoohan always wanted things to go faster. As well as the editing of the episodes, the star apparently

---

lxxxiii See page 288 as to a short (unreleased) film, *Red Reflections*, made by Mival, for which McGoohan provided some commentary.

held the same approach towards the music. "He seemed to take over. I remember Geoff Foot, who was regarded as the leading editor in the business, becoming a little annoyed. Even the first episode was cut again because it wasn't moving fast enough. It became a bit like the TV commercials of today, moving very quickly indeed." Mival remarked that, "McGoohan had very high standards. One of the things about him that impressed me was that despite all the things going on, if he said 'I'll see you at three o'clock,' he was there on the dot. And woe betide you if you weren't there."[69]

Prisoner scriptwriter, Vincent Tilsley, recalled[lxxxiv] writing a scene between McGoohan's character Number Six and an attractive female spy. "(McGoohan) refused to kiss the actress Nadia Gray, which I thought bloody silly. He was constantly making up awkward movements to avoid it. He also made a change in a speech I wrote all about Christianity. He didn't like it at all and completely rewrote it."[lxxxv] Tilsley was asked what McGoohan had been like to work with. "He's an egocentric. He's got a terrific amount of push. With someone as sensitive as George Markstein around, it was inevitable that they would argue. I can't think how they got together in the first place." Tilsley also felt that the idea of Number Six fighting with himself should have been developed throughout *The Prisoner* and not just left to the final episode. "Why is the imprisonment of oneself, the worst aspect of oneself, not hinted at anywhere in the series except at the end? Imprisonment is a two-way thing, in the psyche and by exterior forces. Why was there no evolvement of Number Six's character in the series? Just by being alone with oneself, one can evolve."[70] From Tilsley's perspective, he found the character which McGoohan had created as being unbelievable. In his opinion Number Six's escape, in the final episode, should have been the start of a sequel, showing what the character could do with his new-found freedom. The entire series, to Tilsley, had been effectively a waste of time, merely showing the central character being imprisoned and fighting against real or imagined forces, physical or mental. Tilsley would have preferred the man to crack up, which would have been more credible.

Had there ever been a second series of *The Prisoner*, Tilsley's story *Do Not Forsake Me Oh My Darling* would have been the opening episode. As it was, this became just one of the later episodes and at the writing stage, Tilsley had been given no particular brief or instructions. In order to cover up McGoohan's absence from the production – while filming *Ice Station Zebra* in Hollywood[lxxxvi] – the writer considered various options. One idea was to have a circus visiting the Village and Number Six would go into a magician's box and 'disappear,' until his reappearance at the end of the story. In the end, the Tilsley mind swap device was felt to be a stronger plotline and became the one which was used, allowing Nigel Stock to stand in for McGoohan.[lxxxvii] One interesting variation on Tilsley's plotline being considered was to have the prisoner's mind not only transferred into Stock's body, but to have it 'turned back' to the day before he resigned. The idea would be for Stock to resign once more, with the option of finding out why he was doing it. However, he would discover

---

[lxxxiv] Vincent Tilsley was later working as a psychotherapist and his new role perhaps caused him to re-evaluate the sixties' series. He gave his comments in an interview with the *Prisoner* appreciation society.
[lxxxv] Writer Terence Feely encountered the same problem – see page 141.
[lxxxvi] See page 178.
[lxxxvii] The wild thinking in another writer's mind was to have a secret prisoner held in the Village and eventually Number Six's curiosity gets the better of him and he finally finds the captive to be the late President John F. Kennedy – assassinated in the US in 1963 – although this probably would not have proceeded for reasons of political correctness in any event.

the ruse by glimpsing himself in a mirror and noticing his changed appearance. Behind the mirror, with its one-way glass, would be a darkened room for observers to watch.

Writer Moris Farhi found his work being rejected by McGoohan.[lxxxviii] "He turned it down flat, because I had a scene with him perspiring under torture." The writer never forgot the rebuff from McGoohan, who told him simply and sharply, "Heroes don't sweat."[71] Scriptwriter Terence Feely encountered a difficulty with his story *The Schizoid Man*, which included a scene where McGoohan would have to kiss co-star Jane Merrow.[lxxxix] "(Pat) would not kiss a girl on the set. He had this terribly puritanical thing. I said 'Why won't you kiss a girl?' and he said because I have this tremendous guilt inside and if I did I would not be able to look my wife in the eye.'[xc] The plot of *The Schizoid Man* is that he and this girl know each other so well because of a mind meld. I originally wrote that she would kiss the (fake) Number Six and kiss the real Number Six. Of course she would instantly know which was the real one. No way. 'I'm not gonna kiss Jane Merrow, I'm not gonna kiss her.' We had this raging bloody row, on and on, and in the end I said 'Okay, right, if it can't be physical then it's got to be a mental rapport with her, in that she can read your cards or you can read her cards, whatever. 'Great, great, let's do it.' So that's how that happened."

Feely recalled being asked to write his later story, *The Girl Who Was Death*: "I was on holiday in Cannes. David (Tomblin) and Pat arrived at the Carlton Hotel saying 'Listen, there's something that we think would interest you' and I said 'Oh yeah, what is it? And they said 'We want a two hour special. To be honest we're getting sick of *The Prisoner* always being in The Village. We've got claustrophobic about it. Now we want to get him out and we have this idea that we play a con trick and get him out by having him read a children's story to some kids, then break out of the story into the story he's actually telling. And by this device we get him out of The Village and do a kind of weird out-of-the-Village episode. Could you write it? And I said yes, it's absolutely my kind of writing, love to. But at the end of the day Lew (Grade) would not stake us the money for two hours. He said 'No, I don't care how good it is. I don't even want to see it. I can't fit it into the series. I can't sell it as part of a package. It's got to come down to an hour and just be like any other episode.' And so it came down to an hour."[xci]

Feely described *The Prisoner*'s setting as a "science-warp island where things can happen that can't happen in real life; where they've got techniques that we don't yet have; where they can get inside people's minds; they can manipulate people's minds; where everything we see and everything they use is going to be different and nothing like anything people are used to in that kind of situation. Pat has got a weird mind, you know."[72] He praised *The Prisoner* as a concept: "The series was about creative people for once running the asylum. We were doing what we wanted and showing what the medium was capable of. And also showing what a marvellous tool television is for surrealistic expression. (*Fall Out*) I think was one of the best examples of total surrealism. No prisoners taken."[xcii] [73] Feely concluded, "This was a series built to last. It is only now beginning to be properly appreciated and I wouldn't be surprised if it is still a cult show 20 years from now."[74]

[lxxxviii] Farhi penned an unfilmed *Prisoner* episode entitled *The Outsider*. Another unfilmed script was *Don't Get Yourself Killed*, by Gerald Kelsey. For other ideas not pursued, see the end section of Appendix One.
[lxxxix] However, there was a brief kiss between them in an earlier *Danger Man* episode, see page 83.
[xc] Writer Vincent Tilsley had a similar difficulty – see page 140.
[xci] A planned chase sequence in a maze was cancelled.
[xcii] Feely was also engaged to write for post-*Prisoner* projects – see page 184.

One of the series' stunt actors was Peter Brayham, who recalled how he had accidentally clipped McGoohan during one *Prisoner* fight scene. The star got his own back in a later take when he was on the ground and had to throw Brayham with his feet, over his head, in an action known as a monkey climb. The unfortunate recipient of the move would then have to tumble down some stairs and lay still at the bottom. The fall occurred and moments passed, but there was no sign of movement from Brayham. McGoohan hurried down to the motionless fall guy, by which time other members of the stunt crew had crowded round him. They were all in on the joke, but McGoohan had not yet caught on that the actor was feigning unconsciousness. The star leaned over and asked "Is he all right?" McGoohan's stunt double, Frank Maher, exclaimed, "I think you've really hurt him, Pat." Then as the star leaned in closer, Brayham shot up, grabbed him by the lapels and was about to plant a kiss on him, which apparently was a joke stunt men often used to play on each other.[75] McGoohan realised at the last moment that it was a prank and moved quickly out of the way. Dennis Chinnery, an actor who had been required to fight McGoohan on screen during *The Prisoner*, remembered almost being strangled. The scene had to be redone and McGoohan apologised for being over-zealous when applying force to the Chinnery neck. However, thirty years on, Chinnery expressed fond memories of McGoohan. "It was so exciting. In fact it was one of the most exciting things I've ever done in my life. He was one of the most exciting people that I've ever worked with in the business. He really inspired a terrific sort of energy and enthusiasm and vitality."

Stunt actor Frank Maher looked back on his years of being McGoohan's double from the days of *Danger Man* and also *The Prisoner*. The pair became good friends in their filming days and according to Maher worked closely together, as the double was involved in virtually every scene where the lead actor needed a stand-in. Maher would also appear in many other shots, in which McGoohan was not seen. Such fill-ins and covers were necessary to keep the action moving, while the star would perhaps be engaged somewhere else, filming close-ups or straight dialogue sections. The two men lived nearby and played squash every night. "For solid hours we would smash each other to pieces on the court. I injured him one night. I shoulder-charged him into a wall. Pat couldn't do anything for three weeks. He could only do close-ups and so I earned a fortune." Maher revealed that *Danger Man* was the first series which broke the American barrier. "Pat was being offered the lead parts in *The Saint* and also the *James Bond* movies. He turned them down because of the aspect of kissing ladies on screen. Both Sean Connery and Roger Moore owe him an awful lot!"

The stunt man recalled a day, in the mid-sixties, when Roger Moore had come to the film set where McGoohan was working. "Les Crawford[xciii] was Roger's stunt double. We decided to arrange for Roger and Pat to meet. Late afternoon, Les was doing a *Prisoner* close-up of him hitting Pat. Roger walked on to the set. I said, 'There's Roger.' Pat asked me, 'Roger who?' I said, 'Roger Moore.' Les, being Roger's double normally, went over to Roger to talk to him. Roger had seen what was going on and conspiratorially whispered in Les' ear and tucked, unseen by Les, a money note into his pocket. As shooting began again, the red light came on and the order came to turn over. Les threw a punch but accidentally caught Pat. He hit him so hard it put him, plus two other men who were holding him in the shot, down onto the floor. Pat picked himself up, while Roger walked over and said to Les,

---

[xciii] He also appeared as a cowboy in the *Prisoner* episode *Living in Harmony*.

'Worth it, was it?' Les replied, 'What are you talking about?' Pat of course could not believe that Les had not done it deliberately after hearing Roger's comment. (Pat) had a big lump on his head and many people saw this incident, as they had come to see both him and Moore being together on set. The atmosphere was electric" However, Maher also respected McGoohan's own pugilistic prowess. "He'd be a good man to have with you in a punch-up. He's much tougher than he looks and packs quite a punch. I've had some fair bruises to show for it on the occasions when he's slipped."[76] In the *Prisoner* episode *The Schizoid Man*, Number Six is given a 'twin,' by use of the split-screen effect. This meant that often McGoohan and Maher would have to switch jackets and effectively the double was in the story as much as the star. Maher recalled that he was about to get more than he had bargained for. "In one scene Pat hit me on the chin. It was so hard that I went over a worktop. I ran outside to cool down. I was going to kill him. He came over and put his hands up and said, 'Sorry.'"

Maher's opinion was that compared with the earlier *Danger Man*, by the time of *The Prisoner* Pat had become "a harder taskmaster." Perhaps it was because the star was doing nearly everything on the new series, his double opined. "We all knew we were finishing *Danger Man* and that the character John Drake would go on, into *The Prisoner*. We all knew it was Drake. One night in the pub Pat said to me he would give me a synopsis the next day. He said, 'We won't say it's Drake, but it is.' He also said we would do twenty six episodes. We got to Portmeirion and along with Don Chaffey we were making it up as we went along. We just did assorted pieces, which were put together later. We all chucked in ideas."

Maher, asked about script editor George Markstein, replied, "I only saw George once. He never came on set. However, Pat is a straight man. He wouldn't say something was his idea if it was somebody else's. I do not think George Markstein was involved anywhere near as much as he claimed to be. Pat was in Portmeirion, just the once for thirty one days. I did the rest of the scenes there. I went to Portmeirion three times. I remember the day the penny farthing was wheeled out of the props truck. Pat said to me, 'Ride it.' I nearly broke my neck. It is not true that the bike had any symbolism. It was just one of the strange props that were to decorate the Village and a lot has been attributed to it with the benefit of hindsight."

Maher had plenty of quirky recollections about the Portmeirion filming. "The first week we were up there, there was this little hotel or pub in Tremadoc. The alcohol laws at that time were crazy in North Wales. Running through the middle of the street and the bar was the boundary between two different counties, with different laws for Sunday drinking. I was in the part of the bar that was open the first Sunday evening we were there, with a couple of other stunt guys. Pat turned up in the other bar which was closed. He stood there for ages and was livid. He could see us drinking and was furious that he was unable to buy a drink. In the end the landlord said the poor chap had suffered enough and we let him in on the joke. We of course all had to buy him drinks to make up. Pat used to be annoyed that I did all the stunts. He insisted on doing one piece of action involving running across the sand. I warned him not to, as soft sand can suddenly become hard and I said he could pull a muscle. He did injure his leg and was out of action for a while."

As for the *Prisoner* series' demise, Maher reflected how the decision had brought sorrow to all those involved. He described the feeling of some on the set as "distraught." He added, "At episode sixteen, we were suddenly told that the next one was the last. The series came to a premature end. I didn't know what that last one was about. Neither did Pat! Lew Grade just stopped it. The budget was twice that of any other series at that time. Normally episodes of drama series cost around £35,000 and we were up in the £100,000 region." Maher reflected, "It was a marvellous series. One of the best ever made."[77]

He also claimed credit for the *Prisoner* episode *Living in Harmony*.[xciv] "The idea for a western came from me. In the pub one night I said to Pat, 'Why don't we go somewhere different. It's all in the mind anyway.' Pat replied, 'As long as you handle it all.' David Tomblin and I worked hand in hand on that one together. I did the wardrobe, the posters in the saloon, props, horses and everything. Westerns were my thing. Pat's horse was called Viking. Even my son was in one shot. Young Gary, a child at the time, picked up a hat in the town street at the end of the big fight." On the subject of gunslinging, Maher recalled, "I taught McGoohan and Alexis Kanner the use of their guns. While Pat was in Hollywood[xcv] he said he had got Steve McQueen teaching him to draw. (He) proved to be almost as fast with a gun as me. I was so fast that two years later I beat the fourth fastest draw in the world."

Alexis Kanner revealed how his part in the *Prisoner* cowboy episode, *Living in Harmony*, was offered to him: "Dave Tomblin phoned me up and said 'Wanna do a western?' He had been First Assistant Director on one of the first pictures I had done. At the time, McGoohan was in Hollywood filming *Ice Station Zebra*[xcvi] and of course was ready to do the *Harmony* episode upon his return. Meanwhile, he got in touch with me from there (USA) and said he was practising fast draws with a gun. So I practised a long time as this was going to be a real showdown, not using camera effects. On the western set, when the time came, the crew were expectant and a great deal of money changed hands as to who would be quickest on the draw." Kanner recalled clearly, "On Tomblin's order we were just to draw and fire. The camera was behind Pat's holster and as he fired it would zoom into me. So I had to let Pat draw, as the camera crew went to start zooming in on me. Only one shot was heard, but when the frames of film were counted, he had taken eleven frames and I took seven. So I was one sixth of a second faster than him on the draw!"

The actor also reminisced about the team's end of day habit of winding down at a Borehamwood public house. "Tomblin, McGoohan, Bernie Williams (production manager) et al would stand a metre from the bar, drinking, staring straight ahead and not speaking. The time came when I couldn't take it any more and I cut out a cartoon from the newspaper. This showed the little *Andy Capp* guy where he is propping up the bar. A stranger leaves and says 'Good night' and Capp's comment is 'Amateur!' I put this on the bar and it at least got us talking. Pat then said, 'We've got to blow the place up,' meaning the Village. It was a moment born of a very long period of hardship, on his part, work and creative energy. So he had the right to make that instant decision."

Kanner recalled: "Pat and I used to play squash in a deserted school house in Mill Hill and I started not bothering to go home. I used to try and be first on set the next morning. The studio would be in darkness, but no matter how early I got there, there would be this robed figure waiting. 'How do you feel?' a deep voice would enquire of me and I would tentatively say, 'OK.' His response was, 'Good, because it's going to be another day of

---

[xciv] See earlier mention of Ian Rakoff supplying the idea for a western, page 138.
[xcv] See page 178.
[xcvi] See page 178.

indescribable brutality.'" Kanner had developed a high level of respect for McGoohan, but was alive to his idiosyncrasies and changing moods. "He and I had two dressing rooms in an empty corridor. Further along there was a sign 'Beware, dangerous animal.' I thought they should put it nearer Pat's door. It actually related to Stanley Kubrick's leopard – for the movie *2001: A Space Odyssey* – which incidentally he had to fire as it was too timid. (Our) production occupied two enormous sound stages at Borehamwood. The movie *2001* was off in a corner somewhere!" Kanner also reflected upon McGoohan's condition at the end of production. "He was real tired. He had put out an awful lot of himself. I thought that at the end Pat should rip the Number One mask off and it would be Lew Grade, but Pat didn't think that was funny. We were still shooting scenes a few days before transmission. That's why there were so many editors. I don't think any of them saw all of the footage."[78] [xcvii]

Of course, the anecdotes and memories presented here by the *Prisoner* cast and crew are but a small selection of the many tales which have been told over the years. This chapter now returns to the story of the series and how the end of its television debut run was drawing to a close. There was concern that McGoohan had no proposed ending for the series and at the end of 1967 press reports were claiming that the hugely anticipated finale might not materialise at all. There was by now a media frenzy and the revealing of the identity of the mystery "Number One" was a topic on everybody's lips. One reporter described the finale as "the most eagerly awaited hour of British television to be shown in 1968."[79]

Problems had arisen when McGoohan manoeuvred a break from the production – believed by this writer to be the defining moment in its demise – leaving his MGM Borehamwood team working on an episode to be made without him. The story *Do Not Forsake Me Oh My Darling* saw the mind of Number Six being transferred into the body of another man, played by actor Nigel Stock.[xcviii] Only at the climax of the episode would McGoohan re-appear, both on screen and, in person, back from America. As the actor was leaving for the States – covered later in this book – to star in the movie *Ice Station Zebra* (1968),[xcix] journalist Sean Usher cornered him as he was boarding a jet bound for Hollywood. Usher learned that McGoohan had yet to start creating the script for the series' finale – having "no idea" as to its ending – although the star promised he would start work on it during the flight. The journalist had time to point out that public opinion was becoming sharply divided on *The Prisoner*; probably McGoohan's own thoughts on the writing task ahead were little different. Usher wrote in his ensuing article that the last days of the production were now a nail-biting time for Lew Grade, "the cigar-munching master of ATV." It reported that he had taken a "frightening gamble" in underwriting the "*Prisoner* experiment," with ATV funding. McGoohan was said to be going off to make films, being therefore unable to make any more *Prisoner* episodes even if he wanted to.[80]

The few weeks' grace afforded to McGoohan, enabling him to take leave of absence from *The Prisoner*, were then matched by MGM in Hollywood. This gave the actor much

---

[xcvii] Kanner finalised his comments by revealing a surprising idea for a follow-on *Prisoner* series. He spoke of a follow-on series, with the prisoner going out into the world, but still being within reach of the tentacles of the Village. Kanner was amused by a plan to have his own Hippie character running in a marathon race at the Olympics. A fair distance behind him would be seen the *Prisoner* dwarf butler, running furiously in an attempt to keep up. This demonstrates the bizarre ideas being thrown about at that time.

[xcviii] A party scene used a set from MGM's *The Dirty Dozen* (1967).

[xcix] The producer, Marty Ransohoff, also produced *The Moonshine War* (1970), in which McGoohan took the lead role. While in the states, the actor was reportedly able to have his wife and three daughters with him for much of the time.

needed further time to complete the final trio *Prisoner* episodes,[c] although he declared at the time that he hardly knew where he was. Another writer has advanced that the actor's absence, while in the US, was tantamount to a knell being sounded back home over *The Prisoner*. He refers to the star's return from Hollywood: "A coup d'etat of sorts had taken place behind the scenes. With the production getting increasingly more expensive and bewildering, Grade decided McGoohan's number was finally up and that episode 17 would be the last ever *Prisoner*. Thrown into disarray, McGoohan had just one week to tie up all the loose ends of the series into a climactic episode that has entered history as the most controversial television denouement ever."[81][ci]

In fact, towards the end of the run of weekly *Prisoner* episodes in Britain, the final two *Danger Man* colour stories, *Koroshi* and *Shinda Shima*, were screened instead in some parts of the country, on 5th and 12th January, 1968. Some sources claim that this allowed McGoohan more time to write the final *Prisoner* episode, *Fall Out*. However, this was not necessarily an intentional part of the broadcasting plan. As *The Prisoner* was being shown in various regions on different dates, local scheduling sometimes got in the way and caused transmissions to fall behind. In London there had already been two episodes missed, owing to a presentation of the *Royal Variety Show* and Christmas programming. To restore the balance, the two *Danger Man* episodes were shown in some other areas,[cii] thereby putting the whole country back on track. By 1st March, 1968, the *Prisoner*'s legendary finale had been seen in all of Britain's ITV regions.[ciii]

1   TV Guide, New Zealand, 29th May 1967
2   The Scotsman, 16th July 1977, Cameron Simpson
3   Screenonline, Anthony Clark
4   Hollywood.com website
5   Idols magazine, November, 1988, Graham P. Williams
6   Boston Globe, 13th January, 1985, Ed Siegel
7   Still Dancing: My Story, HarperCollins, 1987, Lew Grade
8   Six into One: The Prisoner File, Channel 4, 1983
9   Christchurch Press, 30th December, 1982, Judith Regan
10 Sunday Telegraph Magazine, 24th March, 1985, Anthony Masters
11 Number Six Magazine, Six of One, The Prisoner Appreciation Society, January, 1988, Christopher Frost
12 The Prisoner Investigated Volume 1, TR7 Productions, 1990
13 Screenonline, Anthony Clark
14 Source not verified
15 Number Six Magazine, Six of One, The Prisoner Appreciation Society, April, 1992, Chris Campbell
16 The Prisoner Investigated, Volume 2, TR7 Productions, 1990
17 ITC press book, 1967
18 Ontario Educational Communications Authority, TV Ontario, March 1977, Warner Troyer
19 Ibid
20 1966, source not verified.
21 Free for All Magazine, Six of One, The Prisoner Appreciation Society, 1999, Rob Beale
22 TV Week, 27th April, 1968
23 ITC publicity material, 1967
24 Interview in Six of One Alert journal, summer 1980, Jon Older
25 Ibid
26 Ibid
27 TV Guide, 1968, Joan Barthel,
28 Boston Globe, 13th January, 1985, Ed Siegel
29 UK newspaper, article by Sally Moore, details unknown

c   The story which came to be shown as the penultimate one, *Once upon a Time*, had already been filmed.
ci Although this is a commonly held view as to the curtailing of the number of *Prisoner* episodes, McGoohan's account was simply that he was "exhausted" and had, in any event, completed the job he set out to do.
cii *Koroshi* and *Shinda Shima* had in fact been shown in the London area almost a year earlier
ciii The screening of *Fall Out* is covered in Chapter Seven.

[30] TV Stars Yearbook, 1966/7
[31] New Zealand TV Weekly, 20th November, 1967, Ad Astra
[32] Source not verified
[33] TV Times, 1967, Anthony Davis
[34] Record Song Book, late 1967
[35] Source not verified
[36] TV Times, 1967, John K. Newnham
[37] Ibid
[38] Number Six Magazine, Six of One, The Prisoner Appreciation Society, January, 1992, Steven Ricks
[39] Film Dope, July 1983, interview By Bob Baker and Markku Salmi
[40] Number Six Magazine, Six of One, The Prisoner Appreciation Society, April, 1992, Chris Campbell
[41] Ibid
[42] Ibid
[43] Number Six Magazine, Six of One, The Prisoner Appreciation Society, January, 1993, Mathew Lock
[44] Interview with the writer, 2006
[45] Number Six Magazine, Six of One, The Prisoner Appreciation Society, January, 1993, Mathew Lock
[46] Interview with the writer, 2006
[47] Letter to the writer, 2002
[48] Ibid
[49] Ibid
[50] Number Six Magazine, Six of One, The Prisoner Appreciation Society, July, 1995, Tony Worrall
[51] Ibid
[52] Six of One Portmeirion convention, 1996
[53] Six of One Prisoner twenty fifth and thirtieth anniversary events, 1993 and 1997, London
[54] Number Six Magazine, Six of One, The Prisoner Appreciation Society, January, 1988, Christopher Frost
[55] Source not verified
[56] Letter to the writer, 2006
[57] Free for All Magazine, Six of One, The Prisoner Appreciation Society, October, 2002, Roger Langley,
[58] Letter to the writer, 2006
[59] Ibid
[60] Ibid
[61] Ibid
[62] Idols magazine, November, 1988, Graham P. Williams
[63] Six of One Prisoner twenty fifth and thirtieth anniversary events, 1993 and 1997, London
[64] Letter to Six of One, The Prisoner Appreciation Society, member Brian Nixon c. 1978
[65] Letter to Six of One, The Prisoner Appreciation Society, member Michael Prendergast, 1977
[66] Leo McKern interview, The Day the Earth Caught Fire DVD, 2001
[67] Inside the "Prisoner": Radical Television and Film in the 1960s , 1998, Ian Rakoff
[68] Ibid
[69] Ibid
[70] Six of One, The Prisoner Appreciation Society
[71] Sunday Telegraph, 24th March, 1985
[72] The Prisoner Investigated, Volume 2, TR7 Productions, 1990
[73] Interview with Terence Feely, by Hugh Conrad, 1985
[74] 100 Years of Science Fiction Interview with Terence Feely, by Hugh Conrad, 1985
[76] Photoplay, May, 1965
[77] Six of One Prisoner twenty fifth and thirtieth anniversary events, 1993 and 1997, London
[78] Six of One Prisoner twenty fifth and thirtieth anniversary events, 1993 and 1997, London
[79] Anthony Davis, The Prisoner In Depth 4, TR7 Productions, 1993
[80] Daily Sketch, 2nd December,1967, Shaun Usher
[81] Cult TV The Golden Age of ITC, 2006, Plexus, Robert Sellers

The *Prisoner* press conference at Borehamwood, 1967

CHAPTER SIX

The Prisoner:
The Schizoid Man

"What's it all about?"
The Prisoner: Arrival (1967)

The middle section of this book takes time out to look at the concept of *The Prisoner* and also to provide some comments made by other writers. In addition, there is an opportunity to cover what McGoohan himself was saying to the media, after broadcasts of the episodes were well under way. Perhaps the most revealing comment from the star – missed by almost all reviews, interviews and writers then and since – had been uttered by him at the 1967 *Prisoner* press conference, covered in the previous chapter. Regarding the meaning of the series, McGoohan declared, "The Prisoner is all about freedom. It's about a top scientist who has vital space secrets in his head and decides he wants to resign. He has no name. He's kept prisoner in an isolated village where he is subjected to various brain-washing techniques." The actor insisted, "The greatest fight before any one of us today is to be a true individual, to fight for what you believe in and stick to that. If I have a drum to beat, it's the drum of the individual."[1]

The title of this chapter comes from the episode in which Number Six is confronted by his 'identical twin'. The actor of course plays both roles, the 'real' prisoner wearing a dark jacket and the 'fake' a light one, for ease of identification. The plot itself provides a useful analogy, as McGoohan must have felt like two different people during the latter days of *The Prisoner*. Also, this chapter allows a study of the largely autobiographical content of the episode, *Once Upon a Time*. Although the story was placed as the penultimate one in the series, it was originally – having been filmed months before *Fall Out* – meant as a 'season closer,' or at least that is what many believe. Whatever is the case, the episode was used by

McGoohan as a 'This is Your Life' presentation, as will be covered later in this chapter. The final episode is also studied, while events surrounding its 1968 screening and the aftermath are covered in Chapter Seven.

Before this writer's analysis is given, it is interesting to look at McGoohan's own 'split personality' comments, which have varied greatly at different times, or when he was speaking to different journalists. At one point he said, "I don't want to be a prisoner, that's why I did the series. It represented man's fight against the bureaucratic establishment. All stories apply to our society and the dangers of being reduced to a number. It had a surrealistic look to it. In the last episode it was revealed that No. 1 was himself. The greatest enemy is ourself. That's who we're prisoners of – ourselves. The only freedom in this world is to have a free spirit."[2] Alternatively, at another time, the actor could sound like a hopeless romantic: "There's love, faith, hope and charity in this world. Everyone is looking for love. Most people are lonely and lost. I always go back to my favourite movie, *It Happened One Night*.[i] It was a beautiful love story, one hard to comprehend these days. Colbert and Gable never touched. There was the blanket between them in the motel. But still it was a love story. In a way I'm guilty of doing a series like *The Prisoner* without injecting a note of hope into it. The guy should have been victorious against the system."[3]

An interview given in Hollywood, in October, 1967, is possibly the most revealing as to the amount of calls and pressures on McGoohan's time, skills and – not least of all – his mind. The actor revealed to the reporter that he was already looking far ahead and would visit New Zealand early in 1968: "The actor's trip, however, will be partly business as he will be taking a serious look at New Zealand as a location for future film production. Patrick revealed these plans to me exclusively in Hollywood last week, where he is filming the multi-million dollar production of *Ice Station Zebra*." The journalist continued with more words from the actor: "I am also writing a novel which is set in (New Zealand) and it is through this that I have gained most of my knowledge of the country."

McGoohan, whose itinerary was not certain, would be flying from London to Japan to discuss two films being planned there, followed by trips to New Zealand and Australia. The actor mentioned his "successful film production company in London, Everyman Films," referring also to the New Zealand Government "(which) I know is keen to get film production going there and this interests me very much." However, McGoohan was reluctant to discuss the novel he was writing: "It's more a hobby than anything. I might even develop it as a screenplay eventually for shooting in New Zealand. I haven't titled it as yet and I don't feel there is any point in going into the plot, but it does relate to the *Treasure of Sierra Madre*."[ii]

The journalist was impressed with the writing project: "Such a book would be a major undertaking for most people, but for the tall, sandy-haired actor it is just one of at least half-a-dozen projects he manages to juggle at once. At present, he is dashing backwards and forwards across the Atlantic to film *Ice Station Zebra* in Hollywood and complete the final episodes of his latest television series, *The Prisoner*, in London. The actor explained, 'It meant reshuffling schedules of both film and television series, but it has delighted me that I have been able to do (the movie). John Sturges (the film's director) has arranged for all my scenes to be shot first and I am able to return to London for a week, then fly back here

---

[i] The 1934 movie starred Clark Gable and Claudette Colbert.
[ii] The 1948 movie starred Humphrey Bogart, in a story about three men discovering gold in the mountains.

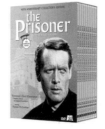

DVDs of *The Prisoner* and *Danger Man*

(Hollywood) to complete my part of the film.'" The journalist closed his article by informing readers that when McGoohan would be returning to London, "he will almost immediately begin a film production of Ibsen's *Brand*, a role that brought him wide acclaim, both on the stage and television in Britain."[4]

Many reporters and writers have covered *The Prisoner*, both in a contemporary way and retrospectively. A US magazine ran a feature on McGoohan's involvement with Disney productions, showing how his screen presence endured, decades later: "For many of us fortunate enough to have been exposed at some time to Patrick McGoohan's unflappable demeanour and clipped, nasal intonation in either of the classic TV series *Danger Man* or *The Prisoner*, this singular actor has come to embody one of the truly invaluable icons of sophisticated, anti-authoritarian masculinity of the 1960s, indeed of the last century." The earlier of the two series received praise, but of *The Prisoner*, the journalist enthused that it was, "A ground-breaking series that has yet to be surpassed for its cinematic flair and invention."[5] More press comments abounded during the first broadcast of *The Prisoner*. "McGoohan (who is originator and executive producer as well as a star) hopes his new baby will demonstrate that thrillers can embody food for thought. Yes, indeed. I offer him a thought right now. You can deck out a load of old hokum with every technical device the electronic age provides – and you've still got a load of old hokum!"[6] Another media reporter described watching *The Prisoner*: "The appeal lies in figuring what in hell is going on..."[7] One more commentator, after labelling the series an "air-conditioned nightmare," wrote: "McGoohan in his new series has made a mixture of *The Fugitive*, George Orwell and the trappings of science fiction – and it should settle down to a potent cocktail, leaving us with an uneasy hangover for the rest of the evening."[8]

Although some say that McGoohan's masterpiece – or muddle – is a conundrum which can never be unravelled, this is not necessarily so. *The Prisoner* can be analysed through its visual symbols. At the start of episodes a formidable bank of filing cabinets is seen. Here, metaphorically, there are enough drawers to house all aspects of the series. Considering themes from any one story can be done by 'pulling out' two or three drawers and studying the contents. However, pulling out too many drawers causes the cabinet to topple over. The moral here, with regard to solving the riddle of the series, is that there are just too many aspects for all of them to be considered together. The episodes present an impressive array of topics: democracy and drugs; torture and technology; power and politics; misinformation and the military; incarceration and individualism; conformity and the community; society and survival; identity and independent thought; force and freedom; religion and rebellion; education and escape; violence and values; science and security; hallucinations and heroism; authority and art; weaponry and will; brainwashing and beliefs; censorship and coercion; jingoism and justice; psychology and peace; loyalty and love; danger and death.

It is therefore no wonder that it has been said that *The Prisoner* works on many levels. Not only does a myriad of topics exist throughout the seventeen episodes, but there is also a multitude of symbols, insignia and devices on view. These include the fearsome white balloons, patrolling under the name of "Rover,"[iii] an outdoor chess game, with human 'pieces' and a quaint penny farthing bicycle. The latter contraption is adorned with a canopy, a combined emblem which is seen throughout episodes: on flags, shop goods and badges worn by guardians and inmates alike. There are jaunty taxis, which take passengers

---

[iii] A name used only briefly in one *Prisoner* episode, *The Schizoid Man*, but one which has stuck.

on pointless local-only journeys; signs and slogans are on view everywhere and covert observation is maintained upon the prison population by means of surveillance cameras, hidden inside statues. A cheerful greeting, "Be seeing you," accompanied by a finger and thumb hand salute, delivered from the eye, belies the internment of the community dwellers – each with his or her own assigned number, but without names. There are silent funeral undertakers, their hearse making sinister appearances right up to the last episode. A dwarf butler is assigned as manservant to each new official in charge, but their head employer is never seen. Various underground chambers are occupied by top-hatted committee members, surveillance staff and observers.

Lines of dialogue employ extracts from Shakespeare, Cervantes and Goethe. Classical music – Bizet, Vivaldi, Strauss – plays alongside pop, including the Beatles. Storylines draw comparison with the works of Kafka, Orwell, Huxley and even Lewis Carroll. In the Village, a prisoner can be given a lobotomy to ensure conformity, or be declared "Unmutual," becoming shunned by the whole community. All mental states can be manipulated – from happiness to madness – so that resistance is turned into obedience. Mind control is enforced through methods and practices which have worrying titles: "Instant Social Conversion," "Therapy Zone," "Embryo Room," "Speedlearn," "Degree Absolute," "Aversion Therapy" and "Appreciation Day." Only the main character, Number Six seems to have a general immunity against being harmed by those in power, although occasionally his exemption is conveniently ignored by a leader wanting to use a more extreme approach to break the will of his captive.

From the initial premise of a man held by an enemy side (which might even be his own side), the episodes grow more abstract, open to all kinds of interpretations and seeming to become a commentary on life in general. The existential conflict between the main character and his captors – even his surroundings – strikes a chord with viewers' own personal experiences. Fears and guilt, being punished or rejected, searching for identity, are all themes which bounce between the viewer and the television screen when watching *The Prisoner*. In the final episode, *Fall Out*, the strangest characters and events of the whole series are witnessed. In a subterranean cavern a public trial occurs, with wigged president, hooded assembly members, dancing Hippie character, a rocket launch, machine guns, a supreme ape figure and a mobile cage. McGoohan recalled, "That last script was written by me very close to the end, in thirty-six hours, just scribbling away and chiselling at it, until eventually I got what we have, which, as far as I am concerned, I think, works. I wouldn't change it."[9]

On our 'trip' – to borrow a drug term from the sixties – through the episodes, we are treated to a holiday atmosphere, while also being aware of the dark secrets of "The Village."

The eclectic climate of the decade is mirrored in the episodes: the Cold War era, the breaking away from the austere fifties and stripping of previously held values, plus the growing trend of crossing borders, moving towards a state of 'internationalism.' With all this 'progress,' Patrick McGoohan prophetically saw an increase in government control, numeralisation and computerisation. Some say that *The Prisoner* foresaw the end of the sixties' new-found freedoms. The episodes may seem to portray one long party, but behind the fancy costumes and pretty surroundings, a darker reality is perceived. If the decade did not know which way to go, then certainly it can be argued that *The Prisoner* also did not know where it was headed.

At this juncture, it assists to look at the very decade which so styled *The Prisoner*, the swinging, sexy, super, sock-it-to-me sixties. It is interesting to reflect upon what events, from around the globe, influenced the style or content of *The Prisoner*. The series' initial pre-production occurred around March, 1966 and the screening of *Fall Out* during the original British run followed two years later. In between, the world was developing quickly and by 1968 much had changed. In 1966, computer assisted instruction first began in US elementary schools and in 1967, electronic music was first generated by computers. By 1969 the information handling capacity of these machines exceeded the amount of brain storage of the entire human race. It is little wonder that McGoohan had a close interest in computers, particularly their future and potential for abuse. The actor would frequently refer to events happening around the world whenever he was being asked what *The Prisoner* was about.

The darkest aspect of the 'swinging' era was the ongoing Vietnam war. Some say that *The Prisoner* alluded to the conflict, there having been a major escalation of the air war in 1966. The events in South East Asia dominated headlines for the rest of the decade and McGoohan commented on prisoner of war newsreels more than once. He was equally vocal on the topics of drugs and relaxed morals, both of which were prominent factors of the sixties: "The powerful nations of the earth who have wealth at their disposal are spending that wealth building tanks, guns, rockets and bombs. Every human being has a responsibility to society and to himself. I think one should be aware of what is happening; that every responsible person should try to resist it. I have never met anyone in my life who didn't have, somewhere hidden in their background, a conscience. The object of the television series, *The Prisoner* was to create a feeling of unrest about life today. It was an abstract expression of the world we are living in and a warning of what would happen to us when gadgetry and gimmickry take over from creative people."[10]

McGoohan's wide-ranging comments drew from the world around him: "I wanted to have controversy, arguments, fights, discussions, people in anger, waving fists in my face. Has one the right to be an individual? I wanted to make people talk about the series. I wanted to make them ask questions, argue and think. More than anything I believe in the freedom of the individual. I thought there was a period in the 60's when the youth were going to rebel and I thought it would have been good. But unfortunately they weren't organised and I think that's sad. Somebody needs to yell a warning. I hope I'm giving some kind of warning. My Village is not 1984, but 1968. People disappear into camps like this. It's not just imagination – it's fact. These camps are actual physical map references. At this moment, individuals are being drained of their personalities and being brainwashed into slaves. The inquisition of the mind by psychiatrists is far worse than the assault on the body by torturers. We read in the paper of crashed spy planes and captured spy boats. And we take it for granted when the patriotic pilots and commanders are paraded in public by their captors as grey, blank-faced old puppets who, without any sort of outward damage, spit at their country and beliefs. It's not fiction. It's a Chinese newsreel. It's as real as the headlines. More than anything else, I believe passionately in the freedom of the individual. I want to yell back: 'That's our right. The loss of one's own individuality is a nightmare.' And if I haven't made my 'yell back' clear in *The Prisoner*, the individual viewer has the right to shout 'Nuts to you Paddy boy.'"[11]

McGoohan filming with the Lotus Seven and Caterham Cars' Graham Nearn, reunited in the third picture down on the right, at the Birmingham Motor Show, 1990

The actor summed up his whole philosophical purpose in bringing *The Prisoner* to audiences:

"I would be arrogant enough to say it's essential for every man to do the equivalent of getting down on his knees and conceding that there is something bigger than he is, within whose shadow he lives. You've got to work to find truth – yourself. Nobody else can show it to you. In *The Prisoner* I tried to create a first-class piece of entertainment, but I hoped it had truth too, because here also I was concerned with the preservation of the individual and his liberty. The stories were all about one man, one scientist's great unflinching battle for survival as an individual in a macabre world in which every move was watched by electronic eyes and all his neighbours were suspect. He had to live under wraps all the time. His individuality was constantly threatened, even his sanity. How can a person be truly individual today? It's a big question. I should never have thought of John Drake as a calm man, but one with a constant potential of eruption. This is essential to any part. The audience must be aware of a man wanting to erupt into action. Temper can be inconsequential or the result of hysteria. Anger at injustice perhaps is nearer the mark than temper. Anger should imply something colder, with a good reason behind it. Our only hope is really whatever our youngsters are after. The wild beauty of a child's mind, a Garden of Eden with craggy peaks is one of the most virile things you can talk about; it is a tremendous responsibility to preserve this in your children and make sure the seeds flower. But they're getting old, some of the 'adolescents.' I mean, I'm in sympathy with any form of rebellion, but when they get to be 35 or 40 what are they going to be – where are they going to go? It takes an awfully long time to dig into what the real rebel is. Surely rebel and revolutionary go together. You've got to rebel with a premise. No one can 'qualify' to be an individual. You know, get a certificate saying, 'I'm an individual.' I don't believe anybody has been able to do that in honesty and get away with it. One of the worst pollutions is the spread of the dissipated word: truth, dissipated by virtue of the fact that it has to please so many people. 'I'll be right back, after this message, to tell you about the end of the world.' I think the first discipline a child should be taught is to continue to ask his own questions and find his own answers."[12]

Some of the 1966 to 1968 headline-grabbing events in Britain can be touched upon here. In 1966 Britain, Prime Minister Harold Wilson led the country after a landslide election victory by the Labour party. There soon followed a freeze on prices and there was trouble with support for the pound[iv] abroad. On the pop music front, The Beatles released their *Revolver* album, as well as videos and singles for songs like *Paperback Writer*, *Yellow Submarine* and *Eleanor Rigby*. They played their last concert in San Francisco. Bob Dylan toured the UK, Twiggy the fashion model came to the fore and London's Carnaby Street was the hot place to buy clothes in the English capital. Movies *Alfie*, *Thunderball* and *Dr. Zhivago* entertained audiences while on the scientific and political fronts, 'soft' moon landings were achieved by the USSR and USA. Rock guitarist Jimi Hendrix arrived in Britain to become the talk of London and on TV new shows like *The Monkees*, *Star Trek*, *Mission: Impossible* and *Batman* began. Mini skirts were raising hemlines and eyebrows, England won the football World Cup and the

---

[iv] The UK standard unit of currency at the time, before decimalisation in 1971. The most common coin was the penny and a there was previously a smaller one, being quarter of its value, called a farthing. The penny farthing bicycle, used as a symbol in *The Prisoner*, was named after these two coins, having a large front wheel and a much smaller rear one.

Various magazines featuring McGoohan on the covers, mainly in *Danger Man* and *The Prisoner*

Chinese leader, Mao Tse Tung launched his Cultural Revolution. The credit card was introduced to the UK, while prices went up in respect of almost everything and the pound dropped a third in value.

The year 1967 brought the Hippie movement, with "Flower Power" to the fore and the "Summer of Love" being enjoyed by the young. London had been dubbed the "Swinging" capital of the world and *Sgt. Pepper* was the Beatles' contribution to the spirit of the times. Meanwhile, Britain was entering a monetary decline, with a huge trade deficit, unemployment figures soaring and devaluation of the pound about to occur. Only the young ignored their own doorstep difficulties. The London School of Economics famously organised its 'sit in' by way of student protest, there was a "Legalise Pot" rally in Hyde Park, with US beat poet Allen Ginsberg attending. The Beatles continued their reign of popularity with the release of *Penny Lane/Strawberry Fields*, while their anthem *All You Need Is Love* was played in *The Prisoner* final episode, *Fall Out.*[v]

The underground *Oz* magazine was launched, 'pirate' offshore radio was outlawed homosexuality and abortion were 'legalised' and theatre censorship came to an end. Movies were released such as *Blow Up*, *The Graduate*, *Casino Royale*, *You Only Live Twice* and *Bonnie and Clyde*. Colour TV broadcasts began in Britain (not on the channel showing *The Prisoner*) and there was a tragic Cape Kennedy astronaut disaster, plus the "Torrey Canyon" oil supertanker catastrophe. The revolutionary Che Guevara died, Dr. Christian Barnard performed the first human heart transplant and China exploded its first hydrogen bomb. The Six Day Israeli-Arab war started, while the US and USSR proposed a nuclear non-proliferation treaty.

Although *The Prisoner* was not on TV screens in Britain any more, the series was soon to be shown in the US and in France. Half a million people were about to gather at Woodstock, in New York State for an extended music festival. On stage, *Hair*, the musical, excited or shocked audiences. At the cinema, *2001: A Space Odyssey*, *Yellow Submarine*, *Bullitt* and *Barbarella* were among the top movies. Apollo 7 performed an eleven day orbital flight, Robert F. Kennedy and Martin Luther King Jnr. were assassinated, Richard Nixon was elected US president and Jacqueline Kennedy married Aristotle Onassis. Elsewhere, Soviet forces invaded Czechoslovakia, students were rioting in Paris and other European cities, Communists in Vietnam launched the Tet offensive and 'pop' artist Andy Warhol was shot, although he survived. The times, as Bob Dylan sang, were a-changin' and the like of them will never be seen again. In today's world of political correctness, technology, mobility and integration, there are new trends, which would not have been imaginable at the time of *The Prisoner*. In the sixties there were reports of war, attempted and successful moon landings, plus looks at the future: how the modern home would be, the gadgets we would use and the huge amounts of leisure we would enjoy. Nowadays, the Internet is often the main point of reference and newspapers become sources of gossip, or pictures of the rich and famous.

McGoohan, through his seventeen *Prisoner* episodes, challenged people to think and to question. Those same episodes have managed to survive the passage of time through four decades, somehow serving the same purpose: to make people look at their own lives, at the way in which the powers that be control all of us and at our own privacy and individuality. These

---

[v] With its Vietnam suggested scenes of multiple airborne helicopters, plus launching of an intercontinental ballistic missile – or moon rocket – and, for the first time in the series, a climax of machine gun massacring.

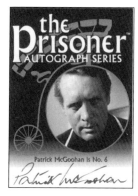

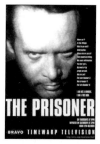
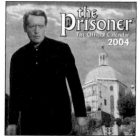

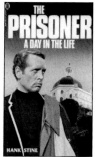

A collection of *Prisoner* and *Danger Man* memorabilia and magazines

are the aspects which are not contained in news bulletins or papers; *The Prisoner* may have reflected the sixties, but the series overall also encapsulated many issues of life in general.

The ultimate message of *The Prisoner* is that the hero (or anti-hero, depending upon one's view) is his own captor, a prisoner of himself. In this way the series cleverly, and possibly unintentionally, has caused viewers to examine their own worlds. *The Prisoner* craves analysis, forcing questions to be raised. Everybody eventually comes up with his or her own conclusions, with any one opinion being as valid as the next. The fairy tale location, the Village, can be regarded as a microcosm of the world and society as a whole. The amorphous guardian balloon may represent our own inner fears, or personal nightmare, being a faceless and formless enemy. The main character's resignation suggests a burdened conscience: whenever a difficult problem or decision is being mentally resolved, brain cells continually process an individual's own reasoning.

So who was Number Six? What was his former occupation? Why did he resign? Why was he taken to The Village, where is it and who runs it? In the penultimate episode, *Once upon a Time*, Number Six is regressed back to childhood. During intense questioning he is brought up to date and finally lurches towards freedom in the finale *Fall Out*. At last we meet the mystery figure, Number One. The prison is destroyed and the man emerges free, his own person. A single closing screen end credit describes him only as *Prisoner*. And yet, when the former Number Six reaches his London home, his front door emits the same electronic hum as did the automatic door of his recently vacated Village apartment. So did he escape, were his experiences all imagined, maybe even a case of mental breakdown? During seventeen episodes, the prisoner has fought many battles, his struggles sometimes taking on mythological proportions, almost resembling an odyssey. As for the meaning of it all, McGoohan instructs us through a key line of dialogue from his *Once upon a Time* script: "Ask on, ask yourself!"

In fact, the autobiographical aspects of *Once upon a Time*[vi] provide a separate and tantalising facet to the *Prisoner* series. The script for this penultimate episode was penned by McGoohan, who locked himself away to write the screenplay. This ran only to thirty six pages, while the normal length for television hour-long productions was around fifty five pages. His personal details were deliberately inserted by him and elements of the story were clearly going to require a great deal of improvisation from the actors. Co-star Leo McKern was concerned about the extent of the ad-libbing which would be required of him, although he found it an interesting challenge. As the script was distributed amongst the crew, props master Mickey O'Toole noticed the shortfall in the number of pages, as well as seeing the name of the scriptwriter on the front: Archibald Schwarz. Not knowing that this was a humorous pseudonym which McGoohan had used, O'Toole went to the star, telling him that the script length was inadequate and that its content was "rubbish." On some pages McGoohan had simply penned what appeared to be nonsense: one example is the words of the nursery rhyme "Pop Goes the Weasel," where the characters just shout "Pop" at each other, repeatedly. In another scene, the pair recite numbers out loud. *Once upon a Time*, directed by McGoohan, presents several scenes, played out in a closed room, with fellow actor Leo McKern as Number Two. McGoohan introduces stages of his own life, through an interrogation by the Village leader. The action in the sealed chamber begins with an early reference to the star's life in the theatre:

[vi] See also later in this book, page 162.

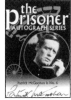

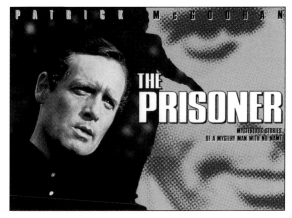

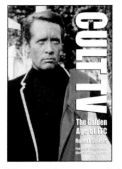

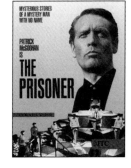

An assortment of *Prisoner* and *Danger Man* memorabilia, brochures and covers.

Number Two: (regressing Number Six back to childhood) Come ahead, son – let's see what you're made of. All the world's a stage and all the men and women merely players. They have their exits and their entrances, and one man in his time plays many parts.[vii]

In a later scene, set at school, the two men are dressed as teacher and pupil, respectively, in attire which would have been the norm during McGoohan's Ratcliffe College days:

Number Two: (wearing headmaster's hat and gown) "Take off your hat in my presence."
Number Six: (removing straw boater) "Sorry, sir."
Number Two: "You were talking in class."
Number Six: "No, sir."
Number Two: "You refuse to admit it."
Number Six: "I wasn't, sir."

Also drawn from Ratcliffe, McGoohan's boxing prowess is remembered in the episode:

Number Two: (in padded helmet, sparring with Number Six) "Come on, school boy! Not too much swing! Keep 'em down! Keep 'em short! Again! Hup! Good boy! Come on, champ! Hit me! Hook! Good! That's it, boy!"

Even McGoohan's banking days are recalled, as he applies for work, with reference being made to his attained maths qualifications and his daily duties as a bank post-room clerk, licking stamps:

Number Two: (conducting an employment interview) "Why, exactly, do you want this job?"
Number Six: "What's a job?"
Number Two: "No respect for tradition for an old established firm of bankers."
Number Six: "I was very good at mathematics."
Number Two: "Yes, of course. My dear boy, you don't expect a man of your talents would be wasted in licking stamps do you?"
Number Six: "Never!"
Number Two: "Congratulations!"
Number Six: "Ask the manager."
Number Two: "Manager?"
Number Six: "The bank manager. He knows I'm good at figures."

A common misconception arises from *Once Upon A Time*, when Leo McKern, as Number Two, delivers the line "Report to my study in the morning *break*." Many who claim that Number Six was John Drake, from the earlier *Danger Man* series, believe the line to be "Report to my study in the morning, *Drake*." Similarly, in the series' opening sequence, "You are Number Six" is heard by some as "*You are, Number Six*," in answer to the prisoner's question, "Who is Number One?" This would support the suggestion that Number Six was regarded as Number One from the outset. Unfortunately the early scripts show that this was not the intention; the initial dialogue response to the question was written as, "You are *our* Number Six."

Scenes from *Once upon a Time* are once more shown at the start of *The Prisoner*'s closing segment, *Fall Out*. By the end of the final episode, McGoohan is seen driving his distinctive open sports car through London. The final shot of the episode is McGoohan's own face, filling the screen, the frame being identical to the one used in the opening episode, *Arrival*. Nobody could doubt that McGoohan's personality was the driving force behind the entire undertaking. An astrologer declared, "One of the more successful Pisceans of this world,

vii *As You Like It*, Act II, Scene VII, William Shakespeare.

McGoohan could go on to higher things. His interest in politics and the law, albeit from an outsider's point of view, may decide him in favour of a series in this vein. I don't think he will ever reach the heights he attained with 'The Prisoner,' but it would be nice if he decided to make a film, even a little one that explained it after all this time."[13]

Instead, McGoohan's comments have remained cryptic: "When I wrote the last episode, everyone thought I was mad. And, in effect, I was! Good thing too, deliberately so! I wanted something oblique. It's up to the public to work it out. To each his own interpretation. I still don't want to give one answer. What I have in my head is an allegorical conundrum. Unravel it yourself!"[14] Lew Grade, the cigar-wielding head of ATV, would not have been comforted by the star's posturing. The 'signing' of the actor and his new series having been done on a simple handshake, surely even Grade's affection for McGoohan would not have led to the company cheque book being taken out, if the series' later idiosyncrasies had been known of in advance. However, in his autobiography *Still Dancing*, Grade mentioned how *The Prisoner* series had become "a great cult series throughout the world." The television and film mogul recalled lunching at CBS, when he presented *The Prisoner* as a new production idea. He showed his lunch guests pictures of Portmeirion, the filming location, and had cemented a deal before the dessert course, with even financial terms agreed. After the first few *Prisoner* episodes had been made, the CBS Vice-President of Programming visited Grade in London and saw what was on offer. Worryingly, Grade recorded the visitor as remarking, "I really can't understand what it's all about." To solve the problem, a meeting was arranged with McGoohan, although this still did not deepen the Vice-President's understanding of the series.[15] It is clear that without Lew Grade and his being prepared to take a chance, the cult series would probably have met with many obstacles before it was permitted to be made for TV viewing, if at all. McGoohan had a hand in sealing the deal with CBS, as he recalled: "We finished … the last episode of *Danger Man* and the next Monday we were shooting *The Prisoner*. I got this first episode together and (Lew had) sold it to Mike Dann of CBS (who said 'I've seen this thing … you appear to have crossed over into something else … but what were all those people doing who were wandering about in the capes, in this Village place?' And I said, 'Well, they've been watching too much television.' To his credit, he laughed like a drain. So that helped the sale I think."[16]

Other writers have discussed *The Prisoner*. In a short-lived publication called *Twilight Zone*, Welch D. Everman stated, "In the amazing final episode, written and directed by McGoohan[viii] No. 6 survives the ultimate test – a traumatic confrontation with his own past – and goes on a surreal journey through the secret labyrinths of The Village and his own mind. Finally, he is offered a choice: freedom, or the position of No. 2. He rejects both, destroys The Village and escapes to London where, unfortunately, life is not very different from the world he just left. No. 6 is as much a prisoner of his own self as he is of the powers that be. Since *The Prisoner*, the anonymous authorities who control television's Village have come up with little or nothing to match the series' power and intelligence."[17] Richard Last provided an opposite view: "*The Prisoner* was a warning of what can happen when gimmickry and camera technique take over from creative thinking. From start to finish this monstrously drawn-out series depended on what should have been purely ancillary devices – a fantastic barrage of sub-science fiction machines,

---

[viii] McGoohan wrote and directed under his own name and also using pseudonyms: Paddy Fitz and Joseph Serf. He also wrote under another name, but which did not appear in the screen credits, being that of Archibald Schwarz: see page 160.

ceaseless camera cutting and the deliberate creation of pretentious confusion. Laid bare, the script had the calibre of a horror-comic strip. Beneath the eyewash, one could faintly discern the glimmerings of a crude rudimentary Orwellian message. This was hopelessly overlaid by the super *Doctor Who* format and undermined by the semi-literate gibberish that frequently passed as dialogue."[18]

However, *The Individualist*, published by *The Society for Individual Liberty*, declared that both McGoohan's series, *Danger Man* and *The Prisoner*, "are easily the most important television productions in existence today. They combine intriguing entertainment with the most fundamental philosophical-moral-portrayal of an independent human being. McGoohan's work at this time is just beginning to be recognised. This recognition will continue to be more penetrating and widespread with the passing of time."[19]

Another organisation, under a 'Libertarian' banner, published analyses of the cult series, commenting: "McGoohan's Village is a portrayal of the essentials of our own society – with its vicious bromides of 'social responsibility,' its dominant ideologies of altruism and collectivism, its conformity, and the paternalistic coercion of the 'Welfare State.' The theme of *The Prisoner* was strikingly clear … the individual versus the collective."[20] One more publication in the series added: "Society, it seems, whether conventional or non-traditional, has little tolerance for individual identity. Thus, by attempting to form an individual identity, the seeker walls himself off from any and all societies; he creates his own prison."[21]

This book's writer was quoted in a French book about *The Prisoner*: "For many, McGoohan portrays the safeguarding of freedom and individuality. It is as though the character of Number 6 represents the never-ending challenge to our struggles in life (with) the establishment. McGoohan himself stands against the erosion of free thought and free choice. His character, Number 6, is frequently applauded as a role-model – a man who is confident, resourceful and honourable. The Village, in which he is trapped, shows us the comfortable lives of its citizens, who are brainwashed and subjected to constant surveillance. The rebellion by one man influences and dares us to find answers to the many questions (being posed). *The Prisoner* series, I have said before, is the sum of its parts and in my opinion it is impossible to choose certain episodes or plots to consider in isolation. I think that (the series) will continue to demand scrutiny and provoke argument and debate. Unlike other television series, *The Prisoner* will always defy classification. I hope that it will continue to be appreciated for its high standards of creativity, original ideas, direction, acting, scripts, music and camerawork. (McGoohan) presents on one side a doctrine of responsibility and conscience. On the other side (the series) represents unrest and unanswered questions. The (final) episode … suggests that we might be in danger of destroying our planet – or our ideals. The statement 'Be Seeing You' can also be spoken as a question – 'Be Seeing You?'"[22]

As a kind of *Danger Man* reprise, in one of the last *Prisoner* episodes *The Girl Who Was Death*, McGoohan again donned his flat cap and raincoat garb, seen in the earlier series.[ix] By then, he obviously believed that he was able to do what he liked with his unique and ever-changing series. As the 'swinging decade' was drawing to a close, McGoohan

---

[ix] For a late action scene in the episode, McGoohan had to hold on to the underneath of a helicopter taking off. He rose with the craft several metres in the air, executing a truly dangerous stunt. In the episode, names of production team members appeared on signs: David (Tomblin) Dough, Brendan (Stafford) Bull and Leonard (Harris) Snuffit. An estate agent's sign in *Fall Out* bore the name Lageu, being that of the set dresser.

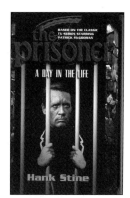
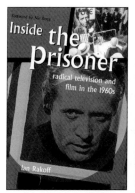

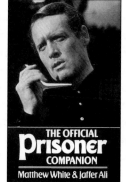
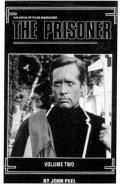
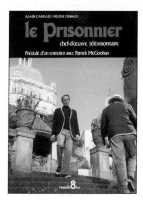
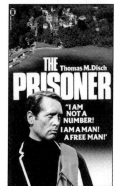

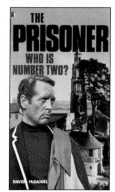

Various book and comic covers relating to *The Prisoner*

contended with more requests for interviews. In his words, "The interview has become a disease, hasn't it? Everybody's out there, doing interviews, writing books. They've got all the answers. It's the great leveller. Boy! I think it's interesting to observe people from a distance sometimes, to work out what they are getting at without the interview. People lower themselves to the level of the interview, on the late talk shows for instance." The actor's words seemed to evince a punitive doctrine for himself and for everybody else. "It would be arrogant to say it's essential for every man to do the equivalent of getting down on his knees and conceding that there is something bigger than he is, and within whose shadow he lives. Because once you go out and say 'I know better than whatever that power or force is' it doesn't work out. And a man has to suffer. It's bad to have it easy."[23]

McGoohan was asked by a journalist, "Do you consider No. 6 was an anti-hero?" the actor replied. "No, I don't. He is a prisoner of society. I think he's like a bank clerk."[x] The actor asserted that the series was originally conceived as an entertainment piece, rather than a parable. "Entertainment itself is a therapy and if one sees something that's good and well done you walk away from it feeling uplifted. I mean even if it's a tragedy, for instance, *King Lear*, if you see it well done you can walk out of the theatre feeling uplifted, although there are dead bodies all over the stage."[24] McGoohan said in another interview that he had real concerns about the safety of the world, with more and more weapons being stockpiled by the super powers and their allies. Eventually he felt that something would have to give, like a volcano. As to the shoot-out ending of *The Prisoner's* closing episode *Fall Out*, he could find no conflict in the way which Number Six used violence to escape to attain freedom. It is of note that McGoohan felt that too often in television shows, there were killings. No wonder the star was always pleased that *The Prisoner* stirred up debate: he seemed to have a fair degree of controversial arguments raging within his own mind. However, one media reporter did not hold back any criticism in his account of *The Prisoner's* seventeen week run. He described the ending: "The truth seemed to be a kind of self-humiliation in which McGoohan discovered that his personal ego was the beginning and end of his troubles. It is unfortunate that the thinking was somewhat woolly – far too obscure to get over to a mass audience. If it failed as a concept it is certainly nobody's fault but McGoohan's. But at least he got the viewing millions out of their Sunday night predictable rut. Technically the series has been a triumph. If its message of the faceless men who control our destinies didn't come through then this is a fault in scripting which should have been seen and remedied months ago."[25]

McGoohan wrote a foreword to a book on cult television shows, commenting how the programmes were made by people who believed passionately in their work and thereby transmitted their enthusiasm to like-minded viewers.[xi] Karen Langley is one such enthusiast, having been secretary of the *Prisoner* Appreciation Society for three decades[xii] and having had contact with fans of the series from around the world. Her belief is that the series has "a particular resonance with women, something which was noticeable during the growing women's movements of the last century," and that this endures. "In *Prisoner* episodes there are women playing strong characters, with storylines raising issues of freedom, or rights of the individual. Patrick McGoohan caused people to think and to

---

[x] As McGoohan once was.
[xi] 1993, see Chapter Eleven , page 251.
[xii] See page 201 as to the society's formation in the late seventies.

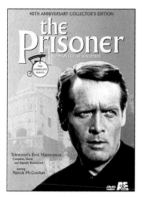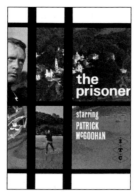

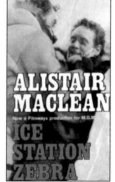

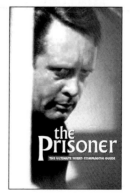

Various book, video and sheet music covers featuring *The Prisoner* and McGoohan's other works

question everything around them. I have been pleased to see in the Appreciation Society – with fifty thousand members having been enrolled during its life – how women at *Prisoner*-based events have always had an equal voice and presence. Apart from *The Prisoner*'s entertainment values, one effect often overlooked is the way it raises consciousness, often with student admirers of the series and especially women."[26]

One recent writer remarked, "No book about television in the sixties would be complete without mention of *The Prisoner*, such was its impact ... between 1967 and 1968. Imaginative, intriguing and allegorical, it's a series that has baffled and engrossed viewers in equal measures for ... forty years. The series has become a cult classic that every TV aficionado simply has to have in their DVD library. At the heart ... was Patrick McGoohan's superb performance as Number Six. Abstract, psychedelic and, in sixties' parlance, 'far out'... the series asked so many questions, with the ... answers open to your own interpretation, that you needed to take a complete rest after watching an episode until your head stopped spinning. It was fascinating stuff and it's not surprising that the programme ... still has legions of devoted fans around the world."[27] As another writer observed, "Up to this point most ITC live-action series tended to focus on one (usually male) central character, a formula ... which was stunningly deconstructed in McGoohan's *The Prisoner*."[28] Clive Donner, an early *Danger Man* director, opined, "*The Prisoner* (was) the granddaddy of all cult TV shows. McGoohan revelled in the fact that many of the allegorical aspects of his pet project flummoxed audiences, who kept watching out of a sheer morbid fascination to find out just what the hell was going on."[29] This, according to a recent reporter holds the main appeal of *The Prisoner*, the series being described as "the first TV show to prove that the journey is more important than the destination. You travel agog, and don't mind when at the end, the answers are incomprehensible or even non-existent."[30]

However, this writer believes that McGoohan achieved something with *The Prisoner* which is often missed by reviewers: he created the vogue for a deeper analysis of mainstream television. Whether *The Prisoner* is dismissed as gimmicky, or acclaimed as one of TV's finest achievements, it continues to invite further analysis. The four decades of media reviews and commentaries by researchers and writers have resulted in what is nowadays a truism: *The Prisoner* is one of the most discussed and debated television programmes of all time.[xiii] Given the series' high cost, the strange subject matter and the risk factor, one can only thank, or blame, the 1960s as being an era in which challenging British television was cherished and cultivated. The sheer professionalism of the product and expertise of the many actors, technicians, artists and composers ensured delivery of a fascinating series. Then of course there is the main man behind the series, without whom *The Prisoner* could have become a standard action-adventure series. Handing an actor and star like McGoohan almost total control over the making of a TV series might have been unprecedented, but he produced something which no other person could have done. Words like "enigmatic," "cult," "classic," "allegorical" and so on are not those usually applied to a mainstream television action-adventure show.

One final aspect of *The Prisoner* which could not have been predicted is how the series is always name-dropped when something is needed for comparison with a modern, quirky TV show. The likes of *Twin Peaks*, *Lost*, *Life on Mars* and others are frequently referenced to *The*

[xiii] In 1969, *Fall Out* was nominated for the science fiction Hugo award for Dramatic Presentation – the eligibility year being 1968 – along with the movies *Charly*, *Rosemary's Baby* and *Yellow Submarine*. The winner of the award was *2001: A Space Odyssey*

Director Don Chaffey turns McGoohan into a pawn on the human chess lawn, in *Checkmate*.

Prisoner, suggesting that McGoohan's unique series has set the definitive TV cult standard for all time. The actor's old Sheffield repertory friend Paul Eddington[xiv] summed up the phenomenon succinctly: "I certainly think *The Prisoner* is one of the most remarkable series ever made and the fact that Patrick was director, producer and star of it is very significant."[31]

[1]   Photo Screen, September, 1968, Joseph Curreri
[2]   Source not verified
[3]   The Spectator, 5th March, 1977
[4]   New Zealand TV Weekly, 9th October, 1967, Ronald Simpson – courtesy of Bruce Clark
[5]   Proof Magazine, Neil Martinson, details unknown
[6]   The Sun, 1967, Richard Last
[7]   The Daily Mail, 1967, Peter Black
[8]   The Daily Sketch, 1967, Robert Ottaway
[9]   *The Prisoner of Portmeirion*, 1985, Max Hora
[10] Collected interviews from *TV Times, Daily Sketch, ITC Pressbook, Woman's Journal, Sunday Times, Daily Mirror, Photoplay and Pace* magazine, printed in *The Prisoner in Portmeirion*, 1999, Roger Langley
[11] Ibid
[12] Ibid
[13] Peter West, *Man of Many Parts*, 1979, astrology magazine
[14] Premiere Magazine, October 1995, Jean Yves Katelan (translations Rosemary Camilleri and Jane Rawson)
[15] Still Dancing: My Story, HarperCollins, 1987, Lew Grade
[16] Lew Grade: The Greatest of them All, 24th and 25th December, 2006, BBC Radio 2.
[17] Twilight Zone Magazine, article by Welch D. Everman, date unknown
[18] UK newspaper article by Richard Last, details unknown
[19] The Individualist, The Society for Individual Liberty, April,1970, F. R. Chamberlain
[20] Different Values: An Analysis of Patrick McGoohan's The Prisoner, New Libertarian no. 34/35, September, 1980, Chris R. Tame
[21] The Prisoner and the Question of Identity, Libertarian Alliance Cultural Notes no. 13, 1987, Lee Roger Taylor, Jr.
[22] *Le Prisonnier*, Alain Carrazé/ Hélène Oswald; Huitième Art, 1989
[23] Pace Magazine, December, 1969, Henry Pelham Burn
[24] 1978, Steven Mori, details unknown
[25] British newspaper, 1968, James Thomas, details unknown

[xiv] Eddington appeared in the opening *Prisoner* episode, *Arrival*

[26] Interview with the writer, 2006
[27] *That Was The Decade That Was*, 2006, Michael O'Mara Books, Richard Webber
[28] Screenonline, Sergio Angelini
[29] The Independent Online, 30th November, 2006, Robert Sellers
[30] The Dominion Post, New Zealand, 25th January, 2007, Jane Clifton
[31] Letter to Six of One, The Prisoner Appreciation Society, 12th May, 1977

CHAPTER SEVEN
The Prisoner: Fall Out

"You are the only individual. We need you."
The Prisoner: Fall Out (1968)

When *Fall Out* brought the curtain down on the British debut run of *The Prisoner*, early in 1968, McGoohan was to be found at his production desk at MGM, tidying up loose ends. He told a journalist, "Now that it's all over I admit we didn't bring it off with all the stories, but I can only blame myself. I agree it hasn't come off 100 per cent. Certainly some of the stories may have been confused for some viewers. My own teenaged daughter was confused. But on the other hand, we've sold it to America and all over the world.[i] As far as I'm concerned it's explained, but I admit a great deal is still left open." The star told his listener that he had left a message for viewers: "You still want to know its message? Then it's this: the most dangerous thing in the world is an attitude of mind. Each episode relates to events happening around us, even though it may be in fantasy. There's a basis of reality throughout – if you can spot it. This is the point of it all … we're all being puppeted. We're all becoming Numbers."[1]

An Austrian magazine quoted McGoohan as saying, "When my experiment fails, it is only my fault." The feature observed that *The Prisoner* had misfired in Britain, but that it was not necessarily only McGoohan's fault. "He did what he did, but the audience, amused by hundreds of corpses on TV, made insensitive by gallons of artificial blood, did not appreciate watching mental tortures." The article closed with McGoohan's own rationale of *The Prisoner*, "The series deals with the loss of humanity, of individuality, something

---

[i] Records held by PolyGram showed that within three decades (later figures from Carlton and Granada, plus video and DVD sales, are not available) *The Prisoner* was screened in sixty countries: Abu Dhabi, Australia, Austria, Bahrain, Barbados, Belgium, Canada, Cyprus, Denmark, Dubai, Eire, Finland, France, Gabon, Germany, Ghana, Gibraltar, Greece, Holland, Hong Kong, Iran, Israel, Italy, Ivory Coast, Jamaica, Japan, Jordan, Kenya, Korea, Lebanon, Liechtenstein, Luxembourg, Malta, Malaysia, Mauritius, Monaco, Morocco, New Zealand, Nigeria, Norway, Pakistan, Saudi Arabia, Sierra Leone, Singapore, South Africa, South America, Spain, Swaziland, Sweden, Switzerland, Taiwan, Thailand, Tunisia, Turkey, Uganda, UK, USA, Yugoslavia, Zambia, Zimbabwe.

McGoohan behind his desk at MGM Studios, Borehamwood

happening to all of us. That's what I wanted to say with it. But it seems I could not make myself understood."[2]

One writer commented, "It is plausible to see *The Prisoner* as a parable of the modern world, an updated, Kafkaesque micro-society in which leisure on a mass scale has brought with it a sheep-like conformity, a 'soft' repression in which 'clean' techniques of mind manipulation are used to discipline troublemakers who assert their individuality." The analysis continued: "Manifestly, viewers were invited to draw their own conclusions, a prospect that excited a cult minority but undoubtedly bewildered most. This was a logical consequence of the series' existentialist strategy of interpolating viewers to recognise their own unfreedom, to confront the jailer within themselves". However, it was argued that the series suffered from "an ideological thinness, an obsessive concern with individual freedom in a setting which is too facile to allow the issue to be treated with the necessary complexity."[3]

Perhaps, in retrospect, the actor could have given out a few pointers along the way, instead of leaving audiences to fathom the content of the series, especially that of *Fall Out*. The symbolism was not popular with all viewers, especially as McGoohan had promised that the final episode would explain what had been happening. Frustrated members of the public tried to make sense of the finale, an "abstract piece of television,"[4] as it was described. According to a recent book, looking back on *The Prisoner*, "(The series) ended abruptly in *Fall Out*, an episode that cast more doubt than light over the proceedings. Initial responses were favourable ..., but as the lack of resolution became ever more apparent, it attracted increasing hostility, at least on its first screening. McGoohan recalled the anger of viewers at that last episode: 'Outraged, they jammed the switchboard at ITV: they had been led on, swindled, double-crossed.' The refusal to explain, the sheer confusion that was engendered, however, have ensured that the series has retained a huge cult following. Key to its enduring appeal is its external location filming in Portmeirion, a setting both photogenic and imprecise; it was, said McGoohan, 'Built in an unusual architectural style, it could well become a place of isolation where people all over the world could be put away.'"[5]

Press articles attempted a debriefing of *Fall Out*, claiming that McGoohan's character had been undergoing a test to see if he, Number Six, could lead the country at a time of national crisis, as prime minister. Another theory was that McGoohan was condemning the futility of war and criticising world powers for stockpiling weapons of mass destruction. The firing of a rocket in *Fall Out* could be seen either as an inter-continental ballistic missile being launched, or even a wish to leave the planet and meet God, somewhere in the cosmos. It was even reported that McGoohan was making "a statement about Vietnam,"[6] the long-running war, involving the US, which occupied much of the sixties and continued into the next decade. The actor would allude to this in some interviews.

One metaphysical angle, peddled by the series' star, about the last episode's interpretation, would have been lost on many audience members, at the time of viewing. McGoohan claimed that when the Number Six character finally met with Number One, he was about to discover that the greatest enemy on earth was his own self. The final scenes in the Village, in *Fall Out*, were tightly-edited to be fast-moving, and the meeting with Number One was only of a few seconds' duration. It was no wonder that the public had no idea of what was being thrust at them. However, McGoohan was unrepentant: "I think there were fifty-two frames of the shot where they pulled off the monkey mask.[ii] I could have held it there for a good two minutes and put on a subtitle saying, you know, 'It's him!' but I wasn't going to pander to a mentality that couldn't perceive what I was trying to say."[7]

To remedy the situation, ATV hurriedly and bravely put out a printed 'explanation' of the *Prisoner* series' final episode, making ready no doubt for an expected onslaught of US audience questions.[iii] It was referred to as a "Plain Man's Guide" and covered each aspect of *Fall Out*. The content was reproduced by ITC New York, as the *Speculative Guide to the Prisoner*, as well as being published in ATV's in-house newsletter. Although unprecedented for a mainstream television show – especially at that time – the broadcasting company was able to fend off viewer queries by providing a copy of the guide. The name of the author was not disclosed, but his article appears here:

The Prisoner was indeed controversial. During and immediately after the London transmission on Sunday, February 4, the ATV Duty Officer logged well over 150 calls – in the main from a confused public. The following day the mail began to flood in. Strangely enough, the trends of the previous evening were reversed with a heavy correspondence in favour of the series. Below, one of our correspondents gives his views on the series and explains what *The Prisoner* meant to him.

'What's it all about, Patrick?' This question was posed by many puzzled viewers who, fattened on a diet of pre-digested television, found thinking for themselves something of a strain. The press were more cautious – their reactions mixed. Was it all hokum? Has Patrick McGoohan taken us all for a ride or was this the most penetrating study – the most vivid of comments on modern civilisation – in the history of British television? The answer, like many aspects of the series, is all in the mind. For example, one may look at an abstract painting and draw from it one's own conclusions. The conclusions I drew from *The Prisoner* – particularly the last episode – were disturbing and frustrating to me personally. Disturbing because, in my interpretation, they reflected my own innermost emotions – frustrating because, unlike Patrick McGoohan, I am not clever enough to find an outlet for those emotions.

A message came through to me. Whether or not the message I got was the one Mr. McGoohan intended, I do not know, but *The Prisoner* made me think. It made thousands of

---

[ii] The ape mask made an evolutionary point – guess whose face was underneath it.
[iii] The US premiere is covered later in this chapter.

ATV Network Limited

DIRECTORS:
LORD RENWICK, K.B.E. (CHAIRMAN)
LEW GRADE (DEPUTY CHAIRMAN and JOINT MANAGING DIRECTOR)
ROBIN D. GILL (JOINT MANAGING DIRECTOR)
JACK GILL (FINANCE DIRECTOR)
SIR ERIC CLAYSON
NORMAN COLLINS
LEONARD MATHEWS
BILL WARD.

A T V House · 17 Gt Cumberland Place · London · w·1

Cables & Telegrams: *Telephone: 01-262 8040*
Ayteevee · London · W·1   *Telex: 23762*

VC/IB.   26th September, 1968.

Mr. R. J. ▓▓▓▓,
▓▓▓▓▓▓▓▓▓▓▓▓▓▓▓▓▓▓▓
▓▓▓▓▓▓▓▓▓▓▓▓▓▓▓▓▓▓▓
07304, U.S.A.

Dear Mr. ▓▓▓,

                          'The Prisoner'
                          ─────────────

        We acknowledge receipt of your communication; its contents have
been noted with interest.

        We are sorry to hear that you found the final episode of the above
series confusing. We felt that, from the point of view of individual
satisfaction, viewers would want to draw their own conclusions and place
upon this episode their personal interpretation.

        However, we thought you might be interested in the enclosed personal
analysis prepared by one of our correspondents who gives his views on
this final programme.

        We are always pleased to hear from our viewers, and thank you for
taking the trouble in writing to us.

                                    Yours sincerely,

                                    Irene Bignall

                                    Irene Bignall (Miss),
                                    Viewers' Correspondence,
        Enc.   ATV NETWORK LIMITED
        ───   ───────────────────────

ATV's letter to an enraged fan, sending an explanation of the final episode

people think – and it made tens of thousands of people talk. Patrick McGoohan has
forcefully shaken the viewing public out of its state of mental lethargy. What did *The
Prisoner* mean to me? Here I give my personal interpretation in the form of a plain man's
guide to 'The Prisoner.'

        The Village: It did not exist in any materialistic form. It symbolised the prison that is
man's own mind.

The Numbers – No. 6, etc.: This represents man's lack of freedom – the stifling of individual liberty by authority.

The Balloon – Rover: Symbolises repression and the guardianship of corrupt authority which, when corruption is finally overcome, disintegrates.

"The Penny-Farthing: Represents the slowness of progress in our modern civilisation.

The Hippy Character (as played by Alexis Kanner): Symbolises youth in rebellion against the establishment and, as in the closing sequence of the young man trying to thumb a lift first in one direction and then in another on a motorway, youth not knowing, or caring, in which direction it goes.

The Former No. 2 (as played by Leo McKern): A former trusted member of the establishment who, having broken away, is accused of having bitten the hand that fed him and is being made by authority to pay for his failures.

The Prisoner starts on US TV, 1968, as pictured on this magazine

The Little Butler (Angelo Muscat): He represents the little men of every community, prepared to follow faithfully, like sheep, any established leader.

The break-out sequence, guns firing – overlaid by the theme, "Love, love, love": This was a protest against the paradoxes which exist in modern civilisation. Man, preaching love, love, love against the holocaust of war. A penetrating comment on the world situation – Vietnam, the Middle East, etc.

No. 1: The unveiling of No. 1 as Patrick McGoohan himself is representative of every man's desire to be No. 1 – to be the top dog.

The shouting-down of McGoohan by the hooded assembly: The inability of the ordinary man to make his voice heard – to put forward his viewpoint to the world."[8]

McGoohan had his own explanation for the end scenes of *Fall Out*, when the 'escaped prisoner,' returns to his London home, "He goes back to his little apartment – and the door opens on its own ... and you know it's going to start all over again. Because we continue to be prisoners. When that door opens on its own, you know that someone's in there waiting to start it all over again. He's got no freedom. Freedom is a myth. There's no final conclusion. We were fortunate to do something as audacious as that, because people do want the words 'The End' put up there. The final two words for this should have been 'The Beginning.'"[9]

Prisoner producer David Tomblin was also questioned about the series' closing episode, with its controversial imagery and symbolism. He was asked if he had contributed to the final script in any way, or whether it was totally McGoohan's work. His reply could not have been clearer: "That was him. He can take the blame for that! When the series came out it wasn't well received and I think that he was disappointed. He never said anything and we never discussed it, but he went off to Switzerland and ended up in America."[iv][10]

[iv] See next chapter.

Meanwhile, if 'preaching' via the medium of television, through *The Prisoner*, had not been enough, McGoohan began speaking out, mid-1968, about social issues, such as those addressed by the film *Poor Cow* (1967), along with movie morals. This was a true-life tale about the dismal life of an impoverished young London mother, living in squalor, one of the new breed of 'kitchen-sink,' docu-dramas. The movie had been an earlier successful and shocking television play. McGoohan found the film version to be "brilliantly made." He sympathised with the central female character, who could not obtain financial support or assistance with accommodation because of bureaucratic barriers. However, the actor felt that some things, which were too 'real,' should not be portrayed on screen.

He questioned, "Where are we going? We've just seen just about everything it's possible to see. I sometimes feel that the only thing left to do is for someone to walk about and urinate through the screen. They'd say this is just life, a documentary about urination. People say: 'We don't want to see it,' but unhappily, we all want to see it. *Poor Cow* (had an extra week) at every cinema. It's all part of the process of evolution, like the Paris see-through nudity fashions. It's part of the ultimate extreme of total exposure – of morals, immorality, everything. Then suddenly – wham! – the curtains will close and we'll all go back into hiding."[11]

When *The Prisoner* was screened in New Zealand, during 1968, a TV critic reviewed the phenomenon. The writer stated that the series was, "brilliantly contrived, the most intelligent and original piece of TV I have so far seen, which opens up barely-explored possibilities. For sheer inventiveness and depth, McGoohan's series was unforgettable."[12] A less enthusiastic reviewer from the same publication thought the series fell down in the writing and construction of its plots, branding it only "A good try."[13] The magazine also carried an interview with McGoohan, conducted in his office at MGM, Borehamwood. The actor volunteered, "The reactions are much as I expected, except for one thing. I've received far more favourable letters than I anticipated. Some have been pretty vitriolic. I had one the other day which began 'You b*st*rd!' and another which said 'I hope the tax man gets you.' But I've been more impressed by those from people who have taken the trouble to analyse what I have been trying to say." The interviewer offered his own take on *The Prisoner*, being that viewers are not watching John Drake or No. 6 or Patrick McGoohan. "We are watching ourselves. The Village symbolises the prison that is man's own mind. No. 1 is our own ego."[14]

Actor Kenneth Griffith[v], who appeared in the last two *Prisoner* episodes made,[vi] told a different New Zealand writer that *The Prisoner* and the Samuel Beckett stage play *Waiting for Godot*, were the only two productions in which he had starred, but had failed to comprehend. "No-one has ever been able to explain it, because Godot was open to so many interpretations. I got around to understanding it – but I couldn't explain it to you because what it meant to me was something very personal. *The Prisoner* is the same. It's an allegory and it's a comment on life. You can read into it what you like."[vii] [15] Griffith spoke of his role in the final *Prisoner* episode, *Fall Out*, as the president of the Village community; wigged and gowned, as if some English High Court judge. He related that McGoohan had left the

---

[v] See also page 191 regarding documentaries made by Griffith in collaboration with McGoohan.

[vi] *The Girl Who Was Death* and *Fall Out*.

[vii] The journalist wrote that his own opinion was that McGoohan was holding up a mirror, in which viewers would be able to see themselves; that the Village symbolised the prison that was man's own mind; the balloon symbolising repression; the butler presenting as the little man in every community, always willing to follow sheepishly; Number One being the evil, corrupting alter ego of each of us.

writing of a lengthy address speech to Griffith, who had to deliver it on screen: "A few days before we went into the studio Patrick told me that he hadn't got time to write his long speech (he was working too hard at the time: writing, producing, directing, acting), so would I write it myself; which I did. That was typical of him. He is a hard man, but he can be an open giver. But his mood and attitude can change in a moment. Yet, overall, he retains his remarkable quality which I value much."[16] Griffith also recalled the props master on *The Prisoner*, Mickey O'Toole, who was once the source of a misunderstanding. The Welsh actor was close friends with film star Peter O'Toole. In an episode in which Griffith was dressed as Napoleon,[viii] he wanted to call one of his troops "O'Toole." He remembered McGoohan rejecting the idea, saying, "Kenneth, I don't think we ought to have any private jokes, do you?" The star had mistakenly thought that his fellow actor was referring to Mickey.[17]

Griffith reaffirmed years later: "*The Prisoner* was an extraordinary experience, basically because of Patrick McGoohan. What he achieved in it was closely married to George Markstein, whom I knew and liked very much. The departure of McGoohan has been a great loss to the British film industry and to British television. But he always, in a strange way, underrated himself. I think he could have made a great contribution to keeping us more vitally alive here in Britain. On *The Prisoner*, McGoohan drove himself into the ground. Apparently nothing else seemed to exist and he worked from early in the morning until late at night. You bloody well had to keep up with him, I tell you."[18] Griffith had not yet run out of accolades for the series and its star: "The series was a remarkable achievement, out of a very unusual and talented man. I have long felt frustrated that he has not continued to create from his genius. When everything that I know about Patrick McGoohan is put into my scales, I am left with great admiration for him and strangely a deep affection."[19]

In his autobiography[ix] Griffith devoted several pages to Patrick McGoohan, describing him as, "One of the most remarkable personalities to have hit the world's television screens. With perhaps Douglas Fairbanks Senior and Peter O'Toole, he is the most dynamic personality that I have ever witnessed on screen. I have long believed that he has woefully, not consciously, smothered his own potential." Clearly believing that McGoohan had squandered his talents, Griffith revealed that he had even once told the actor that he could be as big a star as Steve McQueen and a pin-up to boot. The recipient of the flattery had replied that his daughter had a picture of McQueen on her wall and that young people would never think of her father in that way.[20] Who knows how high up the stardom ladder McGoohan would have climbed, if he had moved to the US at the time of the premiere of *The Prisoner* there, instead of waiting several more years?

In fact, *The Prisoner* was first broadcast in colour[x] on US TV, in the summer of 1968, with a re-run the next year. The series' CBS airing attracted millions of viewers, although it does not seem that McGoohan did anything much to promote the series, nor in Europe, where screenings began the next year. However, the show did well enough on its own and has always enjoyed a glowing US endorsement: "'The Prisoner' is truly that rare commodity – a television classic."[21] The same writer appreciated the star's performance: "Tall and dashing, his cool demeanor and underlying intensity are perfect for a television screen. His performances are completely devoid of histrionic fat. Here, distilled, is television

---

viii The character was originally intended to be Hitler.
ix *The Fool's Pardon* (1994)
x Britain started colour transmissions from 1967, but not on the ITV channels which screened *The Prisoner*.

minimalism at its best."[22] According to *TV Guide*, the Americans were joining the rest of the world in trying to figure out what the new multi-million dollar series was all about. US audiences were clearly rising to the challenge, as they were told that the show had baffled viewers in Britain, when it ended several months earlier. *The Prisoner* was promoted as the most expensive series to be produced for television so far. "The budget is $168,000 an episode, which is an almost unheard of price in Britain. It is now running in thirty four countries," reported one article.[23]

Lifelong McGoohan fan Bruce Clark watched the entire runs of *Danger Man/Secret Agent* and *The Prisoner*, during his home US broadcasts. As North American organiser of the *Prisoner* Appreciation Society, during nearly twenty five years and continuing as its internet webmaster, he accumulated a wealth of material about the actor, as well as having limited direct contact with him. Clark regularly assisted ITC's New York base, or its licensees, with Stateside airings of the series and distribution, including video and laserdisc releases. He also located the 'alternative' versions of two early *Prisoner* episodes and ran a successful one man campaign to cause screenings of the show in his Philadelphia area and in other states.

"I first watched McGoohan's spy series during its several years on US TV, but on June 1st, 1968, I was knocked out by his new show, *The Prisoner*. I know, from my own experiences, that across North America, during four decades, this cult classic has always been hugely popular. Nothing like it had been on US television before and I doubt that it will again. Many people from around the world email me through my website and there's no doubt that McGoohan and his TV shows and appearances – including *Columbo* – are regarded as the best."[24]

Most importantly, 1968 would see stardom beckoning for McGoohan. The actor's name was not unfamiliar in the US, but one writer thought the surname was a drawback. "The name McGoohan doesn't exactly ring a bell. McGoohan isn't exactly the name for an actor to project a hero – or to make a hit with the girls. Pat admits there has been talk of change. 'But,' he laughs, 'If Peter O'Toole didn't change his name, why should I?'" Certainly the Irish handle in no way prevented McGoohan from receiving a leading part in the blockbuster, *Ice Station Zebra* (1968).[xi] In this major Hollywood production,[xii] he played agent David Jones, his character not much changed from the one in *The Prisoner*, which the actor had temporarily left behind in Britain. Directed by John Sturges and based on the Alistair MacLean novel, *Zebra* came to the screen in Super Panavision.[xiii] At last, McGoohan's face was on giant billboards, alongside those of top stars Rock Hudson[xiv] and Ernest Borgnine.[xv] An all-male cast presented tough characters, with McGoohan's being as icy as the polar meteorological station to which was headed, on board a nuclear submarine. A US magazine reported, "Eight million dollars are riding on every 'take.' The big boys are sweating buckets. But the Britisher is cool. Patrick McGoohan is always cool!" The article continued, "Britain's highest paid and most seriously-committed TV actor ... delivers each line with completely professional bearing capped by a feeling of potential instant eruption.

[xi] The movie won an Oscar for Best Cinematography and Effects.

[xii] McGoohan also participated in a short promotional film, *The Man Who Makes the Difference*, featuring the work of John M. Stevens, the second unit cinematographer, who worked on *Ice Station Zebra*.

[xiii] The movie caused *2001: A Space Odyssey* – both Cinerama presentations – to be pulled off the circuit, as MGM were keen to get their new blockbuster into cinemas, even though *2001* was still drawing good audiences and making profits.

[xiv] McGoohan and Hudson would respectively both enjoy later US TV starring roles in the *Rafferty* series and the *McMillan and Wife* strand of *Mystery Movie*. The latter generic series also housed *Columbo*, in which McGoohan appeared several times.

[xv] The lead parts were originally offered to Gregory Peck, George Segal and David Niven (his proposed role being filled by McGoohan).

Handsome, exciting, he shows those Hollywood heroes the way it should be done." John Sturges was quoted as saying, "That man has movie star written all over him." According to the magazine, thirteen episodes of *The Prisoner* had been completed, "before Pat was called away for his stint on *Ice Station Zebra*."[25]

The actor later boasted proudly that *Zebra* became Howard Hughes' favourite movie and that the reclusive film maker and eccentric millionaire watched it over ninety times.[26] In the making of one dramatic scene, McGoohan, or a stunt actor, was to dive and rescue a naval officer from a flooded torpedo room. Being a strong swimmer, the star chose to do the scene himself, although Olympic swimming champion Murray Rose[xvi] accompanied him, in case anything went wrong. All went well, until the two men were up to their necks in rising water. Just before the 'take,' McGoohan whispered, "Now I've done it. My foot's stuck."[27] Rose dived and freed the actor's foot – tightly wedged in a torpedo rack – in the nick of time.

While the release of the film met with good reviews, the success of *Zebra* was not enough to propel McGoohan onto the Hollywood A list. The US press, at the time of McGoohan's 'Tinseltown' debut, described him as "A six-foot, two-inch lance of a man with electric blue eyes and sandy hair. McGoohan is Britain's highest paid television star, distinguished also as a stage actor who won 'Best Actor' award for his performance as *Brand*. But he dislikes the word star and says, 'Call me an actor and I'm flattered. A star can be a mere personality. It takes work to become an actor.'"[28] As for fame, McGoohan told the media, "Taken by itself it's a nuisance because it comes close to destroying privacy, which I regard as one of man's most precious rights." On the subject of TV he confessed, 'It's killing work. I'm getting out of television the moment I can make a clean break." Surprisingly, he opined, "Television's destroying rep, the greatest training ground in the world for anyone in my line. There used to be repertory theatres all over Britain. Since the rise of TV, relatively few have survived."[29]

In *Ice Station Zebra*, McGoohan still appeared to be in his Number Six guise: clipped vocal delivery and a penetrating glare. In one scene in the captain's submarine cabin, there is a battle of wits between McGoohan and Rock Hudson. The latter insists that he has the authority for the running of the underwater vessel, while his top secret passenger claims to have orders from the highest level, to do things his way. The confrontation ends with a fierce outburst from McGoohan who slams his fist down upon the table, Number Six style. A response from Hudson ends with a relatively meek thump of the table with balled fist and the audience is left in no doubt as to who gives the orders.

Variety review: "Action adventure film, in which US and Russian forces race to recover some compromising satellite photography from a remote polar outpost. Alistair MacLean's novel adapted into a screen story is seeded with elements of intrigue, as Rock Hudson takes aboard a British secret agent, Patrick McGoohan; an expatriate, professional anti-Communist Russian, Ernest Borgnine; and an enigmatic Marine Corps captain, Jim Brown. Action develops slowly, alternating with some excellent submarine interior footage, and good shots – of diving, surfacing and maneuvering under an ice field. Film's biggest acting asset is McGoohan, who gives his scenes that elusive 'star' magnetism. He is a most accomplished actor with a three-dimensional presence all his own."

New York Times review: "A top-secret Soviet spy satellite – using stolen Western

---

[xvi] Murray Rose was hailed as the most successful male Australian Olympian of all time, after winning six swimming medals.

technology – malfunctions and then goes into a descent that lands it near an isolated Arctic research encampment called Ice Station Zebra, belonging to the British, which starts sending out distress signals before falling silent. The atomic submarine "Tigerfish," commanded by Cmdr. James Ferraday (Rock Hudson), is dispatched with orders to get to Ice Station Zebra carrying three passengers, a Englishman going by the name of David Jones (Patrick McGoohan), a Soviet turncoat named Boris Vaslov (Ernest Borgnine) and an American Marine officer, Captain Anders (Jim Brown), who is supposed to command the Marine unit assigned to the mission. Jones is problem enough, as he is in command of the mission and he prefers to withhold as much information as it's possible to do from Ferraday, even at the risk of the Tigerfish's safety. Add to that the fact that Anders is suspicious of Vaslov, and Vaslov seems much too inquisitive and is telling even less of what he knows about the mission, and Ferraday has his hands full trying to get these men to the polar ice – 600 miles of dangerous travel – in just two days. When an attempt to break through the ice – coupled with some timely sabotage – kills one man and nearly destroys the boat, the men surrounding these contending parties start to understand just how high the stakes are for everyone. It turns out that the Soviets want what was aboard that satellite as much as the West does; indeed, both sides are frantic to get it, and, just as much, to keep the other side from getting it – and they're prepared to take it by brute force. Once Ferraday and his men arrive at Zebra, they find a disaster and still more mystery, with most of the men dead and the object that Mr. Jones is supposed to secure nowhere in evidence, and he and his two fellow men of mystery suddenly showing their killing instincts quite freely. And with the storm clearing from the Soviet side first, their planes and their paratroops are closing in on Ferraday, and his relative handful of men." (Bruce Eder, All Movie Guide)

McGoohan was offered another film role at this time, "a highly lucrative co-starring role in the David Niven-Deborah Kerr film *Prudence and the Pill* (1968). He declined, saying 'I'm just not in harmony with the subject matter.'" The actor admitted to being prepared to depict romance on screen, as it was "something that you create in the minds of the viewers." Against this, he added, "But sex is the antithesis of romance. It's phoney. I'm against promiscuous sex. I feel this personally and strongly because I have three daughters and I just don't want them to watch this kind of thing."[30]

Throughout this period, McGoohan gave many interviews. In one magazine, there was no introduction, no separating questions, just the unbroken transcription of the actor's comments, with even the interviewer's name being omitted: "The permissive society has come about because scientific knowledge is increasing so much faster than the ability of a thinking human being to keep up with it spiritually. Initially it was the nuclear bomb race, then the moon race. Everything is happening so fast. There is no time for meditation. The Beatles going off with the Maharishi – this is a sort of buffer for them. Meditation has come up like a new detergent that washes whiter and brighter." On the subject of the contraceptive pill, McGoohan felt that this was the most dangerous thing on earth, more dangerous than The Bomb. The actor expressed his belief: "It interferes with the natural functions of the body and we don't yet know medically what the repercussions of its long usage are going to be."

More was offered from the mind of McGoohan: "There are so many young people doing so much good. The Peace Corps, Oxfam, Shelter – these things are going on all over the world because young people are vastly concerned with what is going on around them. I think Hippies are too, in a strange way, and the drug addicts. It's because of their concern and their fear of what is going to happen to them that they are driven to these extremes."

Society's ills were also addressed: "Whenever you get massive material development, you get a breakdown in morality. The Roman Empire was at the height of its material power when its destruction was caused by moral breakdown. My parents gave me certain ideals which I have always had, even when I've been a sinner. I never lose them. The pop scene is the expression of youth, and pop as such is not a bad thing. Drug taking is, I think, the result of a sick society. It's generated by youth; youth is blaming the generation who brought them up and I think the responsibility lies with the parents." McGoohan closed his 1968 interview by turning to newsreel and the ongoing Vietnamese war. "The more we watch, the more inured we become."[31]

Another major interview appeared when *Ice Station Zebra* was being screened in many countries. Mike Tomkies wrote: "Patrick McGoohan came off the film set, his bright blue eyes glaring about him. He'd just done a scene with Rock Hudson and Ernest Borgnine – just about stolen it in fact – and he was still edgy and tense." Perversely, McGoohan told the journalist that he was an idealistic man and so shouldn't really be talking to a journalist. A few short moments later he told Tomkies to come back another day with some decent questions, rather than a series of trivial ones which had all been asked before. Fortunately for the journalist, an hour was set aside and an expansive interview took place.

McGoohan was wearing horn-rimmed glasses, looking donnish. His mood had apparently changed from the previous meeting and he was now more affable. McGoohan was still defending his recent project. "I must have individuality in everything I do. I question everything. I don't accept anything on face value. I argue because by arguing something good often results. As long as you regard what you're doing just as work and the fact of people recognising, lionising and asking you for your autograph just as a social part of the business, you are all right. You have to put it all into its proper context." The actor described himself as having only two gears: "Very low and very high. I wish I could cultivate the middle gear but I can't. At MGM, where my offices are, I allow my desk to get cluttered up for three days. I look at my 'in' tray till it won't hold any more, descend upon it and clean it right up. It's a bad way to work, but it's the way I'm made." McGoohan observed, "In private life I've been known to lose my temper. But if it was the result of working too hard, I always try to go back to what caused it and put it right. I'm not ashamed to admit that I do have a temper. It's essential sometimes." There had been several actors and members of the crew on the set of *The Prisoner* who could vouch for the fact that McGoohan might vent his anger one day, but be utterly charming the next day and full of apologies.

Also in 1968, the actor's next small screen appearance was a brief one on US television. He hosted *Journey into Darkness*, a compilation of two filmed episodes from a British anthology television series of one hour mild horror fantasies called *Journey to the Unknown*, produced by Hammer Films. McGoohan's insert pieces were shot while in the States on the movie *Ice Station Zebra*. His pair of stories – entitled *The New People* and *Paper Dolls*[xvii] – were shown together in the US with McGoohan wearing a dark cape, a là Orson Welles, opening and closing each story. The first drama was about an American couple buying a house in England, the previous owner of which committed suicide after being involved in a satanic cult. They learn that everyone in their new neighbourhood belongs to the cult,

---

[xvii] Episodes 1 and 16, respectively. See Appendix One screenography of McGoohan's TV work for a mention of *Trilogy of Terror*, sometimes apparently confused with *Journey into Darkness*.

which has chosen them as sacrifices. The other concerned quadruplets, adopted by different families, with the ability to share experiences telepathically.[xviii]

In 1969, when *The Prisoner* was repeated on US screens, the series had by then generated three stateside paperback tie-in novels. There was no other North American merchandise, but in Britain three collectable items had emerged: a Dinky Toys model of a Village taxi was on sale, as was a seven-inch music vinyl offering of the series' theme tune[xix] and the third item was simply the published sheet music, featuring a jazzed up version of the title theme, with a cover containing a monochrome *Prisoner* picture.[xx] Also on the musical front, in 1969, British folk singer Roy Harper penned a song entitled "McGoohan's Blues," inspired by the actor and his character in *The Prisoner*, during the series' recent premiere run. The ode lasted as many minutes as there had been *Prisoner* episodes, seventeen in all.[xxi] A few of the lyrics can be included here:

And I'm just a social experiment tailored to size,
I've tried out the national machine and the welfare surprise,
I'm the rich man, the poor man, the peace man, the war man, the beast ...

Harper continued with lines like "The Village T.V. hooks its victims..." and "The Prisoner is taking his shoes off to walk in the rain." The singer eventually declares: "And I've seen all your pedestal values, your good and your bad," challenging through song, in the same way that McGoohan did through television.

Also in 1969, McGoohan briefly made the news, although not in a showbusiness setting. The *Evening News* reported that "Patrick McGoohan had to flee when fire broke out at a Maida Vale hotel today. He was asleep when staff at the Clarendon Court Hotel roused him. He was evacuated with 150 other guests."[32] The actor also had a lengthy interview at the end of the year, with the US magazine *Pace*, at the time of *The Prisoner* enjoying its second Stateside run. The journalist had found McGoohan to be "Like an onion. Not that he brings tears to the eyes, but he comes in layers." The interviewer spent two days with the actor in one of the most direct and pithy exchanges with McGoohan ever to reach print. If the star was hoping that his screen prowess would appeal to prospective US producers and directors, he was not guarded with his comments. The actor proceeded to take the American film industry to task: "*Midnight Cowboy*, don't you think it was a license to fornicate? If you're going to do stuff like that and call it art, well, I still believe in the old fashioned thing of crime and punishment. That film is publicising fornication and if I see director John Schlesinger again I shall tell him so."

The USA was next treated to McGoohan's condemnations. "Man has to be a moral being in order to survive. If there is no morality, he has to create it. I will not read *Playboy*. Those are moral decisions. One must live with the awareness of constant choice. Our hardest battle is recognising what is evil and fighting it. How to sell truth? How to push truth without going over to 'Ultra Brite.' I bought a tube of the stuff to try, by the way. Sex appeal! It didn't even clean." McGoohan also offloaded thoughts which might not have

[xviii] The series, plus compilations, were screened in the US before the UK started a run of single episodes of *Journey to the Unknown*. Two other double episode features called *Journey to Midnight* and *Journey to the Unknown* were hosted in the US by Sebastian Cabot and Joan Crawford., but none of the hosted compilations was shown in the UK.
[xix] This recording was in an altered form, released by the Ron Grainer Orchestra, on the RCA record label.
[xx] In the mid-eighties and again around the time of the series' thirty fifth anniversary, there would be *Prisoner* books, T-shirts, calendars, compact discs, videos, DVDs and posters, plus moving image pens, decorated mugs, computer mouse mats and even pewter bottle stoppers.
[xxi] On the album *Folkjokeopus* © Roy Harper and Carlin Music Corporation.

endeared him to the youth of the day. "How long will they sit there, waiting for the miracle, carried along by the momentum of nothingness? Suddenly there's Mick Jagger. And he says, 'Marriage is for the birds.' So let's have sex, fellows, it don't mean nothing. If my eldest daughter met Mick Jagger she'd sort him out in no time." The actor was well aware of the contention which he had injected into the interview. "You've got to offend a huge mass to save the world." The article even unearthed something of the McGoohan family's Irish roots. The actor declared, "A fellow was telling me his third child is nine years old and showing no signs of being rejected like the book says. My grandmother in Ireland had fifteen! They were so busy living they didn't have time to feel rejected! She'd deliver her own child, tie up the knot and get back to the fields. She didn't have a book. She couldn't read. But she did know music!"

A stern look from McGoohan in *Ice Station Zebra* (1968)

The tirade continued, now entering the obscure territory of *The Prisoner*. "Any man or any woman can have truth inside them as a result of their own private war within themselves. They are fighting themselves. And if they win some of those battles there comes an essence which by the nature of life emanates." The writer concluded, "McGoohan's imagination runs wild. He is nobody's prisoner. He has offered to pay my expenses if I forget about this interview. He doubled the offer. He said it was just more talk, more hot air."[33]

This was a fitting exchange to bring to an end McGoohan's sixties decade. Sadly, the actor was about to quit Britain and also the British television scene which had served him throughout the decade. As *The Prisoner* was frequently repeated in numerous countries over many years – whether *Le Prisonnier*, *Nummer 6*, *Il Prigioniero*, et al, or in its Japanese language version – the series continued to enjoy an extended life, of which most modern TV producers would be envious. Given the commercial tape or disc set releases, perhaps McGoohan, or the studio, did have some foresight in having additional scenes filmed with foreign language writing, on objects like filing cabinets, so that there could be custom-made presentations in certain foreign markets. It was not only the actual global screenings which added to *The Prisoner*'s longevity, but the universal 'message' of the series itself. The man in isolation, the freedom of the individual, the resistance against oppression and so on were the themes which struck chords with students, the socially excluded and even those uncertain of their sexual or religious orientation.

Clearly, *The Prisoner* became a turning point for McGoohan, although what is not widely known is that for the subsequent period, the actor was already preparing more television work and even planning to make cinema movies. His production company, Everyman Films, was holding several "properties." Perhaps it had been his recent Hollywood filming experiences and the ending of the *Prisoner* series in Britain which led to a change in McGoohan's aspirations. He was increasingly talking about made-for-television movies, the relatively new format of US films made exclusively for TV. The genre had been born earlier in the decade, with studios such as Universal and MCA, creating 'pilots,' made with the

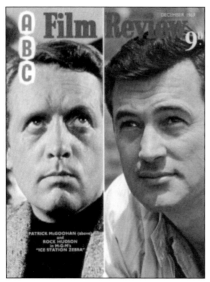

McGoohan on the cover of *Film Review* magazine, 1969

hope of garnering full series. However, it was not until Steven Spielberg's *Duel* (1971) attracted critical attention – as well as grossing millions of dollars – that interest flared in TV movies, during the seventies.

McGoohan recognised 'Tellywood' as the next big opportunity for his company Everyman Films. Perhaps it was the promise of retaining artistic control, coupled with the attraction of gambling on his talent and realising a high return for choosing the right property. With his many years of small screen production experience in Britain, the actor talked eagerly about working within this new American framework: "I intend to go into producing some of these shows myself. With a million dollars spent on them, actors will no longer have to do the hop skip and jump type of TV exposure. I own several properties myself and I intend to go into this sort of deal in a big way."[34] The actor declared, "We're in the era of the special TV first-run movie. Two-hour shows with top stars and million dollar budgets. With that kind of money you can turn out top productions."[35] In the meantime, the actor confided that he still lived the same simple home life with his family, still used the same London pubs and still saw the same old friends "from my broke days." His mantra was, "I only want to be a true individual, to organise my working life so I do what I believe in. I try never to allow myself to become engulfed by outside pressures, though I might sometimes be by my own. We must resist to the last – and die laughing!"[36]

In an interview at this time, McGoohan revealed that *The Prisoner* was his last television series.[xxii] The actor stated that he now planned to tackle the cinema, on the same "all-or-nothing" basis which he had recently applied to his TV productions. First in his sights, he confirmed, was the planned film version of *Brand*. "It could be visually superb," spoke McGoohan of his location idea for shooting in Norway. He also envisaged that his wife, Joan, would play Brand's wife, Agnes, in the film. Surprisingly, McGoohan dismissed *The Prisoner* as "a load of old rubbish, but one does something for a living." The actor continued to speak about his company Everyman Films, formed to undertake "honest commercial ventures." According to McGoohan he would personally finance films which he believed in commercially and artistically. He was on the verge of committing himself to the tune of ten million dollars, as co-producer and lead actor of his next (undisclosed) production.[37]

One Everyman Films proposal was for a feature film entitled *Black Jack*, based on a 1967 book by Leon Garfield. Set in 1749, the movie would follow the adventures of a hardened criminal who, in the opening scene, survives hanging by craftily using a piece of metal tubing as an airway. Left for 'dead,' he would be rescued by a young man, Bartholomew Dorking and, together with a woman called Belle Carter, the pair would embark upon some bizarre adventures, the climax being an earthquake in London, in 1750. The treatment, by *Prisoner* producer David Tomblin and scriptwriter Terence Feely, was worked on during

---

[xxii] A decade later McGoohan would star in the US medical drama TV series, *Rafferty*, as well as future episodes of *Columbo*.

1968.[xxiii] Later, more projects were being discussed, Feely recalled: "Lew Grade gave us – that's Everyman Films – £900,000 to make two movies. One, an action adventure movie of our choice, starring Patrick, was the story of a mercenary sick of his trade. (He) decides to opt out and go to Northern Ireland for peace and quiet. And it's there that he gets sucked into the conflict between the IRA and the British Government. And Pat's got to, in order to survive, come out of retirement and fight harder than he's ever fought in his life. It really was a great action adventure culminating in a fight, a chase fight across fields and things instead of roads."

With regard to McGoohan's intention to bring Ibsen's play, Brand[xxiv] to the screen, Feely revealed: "(Lew) didn't really want Brand but he would give us (it) if we would do the action adventure movie. So we went location scouting in Norway to find a fjord where Brand was going to be done. And then we went to Ireland to scout locations for the action adventure (movie)." Things deteriorated, as Feely remembered: "One day Pat came in with that look in his eye. You read in melodramatic novels about the red light in the madman's eyes. It's not entirely untrue because Pat came in and had this look. I thought uh oh, and I said 'what's up Pat?' He said, 'We haven't got the magic figure.' I said 'Sorry?' He said, 'The magic figure is a million pounds.' I said, 'Yeah I know, but we've got £900,000 and we all know it's more than enough to make Ibsen's Brand and the action adventure movie. Why do we need (more)? He said, 'Because, the million is magic.' I said, 'Well, I tell you what we do; we announce to the trade papers that we've got a million. We know we've only got £900,000 but that doesn't matter.' And he got hold of me, he said, 'Don't you know you can't cheat magic?' And so I said, 'Well what's the answer, what are you gonna do?' He said, 'This afternoon I'm gonna see Lew Grade who loves me like a son. I'm gonna get the other hundred.' Now I afterwards heard what happened. Lew, being an entirely practical man, knew we didn't need the other hundred grand and despite loving Pat like a son, which he did, said 'No.' Whereupon Pat, like Douglas Fairbanks Senior, with one leap landed on the middle of Lew's desk which is about four times the size of (a standard one) and kicked everything off it to the four corners of the room. With the result that when he came in next morning we not only didn't have the million, we didn't have the £900,000 either. So all that work went down the Swanee."[xxv] [38]

A further Everyman project was to be a historical adventure, set in the American West of 1878. The title When Trumpets Call was written by Charles K. Peck Jr., deriving the title from a Kipling poem. McGoohan would have taken the part of a Cavalry lieutenant, he envisaging the production as a television movie, to be bought by CBS.[xxvi] A third script was more in keeping with the actor's recent British work, being a proposal for a TV series entitled Vagabond. The pilot episode script entitled Noises Off[xxvii] followed the adventures of Johnny Quill. This 'man of the road,' with a faint Irish accent (no doubt as to who was to star), does not have a care in the world and is able to mingle with people in pubs, or other social settings, although strictly speaking remaining a stranger. A light comedy, the plot saw

---

[xxiii] The book was filmed by director Ken Loach, in 1979.

[xxiv] See also pages 152, 186 and 192.

[xxv] Feely also enlarged upon a proposed film about a mercenary who wants to quit his lethal occupation and retire away from the action. According to him, Everyman Films scouted locations in Ireland and the production was going to be called The Soldier. The plot was very similar to McGoohan's 1979 television movie The Hard Way, shot in Ireland, in which he played a retired hit man. See above and page 213.

[xxvi] CBS premiered The Prisoner in the US, on 1st June, 1968, as a summer season replacement for The Jackie Gleason Show.

[xxvii] A recent book about the Prisoner scripts gives Noises Off as the title of the series – instead of Vagabond – the name being only that of the pilot episode.

Quill being persuaded to purchase a village pub which was located not far from a noisy missile testing range. As a pilot episode, it was hard to see how this would pan out into a series, or how Everyman Films would have attracted funding.

Former *Prisoner* production manager Bernard Williams remembered how there were at that time plans for new projects: "Patrick wanted to go into independent films. He wanted to make a project, a heavy piece called *Brand*[xxviii] by Henrik Ibsen, which Pat won awards for as an actor on stage in Hammersmith years before he became a star with Rank. And he was very persuasive for me to read this material and it was very difficult material for me to understand, at my age, 25 or 26, but once I got it, it was an all-or-nothing concept. And I believed in what Ibsen was trying to say. So I went off to Norway to look for locations to make this serious movie. That was kind of unpalatable to the commercial side of Lew Grade, because it's a heavy serious piece."[39]

Williams recounted McGoohan's words: "'Well, I'll make a few other movies. I'll make a mercenary movie and maybe we'll make a feature of *Secret Agent (Danger Man)*, or maybe we'll make us a feature of *The Prisoner*.' So while all that stuff was going on, I scouted locations, met Pat in Norway. David Tomblin was preparing a movie called *The Mercenaries* (1968)[xxix] and then all of a sudden Patrick decided he just wanted time; he just wanted to shut down for an indefinite period. So he went to Switzerland to live and we just abandoned those projects. There was too much coming at him. He was getting so many offers from Hollywood. He gave me a pile of scripts. He was offered Robert Redford's role in 'Butch Cassidy.'[xxx] He had a problem doing the movie for some reason, whatever it was. He was asked to direct *William the Conqueror*.[xxxi] He was asked to star in *Kelly's Heroes* (1970). The Beatles thought he was the best thing since sliced bread. They just wanted him to direct all their material after that. They just thought he was really with it and crazy enough to be right for their material."[xxxii] [40]

Last words on the decade that spawned McGoohan's classic TV shows go to former *Danger Man* actress, Barbara Shelley.[xxxiii] She declared: "I always wanted to do *The Prisoner*, but … I was in the USA much of the time. I was making a lot of movies around that time and it is just one regret that I had that I was not in *The Prisoner*. Patrick had a definite quality and everything he was in was like this. I think he had a big say in his own productions and they had a certain quality and status because of him, the man. I know that *The Prisoner* was not well received at first, as people did not understand it, but this is ideal for the making of a cult series and of course *The Prisoner* has become a cult. I think it is because Patrick very cleverly decided not to tie up loose ends in the episodes. *The Prisoner* stimulated the imagination. However, I wish that Patrick had stayed in Britain and done more good television."Amen to that.

---

[1] Daily Mirror, 1968, details unknown

[xxviii] See also pages 152 184 and 192.

[xxix] The movie's credits do not include Tomblin's name.

[xxx] *Butch Cassidy and the Sundance Kid* (1969) starred Paul Newman and Robert Redford.

[xxxi] No completed movie of this title at the time has been found.

[xxxii] The Beatles' *All You Need Is Love* is heard twice in the final *Prisoner* episode, *Fall Out*. The song was first performed, live, on 25th June, 1967, in a satelitte television show, transmitted simultaneously by satellite to five continents and 24 countries. In the following month the song topped the British pop charts

[xxxiii] See earlier, page 76.

[2] Hor Zu Magazine, 1971, translated for writer by Ingrid Augustin

[3] *From The Avengers to Miami Vice*, Manchester University Press, David Buxton, 1990

[4] Source not verified

[5] Alwyn W. Turner, *Portmeirion,* Antique Collectors' Club, 2006

[6] Source not verified

[7] Idols magazine, November, 1988, Graham P. Williams

[8] Associated Television (ATV) guide to *Fall Out*, 1968

[9] Idols magazine, November, 1988, Graham P. Williams

[10] Number Six Magazine, Six of One, The Prisoner Appreciation Society, January, 1992, Steven Ricks

[11] Woman's Home Journal, June, 1968

[12] New Zealand TV Weekly, 1968, J. C. Reid

[13] New Zealand Weekly, 1968, Barbara Cooper

[14] New Zealand TV Weekly, 29th April, 1968

[15] New Zealand TV Weekly, 29th April, 1968, John K. Newnham

[16] Letter to Six of One, The Prisoner Appreciation Society, member Michael Prendergast, 1977

[17] Six of One, The Prisoner Appreciation Society, interview

[18] Ibid

[19] Letter to Six of One, The Prisoner Appreciation Society, 13th April, 1977

[20] *The Fool's Pardon*, Kenneth Griffith, 1994; Little, Brown

[21] New York Times, 7th June, 1985, John J. O'Connor

[22] Ibid

[23] Source not verified

[24] Interview with the writer, 2006

[25] Photo Screen, September, 1968, Joseph Curreri

[26] Internet sources, various

[27] Photo Screen, September, 1968, Joseph Curreri

[28] Ice Station Zebra press book, 1968

[29] Source not verified

[30] Photo Screen, September, 1968, Joseph Curreri

[31] Woman's Home Journal, June, 1968

[32] Evening News, 1969

[33] Pace Magazine, December, 1969, Henry Pelham Burn

[34] Photoplay, June 1968, Mike Tomkies

[35] Photo Screen, September, 1968, Joseph Curreri

[36] Photoplay, June 1968, Mike Tomkies

[37] British newspaper, 1967, Adam Hopkins, details unknown

[38] Interview with Terence Feely, by Hugh Conrad, 1985

[39] Number Six Magazine, Six of One, The Prisoner Appreciation Society, April, 1992, Chris Campbell

[40] Ibid

[41] Interview with the writer, 2006

McGoohan between scenes in the Spaghetti Western *Nobody's the Greatest*

CHAPTER EIGHT
Switzerland, South Africa and the States

"It had to be done and I'd do it again tomorrow."
Columbo: By Dawn's Early Light (1974)

At the end of the sixties, McGoohan left Britain and took his family to Switzerland. They stayed there for around two years, at Vevey – on the shores of Lake Geneva, where his parents-in-law lived. The old town, with its narrow alleys, arcades and shuttered facades, also offered a busy marketplace, packed with stalls, selling foods, crafts and wines. The actor relocated there, claiming that after *The Prisoner* he was exhausted and that he had completed the job he had set out to do. However, he subsequently admitted that he had been forced to go into hiding.[i] In fact, it was also being widely reported at the time that McGoohan had to leave his home country, because of the angry response to the *Prisoner* finale from an enraged public.[ii]

McGoohan gave an interview to a journalist in Britain, who discussed what had happened after the final episode of *The Prisoner* was screened.[iii] It was put to him that he had suddenly left puzzled viewers to go and live in Switzerland and it was suggested that mounting tax problems had driven the star away.[1] The actor denied that he was a tax exile: "I never had a penny in a Swiss bank. I just felt like a change and that I had done all I could in England."[2]

The interview revealed that the budget for the series had been eight hundred and fifty thousand pounds – then over two million dollars – a huge sum for the sixties. An earlier

---

[i] See page 232.
[ii] Some sources relate that McGoohan and his family hid out at a secret North Wales location until the heat died down.
[iii] According to *Prisoner* producer David Tomblin, the series had not been well received and McGoohan was disappointed.

interviewer[iv] was quoted to McGoohan, regarding the recently ended series having taken on a life of its own and having become "an intriguing, baffling detergent opera."

The words of ITC distribution company head, Bernard Kingham, were also put to the actor: "Lew Grade gave McGoohan carte blanche, but drew a breath of relief when the series was finished." The actor was told that Kingham's recollection was that there was originally only to be seven episodes, but that Lew Grade persuaded the actor to make ten more. Kingham had concluded, "The basic idea didn't progress, and McGoohan … admit(s) that he ran out of steam."[v] Conversation about The Prisoner continued, with McGoohan admitting, "I got spoiled, because I had complete control, down to every last nut and bolt." This was almost a humorous repetition of a line of dialogue from The Prisoner, in a scene where Number Six describes how he built his own Lotus sports car, using virtually the same phrase. The journalist learned from his subject that McGoohan felt that acting was his only craft. "I just learn the lines and show up on time." Possibly he was recalling the repertory notice board from years before, with its dictate that there was no excuse for being late. However, the actor once again was saying, "But I will never do another television series, not for all the money in the world. Television is fodder, popcorn."[vi] Finally, McGoohan described how he was presently taking daily three mile walks, at five in the morning; that he needed little sleep and would jot down ideas in his notebook while strolling. He confessed to having a deep need "to be occupied."[3]

The actor's new lifestyle was a dramatic change for him, compared to the one he experienced during the two years of The Prisoner and including his final months in Britain. A journalist writing for a New Zealand[vii] magazine[4] revealed that the actor was now "living in peaceful seclusion in the Swiss Alps … away from prying eyes in London." This time, the reason for the move from Britain was laid at the door of the planning wrangle, which had occurred some months earlier.[viii] The reporter stated that the Mill Hill home,[ix] vacated mid-1968, had been sold in the autumn of that year[x] and that McGoohan was presently living "'incognito' in quite an ordinary house," although his secretary Roger Gambles "declined to say exactly where." The secretary was asked if the actor had been driven out of England because of a lack of privacy. "No, it would take more than that," answered Gambles. He added that the star had "had enough" and was currently "busy preparing films." In the article, the dispute with Barnet Council and former neighbours was highlighted. McGoohan, it was said, was angry that his wife Joan and daughters Catherine, aged sixteen, Anne, aged seven and Frances, aged six, were "goggled at" in their home by passers-by and sightseers. According to the journalist, the actor had begun "to feel too much like his 'No. 6' character in The Prisoner… under constant watch." Cryptically, the reporter ended his piece with a comment about the council's appeal decision, which had gone against McGoohan. The actor was required to remove the six foot high fence he had erected around his home, without planning consent, but the journalist claimed that the ruling "fell on deaf ears." Whether this meant that the actor simply sold up, leaving the offending fence

---

[iv] Daily Sketch, 1st February, 1968, Fergus Cashin – see list of articles at end of book
[v] Kingham also disclosed that McGoohan never collected his profits from The Prisoner.
[vi] As indicated previously, McGoohan would go on to make a TV series in the US – Rafferty – covered later.
[vii] The Prisoner was airing in that country.
[viii] Covered in Chapter Five.
[ix] "Northcote," The Ridgeway.
[x] For the equivalent of fifty thousand New Zealand dollars.

in situ, was not made clear. However, there was no doubt in the mind of the reporter that the bureaucratic tussle had led to McGoohan's upping sticks.[5]

Although the actor was now residing in Switzerland, he made a few trips back to Britain, to deal with business tie-ins concerning a number of African documentaries, which he was making in collaboration with *Prisoner* actor, Kenneth Griffith.[xi] According to Griffith, in a meeting to discuss the production, McGoohan – emulating Lew Grade, the mogul who had originally given the go ahead for *The Prisoner* – thrust a cheque at Griffith and told him to make haste for South Africa to film the story of Cecil Rhodes.[xii] When Griffith said that he also wanted to make a film about British veterans of the Boer War, McGoohan

McGoohan as a Revenue man in *The Moonshine War* (1970)

replied, "Do it," again providing money.[xiii] [6] The arrangement was for him to pay for the film stock, with the BBC financing Griffith to complete the films. McGoohan handled the contractual aspects, while his Welsh colleague filmed the Boer War veterans, men in their eighties. Griffith eventually had so much footage from South Africa that a producer was appointed and four half hour documentaries were broadcast fortnightly. McGoohan was reported as saying: "For people who want to make their own films, the time is ripe to branch out, sow their own field of potatoes." It was stated, "Besides making plans to shoot Ibsen's *Brand* in Norway, he has two film crews in southern Africa working on an unusual series of documentaries on the British Empire, including the Boer War and the lives of Mahatma Gandhi and Cecil Rhodes."[7] Eventually, some work began and other potential producers wanted Griffith to make films for them also. Honourably, he respected the unwritten partnership deal he had with McGoohan and sent a telegraph to the latter. McGoohan replied that he would seek half the profits of any film made. This was agreed and so Griffith was able to work extensively in South Africa, preparing and filming material for various documentaries.

Griffith later expanded upon had happened with regard to the McGoohan-backed documentary films: "Patrick wanted to promote my films, but while working on the first one, he withdrew for reasons which are not clear to me. He also wanted to make a film based on the play *The Prisoner*,[xiv] on the life of Cardinal Mindszenty. He had all sorts of extraordinary and creative ideas, surrealist ideas."[8] McGoohan commented to one writer that during the collaboration with Griffith he had been thrown into a South African prison for talking

---

[xi] See chapter 5 for Griffith's *Prisoner* recollections.
[xii] *A Touch of Churchill, a Touch of Hitler,* subtitled *The Life of Cecil Rhodes* (1971).
[xiii] *Sons of the Blood* (1972) was a four-part documentary, subtitled *The Great Boer War,* 1899-1902. One source states that McGoohan backed and worked on at least eight documentaries with Griffith, including, possibly, films about the Relief of Mafeking and others not completed.
[xiv] The 1954 Bridget Boland play, in which McGoohan appeared, in the 1963 television production.

bluntly about apartheid. "I found out that one of my crew was actually a spy for the government. They threw me in jail. It was an interesting experience. The food was good and I played a lot of chess with a fellow prisoner."[9] Apart from making or financing documentaries, McGoohan began taking steps towards filming the play *Brand*. He travelled to Oslo, as a base from which to scout Norwegian locations.[xv] More sources announced the actor's intention to cast spouse Joan as Brand's wife Agnes, with himself in the lead role. Michael Meyer – translator for the 1959 stage production – was approached to write the screenplay for the film. However, as observed by Dilys Hamlet, the original stage Agnes, the film never happened and nobody knew why.

Interviewer Jeannie Sakol met McGoohan at the Bristol hotel, in "downtown Oslo" and conducted an interview for *Cosmopolitan* magazine, under the heading "ferocious goody two-shoes." Her description of the actor followed: "He moves with the contained ferocity of a tightly-wound spring. Control is perhaps the operative word for McGoohan. His voice comes at you in clipped, staccato jabs, with faint echoes of Orson Welles' fire and the metallic insinuation of Laurence Olivier's Richard III." Ms. Sakol recalled the words of the actor's long-time friend and casting director on *Danger Man* and *The Prisoner*, Rose Tobias Shaw. The advice she consistently gave was, "Look into those bright blue eyes and die!"[10]

After the actor's sojourn in Switzerland, he took his wife and children to live in the United States. This move would mark the start of over three decades of living on the west coast of the country. Firstly there was a short spell at Santa Fe in New Mexico, before the family finally settled in Pacific Palisades, California. Home to movie stars and the affluent, the beautiful district is located between the cities of Santa Monica and Malibu. The suburb, founded in 1922 as a residential community, is technically a town of Los Angeles, but residents fiercely protect the 'village' atmosphere. There are around thirty thousand residents and ten thousand homes. The commercial district has five hundred shops, businesses and professional offices.

The McGoohan dwelling was described by one writer as being "In a prim, private and pricey suburb. Hollywood is 30 minutes away. Home is a Cape Cod style house, a wooden, old-fashioned building, with a small garden, on a tree-lined street of similar homes."[11] Another report clarified that the residence had "no ocean view at all," with McGoohan adding, "Its view is of trees and flowers. It's absolutely enclosed. Very private."[12] A British reporter observed, "When McGoohan is not working he can often be seen in nearly Santa Monica where he pops into a British-style pub for a beer. He sits at the bar, wearing horn-rimmed spectacles, reading the English papers. And he does not like to be interrupted."[13]

Throughout the seventies, the actor would experiment with different types of roles and productions. As he had foreseen, made-for-television movies became more of the McGoohan metier. During the decade he had a steady amount of screen work and his career would enjoy a renaissance in years to come. Meanwhile, the next US film engagement was *The Moonshine War* (1970). McGoohan was offered the part by the producer of the earlier movie, *Ice Station Zebra*. This time, the actor would be filming on a 'set' located in the foothills of the Sierra Nevada. His name received top billing, above that of Richard Widmark and Alan Alda. McGoohan felt some trepidation with regard to being cast in the role of a US Revenue agent, in 1932. "Kentucky? Louisville? Revenuer? It's kinda out of my beat."[14] The actor thought however, that the production would make for a nice holiday for

[xv] See pages 152, 184 and 186.

his wife and children. His lasting recollection was that nobody seemed to know whether the movie was meant to be a comedy, farce, or satire.

New York Times review: "In this comedy drama set during the late Prohibition era, a federal agent attempts to make some real money before the alcohol ban is lifted. He sets his sights on the whiskey cache of an old army buddy, but just before they strike a deal, two ex-convicts frighten the buddy away. The creeps then murder the town sheriff and his deputy and begin looking to get a hold of the moonshine. The agent decides to help his friend defeat the thugs. One of the crooks ends up killing the agent and taking four locals hostage. In exchange for their lives, he wants all the whiskey. The moonshiner acquiesces and tells him that the booze is stashed in a graveyard. The greedy crook races off and begins digging. Unfortunately instead of hooch, he finds dynamite and blows himself up. To celebrate his death and the end of Prohibition, the town decides to have a blow-out of their own. Naturally the buddy provides the booze." (Sandra Brennan, All Movie Guide)

Publicity for *The Moonshine War* described McGoohan as having been "considerably transformed in his role as a corrupt 'revenuer.'"[15] His character was combating an attempt by city gangsters to hijack 150 barrels of aged prime whiskey. The star waxed lyrical about his family, especially his three daughters, then aged eighteen, ten and nine. One of the actor's comments from another time was revisited and revised: "The wild beauty of a child's mind is one of the most unspoiled things you can talk about. It's a tremendous responsibility to preserve this in your children and make sure the seeds flower."[16] The interview revealed that during the *Moonshine* filming, McGoohan was continuing work on a screenplay, as well as editing a TV documentary he had just filmed in South Africa. He was continually on the telephone to Pretoria, where he had a company shooting another documentary.

More information about the *Moonshine* movie came in the form of a seven minute promotional film, *Shooting the Moonshine War* (1970) showing the production on location in a rural setting, with McGoohan's participation. At that time, McGoohan stated that he would be starring in the movie *Tai Pan*,[xvi] about the founding of Hong Kong, as soon as *Moonshine* had been completed.[xvii] [17] However, the actor's next film engagement was in the costume drama *Mary, Queen of Scots* (1971), made by Universal. Alongside top acting names such as Vanessa Redgrave, Trevor Howard, Nigel Davenport and Daniel Massey, McGoohan took on the role of James Stuart, Earl of Moray. The film was extensively filmed on location, in England, Scotland and France and was nominated for five Academy Awards.

Variety review: "A large cast of excellent players appears to good advantage under the direction of Charles Jarrott. Superior production details and the cast help overcome an episodic, rambling story. Mary Stuart (Vanessa Redgrave) emerges as a romantic, immature but idealistic young woman. Her perilous position was repeatedly confounded by the machinations of half-brother (later King) James Stuart (played by Patrick McGoohan), the blunt but well-meant efforts of eventual husband and lover Lord Bothwell (Nigel Davenport), the paranoid homosexual, and bisexual inclinations of second husband Henry Darnley (Timothy Dalton), and the low-key, amiable clerical advisor, David Riccio (Ian Holm). Elizabeth (Glenda Jackson) in contrast had a well-oiled machine of intrigue: advisor

---

[xvi] McGoohan's name was also linked to other movies: *Isabella of Spain* (1971) and *Porgi l'altra guancia* (1974), see Appendix One list of unconfirmed productions.

[xvii] Shooting was scheduled to start in the spring of spring, 1970, but apparently did not commence. A film of *Tai Pan* finally appeared in 1986, but did not involve McGoohan.

McGoohan leads his armed agents in *The Moonshine War* (1970)

William Cecil (Trevor Howard), a power-hungry lover Robert Dudley (Daniel Massey), and the corrupt cooperation of McGoohan and other Scottish factions. The result of such a dramatic imbalance renders Redgrave's character that of a storm-tossed waif, while Jackson benefits from a far more well-defined character. The face-to-face confrontations between the two women are said to be historically inaccurate. The script almost has to have one, and these brief climactic encounters are electric."

New York Times review: "Vanessa Redgrave stars as Mary Stuart of Scotland, with Glenda Jackson costarred as Queen Elizabeth I. The film's sympathies are with Mary, and there are two contrived, wholly fabricated face-to-face confrontations between the two queens (who never met in real life). The film is literally swamped with lavish Tudor decor, perhaps the only completely accurate aspect of the whole project." (Hal Erickson, All Movie Guide)

Another documentary project came to light in 1972, when "an epic film dramatising the true role of the chiropractic profession as the world's leading natural healing art and science" was announced. The news confirmed that "a contract (was) signed this week with Hollywood producer-actor Patrick McGoohan." The report added that McGoohan, a "dedicated chiropractic layman" had scripted the ninety minute film and had agreed to play the part of B. J. Palmer.[xviii] The lead role of chiropractic pioneer Daniel David Palmer was to be taken by veteran US movie and TV star Max Showalter. McGoohan described him as an "actor's actor," adding that "Actors of Showalter's stature are vitally necessary to provide the power to bring to life scenes such as the famous courtroom trial which precedes D.D. Palmer's jailing for the illegal practice of 'medicine.'"[xix 18]

The actor related how he had become involved with the production: "I was making a movie called *The Moonshine War*, when I somehow triggered a disc problem which hit me hard in the back and left leg," McGoohan recalled. "It looked as if surgery was the only way out."[19] Fortunately, a Dr. L. Ted Frigard, a prominent California chiropractor, cured the problem, using no more than standard procedures. However, a more serious problem later struck McGoohan's daughter, Catherine. The medical prognosis was a life of inactivity in a wheelchair, as a result of rheumatoid arthritis, but Dr. Frigard, by then the McGoohan

---

[xviii] B.J. (Bartlett Joshua) Palmer died in 1961 and was the best known figure in chiropractic circles during his lfetime.
[xix] Daniel David Palmer (1845-1913) was the founder of chiropractic. In 1906, Palmer was the first of many chiropractors convicted of practising medicine without a licence. He was sentenced to a hundred and five days in jail, but after serving twenty three of them, he paid the fine originally imposed, in order to be released.

family chiropractor, was able to heal Catherine as well. After a few weeks, the young woman no longer needed her splints, or a wheelchair. She was soon racing with her father in the swimming pool and it was said that the teenager herself was now studying to be a chiropractor.[20]

The successful resolution of these medical misfortunes caused McGoohan to be committed to the two hundred thousand dollar documentary, to be shot in Hawaii. The actor and Dr. Frigard established the Chiropractic Documentary Film Corporation and invited contributions from members of the chiropractic profession, who would share in any profits, plus donations from related professional associations. Among the titles considered for the documentary were *Discovery of Chiropractic* and *Healing Hands*. McGoohan stated: "I am presently engaged in what I consider to be one of the most stimulating and important tasks of my professional life: … a documentary movie about the discovery, development, practice and future of chiropractic … It is our urgent task to destroy for all time the prejudice that has existed for so long. It is our duty to present to the world the exact meaning and function of this profound natural healing force."[21] The documentary was promoted in medical magazines and filming was scheduled to begin in August, 1972. However, by December of that year McGoohan was quoted as saying that support from the profession had been "miniscule." Cancellation of production was also prompted by the confronting of McGoohan by some chiropractic practitioners, insisting that their input was imperative. The actor's response was: "This movie is starring chiropractic and not any fringe group or personality."[22] With that, the project died for lack of support.[xx]

A departure from screen acting came when McGoohan was invited to direct a filmed musical version of Shakespeare's *Othello*, called *Catch My Soul* (1974). The actor was living in New Mexico at the time, as was Jack Good, the film's producer[xxi] and McGoohan stated, "(Good) had heard that I was in the area. Unfortunately, along the way he became a religious fanatic. He converted to Catholicism, then he took the film and had it re-edited. The editor warned me about it and I asked for my name to be removed from the credits, but unfortunately this wasn't done. Moreover, he added eighteen minutes of religious things. Ridiculous."[23]

Good remarked: "It took me weeks of argument before I could even persuade Patrick to direct this picture. He's a genius. But a difficult son of a bitch. I love the man but his indifference to his trappings of success would exasperate a saint."[24]

One critic's comment about the *Catch My Soul* was: "McGoohan directs the whole silly charade with a lack of conviction as to where to place his cameras and how hard to ham it," summing up the production as "lamentable tosh."[25] Another critic disagreed and classed the direction by Patrick McGoohan as "fluid and vividly colourful, to match the strident rock music."[26]

All Movie Guide: "If anyone ever doubts that the '70s were a strange decade for cinema, they have only to watch *Catch My Soul* to find verification. In a way, it's emblematic of the decade, which encouraged a remarkable freedom of expression from its filmmakers; sometimes this resulted in highly individualistic masterpieces; other times it created dreck like *Catch My Soul*. Mind you, a lot of that dreck is highly watchable, in a "what could they have been

[xx] McGoohan made mention of the project a decade later when he was filming *Jamaica Inn* in England. In 1982, he told journalists that his next project was to be a film presenting chiropractic history.
[xxi] Jack Good had written the screenplay and had starred in the original London stage version.

thinking" kind of way, and *Soul* more than fits that bill. Director Patrick McGoohan had been involved as an actor in an imaginative and successful updating of Othello into the '50s jazz world *All Night Long*, so perhaps he thought lightning would strike twice in moving it to a gospel show in the Southwest. He was terribly wrong. The re-setting is ham-handed and ridiculous, and the mixture of direct quotes from the play with contemporary slang is laughable. Laughable also describes every dramatic performance, as do horrible and unbelievable. McGoohan's direction is labored, at best. Still, *Catch My Soul* is undeniably fascinating, a train wreck of a movie that inspires awe and that makes one appreciate a time when awful movies could be so bad in such an interesting way." (Craig Butler)

Time Out Film Guide review: "Lame attempt to film Jack Good's rock opera version of Shakespeare's *Othello*, a folly which started life on the stage. Hampered all the way by McGoohan's languorous direction, which lets each appalling moment of this uncomfortable hybrid of grade-school Shakespeare and grade-school religion sink wincingly in."

There were other reported potential roles from around this time, which did not reach fruition. For convenience, these will be grouped into this section, although they were spread over several years.[xxii] The first of the proposals was an early planned film adaptation of the Frank Herbert science fiction novel *Dune*.[xxiii] McGoohan was also invited to appear in the cinema production of *Flash Gordon* (1980), but according to one interview source he was not prepared to spend six months away from home. In a similar vein, the role of Jor-El in *Superman* (1978) was subsequently taken by Marlon Brando. William Peter Blatty, author of *The Exorcist*, apparently did a deal with McGoohan to have him playing the lead role in an eighties movie of Blatty's 1966 novel *Twinkle, Twinkle, "Killer" Kane*.[xxiv] Another proposed project which did not go far into production was a television screenplay *The Last Enemy*. Written by Tony Stratton-Smith, owner of Charisma Records, work began on a drama which would have had Anthony Andrews and McGoohan in the starring roles. Intending to go further into screen work, Stratton-Smith sold his record company shares and began to clear the decks for his next undertaking. Unfortunately, time was running out and the production went no further. Stratton-Smith died on 19th March (McGoohan's birth date) 1987.[27]

One further prospective undertaking did not come to a conclusion. There was a script presented to McGoohan for an episode in the TV series *Babylon 5*, and it is reported that the actor wanted to take the role offered. On this occasion, although a *Prisoner*-style interrogation scene would have occurred, the actor would have been, for once, interrogator and not prisoner. Owing to an apparent scheduling conflict, this became a missed opportunity for the actor. However, this was not the end of the story and the *Babylon 5* series' creator, Michael Straczynski, again sought out McGoohan for a part portraying the head of the "Psi Force." For whatever reason, the desired appearance did not occur.

To close this section, there were two more unrealised projects. McGoohan was signed to appear in a remake of the 1946 Boris Karloff shocker, *Bedlam*, in 1996. However, the actor did become Dr. Harvey Langston in *Hysteria* (1998),[xxv] a movie so similar to the *Bedlam* subject theme that the movies might be the same item, but with a title change. Another

---

[xxii] See also Appendix One for a list of unconfirmed productions.
[xxiii] A movie of *Dune* did appear in 1984, but without McGoohan's involvement.
[xxiv] Blatty eventually directed the movie in 1980, then called *The Ninth Configuration*, but with different actors.
[xxv] See page 261.

proposition at the time had McGoohan being reportedly picked for a cameo role in the 2000 film *Mission Impossible II*, an offer which it was said he rejected. So ends this short look at a few of McGoohan's other projects which were not carried through, although of course there must have been others.

Returning to 1974, McGoohan's introduction to US television came via the *Mystery Movie* presentations of the *Columbo* detective series. The actor had first met the show's star, Peter Falk,[xxvi] by chance, when both had taken the same flight. Falk was already popular on both sides of the Atlantic, *Columbo* being into its fourth season. He and McGoohan had both enjoyed screen careers and the two men had mutual respect for their professional backgrounds: Falk with his US production experience and McGoohan with a longer history of theatrical appearances. McGoohan insisted that Falk "fought every inch of the way for quality,"[28] and he revealed that they had "hit it off" from the start.

In his first *Columbo* collaboration (there would be several more, covered later) *By Dawn's Early Light*,[xxvii] McGoohan played Colonel Lyle C. Rumford, the proud commandant of a military academy. He is so incensed when the owner of the property wants to turn it into a college, that he plans a murder using a backfiring cannon. The part became McGoohan's favourite role: "It was a terrific part. I made him somewhat more neurotic. I didn't see the commandant as a villain. Not at all. He thought he was doing the right thing. He committed a murder because of his ideals. He would live and die a soldier."[29] The portrayal won McGoohan an Emmy for Outstanding Single Performance by a Supporting Actor in a Comedy or Drama Series (for a One-Time Appearance in a Regular or Limited Series).[xxviii] This – and being involved in a big-budget American show such as *Columbo* – provided the actor with valuable TV exposure.

In the same year, McGoohan took a part in an Italian production[xxix] called *Un Genio, Due Compari E Un Pollo* (1975).[xxx] He played a US Cavalry officer, Major Cabot, but found Italian movie making to be very different in style and tempo. The actor was given vague location instructions and feared that it would be pure chance as to whether he and the film crew would even arrive in the same place, at the same time. There was no production office and McGoohan could find nobody who had heard of the company, or knew any of the personnel involved. Eventually, when filming did occur, McGoohan had to attempt acting while technicians were shouting all around him. In the end, with his voice being dubbed by somebody else, McGoohan dismissed the assignment as being a nightmare and "madness."[30] He later revealed, "I've never seen it. As far as I know it was never released in England and, thank God, never in the United States. It was a spaghetti western … I went to Italy. Very funny actually, most films are post-dubbed. A friend of mine who saw the film told me I had Mickey Mouse's voice."[xxxi] [31]

New York Times review: "Spaghetti western hero Terence Hill plays the title role – sort

---

[xxvi] Coincidentally, the original *Columbo* pilot film *Prescription Murder* (1968), was made at the time *The Prisoner* was being completed in England.

[xxvii] Episode twenty eight in the fourth season, 1974/75.

[xxviii] The award was presented on 19th May, 1975. McGoohan won a second *Columbo* Emmy in 1990 – see later – but it is not confirmed whether he collected either award in person. His wife said that in the eighties he never attended the Academy Awards either.

[xxix] The movie was known as *The Genius* in the US and years later, on video, as *Nobody's the Greatest*. It was released on DVD under that title and also as *A Genius, Two Partners and a Dupe*.

[xxx] The movie won the 1978 Golden Screen Award, in Germany.

[xxxi] Strangely, one of the other character voices in the movie does sound as though it was provided by McGoohan. The actor's voice was in fact dubbed by Robert Rietty, whose voice was heard in both *Danger Man* and *The Prisoner*.

of. A self-styled expert on Native Americans, Joe Thanks (Hill) champions the Indians' cause in the face of white hostility. The action scenes are convincing, even when offset by the tongue-in-cheek nature of the script. The incomparable Miou-Miou shows up as the heroine, while Klaus Kinski tries to take things seriously as a bandit." (Hal Erickson, All Movie Guide)

McGoohan's next *Columbo* appearance was in the episode *Identity Crisis* (1975).[xxxii] The actor played Nelson Brenner and also directed the episode. His character was a wily secret agent, working for a covert government organisation. The camaraderie between him and Falk could be felt on screen. When the villain is being pinned down by the detective, there are some excellent examples of on-screen sparring and the episodes are more entertaining for this. The successful Falk-McGoohan partnership kept up interest in the British star – or perhaps now better termed an American – and the makers of the series were impressed by his additional directing capabilities. This led to his being given the opportunity to steer the last episode of the then fifth season, *Last Salute to the Commodore* (1976).[xxxiii] In the story, the Commodore vanishes at sea at the hands of a greedy family member. This is the first *Columbo* 'whodunnit' where the unveiling of the killer occurs on screen, with all suspects present. The altering of the usual format – where the murder is seen by viewers at the start of an episode – was McGoohan's idea. His friendship with Falk continued in the meantime and the pair reportedly enjoyed some high times together.

Falk spoke in glowing praise of McGoohan: "Peter Falk, the character of Lt. Columbo, and Universal Studios and the NBC network all owe Patrick McGoohan a deep debt. He as much as anybody else I could name is responsible for the success of Columbo. He's the only actor in television history that the first two times he appeared as a guest star won the Emmy both times. He has directed Columbos; he starred in them and, without ever asking for any money; he does an enormous amount of rewriting. He has a tremendous presence; he's got a very good mind. As a matter of fact, when we act together I can actually hear his mind humming."[32]

McGoohan next signed to a major movie production, the adventure comedy *Silver Streak* (1976), co-starring Gene Wilder, Jill Clayburgh and Richard Pryor. Location shooting was in Alberta, Canada and the actor found it to be a complicated process. The locomotive of the title was only allowed so many runs up and down the railway track at certain times of the day. The movie provided McGoohan with the opportunity to portray a debonair villain, art dealer Roger Devereau. There was also an eight minute featurette *Making the Silver Streak*, with behind-the-scenes footage and interviews with some of the main actors, the producer and director, although McGoohan did not apparently become involved.

New York Times review: "While taking a train trip from LA to Chicago, mild-mannered George Caldwell (Gene Wilder) makes the acquaintance of Hilly Burns (Jill Clayburgh). As they indulge in a brief bit of spooning, Hilly tells George that her boss is on the verge of exposing a group of vicious art forgers. Later that evening, George sees the body of Hilly's boss tumbling off the train. Trouble is, no one will believe him – and Hilly, suddenly more furtive and close-mouthed, won't back up his story. Only detective Sweet (Ned Beatty)

[xxxii] Episode thirty four in the fifth season, 1975/76. In the story McGoohan inserted several references to the earlier *Prisoner* series, including a few "Be seeing you" lines and at one point a costume not dissimilar to that worn by Number Six.
[xxxiii] McGoohan would be guest-starring in more *Columbo* episodes, as well as writing and directing – see later chapters of this book – and his daughters Catherine and Anne would appear in two stories.

agrees to investigate, but he too is bumped off. The instigator of these outrages is master forger Roger Devereau (Patrick McGoohan), who with his crony Mr. Whiney (Ray Walston) is planning a particularly diabolical crime. Worse still, they are holding Hilly prisoner so she can't tip off the cops. When George is also targeted for elimination, he manages in slapstick fashion to elude the killers. Falling off the train, he ends up being arrested on some trumped-up charge or other by a local sheriff. He makes his escape in the company of petty thief Grover Muldoon (Richard Pryor)." (Hal Erickson, All Movie Guide)

Silver Streak was a cinema success, being chosen for the Royal Film Performance at the Odeon in Leicester Square in the Queen's Jubilee Year, 1977, attended by the Queen Mother. With McGoohan playing a baddie the audience loved to hate, he came to a rather nasty end, losing out to an oncoming train.

McGoohan taking a break between scenes during filming of *Silver Streak* (1976)

Actually, the script had been offered to the late Peter Finch[xxxiv] and McGoohan had fallen heir to the part. He said of his new role: "I've played many a heel and I've always admired the bad guys played by Edward G. Robinson, George Raft and Humphrey Bogart. They were despicable characters, true, but there was a heroic quality to their badness. When they went out, they went out big. I'd like to do something like that and I'm trying to come up with a mini-series I could do for television, which would give me a string of villainous roles."[33]

Meanwhile, back in Britain, newspapers were taunting McGoohan with rumours that the tax man was after him. The Inland Revenue was reported as saying that they did not know where the actor was and that he would not answer their letters. Everyman Films, the production company for *The Prisoner*, had been placed into liquidation with debts of sixty three thousand pounds, half of which was being claimed in unpaid taxes. It was alleged that McGoohan's other jointly-held company, Drummond Enterprises, had also been liquidated a few years earlier, with debts of forty three thousand pounds, after attempts by McGoohan to finance some South African documentaries.[xxxv] This writer has not discovered any other examples of the company's name being used.

The *Daily Mail* reported that although *The Prisoner* was perceived as an international money spinner, McGoohan had been unable to pay thirty thousand pounds owed by him for UK tax on his share of the profits. Creditors of Everyman Films, at a meeting at Inveresk

---

[xxxiv] Peter Finch was in *Passage Home* (1955) and *Zarak* (1956) in which films McGoohan also took early roles.
[xxxv] Kenneth Griffith visited McGoohan on the *Silver Streak* set and no doubt discussed financial matters with him regarding the South African productions (and see page 191).

Out for a walk with wife Joan

House, in the Strand, London, were told that the company's director McGoohan had been in trouble over tax before. In 1970 when the *Danger Man* series had come to an end after enjoying years of success, the actor's company Drummond Enterprises had reportedly crashed into dissolution. McGoohan at that time was thought to be residing in Switzerland and by 1974 was being reported as living "somewhere in California."[34] The Official Receiver who was appointed claimed that McGoohan did not respond to any communications and the creditors meeting was told that all letters sent to the actor had remained unanswered.[35] Apart from the tax owed in 1974, it was reported that there was a further thirty thousand pounds in the form of debts. Against this, the only assets known of were about five hundred pounds cash and any future receipts from *The Prisoner* series. London accountant Martin Spencer was nominated as liquidator. Other directors of Everyman were said to be David Tomblin, producer of *The Prisoner*, and one (John) Roger Gambles.[xxxvi] To be fair, McGoohan may not have been aware of the British publicity and the story did die down quite quickly.

In fact, the actor returned to England not long afterwards, to play yet one more villain, this time in *The Man in the Iron Mask* (1976). He was cast as the unscrupulous French Minister of Finance, Nicholas Fouquet. The film was shot at Twickenham and on location in France and Dorset. With big names like Richard Chamberlain, Jenny Agutter and Ralph Richardson, McGoohan was able to share the acting honours with an accomplished cast. He tackled the role vigorously and took on dangerous scenes, including fencing, without a stunt double. At one point, the script required a clifftop sword duel. Despite the cliff's crumbling edges, McGoohan demanded that the fight should be shot on the edge of the precipice.

Amazon UK review: "Alexandre Dumas' classic tale of fraternal squabbling makes a more than satisfactory transition to celluloid with this 1976 made-for-television swashbuckler (with) the rather unhip presence of Richard Chamberlain in the lead role(s). This well-lensed action film overcomes a somewhat poky first half to emerge as a terrific adventure, complete with plenty of derring-do, some sharply pointed dialogue, and a wonderful performance by the incomparably malevolent Patrick McGoohan."

During filming of *The Man in the Iron Mask*, the actor had a free day and hired a car. He took his wife Joan, who had accompanied him, for a drive to Sheffield. He did not tell her where they were headed, although she recognised the city as they approached its inner section. After some difficulty with the new one-way system, the landscape having changed considerably, McGoohan finally had to park the car and proceed on foot to find the place for which he was searching. In the centre of Sheffield the actor stood his wife outside Wilson Peck's music shop, making her close her eyes.[xxxvii] He turned her around and asked her to open them again. He revealed that they were standing on the same manhole cover upon

---

[xxxvi] Correspondence from Everyman Films at the end of the sixties was signed by Roger Gambles as "Secretary to Patrick McGoohan."
[xxxvii] The shop – a Sheffield landmark, which sold sheet music, records, musical instruments, and concert tickets, closed in 2001.

which he had proposed to her, over a quarter of a century earlier.[xxxviii]

As the actor returned to the States, an appreciation society was about to be formed around his cult series *The Prisoner*. David Barrie had been fortunate to observe some of the original series' location filming, on an occasion in 1966, while he was in Portmeirion. Then a young man, Barrie was subsequently enthralled by the series when it aired in his ITV region, the following year. Now, a decade later, during the first repeat screening, he wrote to ATV Midlands, asking for other

Photograph sent by McGoohan to the appreciation society for *The Prisoner*, at the end of the 1970s with signed message

fans of the series to be given his contact details. As a result, his name and address were placed on screen, after the broadcast of *Fall Out*, leading to strangers knocking at his door in the early hours of the following morning. Hundreds of letters followed in the ensuing week, pouring through his letterbox. Barrie found himself having to send out circular, printed replies, while the enquiries still flooded in. An inaugural meeting soon followed and a name was decided on, "Six of One."

Barrie recalled starting the society: "There had never been a programme quite like *The Prisoner* before. Here was a series that dared to challenge the viewer to think, to question. Each week, the show dressed up fundamental issues such as politics and education under the guise of popular entertainment. It encapsulated the mood of the sixties, the Bomb, brainwashing and the fear of Big Brother. Patrick McGoohan, star, creator – and everything else – instilled his personal philosophy as the spirit and ethos of the series. Given the money by Lew Grade, the artist was in charge, not the men in suits. What sealed the show's longevity was the final episode, where taking surrealism and chaos theory to new heights for popularist TV entertainment, more questions were posed than answered, whilst it was revealed that Number Six, was indeed Number One: he was indeed a prisoner of himself."

Barrie added: "How could I and many others not be captivated by such a far sighted and profound show? It reflected so well the world we all lived in. It was a breath of fresh air amidst the cosy, stifling conformity of the times. When Six of One was formed, we wrote to McGoohan and he responded in days, wishing us success. Although I've been in the same room as him, I've never desired to meet him. That letter I mailed him expressed my feelings. That was sufficient. A remarkable, but private man. Why should I wish to meet him face to face? There were other ways to demonstrate my appreciation for his creation."

McGoohan's acceptance of the position of Honorary President came by telegram, at the start of 1977: "Profoundly grateful to you and the society for your interest and understanding. Am most honored to accept honorary presidency. Blessings to you all. Half a dozen of the other. Be seeing you. Patrick McGoohan."[36] The society has continued to operate for over thirty years – the actor remaining as Honorary President – with Barrie, this writer and others carrying on throughout the three decades as organisers.

[xxxviii] See page 36.

Hot on the heels of his becoming titular head of the *Prisoner* society, McGoohan was next interviewed in depth about the series in Canada, for the Ontario Educational Communications Authority (OECA). Writer Warner Troyer hosted the thirty five minute show, filmed in March, 1977, in Toronto, before a studio audience and broadcast by TV Ontario. This public television network had shown *The Prisoner* between October 1976 and February 1977, with commentaries from Troyer. In conjunction with the screening, the OECA published two booklets on *The Prisoner*, entitled *The Prisoner Puzzle* and *The Prisoner Program Guide*. These doubled as support literature for psychology and sociology students at Seneca College, in Toronto, where segments of *Prisoner* episodes were being used as study models. Stewart Niemeier, University of Toronto professor, remarked that "The Prisoner is television's first genuine work of art."[37]

The screen interview was relaxed, with McGoohan shamelessly playing to a captive audience of students and smoking cigarettes throughout the chat. At times, an audience member would join in with a comment, or ask a question, or McGoohan would ask the students what they thought, or if they agreed. Ever the entertainer, the actor referred to the objection he had taken to having to sign in, to gain access to the studio. "That's prisonership, as far as I'm concerned and that makes me mad! And that makes me rebel! And that's what *The Prisoner* was doing, rebelling against that type of thing!" The guest bemoaned the fact that these restrictions have to be lived with, saying, "That's what makes us prisoners!"

A decade had passed since McGoohan had made his cult TV series, but this was the first major interview with him about *The Prisoner*. Although it would be interesting to include many of his comments, the series has been adequately covered earlier in this book. Therefore a short exchange is included here, to give McGoohan's views on one recurring topic. He was asked about the series' conclusion and responded that he made Number One an image of Number Six, "His other half, his alter ego." When the actor was asked, "Did you know when you first outlined the series in your mind ... that Number One was going to turn out to be you, to be Number Six?" his reply was "No I didn't. That's an interesting question." Troyer queried when McGoohan had found out and received the reply: "When it got very close to the last episode and I hadn't written it yet. I had to sit down this terrible day and write the last episode and I knew it wasn't going to be something out of James Bond. In the back of my mind there was some parallel with the character Number Six and the Number One character and the rest. I didn't even know exactly, till I was about a third of the way through the script, the last script." The actor admitted using simian symbolism as "we all come from the original ape. The bestial thing and then the other bestial face behind it which was laughing, jeering and jabbering like a monkey."[38]

In complete contrast, despite earlier claims that he would never do another TV series, McGoohan was about to embark upon a US medical production, *Rafferty* (1977) – a thirteen part run of hour-long stories – playing a widower, Dr. Sid Rafferty. Publicity for the show ran: "Come hell or hospital foul-ups – no one steps between Rafferty and his patients!" More promotional spiel declared: "Rafferty will step on anyone's toes, to get his patients on their feet!" The series was filmed at the Warner Brothers studios in Hollywood. Executive producer Jerry Thorpe described McGoohan as "a consummate performer." He added, "There's an enormous amount of spontaneity in his acting. He finds fresh ways of doing clichés. And he has a low-key sex appeal. Many secretaries around here who have watched the show have said 'God! He's attractive!' He is a searching man and discerning. His

standards are inordinately high. If there's anything people find abrasive, it probably grows out of his shyness. He doesn't like people poking into his private life."[39]

McGoohan was even able to direct one episode, *The Wild Child*.[xxxix] The actor clearly had a hand in the way that scripts were crafted and even within the constraints of a hospital TV drama, he soon wanted to take storylines into unusual areas.[xl] The storyline took Sid Rafferty away from the hospital, removing the main character from the usual hospital set. With the doctor travelling on a bus, the story's director had more latitude. Another of McGoohan's suggestions was for a plot to involve the good doctor being called out to an Indian reservation, or having to treat a patient on a boating trip. These script devices presented a compassionate side of his character, in contrast to the villainous parts the actor had played of late. Dr. Sid Rafferty cared about people, not governments; he was dedicated and committed, working for the good of all. In the story *Walking Wounded*, a line of dialogue seemed to have been influenced by McGoohan's earlier *Prisoner* series, or the actor's own medical experiences. There was an apparent humorous reference to Number Two's attempts to extract Number Six's resignation secret, or perhaps McGoohan's and his daughter's real life chiropractic treatments. Dr. Rafferty was applying firm pressure to a police officer's painful back, causing added discomfort and producing the incongruous retort: "You know, if you had the secret to the Neutron Bomb and they did that to you, you'd tell them anything they wanted to know." In another story, the doctor meets a girl with a dog called "Rover." McGoohan's line in reply is, "Rover, now that's my idea of a name for a dog," harking back to the fearsome white balloon, so-nicknamed in one *Prisoner* episode.

A source at that time described McGoohan as being partly grey, keeping in shape playing racquetball at a local gym, shooting occasional pool and playing chess. The actor seemed to be at ease with his current lifestyle and surroundings. He volunteered, "Joan doesn't play chess. Gin rummy is her game. She's very good at it. I t'ink we're runnin' neck and neck. We'll play ten games. If she wins, we go away for a weekend."[40] Daughters Anne and Frances were in their late teens. Catherine had been married for some time and was living in Fresno, having already had offspring of her own. *Rafferty* was being scheduled for Monday evenings, opposite NFL (National Football League). McGoohan said, "If O.J. (Simpson) is on, I'll be watchin' him. I'm not denigratin' my show. I never watch my show, except when I have directed it." McGoohan admitted, "I'm an insomniac. I sleep four hours maximum. I get up at 2.30 a.m. I read or write and then I'm out of the house to walk on the beach. It's lonely then, just people with their dogs and some surfers." Even with *Rafferty* presently occupying his time, the actor confessed, "I want to have my own film company. I want to do stage work in Montana. And I want to pay my wife back. She quit acting shortly after we married. She didn't resent quitting, but she still quit so I could work. She's a big lady in that sense. The time's come for the resurgence of her career. I want to write a play for the two of us."[41]

Over the course of the first season of *Rafferty*, the critics became hostile. The show was cancelled and only ten of the filmed thirteen episodes were screened (although the series had full exposure in the UK). Medical TV series come and go and *Rafferty* was 'struck off'

[xxxix] Some sources wrongly refer to McGoohan's directed episode as being *The Outcast*. He was in a story of that name in *The Adventures of Sir Lancelot*. There was also an episode so called in *Assignment Foreign Legion*, although McGoohan did not appear in it, but did have a part in another episode in the series called *The Coward*. These two fifties shows are covered earlier in this book.
[xl] It will be recalled that McGoohan had directed the *Columbo* episode *Last Salute to the Commodore*, see page 198.

for falling ratings. Summarising the medical series in an unofficial publication at the time, US fan Karen Esibill offered praise, "If there is one constant in the otherwise erratic career of Patrick McGoohan it is that most of his characters are a continuation. Whether hero or villain, they all possess a remarkable amount of McGoohan's own awesome personality. So, it's of little surprise that after turning down offers for years, he decided to return to a television series as the abrasive, wilful and very appealing Dr. Sid Rafferty. Typical of McGoohan's strange habit of revealing glimpses of his private life via his film work, the pictures on the office wall of the late Mrs. Rafferty are actually photos of the very much alive, real-life Mrs. McGoohan."[42]

Looking back on *Rafferty* in later years, McGoohan commented in interview that the series had not been a particularly pleasant experience. He felt that he was being subjected to the 'conveyer belt' system of making TV shows. Although the rebellious nature of the doctor was appealing to the actor playing him, there were too many executives to deal with and, in the end, the actor could only identify with the series to the extent that the personality traits of Sid Rafferty were close to his own. However, the automated production methods were the dominant factor, and the role alone was not enough to leave the actor with any happy memories of *Rafferty*. Although McGoohan might have had a negative opinion of the series, this writer found a lot of good in several of the episodes. Apart from the twee beginning of each story and the sickly opening tune, various segments had their merits. In addition, this was the first lengthy piece of exposure of McGoohan on TV, since he discarded the almost identical character of John Drake and Number Six. However, McGoohan remained highly disapproving of *Rafferty*: "(It) was a disaster. That was the most miserable job I've ever done in my life. You (got) all sorts of promises up front that it's going to be a certain style series … and the scripts are monstrous pieces of garbage. I wanted him to be a roving doctor. And they promised me that this would happen. And instead of that, I was spending all my time walking up and down f**king hospital corridors! I said get me out of this f**king hospital!"[43] The actor's final comments on *Rafferty*, some time later were uncomplimentary: "I prefer to have that one buried with a stake through its heart,"[44] and "(*Rafferty*) was probably the most horrendous experience of my life."[45]

With the end of *Rafferty*, McGoohan proceeded to reappraise some of his past productions. Journalist Arnold Hano, in a 1977 interview, reminded the actor that he had appeared in a compost of bad films in England. McGoohan winced to be reminded of *High Tide at Noon, Hell Drivers, The Gypsy and the Gentleman, Nor the Moon by Night* and *Two Living One Dead*. "Junk," offered McGoohan, "all of them. There's nothin' there a civilised man would want to be reminded of." Instead, he announced his intention to 'remarry' his wife Joan. "We were too busy for a Church ceremony (when) I was rehearsing for Petruchio in *The Taming of the Shrew*.[xli] I said to (Joan), 'I promise you a white weddin' sometime, but not now.'"[xlii] [46] McGoohan now presented the love of his life with a special ring, in reaffirmation of their long partnership. "A white ring for a white weddin.' My wife is dark, a dark angel. The ring is white jade."[47] Another report described the married couple as living "quietly in Pacific Palisades and even more quietly in Montana where, surprisingly,

[xli] Paul Eddington, who later appeared in *The Prisoner*, was Tranio in the same production. McGoohan was quoted as saying that Joan played Ophelia – purportedly referring to *The Taming of the Shrew* – but the character appears in *Hamlet*, not *The Taming of the Shrew*.
[xlii] Some interviews and some sources refer to the wedding taking place between *The Taming of the Shrew* and *Hamlet*, or between *The Taming of the Shrew* and *The Rivals*. However, neither Shakespeare play was being produced in May, 1951, only *The Rivals. Hamlet* had been produced in January, 1951 at the Sheffield Playhouse, but *The Taming of the Shrew* was not until January, 1952.

McGoohan has planned a ceremony that seems somewhat alien to the rebellious instincts in which he glories. On a chilly 1977 May day, high in the mountains, he and Joan will be married again. She will be in white. It will be their 26th wedding anniversary." The affectionate husband commented, "You can be a rebel but you can also be a romantic. This is a reaffirmation of love. I owe it to my wife, this is what she wants. If you owe your wife so much and this is what she wants to do, you do it."[48]

[1] Sunday Telegraph Magazine, 24th March, 1985, Anthony Masters
[2] You, The Mail on Sunday Magazine, March,1983, Mike Bygrave
[3] Sunday Telegraph Magazine, 24th March, 1985, Anthony Masters
[4] TV Guide, New Zealand, March, 1969
[5] Ibid
[6] The Fool's Pardon, 1994, Kenneth Griffith autobiography
[7] Pace Magazine, December, 1969, Henry Pelham Burn
[8] Source not verified
[9] New Zealand television review, 1984, details unknown
[10] Cosmopolitan, December, 1969, Jeannie Sakol
[11] TV Times 1977
[12] TV Guide, 17th September, 1977, Arnold Hano
[13] The Sun, 1977, Lee Bury
[14] Classic Images Magazine, 1987, Barbara Pruett
[15] Publicity material for The Moonshine War, 1970
[16] Ibid
[17] Hollywood paper, 6th October, 1969, Sheilah Graham, details unknown
[18] Chiropractic Economics Magazine, online History Section
[19] Chiropractic Journal, c.1970
[20] Ibid
[21] Chiropractic Economics Magazine, July, 2004
[22] Ibid
[23] Premiere Magazine, October 1995, Jean Yves Katelan (translations Rosemary Camilleri and Jane Rawson)
[24] The Sun, 17th November, 1973, Fergus Cashin and Chris Kenworthy
[25] British film magazine, 1973, details unknown
[26] British newspaper, 1973, details unknown
[27] Turn it on Again, November 2004, Backbeat, Dave Thompson (thanks to Patrick Ducher for details)
[28] The Columbo Phile, Mark Dawidziak, 1998
[29] Source not verified
[30] Classic Images Magazine, 1987, Barbara Pruett
[31] Premiere Magazine, October 1995, Jean Yves Katelan (translations Rosemary Camilleri and Jane Rawson)
[32] The Steve Wright Show, BBC Radio Two, 25th October, 2005
[33] Cutting supplied to writer, details unknown
[34] Daily Mail, 22nd August, 1974
[35] The Sun, 22nd August, 1974
[36] Telegram to Six of One, The Prisoner Appreciation Society, 11th February, 1977
[37] The Spectator, 5th March, 1977, Billy Oliver
[38] Ontario Educational Communications Authority, TV Ontario, March 1977, Warner Troyer
[39] TV Guide, 17th September, 1977, Arnold Hano
[40] Ibid
[41] Ibid
[42] Ibid
[43] Anglofile, spring 1985, Bill King
[44] TV Guide, 17th September, 1977, Arnold Hano
[45] Boston Globe, 13th January, 1985, Ed Siegel
[46] Ibid
[47] Ibid
[48] TV Times, 1977

McGoohan as Colonel Mike McCauley, OSS in *Brass Target* (1978)

CHAPTER NINE
Alive and Well in California

"We don't make good citizens, but we make good prisoners."
Escape from Alcatraz (1979)

Rafferty was given a US air date in September, 1977, by which time McGoohan had once more teamed up with *Prisoner* co-star Alexis Kanner, who was French-Canadian. Filming on Kanner's self-produced movie *Kings and Desperate Men*[i] (1981 Canada; 1983 US; 1984 UK) took place in and around Montreal, with some shooting in Quebec. Work continued into 1978, but future camera and post-production work would delay release of the movie for a few more years. *Kings* would be Kanner's single mainstream cinema directorial release, marking also the only other occasion when he worked with the former *Prisoner* star.[ii] There were many times that McGoohan did screen work in Canada, or had connections with the country: his early film and TV appearances there; the 1967 *Prisoner* world premiere in Canada; the Ontario Educational Communications Authority (OECA) *Prisoner* courses; the Toronto Warner Troyer TV interview; *Silver Streak* (1976); *Scanners* (1981); *Hysteria* (1998). The latter three productions, involving locations in Alberta, Ontario and Quebec, are covered later in this book.

Kings and Desperate Men had echoes of *The Prisoner*, in that director Kanner was developing as a creator and performer, just as McGoohan had done a decade earlier. Using his own name and pseudonyms, Kanner modestly avoided crediting himself with the entire actor-writer-director-producer-editor profile. Clearly, he was treading a McGoohan-inspired

---

[i] The title was taken from the John Donne poem *Death Be Not Proud*: "Thou art slave to fate, chance, kings, and desperate men."
[ii] They would both appear a few years later in a *Prisoner* TV documentary, *Six into One: The Prisoner File*, but not together.

path, wanting to be more fully engaged in movie production. Kanner had been involved in a number of fringe engagements and had notched up several important supporting cinema and television screen roles. However, *Kings* was the most ambitious project that he had undertaken. The movie is idiosyncratic and multi-layered, lasting for almost two hours. Its first half has a fast moving build-up, a fair level of action and a kaleidoscope of different types of scenes introducing the characters. In the second half, however, the events are presented in real time. The terrorists and the forces sent to capture them (an actual squad of trained officers, claimed Kanner), plus the kidnapped members of the main character's family, are linked by a live radio broadcast. The radio host John Kingsley (McGoohan), husband of the abducted wife and father of the children being held with them, is confronted by the edgy leader of the terrorists, Henry Miller, played by Kanner. A 'public trial' takes place over the airwaves, but the terrorist gang become jumpy and a judge, also being held, dies. Audience sympathies switch between the husband and parent who might be about to lose his family, the terrorist spokesman who presents as a sympathetic figure and the hostages. Clear principles are muddled within this morality tale. Kanner voiced the opinion that the world was moving into an uncertain age, with murders and atrocities occurring with a greater frequency. As for McGoohan's performance, there is a tenderness displayed at some points – when speaking by phone to his kidnapped wife and children – not evidenced in his other film roles. Admittedly, some servings of comedy ham from the actor are more funny-embarrassing than funny-effective. Nevertheless, there are some magical interludes on screen between McGoohan and Kanner.

The critics were generally impressed: "Alexis Kanner's bold, brash and sometimes brilliant film ... has (been) produced, directed and written (by him). The compelling picture ... throws in ideas like popcorn into a saucepan. Some of them expand, others merely explode. But it is always an edgy, exciting thriller that is laced with the blackest of comedy. McGoohan invests (his character), the lordly presenter, with the studied eloquence of a ham actor who has quit the boards and fled to a country in which accent and voice training make him instantly employable. The performances are ideally matched, McGoohan in particular cleverly balanced on the very edge of caricature."[1]

"(In) Alexis Kanner's sleek, dazzling political thriller ... an attorney (played by Kanner himself) has turned terrorist in a desperate ploy to correct what he considers to be a gross miscarriage of justice. What sounds like a conventional TV movie plot (is) turned into an exciting tour de force. (It) is not simply an anti-terrorist brief; it respects the attorney's fervent sincerity, even if it deplores his methods and increasingly suggests that he's built his case on shaky ground. (The film) is worthy of Oscar consideration in several categories."[2]

Various other magazines and newspapers also rated the movie highly: "It is without doubt once of the most compelling films I've seen all year," said Films magazine. Time Out described "An innovative and compulsive psychological thriller ... it is remarkable." The Observer billed the two lead actors as "electrifying performers". Amid several other similar reviews such as "No-one will forget it," or "Crackles with a sardonic wit that sparks," the Sunday Times' own extolment was that the film "tingles with an edginess and is combustible with ideas."

With the Canadian premier's wife Margaret Trudeau[iii] also appearing in the movie, as McGoohan's wife – her first film role – there was plenty of publicity surrounding *Kings*. One

---

[iii] At the age of 22, she became the youngest First Lady in the world at the time of her marriage to Pierre Trudeau.

critic wrote off the film saying that Kanner had bitten off more than he could chew: "The film's sole appeal is the talented McGoohan, whose contempt for his captor (Kanner) becomes very convincing by the time the plot wraps up. Other than that, this mod-looking thriller borders on the ridiculous."[3] Ms Trudeau recalled her part, describing the offer to act and the fee as "unbelievable." However, the actress encountered problems, including "the natural animosity between myself and Patrick McGoohan, that was obvious even before we started work together." Ms Trudeau gave an account of the film set – built on the top floor of Montreal's Four Seasons Hotel – where the actors were also staying. "I was surprised to see distinctly frightened look in (McGoohan's) eyes. Perhaps he was shy. Certainly he gave the impression of mistrusting me profoundly." It is even possible that the actor was failing to hide his disapproval of a person he regarded as inexperienced.

According to Trudeau, as shooting was due to commence, she was greeted by her leading man asking her nastily, "What are you doing here?" She had previously thought of McGoohan as a person she admired. Now, she was describing him as "a big surly man, with an awful temper." She decided to take him to task, asking for mutual respect and for him to make allowances for her need to learn the acting craft. Given that Ms. Trudeau was the wife of Canada's leader and a figure of great interest to the press, she was naturally receiving more media attention than McGoohan. "As he became more frustrated he took it upon himself to cut my lines. Every time I had a big scene coming up he would call me over, take out a fat black pencil and, putting his hand out for my script, start removing lines. I soon sensed that both he and the director were really playing a game with me in order to get me into the right mood for the script. I was supposed to be a terrified, confused and hurt woman – and by the time Patrick McGoohan had finished with me, I certainly was."

At the latter end of shooting, on Christmas Eve 1977, there came the final bust-up. According to Trudeau, "By now McGoohan was storming around, shouting that he would get me fired unless I did what he said. He announced 'We can replace you this instant. We'll shoot any girl in what you're wearing, from the side. There must be ten girls walking down Sherbrooke Street at this moment who could step in here and do what you're doing – far better than you're doing it.'" Trudeau had one card to play, as related in her autobiography. She decided to meet McGoohan's threat with one of her own, to leave the set, along with her raincoat, which was her own property. Thus it would not be possible for the costume item to be replaced, on Christmas Eve. The actress claimed that this worked, "He gave me no more trouble." Trudeau found Kanner "a bit of a megalomaniac in the way he saw himself as Orson Welles – leading man, supporting actor, writer and editor. He couldn't delegate and became ever more possessive about the film and in the end it took three years before he deemed it ready for release."[4] Her final thoughts were that her fellow actress on the movie, Andrea Marcovicci, shared Trudeau's sense of exasperation over McGoohan. Ms. Marcovicci said, that McGoohan was the hardest man she ever had to work with.

Some critics found *Kings* to be exciting, fresh and innovative. However, respected US film reviewer, Leonard Maltin, gave the film a low rating: "Interesting premise sabotaged by poor direction, choppy editing. McGoohan overacts shamelessly."[5] Leslie Halliwell's opinion was, "Indulgently scripted, directed and acted, and dreary to watch."[iv] [6] However, Kanner was in no doubt that he had extracted a memorable performance from his co-star. The

---

[iv] It was not until the autumn of 1984 that *Kings and Desperate Men* had its British premiere, at the London Film Festival. Kanner flew in from Canada to attend the event. Unfortunately, only a limited cinema run and two video releases occurred.

actor-director told this writer: "I think Patrick gives the greatest performance of his life and he has said so in the press. In one interview, unlike Patrick, he said to an American newspaper that he thought now that he could die happy because he knew that there was a record on film of his best work for his grandchildren to see. And he was tremendous. Those kind of parts don't come along very often and when they do, they are not often in the hands of a film-maker who is also an actor who is devoted to getting the best performance on screen and was willing to make bad cuts to save the best takes and edits, just because it's more important that the actor comes over well. Patrick gave a very intense performance. I said (to the editors) we'll go for the best takes, where he's absolutely breathtaking."[7]

When the movie was completed, Kanner waited with nervous anticipation as to what would be McGoohan's reaction. "He saw the final result and was thrilled. I know he is sensitive to watching himself on screen and usually he doesn't like his own work. His is a risky performance, which he takes to the edge. His character is an actor who trained to be Laurence Olivier and ends up a talk-show host on a North American radio station."[8] During Kanner's UK promotion of *Kings*, he said there was never any doubt in his mind that the main role of John Kingsley could be played by nobody but McGoohan. "I was delighted when his agent said that he would be very proud and happy to do it."[9] McGoohan began to show his hands-on interest in the movie. According to Kanner, "He wanted to know where the cuts would come, where the scenes would end. Directing him was excellent. Sometimes it wasn't necessary for us to use words. He knew what I was going to say and just did it."[10]

The real-life Mrs. McGoohan had ceased her acting career over twenty years earlier. Latterly, she had moved into selling real estate, nobly allowing her husband to continue his acting career, with no regret on her part being expressed. Her entry into the world of real estate had occurred when the family moved from New Mexico to Los Angeles. Joan did not think the realtor who handled the sale did a good job and was sure she could do better. She eventually progressed to selling high value Californian properties, earning a lucrative living for the McGoohans, as a realtor. In the early eighties, Joan was the top sales person for her firm.[v] This apparently caused her husband to attend the only cocktail party he ever went to in his life. McGoohan told a journalist, "This year she has sold twenty eight houses and not one of them went for under half a million. The other day she sold one in Beverley Hills to a Saudi for a million. The chap showed up with a suitcase packed with cash then squabbled for hours about whether the second hand washing machine went with the house. Mind you, I've told Joan that when she starts making more than I do, she has to quit."[11]

In California, property selling is a highly remunerative activity. Expensive homes are there to be bought by the rich, or viewed during arranged bus tours of celebrity homes. Joan McGoohan established herself in the high value real estate world and soon rose up the partnership ladder. She became responsible for handling multi-million dollar properties and as Internet pages attest, her world of house sales is a fascinating one. Joan also immersed herself in the property selling phenomenon, known as "open house," a marketing exercise during which affluent streets become host to an "acquisitive carnival." Flags flap in front of residences – all valued in excess of a million dollars – while signs and arrows point house hunting hordes to available properties. It is not only buyers who tread the trail, but also the curious and even the stars. Joan recalled that Steven Spielberg, Dustin Hoffman and Richard Dreyfuss all wandered through one of her open houses during a single day. She also

---

[v] In later years, daughter Anne's name would also appear as a realtor within the company.

remembered a Pacific Palisades home which she was able to sell for over thirteen million dollars to a businessman who hadn't even intended to buy in that price range.[12] One house, built a hundred years ago in the grand American Colonial style and listed at over four million dollars was singled out by Joan, who said it felt "Just like Mill Hill," the place where the family had lived, in England.[13]

Now, a quartet of screen productions were once more about to feature husband Patrick's acting talents: *Brass Target* (1978), *Escape from Alcatraz* (1979), *The Hard Way* (1979; for TV) and *Scanners* (1981). These involved filming in several countries, including the USA, Ireland and Canada. The plot behind *Brass Target* was based on *The Algonquin Project*, by Fred Nolan. McGoohan's role was as the quirky Colonel Mike McCauley, who was involved in a conspiracy against General Patton after World War II. In *Brass Target* his

McGoohan with co-star Alexis Kanner during filming of *Kings and Desperate Men* (1981)

role was a minor one, his demise occurring early on in the picture by an unpleasant piece of garrotting, so he 'sat out' the major part of the movie. A newspaper review unkindly commented, "McGoohan is the most fun, playing a spirited game of guess-the-accent."[14]

New York Times review: "What if General George S. Patton didn't die in a car accident, as history tells us, but at the hands of a paid assassin? That's the premise of Brass Target, another in a series of espionage thrillers that speculates on the fates of real-life figures from World War II. Three Allied officers in occupied Germany steal Nazi gold with the help of OSS officer Patrick McGoohan. Patton (George Kennedy) personally supervises the investigation of the theft, assisted by Major Joe DeLuca (John Cassavetes). Soon, however, a professional assassin (Max Von Sydow) is on their trail, Patton is killed on the orders of his own staff, and only DeLuca and his lover (Sophia Loren), who is also involved with the assassin, are left alive for the finale." (Don Kaye, All Movie Guide)

McGoohan was next to become the feared Warden[vi] in the big budget movie *Escape from Alcatraz* (1979), co-starring Clint Eastwood. This had parallels with *The Prisoner*, the brutalising island regime and its detrimental effect upon inmates being the driving force of the film, apart from guessing whether Eastwood would escape or not. McGoohan's sinister performance was described as "enjoyably melodramatic and sadistic." The actor described his role as the Warden: "He's a very cold, ruthless, strict man. A very harsh man with no compassion whatsoever. From the very first meeting it is implied that there's an immediate personality clash between the Warden and Clint Eastwood's character. Therefore the Warden wants to do anything he can to demoralise Mr. Eastwood's character and he does everything remotely possible."[15] McGoohan was asked also about the small bird, kept as a pet, by his character. "A lot of paranoiac people keep gentle things to balance their paranoia. So in his office he's got a bird in a cage, some fish in a tank and he looks after them carefully and plays with them a lot of the time. Personally I think he's a nutcase!" The actor admitted that the current role was

---

[vi] The character's name was not revealed.

Scene from the TV film *The Hard Way* (1979)

not particularly enjoyable, but accepted that all kinds of parts had to be taken by an actor such as himself.[16]

The movie was highly successful, its tagline being one of the Warden's scripted comments: "No one has ever escaped from Alcatraz. And no one ever will!" He proudly boasts to Clint Eastwood's character, "If you disobey the rules of society, they send you to prison; if you disobey the rules of the prison, they send you to *us*. From this day on, your world will be everything that happens in this building." A fan of the movie wrote: "In the 29 years of Alcatraz's existence, and despite the strict measures, 39 captives tried to escape from America's premier maximum-security prison during its existence... Thirty six of whom failed ... This script is about the other three, of whom nothing is known ... They may have drowned in San Francisco Bay, or they may have got away." Another admirer of the film commented: "Eastwood and McGoohan ... both give fantastic performances. It is a top-notch movie ... and I'd highly recommend it."[17]

New York Times review: "No one can escape from Alcatraz, right? Try telling that to lifer Frank Morris (Clint Eastwood). This Donald Siegel-directed nailbiter is a re-enactment of Frank Morris' 1962 attempt to bust himself and two other cons out of The Rock. Eastwood, as Morris, tilts with nasty warden Patrick McGoohan for a while, befriends several fellow prisoners, and picks the guys with whom he'll make his escape. Among his break-out buddies are the Anglin Brothers (Fred Ward and Jack Thibeau), with whom he'd served in other lockups, and several others who've got their own special reasons to despise the sadistic McGoohan. The film leaves open the possibility that Morris might just have made it." (Hal Erickson, All Movie Guide)

McGoohan returned to Ireland in the same year, to shoot *The Hard Way* (1979), a TV movie[vii] about two ageing assassins.[viii] One assessment described the film as "a very well made low budget minimalist neo noir set in Ireland. McGoohan and Van Cleef are very effective in their roles as underworld hit men. Sparse dialogue and good cinematography. Direction is slow but assured and suits the tone of the story well." Another summary was concisely given: "What a brilliantly empty piece of nihilism and what a brilliant combination McGoohan and Van Cleef turned out to be." One more appreciative appraisal was: "Any 'Prisoner' fan will see parallels between aspects of this plot and McGoohan's previous series: an agent who wants to give up his covert work but is not let off the hook so easily by his masters. The agent decides to leave anyway and is pursued relentlessly by his former bosses. An understated, interesting study, worth a look."[18]

The Hard Way was unusual material for McGoohan, as one observer of the production commented in her review: "The man who talks so easily about immorality, amorality and dishonesty, is playing the part of a hired killer. Admittedly, McGoohan's character, John Connor, is trying to retire and make amends with his conscience. There's a great deal of McGoohan in this part. The brooding tough guy at the crossroads of his life. The struggle with his conscience and with his morality. The loner, the solitary man."[19] Writer Jenny Rees was told by McGoohan that he had instantly been attracted to the part. "I suppose it was because I'd avoided parts that had anything to do with guns before."

The reporter found that on set McGoohan had a reputation of being so changeable in mood that people did not know what to expect on any given day. Even his voice would change from the clipped *Danger Man* style to the broader Dublin tones, before moving off into a tough New York-style. He was asked the obvious question by the interviewer, regarding his reasons for leaving Britain. Curiously, he mentioned the fence which Mill Hill's local council had required him to remove, many years earlier. Ms. Rees went on to reveal more about the actor's life at this point in his quiet Pacific Palisades neighbourhood. She learned that in his garden, where his den was situated, he wrote poetry, novels and film scripts.[ix] McGoohan was reflective about *The Hard Way*, saying that he just looked for good scripts and had never been ambitious. The only things important to him were his wife and three daughters. He expected to retreat more and more into a quiet way of life, spending time at the family log cabin in Montana, where McGoohan would fish for trout. The actor revealed, "Anyone can be an individual in society. Only you may have to make sacrifices. I think I classify myself as an individual rather than a rebel. I'm an actor because it's the best way I know to make a comfortable living."[20]

New York Times review: "Patrick McGoohan does his patented 'carrying the world on my shoulders' bit in *The Hard Way*. McGoohan is cast as Conner, a worldly, weary professional assassin. On the verge of retirement, he is cajoled by former associate McNeal

[vii] An ITC film, produced and directed by Michael Dryhurst, with John Boorman as executive producer.
[viii] The rival hit man was played by Lee Van Cleef.
[ix] Sadly, one whimsical screenplay which would have made an entertaining movie never reached fruition. McGoohan said at the time, "It's about a young man who inherits a vacant lot in Manhattan, between two skyscrapers, and builds himself a log cabin, which he fills with his collection of moths and butterflies and where he grows a herb garden. He becomes a national folk hero.."

McGoohan signs autographs for fans during filming of The Hard Way (1979)

(Lee Van Cleef) into doing one last job. Expecting a routine assignment, Conner is in for quite a jolt when he learns the identity of his target. Co-star Van Cleef effectively matches and sometimes surpasses McGoohan's trenchant cynicism." (Hal Erickson, All Movie Guide)

During filming of The Hard Way, McGoohan reportedly suffered a painful abscess under a tooth, distorting his jaw and the left side of his face. This was revealed in a showbusiness article, describing the actor as a "mystery man," who had granted only one other interview in the preceding twelve years. It was therefore claimed that the current interview would be the last for at least a decade, with the actor being likened to an island, remote and craggy. McGoohan was described as generally looking good, although a little fleshier than in his heyday. The mid-Atlantic accent, it was observed, had not diminished, nor the Gatling-gun delivery. The actor was said to be fidgeting constantly, as he smoked, crossing and uncrossing his legs, while his expression was unchanging. As seen in examples of other interviews with different journalists, McGoohan would be either utterly charming and comfortable, or on edge and abrupt. In the present interview, he seemed to be in the middle, answering often in generalities. "To be a star, you have to be more than I was prepared to do. You have to sell your soul, and I mean sell. Too many guys are prepared to trade their wife, kids, homes and happiness, just to see their name up in lights. Not me."

Asked about his disappearance from UK shores, McGoohan said simply that he took off for New Mexico and stayed there for three years. "I'd had enough," he offered, without further explanation. The actor ruminated that he was now not likely to reach stardom level. "I've done things and played some parts that I have regretted, simply because I was starving or broke." He closed with the revelation that he was, "where I want to be at the moment," adding, "I wanted to write poetry, take a closer look at myself, read, think and write."[21]

Completing *The Hard Way*, McGoohan returned to the States, where he said he would soon be spending most of his time on a small chicken farm which he owned in Montana. Raising poultry was surprising, given his earlier years of illness, caused by asthma developing from an allergy to feathers. Although he told the press that he was not giving up acting, he stated that he intended to spend most of his time on the farm hidden in the vast forests of Montana. "I like eggs. It's marvellous when you get 3000 eggs incubating at the same time. You have to wear earplugs from the noise all the chicks are making in pecking out of the shells. I may even make a movie of the chicks hatching." Of his two former refusals to take on the role of James Bond, McGoohan said "After Connery quit and after George Lazenby's brief spell as Bond, I was offered the role again. I still didn't like the character. I'd rather do chicken farming."[22]

Meanwhile, a Canadian interview was appearing in 1979, also confirming that McGoohan was giving up acting to farm poultry. "He's escaping to his secret hideout, a log cabin in the woods of Montana." The actor was quoted regarding his next intended project, the filming of thousands of chicken eggs hatching: "I'm going to have a 150 mm camera and shoot that happening. I'm also going to have a high speed camera and film the catching of trout in one of the two rivers which run through my piece of land." According to the report, McGoohan "slips away to his cabin several times a year, to join his partners in a small film company making documentaries." As soon as the actor had finished *The Hard Way* (1979) he would be back to his cabin in the woods, it was said, in the pursuit of privacy.[23]

Also in 1979, a humorous pop song was recorded as a tribute to the star, entitled "I Helped Patrick McGoohan Escape."[x] A promotional video[xi] was also filmed, the assistant director being Simon West, who was later named to helm a movie remake of *The Prisoner*, covered later in this book. Singer Ed Ball fronted first The Teenage Filmstars and later The Times, before going solo, offering various, and different versions of his ditty:

(First verse) *Once long ago, lived a man, who made a TV show,*
Spent all his savings, every penny, so that we could know.
But this poor man had few fans and his boss wouldn't pay him.
So I thought up a way to help him escape.
(Chorus) *I, I, I, I helped Patrick McGoohan escape.*
Now he's hiding from the human race.[xii]

In fact, the late seventies produced myriad magazine articles and a mass of information about *The Prisoner*, opening the floodgates as to details about the series, never before available. 'Fanzines' chose the cult show and its iconic Number Six character for artwork

[x] The song was re-issued several times – and on albums – the latest being at the end of 2006.
[xi] The 1982 video used costumed members of Six of One, in Portmeirion, North Wales, in the spring and this writer, in London, during the summer, driving his *Prisoner* replica Lotus Seven sportscar, on an airfield and around Westminster, London, to recreate the series' opening sequence.
[xii] Lyrics © Ed Ball.

and features.[xiii] Many a fan was interviewed by the press in his or her home area, for local, or regional, newspapers and conventions in Portmeirion attracted much publicity. Media reports were describing the series as "The TV show that just won't die." Although rescreenings had recently ended in Britain, already fans were clamouring for yet another repeat of the episodes, with home video recorders not yet being widespread in the country. This was the era of the 'punk revolution' and, paradoxically, *The Prisoner* did not stand as comfortably alongside the Mohican-haired and safety pin-adorned rockers, as it had once done with the former decade's Hippies and protesters.

However, lengthy and in-depth articles appeared about the series and it seemed that *The Prisoner* was being discovered for the first time. Populist television programmes began finding spots in their series for a look at the show and travel programmes would mimic scenes from episodes when visiting Portmeirion.[xiv] Even radio breakfast shows would make comments about *The Prisoner*, or play the theme tune and in London marathon screenings of episodes were arranged. By the early eighties, the series' Appreciation Society was approaching its fifth birthday. At this time, many of McGoohan's recent films were appearing on television and a "Best of British" celebration from ITV included the *Prisoner* episode *The Girl Who Was Death*. Numerous interviews with the star were published in newspapers and even a *Prisoner* themed night occurred at a club in central London, attended not only by fans and media people, but with even the odd actor, pop star, or music group members in attendance. At this point at last, the first commercial videos of the series went on sale.

In sharp contrast, along came the horror movie *Scanners* (1981).[xv] To find McGoohan involved in this occasionally gory, Canadian production was unexpected. The film, directed by David Cronenberg, included scenes of graphic violence, delivered via state of the art special effects techniques. The reported story behind the project was that McGoohan had written a script for the producers of *Scanners*. When he delivered this, they asked if he would be available to appear in their movie, which was in pre-production. McGoohan's performance in the film is nowadays regarded by some as being amongst his best, despite the actor's difficult relationship with the film's director. The actor, as Dr. Paul Ruth, is asked by one of his 'patients' what is a scanner. He replies, "Freak of nature, born with a certain form of ESP; derangement of the synapses which we call telepathy." Ruth needs to 'infiltrate' an organisation's computer, telling the scanner working for him, "… you … have a nervous system. And so does a computer. And you can scan a computer, as you would another human being." The man is being mentored by Ruth, who co-opts him to ferret out a dangerous, rogue scanner (played by Michael Ironside), a psychopath seeking world domination.

Evaluations of the movie – McGoohan's first in the new decade – were positive: "Scanners is a film about a group of human mutants that are able to basically make people go mad, and finally they can make their minds actually explode. Supposedly created out of

---

[xiii] A Marvel comics adaptation of *The Prisoner* was even considered and two different prototypes, amounting to nearly 40 pages, were commissioned, although the project did not eventually go ahead.
[xiv] The resort's creator, Sir Clough Williams-Ellis, died in 1978. Sadly, Portmeirion's main hotel building was destroyed by fire in June, 1981 and was not restored for several years. In 1982 the first *Prisoner* information centre was opened there, operated by Max Hora, a Six of One organiser.
[xv] The film won the Saturn Award for Best International Film, awarded by the Academy of Science Fiction, Fantasy and Horror Films, USA and the 1983 Fantasporto International Fantasy Film Award for Best Film (Fantasporto is the Festival Internacional de Cinema do Porto, Portugal).

the scientific work of a scientist working on a product for pregnant women ... the scanners ... are divided into two factions. One is out to destroy all other scanners and the other works for the labs that created them. This is an intensely philosophical film filled with many thought-provoking questions and issues. Patrick McGoohan plays the fatherly scientist with style and finesse."[24]

The movie spawned two sequels and a number of DVD releases, including a recent combined special edition set.

New York Times review: "The title of this David Cronenberg sci-fi horror film refers to a group of people who have telekinetic powers that allow them to read minds and give them the ability to make other people's heads explode. The children of a group of women who took an experimental tranquilizer during their pregnancies, the scanners are now adults and have become outcasts from society. But Darryl (Michael Ironside) decides to create an army of scanners to take over the world. The only person who can stop him is his brother Cameron (Stephen Lack), who wants to forget that he was ever a scanner." (Matthew Tobey, All Movie Guide)

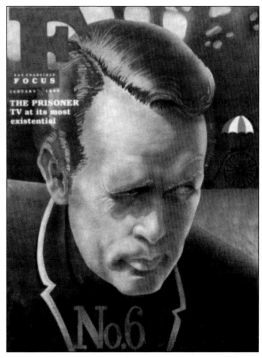

Cover of *Focus* magazine during a US *Prisoner* TV re-run in 1986

Director Cronenberg acknowledged McGoohan's performance in *Scanners*, but cited the star as a negative factor whilst making the movie.[xvi] He referred to the actor's self-destructiveness and implied that McGoohan suffered from self-loathing. He even included a quote from the star himself, reportedly having commented that if he did not drink, he would probably kill someone. If, years later, McGoohan was ever asked about the *Scanners* director, he would simply ask, "What was his name again?"[25] The actor however described the movie as a small-budget film. "They make commercials for more than that one cost."[26]

If Cronenberg's views on McGoohan's drinking were correct, this might explain how the actor reportedly came to be arrested for alleged drunken driving, within a few months of finishing work on *Scanners*. In July, 1982, the news emerged that he had been arrested and detained by police after driving erratically on the Pacific Coast Highway, near Los Angeles. It was said that the actor did not pass a sobriety test and was subsequently booked and released from West L.A. Jail on one thousand dollars bail. Another report said that his licence was suspended and that he had been charged not only with drunken driving, but also driving with a suspended licence and driving without a licence. In the event, McGoohan was said to have pleaded 'no contest' and was fined three hundred and ninety dollars, as well as being placed on three years' probation. In September, 1982, a newspaper claimed that the actor's driving ban had led him to negotiate buying a taxi firm near his new Santa Monica home.[27]

[xvi] In his book *Cronenberg on Cronenberg* (1992).

Around the same time – this writer having taken over operation of Six of One, the Prisoner Appreciation Society, a year earlier – contact with McGoohan was maintained. The actor telephoned sporadically, although his approach was initially guarded. It was soon discovered that McGoohan's caution arose from an earlier Six of One interview – when he was filming *The Hard Way* (1979), in Ireland – conducted by a former organiser of the society. The conversation, tape recorded in the actor's Dublin hotel, was later published in written form, in several successive society mailings, with McGoohan's approval. However, the actor had directed that the actual recording was only to be used for transcription, stipulating that the tape was neither to be copied, nor distributed, in any way. Contrary to McGoohan's wishes, the full conversation was subsequently circulated and later sold by the organiser, in audio cassette and compact disc form. When the actor had received his copy of the society's summer 1981 mailing, with its featured interview audio cassette, he was angry and quickly sent the original interviewer a telegram, "Under no circumstances shall that tape be given to anyone."[xvii] Now, when presently calling this writer, McGoohan would invariably ask whether the listener had a recorder running, commenting, "I wasn't happy about that tape, you know."

The audio reproduction of the conversation soured relations with McGoohan, although there was little which could be done by him, or this writer. It was, however, a source of regret that within only a relatively short time of the actor having affiliated himself with the society, he should become so swiftly disaffected. As to the previous organiser (who had since left), McGoohan said, "I want nothing to do with him." Consequently this writer always verified with the actor during subsequent calls – no recordings ever being made – that it was in order to publish parts of the conversations. In this way, appreciation society publications were able to contain occasional 'transcripts' of what had been said and these were sent openly to McGoohan. The actor never objected to the written format and sometimes would even generously dictate a message by telephone to be used in print, or would send written greetings, to be reproduced.

On a more positive note, McGoohan always expressed enormous thanks to the Appreciation Society during his telephone calls. He said that it was amazing how Six of One had kept up *The Prisoner* series' profile. The actor was pleased with the society's work and to hear that episodes were at that time being repeated yet again in Britain. He commented, "I had in mind *Nineteen eighty-four* when it was made." The message which McGoohan then offered to his fans was, "I wish to thank them for their support and dedication, far from being 'The Prisoner,' Patrick McGoohan is alive and well in California – and getting younger every day!"[28]

1   Sunday Telegraph, 23rd December 1984, David Castell
2   L.A. Times, details unknown, Kevin Thomas
3   TV Guide, 4th July, 1987
4   *Consequences*, Margaret Trudeau; McClelland & Stewart, 1982
5   *Leonard Maltin's Movie Guide*; Signet (annual)
6   *Halliwell's Film & Video Guide*; HarperCollins, 1999
7   1996 Six of One Prisoner Convention, Portmeirion, North Wales, interview by the writer
8   Ibid
9   Six of One, The Prisoner Appreciation Society interview, ICA, London, 25th November, 1984

xvii McGoohan was unaware that several hundred other copies had already been produced and circulated to all *Prisoner* society members, who were ignorant of their honorary president's restriction.

[10] 1996 Six of One Prisoner Convention, Portmeirion, North Wales, interview by the writer

[11] Source not verified

[12] New York Times 21st September, 1988, Anne Taylor Fleming

[13] Los Angeles Magazine, June, 2000

[14] Source not verified

[15] 1978, Steven Mori, details unknown

[16] Barbara Paskin article, January 1979, details unknown

[17] Internet Movie DataBase

[18] Ibid

[19] Daily Mail, 6th April, 1979, Jenny Rees

[20] Ibid

[21] Daily Mirror, 24th March,1979, Edward Macauley

[22] UK newspaper, 1979 article by Dan Ehrlich, details unknown

[23] TV Guide, 13th October, 1979, Marianne Gray

[24] Internet Movie DataBase

[25] Premiere Magazine, October 1995, Jean Yves Katelan (translations Rosemary Camilleri and Jane Rawson)

[26] Classic Images Magazine, 1987, Barbara Pruett

[27] Source not verified

[28] Telephone call to the writer, 1982

Signed photo of McGoohan as Joss Merlyn in *Jamaica Inn* (1982)

CHAPTER TEN
Eighties

"That's the game that I play. You see, that's what they buy tickets for."
Kings and Desperate Men (1981)

McGoohan returned to England in 1982, late autumn, to film *Jamaica Inn*. The made-for-TV movie, with co-star Jane Seymour, concerned the activities of a murderous wrecking gang, operating off Britain's south west coast. This remake of the 1939 Alfred Hitchcock version, from the Daphne du Maurier novel, saw McGoohan as an unshaven, slobbering, tousled haired villain. New York Times review: "This remake of the Alfred Hitchcock adventure stars Patrick McGoohan as the head of a crew of smugglers; Jane Seymour plays his niece, who discovers the secret history of the title inn." (Jason Ankeny, All Movie Guide)

Peter Graham Scott[i] described[1] his involvement with the project as an in-house producer/director with HTV. He chose to cast McGoohan as the villainous Joss Merlyn and invited his return from California. With filming taking place on a hillside set on Dartmoor, the production was planned as a three hour costume thriller for British TV and a four hour special in the United States. Graham Scott revealed, "I suggested (Patrick) for the part and when the makers queried whether he wasn't just that chap from *Danger Man*, I retorted that he was much more than that. I pointed out that Patrick had done *King Lear* at age twenty three in Sheffield[ii] and a few years later was on the West End stage in the play *Serious Charge*. It was in this theatrical production that I first saw him, with Patrick playing a vicar accused of being a homosexual. (Patrick) always saw to it that the details were right. He also had a good sense of what would work and what wouldn't. In *Jamaica Inn*, his performance could have been hammy. He was a villain and as Jane Seymour's uncle he chose to rewrite some of the script and got involved in shaping his part. He would growl, 'It wasn't I,' and Jane would reply, 'It

---

[i] Graham Scott had worked twice before with McGoohan, as director on *Danger Man* and *The Prisoner*.
[ii] The play does not appear in the Sheffield Playhouse history and no record this writer has found places McGoohan in the cast of *King Lear*.

McGoohan with Ivor Wilkins, his driver
while *Jamaica Inn* was being filmed

was you.' He hammered her and then she hammered him back." The producer added, "During all the filming Patrick was very accommodating and was really calm and polite. I recall one day when we were near the end of a day's work, about six in the evening. An actor was saying, 'I can't say this line,' and I replied to the actor, 'Just think of the money.' Patrick's voice behind us barked, 'You haven't done your homework.'"

Graham Scott continued, "Another aspect to Patrick was that he didn't want people coming up to him for autographs and so I would be ordered to have breakfast with him on the set of *Jamaica Inn*, to fend off signature hunters and admirers." The director concluded, "He would always find a way round a part and for example in *Jamaica Inn* he was over the top because he said it was a melodrama and so he had to be melodramatic. He cried real tears in the scene with Jane Seymour while professing to her, 'It was not I.' He always brought life to a part in this way. My cameraman was a cheeky young chap and he said to Patrick, 'I never understood why you wanted Peter to direct your *Prisoner* episode.' I was expecting a reply to say how impressive I was, but Patrick just quipped back, 'He was quick and he was cheap.'"[2]

Jane Seymour took the role of Merlyn's niece, Mary Yellan. The Jamaica Inn of the title was a lonely tavern, on Cornwall's Bodmin Moor, the notorious meeting place for the murderers and smugglers, led by Mary's uncle. As the head of the thieving band, McGoohan was joined by actors Trevor Eve, John McEnery, Peter Vaughan and Billie Whitelaw. According to Graham Scott, when *Jamaica Inn* was shown on ITV in May, 1983, it was "a resounding success, repaying all our effort. Jane Seymour, Patrick McGoohan and Billie Whitelaw were acclaimed and the show was number five in the National Top Ten that week."[3] During the film's US run, *Hollywood Reporter* offered praise, "Impressive action sequences, a suspenseful story, cogent performances and vigorously effective execution."[4] The US magazine *People* applauded McGoohan's performance, saying that he "held our attention better than any villain since Sweeney Todd and deserves the highest honor in television today."[5] *Jamaica Inn* won a drama award at the New York Television Festival.

With McGoohan back in Britain, the media wanted a piece of him. Generously, this time, the actor talked at length to the press and there was a lot to catching up to do. Was there any scandal? Was the tax man still after him? Were there any rifts in his thirty four year marriage? Had he dropped his moral stance and played any sexy roles? The answers were of course unchanged and no amount of probing by the press could elicit any new responses. "I've got everything I ever wanted at home,"[6] McGoohan attested, adding that he felt that he was still on his second honeymoon. He claimed to have given up drink for good and his life was firmly rooted to morality and integrity. The actor now had two married

VOICE	: Hello, Roger this is Patrick. Patrick McGoohan.	Roger	: Oh, that's excellent.
Roger	: Hi, how are you?	PATRICK	: Is that O.K.?
PATRICK	: I'm fine.	Roger	: Yes that's fine, that's super.
Roger	: It's great to hear from you again.	PATRICK	: THERE'S A BIG "THANK YOU" IN THERE.
PATRICK	: How are things with you Roger?	Roger	: Right, that's understood.
Roger	: Fine. As you know, it's our Convention Friday, this week, in Portmeirion.	PATRICK	: I WANT TO THANK THEM FOR THEIR DEDICATION. AFTER 15 YEARS IT'S AMAZING.
PATRICK	: Ah, yes.	Roger	: Well the dedication you put into the programme 15 years ago was what counted.
Roger	: Would you give me a message for the members on Friday when I see them? There'll be a few hundred of them and I know they would like to hear just some message from you - as to how you feel about Six of One now, and whether you have any wishes for the weekend.	PATRICK	: "The Prisoner" is really taking off now.
		Roger	: It really is.
		PATRICK	: I had in mind 1984 when it was made - now it's getting nearer and the message is even more clear.
PATRICK	: You want it now?	Roger	: Yes, well do you know that probably next year, 1983, they will be re-showing it in England on Channel 4, networking it? So it will have a very wide new following from people who were too young to appreciate it even 5 years ago.
Roger	: Yes, because there isn't much time now. You could send a telegram, but alternatively it would be easier if you could give me a message now and I could tell them, I would be able to pass it on.		
		PATRICK	: They're re-running it over here at the moment. I'm very pleased with the interest being shown.
PATRICK	: Have you got a tape recorder on?		
Roger	: I haven't got a tape recorder on.	Roger	: That's great. We really like to hear from you, get your side of things. You've been receiving the "Escape" magazines?
PATRICK	: Because I wasn't happy about that last tape you know.		
Roger	: No, no.	PATRICK	: Yes I've got those, yes.
PATRICK	: Well, the message is: TELL THEM THAT I WISH TO THANK THEM FOR THEIR SUPPORT AND DEDICATION. THAT FAR FROM BEING "THE PRISONER", PATRICK McGOOHAN IS ALIVE AND WELL IN CALIFORNIA - AND GETTING YOUNGER EVERY DAY!	Roger	: Well thank you for phoning and talking to me.
		PATRICK	: Thank you. I appreciate it. Goodbye now.
		Roger	: Keep in touch.
		PATRICK	: I will.

Telephone call from McGoohan to the writer, 1982

daughters and was grandfather to a six year old. He was making efforts to fit himself into the patriarchal role, relating tales of admonishing visiting young Californians for not observing the required level of courtesy, when calling upon the family. There was to be no 'west coast lifestyle' infiltrating the McGoohan household and this was made clear to all who stopped by.

Many of the interviews, mainly conducted in London, were of the tabloid variety. Talk centred around marriage and divorce, with the actor's Catholic background coming to the fore. McGoohan re-aired his stories about meeting wife Joan and their Sheffield courtship. One interview ended with the actor bursting out laughing when asked if he had ever been tempted to be unfaithful. Another reporter remarked that the "nightmare to interview" reputation of the man had again proved groundless. The actor was found to be approachable and was even prepared to talk freely about *The Prisoner*, a decade and a half after its making. McGoohan was perhaps trying to repair the damage which he said had been done recently by a reporter in Los Angeles, who had written an offensive article about him, covered in the next paragraph. This, he claimed, had even led to his being refused a packet of cigarettes in a shop on the south west tip of Britain.[iii][7] Another journalist observed that the actor's absence from Britain for a long period had made him sensitive to differences in the country. McGoohan acknowledged that he had sensed a change in the national mood, commenting, "Things are a lot tighter. The message that Britain is in a mess and that something has got to be done seems finally to have got through to people."[8]

[iii] Health reasons would later dictate the giving up of tobacco for McGoohan, as had already been the case with alcohol.

Left: Time Out magazine cover during *Prisoner* cinema marathon in London, 1982. Right: McGoohan in the UK TV show *Greatest Hits*, 1983

The offensive article, to which McGoohan had been referring, was one penned by Ivor Davis in the *Daily Express*, although the interview had been conducted in Hollywood. It began, "To Patrick McGoohan, interviews are only marginally less intolerable than an over-diluted scotch, so the humour is in limited supply." The writer went on to describe the "snarling countenance of the taciturn actor." Summing up McGoohan's personality and appearance as "irascible," the columnist contrasted his subject's earlier neat and clipped TV style with the present look of "a rumpled poet." The article led to Joan McGoohan demanding to know from her husband the interviewer's name, so that she could take him to task. Both the actor and his wife were clearly offended by the interview. In examining McGoohan's new role as Joss Merlyn, Ivor Davis dipped in and out of topics such as *The Prisoner*, even suggesting that the actor had last been in Britain to try out for the part of James Bond.[iv] Davis reported that after *Jamaica Inn*, McGoohan would be off to Hawaii to direct and star in a movie about the founders of chiropractic treatment. The story of McGoohan being paralysed during the making of *The Moonshine War*, reported by journalists a decade earlier,[v] was included by Davis in his article. "'They shoved me into a station wagon and sent me to hospital for an operation on my spine.' On the way, the driver pointed out a chiropractor's office and said: 'That fellow fixed my elbow.' McGoohan yelled, 'Stop the car' and was dragged upstairs to meet one Dr. Ted Frigard. After eight hours treatment the actor was able to walk out under his own steam and later the doctor saved McGoohan's daughter's life as well."[9]

Davis even attempted a put-down of *Prisoner* fans, commenting that McGoohan approached them with disdain. The publishing of the interview and this comment subsequently in the UK *Daily Express* newspaper, led this book's writer to send a corrective letter to the newspaper, which was printed a day or so later: "In his article on Patrick

---

[iv] This was the second time, within the British press, that McGoohan had been hailed as the new Bond character, both at the time of the first 1963 movie *Dr. No* and after Sean Connery had stepped out of the role (*You Only Live Twice*), before Roger Moore took over (*Live and Let Die*). McGoohan even said that the part was offered to him after George Lazenby's single appearance as Bond in *On Her Majesty's Secret Service*, see page 215.

[v] See page 194.

McGoohan, Ivor Davis says that he treats his *Prisoner* fans with 'disdain.' In fact, when we of the Appreciation Society held our recent convention in Portmeirion, Patrick phoned us from America thanking us for our dedication. His support for the club has been unceasing ever since it was founded in 1977. He has sent us telegrams, phoned us and even made himself available for interview. I very much doubt that Mr. McGoohan would accept an Honorary Presidency while feeling 'disdain.'"[10] However, a number of more informative press articles also covered the making of *Jamaica Inn*. In fact, the arrival back in England of the actor created a fair amount of media interest. Often McGoohan would be self-effacing with regard to *The Prisoner*, saying, "I'm surprised anybody watched it."[11] Another article, supposedly covering the Cornish movie, was instead slanted towards *The Prisoner*. The actor was quoted as describing his sixties production as "the only TV series to be the subject of a Doctor of Philosophy study and to be denounced by Russia as anti-Communist propaganda."[12] The subject of McGoohan's chiropractic movie plans cropped up again and the journalist commented that the actor was working for free and as a thank-you gesture. It seemed that his hopes of producing the movie had stretched over several years, he having told an earlier columnist that the film was about to occur immediately, on location in Hawaii.

Meanwhile, the *Jamaica Inn* trip allowed just one British television appearance, which saw McGoohan meeting up with his UK *Prisoner* fans, on 25th October, 1982. This writer, together with other Six of One members, came face to face, at long last, with the society's Honorary President. The ITV show about to be filmed was *Greatest Hits*, a nostalgia-based production, which would highlight the year 1968.[vi] On the set, there was a hushed, reverent air as people asked continually, "Has McGoohan arrived yet?" Rehearsals occurred without the actor being present. A *Prisoner* style parade was staged, with costumed fans walking down the audience aisles to meet a Village taxi vehicle. Amidst waved large placards and blown-up photos of McGoohan's face, two giant white balloons bounced around. By 9 p.m. *The Prisoner* contingent was seated on the replicated cult series' set and the atmosphere was electric. Host Mike Smith, at 9.20 p.m., finally called for applause as McGoohan's name was announced and cameras rolled. This writer recorded at the time: "Time slowed, but pulses set a new record. Onto the studio floor strode McGoohan, towering over the table umbrellas and having to duck to get under one and seat himself by the interviewer. His eyes surveyed the society members for the first time. A smile flashed and a 'Be seeing you' hand salute greeted the faithful. Was this really happening?"[13] The star was dressed in a casual suit, wearing a beard and his hair long. When he answered the first question, his voice was made of gravel, one octave lower than expected. After a perfunctory interview, McGoohan rose to leave, shook hands, signed autographs, and was gone. He was on call early next day for more *Jamaica Inn* filming. The actor had only ever once before been placed amongst *Prisoner* fans in this way, the previous time being five years earlier, for the Warner Troyer Canadian interview.[vii] The *Greatest Hits* show went out on primetime British TV, in the following March.

McGoohan's UK filming trip was followed by an assignment in New Zealand, where, accompanied by his wife, the actor was making his latest film *Trespasses* (1987).[viii] McGoohan played a Calvinist widower, Fred Wells, whose daughter Katie is enrolled into a

---

[vi] Technically this should have been 1967, but the later year conveniently fitted in with something else the producers were presenting, within the same half hour slot.

[vii] See page 202.

[viii] The production, under the working title *Finding Katie*, was in 1983, but the film was not released until much later.

Programme for the US play, *Pack of Lies* (1985)

dubious local religious cult. Shooting was done at Wainiauku Farm, appropriately the site of a former Hare Krishna community. As with many such screen sects, an initiation practice required some carnal indoctrination. Following a scene of sexual induction into the group, the tone of the film was downbeat. One wonders whether the early *Trespasses* script promised at first look to be a more powerful drama. Certainly, McGoohan spoke strongly in favour of his role, although some might regard the film as being a lesser entry in the star's oeuvre.[ix]

New York Times review: "Fred Wells (Patrick McGoohan) is a sullen introvert who still resents the death of his wife in childbirth 25 years earlier. His daughter born at that time, Katie (Emma Piper), runs away from his ravings about sin and damnation and escapes to a hippie-style commune where an unscrupulous guru ends her virginity in a supposed sex ritual. When the arrogant guru is murdered, a shy young man enamored of Katie is first sought by the police – but the real culprit seems to be her father. The undertones of incestuous desire on the part of the father, and the human reactions when the reality of that tendency is faced, are handled well in this psychological drama." (Eleanor Mannikka, All Movie Guide)

The story goes that the star had been approached by the film's producers in 1981 and that he had rarely been so instantly attracted to a screen role. Despite heavy commitments in Britain and America he was determined appear in *Trespasses* and became enamoured with New Zealand. It was to him one of the few countries left in the world where a man's handshake and his word meant something. "When you make a friend in New Zealand, it's for life."[14]

McGoohan's performance was reviewed by *Variety* magazine and described as "possibly the finest of his career,"[15] giving even a hint even of an Oscar nomination. The New Zealand production was the only involvement which McGoohan enjoyed with that country's film industry. While he was making *Trespasses*, he told the Christchurch press that *The Prisoner* was a part of history and he would never make another such series.[16] In another interview, with journalist Marie McNicholas from New Zealand *Woman's Weekly*, McGoohan enlightened her that he had been taking a back seat from acting so that his wife could pursue her blossoming career in real estate. "That means doing the housework so she can go out to work." Joan revealed: "(Patrick) does most of his writing in the kitchen." The interviewer noted that the McGoohans had a refreshingly stable and sharing marriage – "more so since Joan went out to work after twenty four years at home rearing their three daughters."

[ix] The video release title was *Omen of Evil*.

Above: Autographed photo, mid-eighties
Right: McGoohan snapped by a fan during the
run of the US play, *Pack of Lies*

This second interview proved to be something of a rarity, with Joan for once being the prominent figure. "With Patrick just sitting at home," said Joan, "I insisted that he take on some of my old roles, so he went to the supermarket, did the shopping and he enjoyed it." Significantly, Joan believed that the McGoohan marriage had worked not only because she and her husband had been good friends, but that "Patrick's career has never been the most important thing." She added, "I think he is surprised when other people find me intelligent."

Mrs. McGoohan also disclosed in the interview that living in L.A. had given her and her husband the respite they wanted from the public eye. It was further admitted that the couple had never mixed with the celebrity set. "We have never been part of show business. Patrick is not in show business. He's just doing a job, doing his work. He hates going to parties, so he always turns down invitations. We've never been to the Academy Awards. Patrick won't go with all those crowds. Absolutely not." Talk again moved on to *The Prisoner*. "I don't think at the time we really appreciated it. All I knew was that Patrick was working around the clock, killing himself." The interview ended with the often-heard claim that McGoohan was currently making plans for a new film. In this latest case it was going to be New Zealand which would be the country to which the actor would return, to shoot a film on the South Island. The production was going to use all indigenous actors and have a New Zealand storyline,[17] although this became another unrealised project.

When McGoohan returned to Los Angeles he gave another interview. This time, writer Mike Bygrave noticed that, "The famous voice, with its indefinably mid-Atlantic accent, turns out to be a deliberate creation. In person, the Irish in him breaks through." McGoohan, like his parents, had criss-crossed the globe in search of their respective dreams, according to Bygrave. The reporter also disclosed that McGoohan wrote a love poem to his wife every day. The actor had always spoken over the years about his private writings of verse and prose. Nothing of these has been seen in publication and the actor has always declared that his written efforts are for his family and friends only. Over several

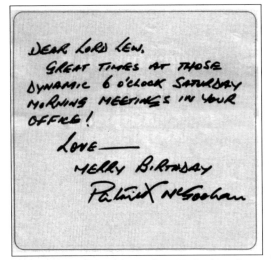

Variety 80th birthday message from McGoohan, for
Lord Lew Grade, 1986

years he would claim to do two hours of "scribbling" each day, before his long pre-dawn walks. Although he always shrugged off his literary attempts, he would admit to having written "probably thousands" of poems, describing them as too personal to publish. "They're notes, scrambled words that I jot down over my scrambled eggs on the edge of the newspaper or whatever. Joan liked these peculiar messages and I kept up the habit. Later, because I've always tried to write formal verse, I try to unscramble them and see if I have a poem." Each time a large enough bundle of poems or writings was amassed, McGoohan would reportedly have them bound and would give them to family members and close friends.[x] The actor, always ready to declare publicly his love for Joan, would often comment, "I've married my first wife and my last wife!"

In McGoohan's intimate conversation with Mike Bygrave the actor admitted that he had become a quieter family man of late, in contrast to the way that he used to drink "a lot." His interviewer was even invited 'backstage' at the actor's home, which he described as "no movie star's mansion." McGoohan's pride was expressed to the columnist with regard to his daughters: Catherine, being married to a film producer and having provided the first grandchild, Frances managing a clothing store and Anne studying child psychology.

The eclectic pursuits and lifestyles within the McGoohan household made it obvious that the film and TV work of the head of the family was not the primary concern. Although McGoohan expressed to his jotting guest that he had no regrets about leaving the stage, he did accept that he had done "an awful lot of crap." The actor alluded to numerous scripts he had written, short films he had made and other projects of his which nobody would ever screen, or finance.[18]

One notable undertaking was being set up at this time, although it never reached fruition. In 1983 the Royal Exchange Theatre in Manchester, England, advertised that McGoohan would appear as Captain Ahab in the stage production of *Moby Dick*. Later, the actor withdrew after the billing had been advertised, but before rehearsals were to begin. This caused recasting of the lead and also ticket refund offers had to be made. The theatre's publicity director wrote a letter to all season ticket holders: "We have received the distressing news contained in the press statement which we have had to issue today that Patrick McGoohan has broken his agreement and withdrawn from the play. After a quarter a century away from the theatre he has told adapter and director Michael Elliott that he no longer has the confidence to act on the stage. Mr. Elliott, whose association with Patrick McGoohan goes back to his spectacularly successful production of *Brand*, in 1959, said, '*Moby Dick* continues in the theatre's autumn season. The part of Captain Ahab is a marvellous one and will attract actors with reputations even greater than Patrick McGoohan's.'"

[x] Actor Alexis Kanner told this author that he had seen some of McGoohan's written work and that it was "marvellous."

McGoohan as Stewart, in the 1985 Broadway play, *Pack of Lies*.

Any claim that McGoohan lacked confidence was proved wrong by his appearance, two years later, on the New York stage.[xi] In fact, a different account of the withdrawal from *Moby Dick* was given by erstwhile *Brand* translator Michael Meyer. He claimed that Elliott had recently seen McGoohan on TV in *Jamaica Inn*. The director felt, it was said, that McGoohan could no longer act. Whatever the truth, there was a strong feeling of dismay from many fans that the man they venerated would not be coming back for live public performances in England.

However, Britain was at least to see McGoohan once more on TV screens, with a revival of *The Prisoner*. In November, 1982, the country received its newest and fourth main TV channel. Channel 4, with its S4C Welsh counterpart, announced that it would start its life

---

[xi] See later, page 237.

ⓣ Telemessage

KEB3446 NKX411 IOB490 4-029482T007   07 JAN 1987/2242

OUR DOUBLE BEST WISHES TO ALL ON THIS DOUBLY HAPPY OCCASION
PATRICK MCGOOHAN
ALEXIS KANNER

Message from McGoohan and *Prisoner* co-actor Alexis Kanner sending best wishes to Six of One on the society's 10th birthday

by bringing back many action-adventure TV shows from the sixties. The long-forgotten favourites would include cult shows like *The Avengers* and of course McGoohan's sixties series. Therefore, in 1983, *The Prisoner* enjoyed its first ever 'national' UK screening,[xii] on Channel 4. The original broadcast of the series in the sixties on ITV had been regional and so had been the repeats in many different areas, in the late seventies. It must also be remembered that *The Prisoner* had not been screened on British TV in the meantime and the series was not available on video. There was a partial release, by Precision Video, which offered a few episodes, inappropriately joined together as feature-length presentations. Channel 4 also transmitted the original half hour *Danger Man* monochrome episodes, although the later one hour stories were never presented. With *The Prisoner* re-run, the last episode's closing moments just crept into the start of 1984, the Orwellian year in which McGoohan always claimed he had set the show.

Along with latest *Prisoner* screening, a documentary[xiii] was commissioned by Channel 4. Filmed in 1983, *Six into One: The Prisoner File* offered a format which would purportedly set it apart from the traditional style of clips and talking heads. Despite these bold intentions, the programme became a collection of interviews with cast and crew, interspersed with episode extracts, presented by a host pretending to unravel the mystery of *The Prisoner*, as if for the first time. The programme was broadcast immediately after the final *Prisoner* episode, *Fall Out*. The late night slot may have meant that viewing figures were not optimum and the documentary was never screened again.[xiv] The makers of *Six into One: The Prisoner File* visited McGoohan in California. At his initial meeting with them revealed that he was not happy with the proposed format. As time was short – the actor was also declaring that he would not appear in a programme which included *Prisoner* script editor George Markstein – there was clearly a problem. The next day, after sleeping on it, McGoohan spoke to the film makers in a Santa Monica restaurant. He agreed to go ahead with the idea, even to the extent of getting involved with the production. He called David Tomblin and Lew Grade, both of whom had declined to appear in the film, and secured interviews with them for the programme makers.

Unfortunately, upon the documentarists' return to London, they were about to find that McGoohan would present them with a volte-face. They again met with him, this time in Paris, over Christmas 1983, to show him a rough cut. He allegedly hated what had been put together and insisted upon a catalogue of changes which could not be considered. The story goes that out of about fifty two minutes, McGoohan endorsed only two. Worse still, his

---

[xii] Some areas of Britain were not initially able to receive C4 transmissions.

[xiii] See also footnote on page 207.

[xiv] Attempts to release the documentary during past years – most recently on a 2006 German DVD set – were reportedly blocked by McGoohan, who did not want it shown ever again.

Left: 1987 cover of a US programme guide. Right: A fan photo taken of McGoohan in the late eighties

position hardened, with a demand that the item should not be screened at all, the order coming a few days later, by telephone call from the States. With Channel 4's lawyers looking at the programme under threat of being sued, the production team could only wait for a ruling. In the end, a 'broadcast and be damned' decision was made by Channel 4, given that a sixty thousand pounds budget had been spent and that it was felt there was no 'libel' issue at all. This is not to say that the makers of the documentary were unsympathetic to McGoohan's sensitivities. They sided with him in some ways, feeling that McGoohan's own view was right, that only he could construct an intelligent and all-encompassing statement on the series and its making. Their consensus was that such a film would be both "biased and brilliant." The team regretted that their film was not the one which the actor wanted.[xv]

After communications between the *Six into One* makers and McGoohan had ended, the actor surprised everybody by proceeding to shoot his own film, although Channel 4 could not use the footage, for legal reasons.[xvi] As the actor's film, which came to be called the *L.A. Tape*[xvii] subsequently revealed, McGoohan wanted to use the British documentary as a springboard for a new project he had in mind. He had seen in the past how being in the right place at the right time, or forming a beneficial association, could cause new doors to open. He no doubt saw this as his big chance, in the early part of the eighties, when he was not over-stretched with working assignments. Thus, his liaison with the documentary makers led to his making a personal film, which would otherwise never have been created.

The *L.A. Tape* is the most concentrated dose of McGoohan ever to appear on film, although it has never been released for public consumption. His intimate offerings covered all aspects of *The Prisoner*, during about forty minutes of interview. McGoohan corrected the idea that the former *Danger Man* character became the man who resigns his highly confidential post in the new series: "(He) was meant to represent anyone in a position

---

[xv] An account of the documentary history first appeared in Six of One's *Number Six* magazine, by Chris Rodley.

[xvi] It was said that a ruling by Equity, the actors' union, prevented his film from being broadcast in the United Kingdom.

[xvii] See footnote on page 126.

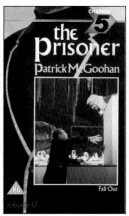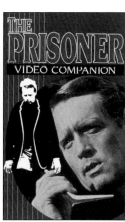

Prisoner video covers from late 1980s onwards

where they had access to vital information of national importance, such as a scientist, or top government official, or even a secret agent." The actor explained how the scripts materialised: "A writer could come along and it was food for thought for him: it sparked, if he did have a good story in him that he might have sold as a film, or put into a book. Here was material that this idea could fit into with this Village. In fact, he might be able to play with it better within that structure than elsewhere."

The long lasting working relationship with David Tomblin was covered: "(He) and I became great friends instantly on the first location of the first lot of the *Danger Man* thing, thirty nine half hours. It was the happiest location I've ever been on. Everyone on that crew became friends immediately – it was really amazing – and stayed friends for many years and worked together for many years." Rarely, McGoohan even revealed his own view of *The Prisoner*: "I suppose (*Once upon a Time*) is a favourite one of mine. It's a little bit autobiographical.[xviii] It's always nice to get that stuff out of your system. You certainly can't blame anybody else if you get (things) wrong and it does save a lot of discussion between the director and the person playing the leading part. The danger of it is always that one has to be extra self-critical and it's essential to have someone behind you." However, the autobiographical element was not the main aspect of the series, or its two-part finale. The actor highlighted something more abstract: "This was not an action adventure show, it was an allegory and an allegory is a story in which people, places, happenings, conceal a message and there is a symbolism. So therefore there's an enormous latitude what one can do with it."

McGoohan recalled the ending of the series and the controversy which the final episode caused: "Everyone wanted to know who Number One was. When it turned out to be the evil side of myself for twelve frames of the camera on one occasion and eighteen on another, they were outraged. But I mean what is the greatest evil? If you're going to epitomise evil, what is it? Is it the Bomb? The greatest evil that one has to fight constantly every minute of the day until one dies is the worser part of oneself. And that's what I did and I'd do the same again." His closing thoughts on the debacle were delivered: "People like a good solid story that ends up the way it should and this one didn't of course, so there was an outcry. I nearly got lynched. I had to go into hiding and they thought they had been cheated. I don't think

---

[xviii] See also earlier in this book, page 162.

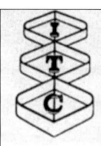

INTERNATIONAL

TECHNICAL

CO-ORDINATION SERVICES

Dear Roger Langley

May I extend to you and all of Six Of One hearty congratulations on your double anniversary. Ten years of Six Of One and even longer, twenty one years of the ITC Entertainment production of "The Prisoner'

It seems only yesterday as Print Acceptance Officer for ITC when I used to sit with Patrick McGoohan and view the first prints from the Laboratories.

My very best wishes

Don Mead

Don Mead
PUBLICITY MANAGER

ITC publicity manager writes to congratulate Six of One and to recall having viewed the first *Prisoner* prints with McGoohan in 1967

they'd been cheated, it's just that they still had this idea, God love 'em, that it was John Drake and it was a secret agent story and it was a *Danger Man* story, or it was a *Saint* story, or a James Bond story."[19] McGoohan's behaviour during the *L.A. Tape* is eccentric and the actor's 'performance' ranges from conceited to charismatic, his own description of the film being "crazy." The off-camera gentle voice of a female interviewer is thought to be that of one of his daughters. At one point McGoohan picks up a pair of laced baby's tiny shoes, dangling them from his finger, questioning what they are for. The message being delivered is that the person on screen has more tricks than anybody knows, can never be analysed and does not give a fig about what will be thought of his 'one man show.'

The *L.A. Tape* was made by McGoohan under a fair amount of time pressure, given that the British *Prisoner* documentary was in the final stages of production. Perhaps it was this factor which gave rise to the most unique and exciting content of the actor's film: there are several quirky sequences where McGoohan presents his own antics at various places within the local area. Initially, the actor is seen under a pier, on the beach, taking down wire coathangers which are dangling above him. The objects seem to have been left there for him, as if some sort of clues. Later, walking along the shore, he draws the shape of the hangers in the sand, using a long stick, before waves pour in and obliterate his work. In another sequence, the actor is travelling in an open elevator on the side of a building. With a hand-held camera being pointed at him in the compartment, the background is visible while the cab is descending. McGoohan, his face in tight close-up, loudly counts down numbers, as he once did in *The Prisoner*. The song *English Country Garden*, performed by Julie Felix, plays over this section. At another point, McGoohan is walking across a footbridge, while the Beatles' song *Come Together*[xix] is heard. Suddenly the actor 'disappears', like a magician (Orson Welles would have approved) thanks to a simple camera trick. Next, McGoohan is seen in an empty room, his feet making a hollow sound on the wooden floor. He repeatedly goes over to a mantelpiece, deep in thought, before pacing over to the far wall, confusing and confounding himself and the viewer. These non-interview parts of the actor's film end with him delivering a monologue about *The Prisoner*, and then closing with key moments from the series' opening sequence. McGoohan's voice is fighting against the wind noise, the man claiming that the idea for *The Prisoner* had been in his head since he was seven years old: the individual fighting against the establishment. The images of the present-day McGoohan and his former screen character Number Six now merge. The actor strides defiantly into the sea, his *Prisoner* voice trailing over him: "I am not a number. I am a free man!" The star's performance is a remarkable piece of McGoohanesque directing and audience-pleasing.

During the *L.A. Tape*, McGoohan even outlined a future project. He described his plan for a film about a society of tomorrow, which no longer relies upon spoken language, for communication, using only the power of projected thought. When the means of contact breaks down, the telepaths need to consult a 'lesser' tribe, who live in exile. Their group is made up of people who once rebelled and would not conform to modern society rules, shunning all the 'goodies' which the others enjoyed. The exiles have been living in caves on a subsistence level, but now their 'superior' counterparts require their help to survive. The title of the film was to be *Stop*, although the project did not ever start.

In Channel 4's own documentary, *Six into One: The Prisoner File*,[xx] after a clip from the series was shown, a bearded McGoohan was seen walking along a Californian beach, stick in hand. This sequence mirrored the one which the actor shot himself separately, for the *L.A. Tape*,[xxi] although the British sequence was shot first. The actor's memory of adverse reactions to *The Prisoner*, expressed in the 1983 documentary, was, "I was not angry, I just had to go and hide myself, in case I got killed!" McGoohan remarked that *The Prisoner* could be watched, with long intervals in between, time and time again. He advanced that as one's own experience in life grew, the allegory presented by the episodes began to

---

[xix] Their anthem *All You Need Is Love* had been included twice in the final *Prisoner* episode, *Fall Out*

[xx] For several of the other interviews in the documentary, with *Prisoner* personnel, see the section starting on page 126.

[xxi] Cryptically, the makers of *Six into One* chose to end their programme with the presenter telling an unseen assistant, "Run the tape that came from L.A. this morning."

The *Prisoner* human chess game, created by the appreciation society in Portmeirion

change and new dimensions could be found in the series, leading to one interpreting things differently. As the Channel 4 evening's close-down occurred, the screen split into four segments of *The Prisoner*'s famous canopied penny farthing bicycle emblem, which then disappeared from each of the corners of the nation's screens. McGoohan had ended by saying that he wanted people to be affected by the series, to question it and everything, their lives, their surroundings. After the documentary, one was left pondering as to how the great man might have made the series anew, nearly two decades later. Indeed, now another twenty years on, the same question can be considered. Given the modern landscape, with terrorist events worldwide, countries at war and threats of weapons of mass destruction, global issues do not seem to have lessened. With today's vast planetary communication network, even the watchers are spied upon by increasingly more sophisticated practices and devices. Perhaps this is the reason why the idea of a *Prisoner* movie or sequel has stalled after development of scripts. Modern audiences are used to seeing computer-generated spectacles, explosive action and gadgetry which enable heroes to escape from any situation. The 'impossible mission' hi-tech style of movie today would expect a prisoner such as Number Six to be able to outwit any captor and to escape from any situation, against improbable odds.

Meanwhile, McGoohan's next movie, *Baby: Secret of the Lost Legend* (1985), saw him playing a professor of palaeontology. The film's plot involved an infant dinosaur being found alive, something which the actor said he regarded as delightful.[20] The prehistoric beasts were being made by Carlo Rambaldi, who had created the famous alien for the Steven Spielberg movie *E.T. The Extra-Terrestrial*.[xxii] The production of *Baby* was undertaken by Touchstone Films, the adult arm of Walt Disney and was reviewed by the magazine Time Out: "Patrick McGoohan is terrific as a nasty, glory-seeking cryptozoologist following up rumours of a Brontosaurus family defying history and living it up deep in the African Congo. The Bronts are brilliant and entirely credible. This, along with some snappy dialogue, makes

[xxii] McGoohan once said that he thought *E.T.* was one of the best actors he had come across.

for highly competent family entertainment."[21] However, McGoohan claimed to be stuck in the Ivory Coast for three months, dealing with snakes, insects, heat and humidity. "I wouldn't invite Hitler to the Ivory Coast. It was awful. One hotel that was tolerable. During the shooting I had a couple of days when I wouldn't be needed so I flew home. It's a thirty five hour flight. Joan was waiting at the airport and I remember saying, 'Just give me a little kiss. A quick peck and I'll turn around and go back.' We had dinner and I went back on the plane for another thirty five hours. But it was worth it."[22]

New York Times review: "(A) story about a 10-foot baby dinosaur in dire straits in Africa because Dr. Eric Kiviat (Patrick McGoohan), an evil paleontologist, is after it with a vengeance. He is the nemesis of Dr. Susan Matthews-Loomis (Sean Young) – determined to save the baby from its hunters – and her husband George Loomis (William Katt), a sportswriter who shares her protective instincts. Kiviat has recruited a revolutionary army to help him capture the baby's mother – which they manage to do without killing her. The army has already shot down the father dinosaur, and so their own instincts are far from protective. As the husband and wife and baby dinosaur are united at last in their attempts to survive, the next step is to recapture Mom dinosaur and get away from the army and Kiviat, not an easy feat." (Eleanor Mannikka, All Movie Guide)

McGoohan's following film project was a television production for the Public Broadcasting Service's *American Playhouse*. He played a Colonial New England magistrate in *Three Sovereigns for Sarah* (1984).[xxiii] The actor reportedly inherited the part from James Mason, who died that year.[xxiv] McGoohan insisted that he was definitely not planning to do any more *weekly* series, "I've done enough, don't you think. Once you do a successful series you get branded. It's going to take me the rest of my life to live down *Secret Agent* and *The Prisoner*."[23] *Three Sovereigns for Sarah* was described as a "minor classic" and "gripping drama" and "utterly compelling." The three part presentation told the story of a trio of sisters convicted of sorcery during the 1692 Salem witch trials. When the mini-series was broadcast, McGoohan was being seen once more in a costumed role, this time under a heavy judicial wig.[xxv] New York Times review: "The brutal Salem witch trials provide the setting for this provocative drama that presents the story of an accused woman who survived the ordeal. Like her two older sisters, poor Sarah faces a trial herself. The sisters were tortured, found guilty and burned. Despite her fear, Sarah proves that her family is innocent of the charges. This film originally appeared on PBS television's *American Playhouse*." (Sandra Brennan, All Movie Guide)

The middle of the eighties brought some surprising news. Alexis Kanner reported that a film remake of *The Prisoner* was now planned, following a long period of speculation.[24] He stated that a crew had appeared in California, prior to his recent visit to the UK, for the premiere of his movie *Kings and Desperate Men*.[xxvi] It was said that the film unit had already contacted his agent and it was claimed that reservations for Portmeirion had been blocked out in the hotel's diary for a year or two. This gave rise to suspicions that a production team would be taking over the resort. Kanner further stated that he had actually been doing work earlier that year with McGoohan. "Pat and I have drawn up material for a movie, set today

---

[xxiii] The TV film was helmed by Philip Leacock, who had previously directed the 1957 McGoohan movie *High Tide at Noon*.
[xxiv] The fourth and last time that a part apparently came to McGoohan after a fellow actor's illness, the previous times being in early plays and at the time of the movie *Silver Streak*, when Peter Finch died after his final film, *Network* (1976).
[xxv] He would return as a judge, unwigged, over a decade later, in *A Time to Kill* (1996).
[xxvi] See page 207.

which, if the mood strikes him, he'll make."[25] This rumour about a *Prisoner* sequel would be joined by many others, during the next two decades.

The second half of the eighties saw McGoohan returning to his first love, the stage. Following a Boston opening,[xxvii] the New York production of *Pack of Lies*, written by Hugh Whitemore, was presented at Broadway's Royale Theatre, for a hundred and twenty performances, from 11th February, to 25th May, 1985.[xxviii] It was considered that the actor would be a good choice for this story about a real-life spy scandal from the early sixties. However, an initial concern was expressed about a possible objection from the British actors' union, Equity. McGoohan rejected this: "I can't possibly see why. I was born in Astoria, Queens. I carry an American passport. I spent many years in England and I have a great affection for it. But I am an American."[26] The actor saw his return to the stage in *Pack of Lies* as another turning point in his career. Over many years, he expressed the feeling that his work in film and television had not been all it might have been. McGoohan was clearly reflecting upon recent years and felt that he should have done more interesting things. "I don't want to do any more *Brass Targets*."[xxix] [27] Now, the actor was stepping into the role of Stewart,[xxx] an icy MI5 operative, who requires an ordinary suburban family to give him access to their home, in the London suburb of Ruislip. This will permit spying on the neighbours across the street, who are under scrutiny. They are suspected of trading military secrets with Russia, but they also happen to be the best friends of the family in whose home Stewart character has set up camp. Commenting on his character's duplicity and deceit, McGoohan enthused, "It's a bit like riding a bike. You never forget how to do it." On the other hand, the actor noted, "You can ride the bike for a bit, along nice quiet country lanes, but then trying to ride it around Times Square needs a little more practice!"[28]

Re-experiencing live theatre audiences, during the play's try-out in Boston, had been alarming for McGoohan, after a twenty five year absence from the stage and also soon to be making his Broadway debut. However, by the time of the New York opening, he had settled into the part and was looking forward to a long run. Aged fifty seven, the actor was enjoying the risk involved with theatrical work, although when describing his performance he used the word "petrified." McGoohan recalled his early days on stage when he would mentally shut out the audience and concentrate upon the area around him, the footlights offering a kind of invisible barrier. "Looking out? I never would. Never. Not even when taking a bow. I try to keep that imaginary wall. They can see in, but theoretically I can't see out."[29]

The actor told another journalist that he had the acting fever back again: "I want to do more on the boards. I think I've been negligent in not going back to the stage oftener. It takes you back to the very basics of our business. Before cameras were invented and before sound was invented, we had people walking around on wooden planks and saying words. The basic function of our business is standing up on a little raised platform and saying words with people watching and listening. That's the lifeblood of our business and it's good to get back to that now and again to remind you of it. You're not protected by cameras; you're not protected by retakes. If you make a mistake, they're all watching you make it and that's a good challenge. It gets the adrenalin going."[30]

[xxvii] At the Wilbur Theatre, 14th January, 1985
[xxviii] There were also previews at the Royale, from 7th February, 1985.
[xxix] It was reported – by Michael Meyer, translator of the 1959 *Brand* in which McGoohan appeared – that around 1985 McGoohan also appeared in Ibsen's *The Master Builder*, in Los Angeles, a semi-professional production for which no details have ever been found.
[xxx] McGoohan was nominated for the Drama Desk Award for an Outstanding Actor in a Play.

McGoohan was interviewed on American television – a rare occurrence indeed – for *The Today Show,* about *Pack of Lies,* with other TV reports on the play also occurring at this time in the USA and Canada.[xxxi] The *Philadelphia Inquirer* said of *Pack of Lies,* "McGoohan, charming and bitterly cool (gives) a smart, powerful, superbly paced performance. The role is perfectly suited to the gray-haired actor who spent much of the 60s sparring with spies in *Secret Agent.*"[31] During other non-TV interviews at this time, McGoohan announced that he had written a screenplay for a movie based on *The Prisoner.* The working title was *Prisoners* and he anticipated that shooting would begin at the end of the year. The actor's premise moved the action to the twenty second century, a period in which the characters would dress in Regency style costumes. With an alternative title of *Century 22,* the outline demonstrated that McGoohan's fertile mind was still exploring ways to experiment with the medium of film. With regard to his *Prisoners* project, McGoohan's attitude was unchanged since the sixties. He said that if it did not succeed, people would have him to blame and nobody else.

Also in 1985, Canadian network CBC-TV began a rescreening of *The Prisoner,* on Sunday mornings. This created renewed North American interest in the enigmatic actor. One writer commented that the showing almost guaranteed *The Prisoner* a small, if discriminating, audience. Another US freelance journalist – also a member of the *Prisoner* Appreciation Society – Tom Soter, interviewed McGoohan during his New York stage run, but not regarding the play; he wanted to discuss the sixties cult TV show. "So it's about *The Prisoner* you want to talk?" asked McGoohan, "Well I hope I can remember something about it." This may have been a ploy to throw the interviewer off balance, bearing in mind that the actor had spoken extensively about *The Prisoner* only two years earlier.[xxxii] Or perhaps the actor was just breaking the ice, preferring to concentrate on the new play. "We're at that awkward stage when you've just learned the lines and therefore haven't been able to do anything with them." Most of the conversation covered the well-trodden ground of *The Prisoner,* until the interviewer asked the actor what he liked to read. "Anything, really, that's decent writing, whether it's Ray Bradbury, or Milton. Bradbury happens to be one of my favourites as a modern-day writer. I've got a large garage of books, of all shapes and variety."

When asked about his daughter growing up to become a film-maker, McGoohan dismissed the story, "It's all highly exaggerated. We used to fool around a great deal together with a super-8 camera. We used to use it as if it were a professional movie. It was on a proper tripod and we edited it properly and put proper music on it."[32] The meeting was one more example of the actor – almost in every year, across three decades – being prepared to chat and give interviews, although often returning practised answers. In view of the many comments given by the actor to a small army of journalists, or TV hosts, the myth which grew up about the man who rarely gave interviews must by now have been proven false.

McGoohan continued to return to the British Isles from time to time to see members of his extended family and to meet up with old acquaintants. Jimmy Millar, the actor's dresser during TV and theatrical productions, was a long standing friend.[xxxiii] McGoohan had given him the *Prisoner* piped blazer, which the star wore in the series as Number Six, along with other costumes from the series and also the earlier *Danger Man* show. On one occasion when the

[xxxi] The actor also participated in a 1985 tribute, on National Public Radio, following on the death of Orson Welles, that same year.
[xxxii] In his self-produced 1983 interview known as the *L.A. Tape,* see page 231.
[xxxiii] Jimmy Millar went to Portmeirion during the 1966 *Prisoner* shoot and even appeared, uncredited, in two episodes: as one of the escape committee in *Checkmate* and as a Napoleonic soldier in *The Girl Who Was Death.*

actor was visiting Millar, he stated that he fancied walking to the local fish and chip shop, to eat the food hot on the walk back.[xxxiv] It was raining at the time and the visitor did not have a topcoat with him and so Millar produced an overcoat which McGoohan had worn in both *Danger Man* and *The Prisoner*. The actor was surprised and touched that it had been kept and looked after for so long. After Millar's death, McGoohan confided to this writer how much he missed his old friend. It was clear that each man valued the other and there was both sincerity and mutual respect. According to one reporter, "(Millar) is never far from Pat at any studio where McGoohan works. And it is impossible to talk to 60-year-old Jimmy without hearing an amazing eulogy of his boss: of Pat's generosity, sensibility and professionalism."[33]

A member of the *Prisoner* Appreciation Society[xxxv] visited, some years later, Millar's lady friend, as he described her, in London. He was shown a lengthy letter from McGoohan, in which the actor wrote about his close bond with Millar, referring to him as a father figure. The actor had sent his friend many snapshots from the USA, of himself and his family. Millar's companion said that McGoohan sent huge amounts of flowers at the time of his old friend's funeral. In the end she had to ask the florist to stop sending them, so that the rest of the money the actor had paid for flowers could be diverted to charitable sources.

At least a few small anecdotes and family photos[xxxvi] have been preserved in this way, which is fortuitous, as personal information about McGoohan has rarely surfaced over the years. The actor has changed his publicity agents on occasions and has declined invitations to appear at events, demonstrating that his personal life remains precious to him and is not for public consumption. The star's strong marriage, close and extended family ties and life-long friendships, all reveal a man respected by those around him. Not for McGoohan the usual tabloid press articles of scandal, or marriage breakdown, or errant behaviour, as occur sometimes with screen celebrities. Perhaps these qualities in the man are the reason that appreciation of him endures, with his work being the main focus, not the 'kiss and tell' type of profile which often appears in the popular press.

By the end of May, 1985, the New York run of the play *Pack of Lies* was coming to an end and, sadly, no more stage work was ever to be undertaken by McGoohan. The actor next began filming on the television movie *Of Pure Blood* (1986), shown as the CBS *Sunday Movie*. He played Dr. Felix Neumann in the film, which had actress Lee Remick in the lead role and also Catherine McGoohan in the cast.[xxxvii] Later released on a commercial tape, the sleeve notes gave a brief outline of the film: "A successful New York casting director returns to her homeland, Germany, to rescue a baby granddaughter from the revived remnants of a Hitler-era plan to produce a Master Race of pureblood Aryans, and in so doing learns some terrible truths about herself." Designed for "mature audiences," the Warner Home Video caption read: "1940, Wartime Germany, in Steinhoring, a race of Aryan children were being bred. In 1986, one of them is asking dangerous questions."

New York Times review: "Four decades have passed since the end of WW II, and a woman returns to Germany, her birthplace, in an effort to discover the circumstances surrounding her

---

[xxxiv] Just as he had done years earlier, with fiancée Joan, see page 35.
[xxxv] Peter Jones, in 1985.
[xxxvi] Some of these photos taken by Jimmy Millar appear elsewhere in this book.
[xxxvii] She would also appear with her father in a later episode of *Columbo* – see next chapter.

son's death. She stumbles upon a covert Nazi organization who, through a selective breeding program, intend to create a new master race." (Mark Hockley, All Movie Guide)

Also in 1986, Sir Lew Grade celebrated his eightieth birthday. McGoohan placed a congratulatory message in *Variety*. The affectionate greeting, along with several others placed by a selection of screen luminaries, stated, "Dear Lord Lew, Great times at those dynamic six o'clock Saturday morning meetings in your office!"[34] The TV mogul's last words on *The Prisoner* in his autobiography[xxxviii] were that the series was still "highly popular and continues to fascinate audiences all over the world." He could easily have applied this description to the show's star.

In 1987 a more traditional type of television engagement came McGoohan's way. He was offered a part in the long-running mystery-detection series *Murder, She Wrote*, starring Angela Lansbury. In the episode *Witness for the Defense*, McGoohan took a role as guest villain, playing an unscrupulous attorney, Oliver Quayle. Although his performance was highly entertaining, this was not the kind of setting which would see him receiving any awards, public acclaim, or a rush of new work offers. *Murder* followed a tight formula and a strict schedule, of the kind which McGoohan had previously denounced. At least his inclusion showed that he was determined not to be found 'resting' and that his name was still an interesting one to TV producers. Of course, a potentially prejudicial side of television is that it can cause actors' faces to become too familiar. A man like McGoohan could find it risky, playing baddies in several similar TV productions. This may have been the case with the several *Columbo* episodes in which he starred, even though these were spread over many years.

As *Witness for the Defense* was being screened, interviewer Barbara Pruett – a former member of the *Prisoner* Appreciation Society – spoke with McGoohan. She later wrote an article, which described the actor's traits: "Warmth, humour and kindness gleam through, as does a volatile temper, stubbornness and impatience. But what shows most strongly is the intense desire for privacy and his strength to follow his own individuality. There is little in print that adequately conveys the private personality or thinking of Patrick McGoohan. Occasionally, an interview will contain enough depth to provide an insight into what the man thinks. But it never goes deeper. You almost never learn how he arrived at his thoughts and beliefs. It's impossible to talk at length with him, without coming away from the conversation impressed by the versatility and intellect of the man. He has a natural interest and curiosity about almost everything."[35]

Also in 1987, McGoohan was seen in a spoof Channel 4 TV production, called *The Laughing Prisoner*. The actor was not live – a few scenes of him in *The Prisoner* being used to suggest his presence – during this latest offering, twenty years on. The one-hour show was filmed to a large extent in Portmeirion, with new *Prisoner* characters and using other hallmarks from the original cult series. The *Laughing Prisoner* was born out of a Channel 4 well-respected live music series, *The Tube*. Its premise was that the presenter of each week's edition (Jools Holland) would suddenly 'resign,' and be 'abducted' to the Village. The action was interspersed with scenes – Stephen Fry, Hugh Laurie and Stanley Unwin appeared – or songs performed by groups, outside several of Portmeirion's decorative buildings. When the show was repeated a few years later, it was revised, with some of the bands missing. A little

xxxviii *Still Dancing*, 1987.

later, the *Beatles Anthology* series also involved filming in Portmeirion, the group members having long been on record that they were *Prisoner* fans.[xxxix] This is a convenient point to mention that many pop promotional videos have used *Prisoner* imagery, or have been filmed at the North Wales resort. Additionally, many bands have released records with *Prisoner*-inspired lyrics.

At the end of the eighties, the first full book[xl] dedicated to *The Prisoner* was published in France, written by Alain Carrazé and Hélène Oswald. The actor gave an interview to Carrazé,[xli] during which McGoohan amended some of his explanations of the symbolism within *The Prisoner*: "The balloon represented the greatest fear of all – the Unknown. Or the invasion of privacy. Or hidden bureaucracy. Or interviews. Or death. Or taxes. Or whatever. It's all a joke. But there comes a time when rebellion is necessary. The last episode was by no means gentle. There were machine guns, people died. Revolution time. Set against the background of The Beatles singing *All You Need Is Love*." Asked by Carrazé if the actor was a prisoner, he replied, "Of course, but on parole."[36]

[1] *British Television: An Insider's History*, Peter Graham Scott; McFarland, 1999
[2] Interview with the writer, 2006
[3] *British Television: An Insider's History*, Peter Graham Scott; McFarland, 1999
[4] Hollywood Reporter, 1985, details unknown
[5] *British Television: An Insider's History*, Peter Graham Scott; McFarland, 1999
[6] Sunday Mirror, October, 1982, Trudi Pacter
[7] Sheffield Telegraph, October, 1982
[8] Source not verified
[9] Daily Express, October, 1982, Ivor Davis
[10] Daily Express, October, 1982, printed letter from this book's writer
[11] Source not verified
[12] Manchester Evening News, January, 1983, Judith Reagan
[13] Escape Magazine, Six of One, 1983, Roger Langley
[14] April, 1984, New Zealand, details unknown
[15] Variety, 1987, details unknown
[16] Christchurch Press, 30th December, 1982, Judith Regan
[17] New Zealand Woman's Weekly, February, 1983, Marie McNicholas
[18] You – The Mail on Sunday Magazine, March, 1983, Mike Bygrave
[19] The L.A. Tape, 1983, Patrick McGoohan
[20] Ibid
[21] Time Out Magazine, 1985, details unknown
[22] USA Today, 7th February, 1985, Laura White
[23] TV Guide, 20th April, 1985
[24] Six of One, The Prisoner Appreciation Society interview, ICA, London, 25th November, 1984
[25] Six of One Prisoner twenty fifth and thirtieth anniversary events, 1993 and 1997, London
[26] New York Post, February 1985 by Martin Burden
[27] Ibid
[28] The Philadelphia Inquirer, 19th February, 1985, Steven Rea
[29] Classic Images Magazine, 1987, Barbara Pruett
[30] Philadelphia Enquirer, 19th February 1985 by Steven Rea
[31] Ibid
[32] Video Magazine, Jule, 1985, Tom Soter
[33] TV Times, September, 1967, Anthony Davis
[34] Variety, 24 December, 1986
[35] Classic Images Magazine, 1987, Barbara Pruett
[36] *Le Prisonnier*, Alain Carrazé/ Hélène Oswald; Huitième Art, 1989

[xxxix] See earlier recollections of *Prisoner* production manager Bernie Williams on page 186.
[xl] *The Prisoner Companion* was published in paperback by Warner Books, in 1988, in the USA – with a corresponding British edition published by Sidgwick & Jackson – but this was monochrome and mostly text. The 1989 French book *Le Prisonnier*, mentioned in the above text, was a large hardback, with colour photographs throughout and so is regarded as the first substantive, commercially published Prisoner book.
[xli] See also page 261.

Invite to the official *Prisoner* shop opening in Portmeirion, 1999

CHAPTER ELEVEN
Nineties

"It's all for nothing, if you don't have freedom."
Braveheart (1995)

The *Columbo* seasons had halted in the late seventies, but series star Peter Falk revived the show late in the eighties. So it was that McGoohan and his long-standing friend Falk were once more using their strong personal bond as a basis for producing another exciting *Columbo*. The story, *Agenda for Murder* (1990),[i] was directed by McGoohan and he also played Oscar Finch, an unscrupulous attorney and political adviser. Both he and Falk won Emmy awards: Falk's was for Outstanding Lead Actor in a Drama Series, while McGoohan's – his second[ii] for a *Columbo* appearance – was for Outstanding Guest Actor in a Drama Series. In the story, murderer Oscar Finch removes the only man standing in his way, making his death look like a suicide. Reviews were enthusiastic, one writer lauding McGoohan for acting in a way which outshone even his strong direction of the episode. "He's so magnetic, yet so endearingly quirky, that he and Falk make a near-perfect pair. Opposite in look and style, yet similar in individuality and strength, McGoohan and Falk restore this new *Columbo* to a level equal to its glory days."[1]

In his autobiographical book, Peter Falk repeats almost verbatim his words written for this book's forward and spoken by him on radio,[iii] regarding McGoohan's involvement with *Columbo* and the particular episode *Agenda for Murder*: "I ... sent ... the script ... to a man who I considered the most underrated, under appreciated talent out there. The first two times that he appeared in *Columbo*, he won an Emmy for 'Best performance by a guest star in a TV series.' No other actor in the history of television has had that honor. The *Columbo* franchise, myself, Universal Studios, and the NBC network – we are all indebted to Patrick

---

[i] Episode fifty in the ninth season, 1990.

[ii] See earlier, page 197. The 1990 award was presented on 16th September, but it is not known if McGoohan attended.

[iii] The Steve Wright Show, BBC Radio Two, 25th October, 2005, see earlier in this book, page 198 and endnote 32.

Top Left: Replica of the *Prisoner* sports car, produced in 1990, by Caterham Cars. Top Right: Photo of McGoohan taken by Arabella McIntyre-Brown during the Motor Show. Left: McGoohan at the Birmingham Motor Show in 1990, with Graham Nearn. Right:McGoohan sitting on the sports car at the Motor Show

McGoohan for his huge contributions to the show. He did everything. He wrote, directed, acted and he did them all brilliantly. He single-handedly lifted the show to new heights."[2]

The unmasking of the murderer is not the principal factor in a *Columbo* plot. Viewers have usually seen the dastardly deed being perpetrated and so the identity of the culprit is known. What is most important, awaited by the TV audience with relish, is the wily detective's inevitable confronting of the villain, to reveal how he or she committed the crime. The murderer is often supremely confident, challenging Lieutenant Columbo to present his crucial piece of evidence. In *Agenda for Murder*, a bite mark was left on a piece of cheese at the crime scene, but as the murderer – attorney Oscar Finch played by McGoohan – knows, this is unsupported by any independent forensic details. However, in the closing scene, Columbo plays his ace, showing Finch a piece of chewing gum recently discarded by the attorney, with the same teeth impressions.

Falk commented gleefully on the incriminating incisors: "Pat loved the bite mark evidence clue. We knew that it would give us a knock-your-socks-off, smashing final scene. Pat agreed to play the murderer, he agreed to direct; and as for rewriting, that came with the territory ... he did that automatically."[3] As Falk succinctly put it, "What a lovely way to introduce to the 15 million viewers the evidence that an hour later will nail the killer."[4] The two actors, both being contemporaries from the start of their stage careers (their ages just a few months apart) never worked together on any production outside

such a Falk-McGoohan Hollywood partnership can only

:ar Finch brought him more public attention. It is reported
s favourite west LA bookstore, to buy what he described
; a prolific poet himself. The store assistant normally
t because of the recent award felt brave enough to bid
onoured *Prisoner* quip, "Be seeing you." Without missing
Six-style hand salute, with the comment, "And you."[5]
n, in 1990, to attend the Motor Show at the National
e was being presented with a sports car – a replica of the
ch he had driven in *The Prisoner*. The press reported:
Os TV hit *The Prisoner,* made a rare and show-stealing
delivery of a brand new limited edition 'Prisoner' Super
Show. The Californian-resident actor said: 'The Super
ial. Back in 1966 when we were preparing (the) series,
ning out of the ordinary. A vehicle to fit his personality
e *Prisoner* represented; standing out from the crowd,
and a touch of the rebel.'"[6]
had been taken over from Lotus, many years earlier, by
later company had recently decided to create a model
th various other features included, plus attention to
e, the facsimile was an attractive purchase. The icing
engraved plaque, affixed to the dashboard, with McGoohan's own
embossed 'signature' and a limited edition number stamped upon the plate. The actor's own
personal vehicle was, naturally, number six. Caterham Cars' managing director Graham
Nearn made the presentation, being 'reunited' with the star after nearly a quarter of a
century. Nearn had appeared in the final *Prisoner* episode as a mechanic in overalls,
delivering the free man's roadster to his London home, in readiness for the owner's
triumphant return.

Although McGoohan's visit to England was brief, he gave an interview to BBC radio
presenter Simon Bates. He was asked about his sports car gift. "This car is more than just a
car; it represents the symbol of the character that I played in *The Prisoner*. It has a sort of
simplicity about it and a slightly rebellious spirit." Toying with Bates, McGoohan claimed
that he had turned down the lead role in the TV series *The Saint* because he did not like
the vehicle which was being offered the hero, it being a Volvo two-seater. "Not that I've got
anything against a Volvo, but it wasn't quite the car for *The Saint* I thought." He was asked
whether that was much of a reason for turning down a lucrative part. "It means that the
whole concept of everything to do with the style of the show is going to be wrong, from the
word go. I'm not denigrating Roger Moore in any way. He did a good job." The actor had
obviously forgotten that in his *Danger Man* screen days he had at times driven a lowly Mini.

Bates asked McGoohan what he considered himself to be. "Mainly a writer. I write all
the time and I have a couple of books, one which will come out if I stop revising it, next
year." Seizing upon this, Bates asked if more could be learned about the book, but his
request was denied. "I'm still revising it and it's sort of meddling with the unborn child. It's
fiction. It's called *Oasis*." The actor declined to tell his interviewer what the book was

Above: Cover of the DC Comics *Prisoner* graphic
novel, its story set at a later time
Right: An image of the Number Six character, much
older, from DC Comics, artwork by Dean Motter.

about, but he did say that he was writing another book, called *Escape*.[iv] McGoohan admitted
to feeling once more like switching countries. "I'll probably make a change shortly, I haven't
decided where yet. I kind of like the feeling of coming back here (Britain) again. This is my
first visit for eight years and it does feel very nice. I live in a place called Pacific Palisades
which is north of Los Angeles and inland of Malibu. It still has the atmosphere of a little
village, a small country town. If you haven't got the cash they'll say 'Well, pay me next
time.'"[v] Bates next asked his guest about his noticeable absence from UK screens. Was he
still professionally active? "I am, I think, one of the few actors that's been fired by his agent
for turning down parts." McGoohan refused to elaborate, although it was known that he
had changed agents more than once. "There's one person I don't turn down, that's Peter
Falk. He called me in recently for a *Columbo* and we did it.[vi] I wrote and directed and acted
in it. I enjoy the work enormously and Peter is great to work with. It's the easiest form of
work, particularly when you're working with someone as simpatico as Peter is and we have
a very good rapport. It works extremely well." However, the star's return to *Columbo* had
not yet seen the end of his connection with this show, as there were still two more important
contributions to the series in the years ahead.

Meanwhile, asked by Bates if he recalled working on *The Prisoner*, McGoohan replied,
"I can remember every shot. I can remember every lens. If I saw two minutes of any
particular episode I could tell you exactly how it progressed shot by shot from there on. It's
embedded profoundly in the subconscious, never to go away." The actor's closing comments

[iv] At the time of this biography, no books written by McGoohan have yet been published.

[v] In the opening *Prisoner* episode, a Village taxi driver says the same thing to McGoohan's character:

[vi] This related to the *Columbo* segment *Agenda for Murder*, mentioned earlier in this chapter. The episode had already been made at the time
of the Bates interview, but was not screened until the following year.

became introspective and serious. "*The Prisoner* never escaped. You're a prisoner of something. Everyone is a prisoner of something. You escape when you're released, I suppose, by death. It's the final release and as to how and where you go and what happens thereafter, depends on what sort of prisoner you were." Bates closed the interview by asking McGoohan, "It's still rattling around in the mind, isn't it?" The actor replied, "What, the concept? Of course, yes. Yes, that goes into everything, does it not?"

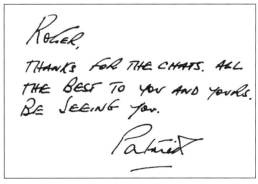

Message to this writer from McGoohan in 1992

McGoohan confirmed that he was intending to use the presentation Lotus vehicle in an up and coming thriller. "I'm working with a friend on a new project. It won't be called *The Prisoner* but it will be from the same stable." Having seated himself in the newly-presented, low-slung roadster, for press photos at the Birmingham Exhibition Centre, the actor stated, "It feels very emotional getting back into the car. It has brought back a lot of memories. The old car was great fun to drive. I'm looking forward to driving the new one." As to the new project, all the star would offer was, "That's still at the earliest stages of development."[7]

Another interview, at the time of the vehicle presentation, was given to an organiser within the *Prisoner* Appreciation Society, who spoke with McGoohan at the NEC Motor Show. He asked initially about the influences which led to the actor creating his cult series, to which the actor replied, "Anyone who has ever been up against bureaucracy, in any form, or up against prejudices, which sort of shackle us unjustly ... It's the buffeting of the frustrations with which we live – the fact that there is no such thing as totally smooth sailing, no matter what walk of life you lead." Challenged about the symbolism in the series, McGoohan explained, "I've always been fascinated by the penny farthing. The canopy was just jazz for the Village, because everything was jazzed up, like the capes and the umbrellas. The penny farthing has always fascinated me because it's always such a primitive, but extraordinary, piece of equipment. For me, it sort of symbolised progress. Anyone who's been in a traffic jam, you could almost get home quicker on a penny farthing, so it symbolises progress. Are we going so fast that we can't keep up, you know?"

McGoohan was asked about the Appreciation Society for *The Prisoner* and the actor confirmed that he always received his Six of One quarterly mailings. "They are professionally laid-out magazines. These people could start their own publishing company." The actor has continued to receive the publications over the following thirty years. In fact, since he accepted honorary presidency of the society, early in 1977, McGoohan himself has become effectively one of Six of One's longest standing members. Finally, the interviewer explored the possibility of an independent writer producing a biography of the actor. This did not find favour with McGoohan either. "No. I like reading biographies of the big guys, from way back. I mean, biographies now, they fall like, out of the sewer! Left, right, centre – everyone in the world's got a biography! You walk into the biography section of any large bookstore and the shelves are full of them!"[8]

THE TALLY HO Oct. 92.

Special 25th. Anniversary Edition

PRISONER BONANZA

Not since the six-
ties has so much
interest been gen-
erated by televis-
ion's famous classic,
"The Prisoner".

The series has come
of age, celebrating
not only its 25th.
anniversary, but also
drawing a whole gen-
eration of viewers.

The unprecedented
emergence of mer-
chandise confirms the
confidence of manuf-
acturers and distrib-
utors that this time

Six of One's 25th *Prisoner* anniversary publication

The presentation *Prisoner* replica vehicle was not actually delivered to McGoohan until the May of 1991. Christopher Tchorznicki was the US representative for Caterham Cars and took the sports car to the actor personally. He drove it from Caterham's Massachusetts base down to the home of the star's daughter Anne, in Richmond, Virginia. Tchorznicki recalled the events of the motor show and the car hand over: "Patrick never took delivery of the car, chassis number six, in the UK. The presentation was for the press and I think it was chassis number one. Graham Nearn then shipped the kit to me and I assembled it and delivered it to Patrick. He drove it around for a day and I took photos of him doing so. He really enjoyed himself and the car. He left it with his son in law, who still has it today."[9]

McGoohan's next British filming engagement was the television play *The Best of Friends*, which was screened by Channel 4 at Christmas, 1991. The play was also shown in North America, in October, 1992, under the umbrella heading of the Mobil-sponsored *Masterpiece Theatre*. Although this was not a live stage production, McGoohan was enjoying the close substitute. He took the role of George Bernard Shaw, appearing opposite Sir John Gielgud – then aged eighty eight – within the format of a four act play. The drama presented 'conversations' between the original real-life characters, taken from their letters written to each other. The action covered twenty five years in the lives of the playwright Shaw, Dame Laurentia McLachlan, the Abbess of Stanbrook Abbey (Dame Wendy Hiller) and Sir Sidney Cockerel, curator of the Fitzwilliam Museum at Cambridge University (Gielgud).

Dear Roger,

I had hoped to engineer a break at the last moment, skip over to London, unheralded, for this very special occasion and, despite my dread of such things, make an appearance.

Unfortunately there's so much going on, not the least of which is preparation of the next series, that it became impossible.

A note of gratitude, transmitted with this, had already been drafted to cover the contingency.

I can't think of anyone better than your goodself to accept the award on my behalf and I should be most grateful if you would.

Still hoping to be over in London in a few weeks, at which time we'll break bread.

Warmest regards to you and yours,

TO ALL THE INMATES HERE PRESENT:

Why should THE PRISONER be confined twenty-five years for having one crazy idea? Give him a break - he has earned some freedom and is working on his ESCAPE: See it soon on your surveillance screens.

Nevertheless, while still incarcerated, he is most grateful for recognition of having successfully survived so long a sentence.

Warm regards to all concerned.

Patrick McGoohan.

Left: Fax from McGoohan for London celebratory *Prisoner* event, 1993. Right: Message from McGoohan for *Prisoner* society members, 1993

The presentation was adapted from an original stage play by Hugh Whitemore and the main actors in the production were described as "Three old pros." However McGoohan, a mere sixty three years of age, alongside his octogenarian colleague Dame Wendy Hiller, could not compete with Gielgud's seniority.

On screen, the character McLachlan says, "True friendship is one of the subtle and beautiful forces that glorify life." The play covered nearly three decades of correspondence between the characters and the way that the principals maintained their alliance in a sincere way. Greg Quill of the *Toronto Star* wrote "A precious, uplifting play. It will not satisfy conventional, modern TV appetites and it won't win any ratings. Savor it now. Treats as succulent as this have all but disappeared from television."[vii][10]

A less savoury sixty-fourth 'birthday greeting' awaited McGoohan, in March, 1992. The gossip-mongering National Enquirer[viii] – "the largest circulation of any paper in America" – incurred the actor's displeasure by printing a lengthy account of his emergency hospital surgery in the preceding month. Reporting that the star had come close to death, it stated, through no less than three writers, that McGoohan was fighting back from the brink of death as a "thin and trembling old man." Allegedly the actor had developed a deadly case of pneumonia and had been transferred to the intensive care unit of the Saint John's Hospital, in Santa Monica. The ailing star was described through the words of his daughter Anne, who reportedly confided as to her father's condition:

"He'd drift in and out of consciousness and he was rambling incoherently like a madman." After intestinal surgery at the end of February, McGoohan was reportedly down to a hundred pounds and was "as weak as a kitten." The story continued, "Joan sat by Patrick's bedside, holding his hand and wiping his forehead with a washcloth, every day and night. She stayed overnight, sleeping in a recliner by her husband." The *Enquirer* claimed that for years McGoohan had been a hard drinker and a junk food addict who often ate on the run. It was said that doctors blamed his bad diet for contributing to his internal

vii A DVD of *The Best of Friends* has been released.
viii See also page 225.

Above: This writer receiving McGoohan's award
from Frank Ratcliffe of PolyGram, formerly ITC
Right: Autographed photo of McGoohan, mid-1990s

problems. After the initial scare was over, the actor was quoted as admitting, "I just thank God I got a second chance."[11]

By the end of the year, with his health restored, McGoohan made his way back to England and while there he telephoned this writer. The actor announced, from his hotel in the capital, "I wanted to feel the heartbeat of London and to get damp." Certainly, at the time, Britain was experiencing very rainy weather and the climate must have been markedly different from the actor's home setting. This writer enquired after McGoohan's health and the Californian replied, amusingly, that he was "Well," adding, "But wet. It's pissing down."[12] During a long ensuing conversation, there was mention of a recent interview, attributed to one of the original *Prisoner* writers. McGoohan was unhappy about remarks which had apparently been made and felt that the particular person could never have held the kind of background information he was claiming to possess and also that some inaccurate statements had been made. On request, a copy of the interview was provided to McGoohan by this writer, the actor stating that he intended to take whatever action he deemed appropriate.

Around the same time, this writer of this book spoke to McGoohan on a few more occasions and a good rapport developed. Although the actor had maintained contact during the preceding decade and would continue to do so for a decade more, the present series of conversations bore much more of a personal slant. Dismissing the *National Enquirer*'s account of his ill health, McGoohan said that he had roared with laughter. He seemed at ease with the topic, and yet earlier in the year he had expressed anger when one of *The Prisoner* Appreciation Society's publications had made mention of the reported health scare. At that previous time, the writer's attempt to explain to him that his fans were only concerned about his well-being and not any scandal story, had fallen upon deaf ears. In addition, the actor was unhappy with assertions made by some *Prisoner* actors or crew members as to the extent of their involvement with the production. Firstly, McGoohan insisted that he had chosen Portmeirion as the filming location and no other person. He also belittled claims made by some as to the interpretation of the cult series, or its 'meaning' or 'message'. Finally, the actor's displeasure was evident as to undue levels of attention from devotees. He expressed a sense of being unable to 'escape' from the series and feeling 'imprisoned' by over-active fans.

However, the next day things were calmer and McGoohan rang again, saying, "Hey, it would be lovely to see you before I leave. How hard is it to get to (you)?" This writer was half afraid to suggest a meeting, owing to some of the tough comments McGoohan had been firing at him. The actor laughed, "Yes, I'm such a nasty man!" A few days later, still in London, McGoohan called for one more friendly conversation, before his departure. He had read the *Prisoner* interview which had been provided to him. This had given him cause for concern but was now amusing him. McGoohan laughed that the interview with one of the *Prisoner* scriptwriters seemed to have taken

Fan photo in casual setting, late 1990s

place "probably after a few drinks, by the sound of it. It's quite incredible what he says; it's a pack of lies; it's libellous." McGoohan sounded relaxed. He spoke of how he had to watch his diet, which he claimed was difficult, with so many good cooks in the family. He mentioned his grandchildren and turned to the subject of work. Talk turned to marriage and the writer pointed out how he had first met his wife in Portmeirion, *The Prisoner* filming location. "That sounds like a good basis for marriage," commented McGoohan.[13]

The Prisoner was celebrated in a special twenty fifth anniversary event which took place in London in 1993. There was a similar London event held for the series' thirtieth anniversary in 1997.[ix] For the former event, McGoohan asked this writer to accept and receive on his behalf an award for *The Prisoner*, given to him by the distribution company ITC and also the series' Appreciation Society. A fax[x] was sent by the actor to this writer, with a second one containing a message for the assembled fans. The star's comments announced that he would be unable to attend, but he delivered some warm greetings. McGoohan also telephoned this writer, stating that he had arranged the booking of a flight for attendance at the event, but there had been terrible storms, with phone lines to his home knocked out and connected problems. At the time of the anniversary, Channel 4 repeated *The Prisoner*. This writer prepared for the screening a four page information supplement about the series and over twelve thousand of these were sent to enquirers who responded to the on screen offer.[xi]

Also in 1993, a book was published on television shows, called *Cult TV*. McGoohan agreed to provide comments for the foreword, as he had done with the earlier French *Prisoner* book. For the new publication, the actor stated that cult shows are viewed "time after time, without diminution of enjoyment. Why? Perhaps the answer is that these programmes were made by enthusiasts, who believed passionately in their work. The energy of their belief is transmitted to a select audience, sympathetic to the theme and hungry themselves for an enthusiasm."[14]

[ix] Coverage of both events appears earlier in this book, See page 126.
[x] See page 249.
[xi] Posted from within Six of One by Bill and Angie Faupel, from the society's then Harrogate address.

Mid-1990s McGoohan magazine covers: *Globe Hebdo*, *The Big Issue*, *TV Zone* and *7 A Paris*.

In the spring of 1994, when it was McGoohan's sixty-sixth birthday, this writer thought it amusing to send the actor a fax, for a change. A birthday message from the *Prisoner* episode *Hammer into Anvil* was quoted to him: "May the sun shine on you today and every day." The line of dialogue brought forth a speedy phone call from the actor, "I'm ringing to thank you for the lovely fax. It was most appreciated." McGoohan then laughed, referring to the *Prisoner* society's name "Six of One" and his age, joking: "I am now sixty-six of one and none of the other." Discussion turned to current rumours of a *Prisoner* movie, at a time when suggestions were being made in the media that Portmeirion would not be used as a location. McGoohan commented, "If anyone makes a film of *The Prisoner* and does not use Portmeirion, it would be idiotic. Anyone who does the movie would need to use parts of the original concept. Of course there could not be an allegorical conundrum – as I did with the series – in a movie. It wouldn't work for a film."[15]

Later in the year, the British television channel BBC2 screened a documentary *The Persuader – The TV Times of Lord Lew Grade*,[xii] with a selection of old shows from the mogul's past companies, including *The Prisoner*. The tribute was hosted by actor Leo McKern – who starred in three episodes of the series, and McGoohan also participated. Although some of the anecdotes have been mentioned in the earlier *Prisoner* section of this book, it is interesting to note the revised, contemporary remarks of both TV boss and actor, nearly three decades on. McGoohan recalled, "I went to see Lew Grade and said 'I do happen to have a little idea and in (this folder) here Lew you've got an outline for a story.' (It had) drawings and descriptions of things and I think he became somewhat alarmed when he saw all these pages going by and said 'Pat why don't you just tell me about it for a while?' So I did that, I closed the (papers) and wandered around the office and started to talk and he listened until I'd finished. I sat down and then he got up, puffed on his cigar, marched around a little bit and then he turned on me and said 'Pat, it's so crazy, it might work.'"

Grade was interviewed on screen by his nephew, TV executive Michael Grade. The elder revealed: "There were problems. After viewing the fourth *Prisoner* episode the president of CBS came over to England to see me. He said, 'What's it about? It's wonderful, it's tremendous, something different, but what is the story about, what happens?' I said, 'Well the best way for me to make you understand what it's all about is for you to meet with Patrick McGoohan.' And I arranged the meeting and he went up to Wales to where they were shooting. I think he was there two days, then came back and he said to me, 'I don't understand that Patrick McGoohan.

[xii] The documentary was repeated in 1996, as part of Grade's ninetieth birthday celebrations.

Do you have problems with him?' I said, 'I never have any problem at all with Patrick McGoohan. He's wonderful.' (He asked) 'But how do you do it?' (I replied) 'I always give in to what he wants.'"[xiii] McGoohan affirmed in the documentary that the TV boss always stuck to their deal: "What I have to say about Lew Grade, rightfully Sir Lew Grade, rightfully thereafter Lord Grade, is that from the very moment he said 'Go,' and shook my hand, we never had a contract, he never interfered in anything that I did, never bothered me, it was marvellous. I can't conceive of anybody else in

McGoohan at *Braveheart* premiere, Stirling, Scotland

the world then or now giving me that amount of freedom with a subject which in many respects I suppose you might say was outrageous."[16]

At the end of 1994, McGoohan's name was linked to *A Christmas Carol*, being performed at the Birmingham Theatre in Michigan. The advance details proclaimed that the actor would be starring, although no appearances by him apparently ever occurred. Possibly the advertisements were produced before any confirmation was forthcoming from McGoohan that he would appear. However, another quartet of cinema films was about to engage the actor, during the second half of the decade. These were: *Braveheart* (1995), *The Phantom* (1996) *A Time to Kill* (1996) and *Hysteria* (1998), returning the actor to the big screen after a gap of ten years.[xiv] His role in *Braveheart*[xv] was heralded as "a triumphant return to the big screen."[17] Cast as the evil King Edward Longshanks, McGoohan admirers saw the actor really excelling in a part blessed with exceptional dialogue. The movie starred Mel Gibson as the thirteenth century Scottish hero, William Wallace. His fight against the tyranny of McGoohan's King Edward I and *Braveheart's* epic power and scale garnered several Academy Awards. The *Guardian* referred to McGoohan's Longshanks as, "A rasping tyrant who recognises that to rule you need to put your rod of iron where it hurts most." As to the actor's performance, this was said to be "smooth, not overplayed, but expressed with suitable quiet venom."[18] While good notices were received all round, one music magazine referred to McGoohan giving a "brilliantly loopy cameo."[19] The actor made much of the role of the malevolent "Longshanks," one of England's most ruthless leaders. At one point a soldier informs the monarch, "The archers are ready Sire." The King replies, "Not the archers. Use up the Irish. Arrows cost money, the dead cost nothing."

Fellow actor and director Mel Gibson said of McGoohan that "he is a very intelligent actor whom I admired as a kid. I watched *Danger Man* and *The Prisoner* and all these things on television which he conceived. So I was really flattered when he agreed to do this." Gibson referred to Longshanks having subdued Scotland and how the king had the power to make everybody feel like a subject, adding "Patrick has the capacity to do that. His performance as Longshanks is very sinister."[20] The film also reunited McGoohan with his

---

[xiii] A similar story was related by Lew Grade years earlier, see page 109.
[xiv] The previous movie had been *Baby: Secret of the Lost Legend* (1985), but the actor was involved with several TV productions in the meantime.
[xv] The movie won an Oscar for Best Picture and many awards from other sources.

Left: Sony 1993 French *Destination Danger* video release Centre: 30th *Prisoner* anniversary postcard 1997
Right: Postcard with *Prisoner* dialogue to celebrate 30th anniversary

old *Danger Man* and *Prisoner* producer, David Tomblin, now first assistant director on *Braveheart*. Location filming occurred in Scotland and Ireland, with several ancient sites being used. The seventy million dollar budget was by far the biggest, longest and most expensive production of all the films in which McGoohan had ever participated.

Variety review: "Gibson's direction meanders at first but takes hold once the fighting starts, and while the movie is indeed a long sit, from that point on it's far from boring. The battles, barring some unwelcome slow-motion shots, are spectacular, with almost balletic stunt and second-unit work all around. The director also pulls the camera back to capture the grandeur and scope of the conflict, which, again, is diminished only through repetition. Marceau and McCormack both cut striking figures in limited femme roles amidst the carnage, while McGoohan perhaps overplays his hand slightly as the villainous king, a figure notable principally for his utter amorality."

New York Times review: "Mel Gibson came into his own as a director with Braveheart, an account of the life and times of medieval Scottish patriot William Wallace and, to a lesser degree, Robert the Bruce's struggle to unify his nation against its English oppressors. The story begins with young Wallace, whose father and brother have been killed fighting the English, being taken into the custody of his uncle, a nationalist and pre-Renaissance renaissance man. He returns twenty years later, a man educated both in the classics and in the art of war. There he finds his childhood sweetheart Murron (Catherine McCormack), and the two quickly fall in love. There are murmurs of revolt against the English throughout the village, but Wallace remains aloof, wishing simply to tend to his crops and live in peace. However, when his love is killed by English soldiers the day after their secret marriage (held secretly so as to prevent the local English lord from exercising the repulsive right of prima noctae, the privilege of sleeping with the bride on the first night of the marriage), he springs into action and single-handedly slays an entire platoon of foot soldiers. The other villagers join him in destroying the English garrison, and thus begins the revolt against the English in what will eventually become full-fledged war. Wallace eventually leads his fellow Scots in a series of bloody battles that prove a serious threat to English domination and, along the way, has a hushed affair with the Princess of Wales (the breathtaking Sophie Marceau) before his imminent demise." (Jeremy Beday, All Movie Guide)

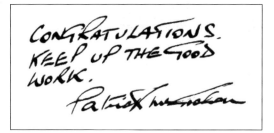

Congratulatory message from McGoohan 1990s

McGoohan attended the UK premiere[xvi] of *Braveheart*, which was held at Stirling, site of William Wallace's famous battle with the English army. The event included an evening reception at the castle, following the movie's screening.[xvii]

Mel Gibson donned full Highland garb for the occasion, in contrast to his older co-star, whose arrival from the rear of a plain car was in casual jacket, shirt, tie and slacks. Clasping papers and a light raincoat, McGoohan stepped out into the drizzly autumn Sunday, more resembling one of the university's lecturers than an invited celebrity amongst so many dinner-suited male guests. The premiere was covered by Sky News and the Stirling Observer, but McGoohan passed almost unnoticed, with no interview or comment. He gave a brief smile to the crowd to his side, assembled behind police barriers outside the Cottrell Building, greeting them with "How are you?" One attending Scot from the *Prisoner* society commented: "Eagerly I shouted a welcome ... He quietly said hello to me, but did not stop to talk. And then he was gone. Soon afterwards, Mr. McGoohan appeared on an overhead corridor, only a short distance from me. He was alone. Our eyes met."[21] Other attending members fared less well, not even obtaining a fleeting glimpse of the actor. This writer was in contact with the university and newspaper and both sources stated confidently that McGoohan had not been there at all, such was the almost anonymous nature of his presence.

However, while McGoohan was involved with promoting *Braveheart* generally, he gave an interview which appeared in several press publications. Before addressing present projects, coming plans and his state of health, McGoohan reflected upon his past and surrounding circumstances: "I didn't leave England because of England. After *The Prisoner* I just wanted a break from it all. One day I just said, 'Let's go!'" The actor referred to giving up "hard drinking" and having undergone a life-threatening colon operation which left him in a coma for some weeks. Although McGoohan had previously complained bitterly about a *National Enquirer* report of his having been in hospital, he now referred positively to the article: "I had a wonderful male nurse who came in when I was at death's door and told me I'd been quoted as saying 'If God gives me one more chance, I'm going to be a good boy.'" The actor claimed that the quotation was false and that "those words wouldn't have been dragged out of me by all the horses in the chariot race in *Ben Hur*. It was a giggle. I had the last rites a couple of times."

The journalist observed, "His peers in the sixties may have faded into obscurity, but Patrick has managed to survive in the treacherous waters of international celebrity status and betray none of his integrity. The fiercely private Irishman has spent the past twenty years living quietly in California with his wife, Joan Drummond, preserving his anonymity." McGoohan offered his own views on the LA lifestyle: "In Los Angeles, famous people are

---

[xvi] 3rd September, 1995. The US premiere had been on 19th May, 1995, in Los Angeles; it is not known if McGoohan attended.
[xvii] At the MacRobert Centre, within Stirling University.

January 22, 1998

Dear Roger,

I have your fax.

Let me make it most clear.

Whatever this spurious campaign, it was not requested
nor desired by me.

I do not wish to petition Polygram Films.

You guys do whatever you want, as you usually do.

But please be kind enough not to mention my name
in association with this farce.

Thank you.

Kind regards,

Patrick

Left: Poster produced at time of *Prisoner* 30th anniversary Right: Fax from McGoohan, January 1998, to this writer

ten-a-penny. My friends are not in the business. They're carpenters and plumbers, nothing to do with the business at all. I never go to cocktail parties. I like to have a beer in a local pub with some of my friends." The actor also spoke affectionately of his three daughters and five young grandchildren.

The interview also highlighted the latest *Prisoner* movie plans, with an eighty million dollar budget being mooted. It was announced that McGoohan was writing the screenplay for the big screen version.[xviii] McGoohan was happy to describe the proposed new *Prisoner* movie as "very exciting" and "a very big film." The finance was coming from PolyGram and the film was planned for release in 1997. McGoohan revealed: "We're negotiating for someone who will be wonderful in it. I can't say who, but he is a fan of the series and a big star, someone I've had in mind from the beginning." The actor hinted that Mel Gibson was his first choice for the title role in any *Prisoner* movie. "Obviously I can't play it because I'm too old, but I'll be playing the father of *The Prisoner*, or the grandfather, depending who does it. I'm writing two scripts, father and granddad."[22] McGoohan announced that the film crew, including himself, would return to Wales in 1996[xix] to shoot *Prisoner* movie scenes in Portmeirion. Because of this, he intended to catch up on the series. "Normally when I finish with something, I finish with it. If I see myself I want to throw up! But I shall be doing some re-watching in the near future." The actor was in good humour and felt moved to explain why his interviews were few and far between. "I am reclusive perhaps. I always feel that interviewers have been looking for the wrong things – news that is salacious – so I avoid it mostly. But I love people, I adore people. The papers just want someone who's been married for five minutes and has got divorced. That's not me."[23]

Another interview McGoohan gave in 1995 was for a French magazine *Premiere*,[xx] conducted by Jean Yves Katelan: "Mostly I've been writing these last ten years, and I've

---

[xviii] The actor was at this point being interviewed in County Kerry, Ireland, which was a potential filming location.
[xix] See fax McGoohan sent to the hotel, page 257.
[xx] The version provided here is a translation from the French.

P	*Hello, is that Roger?*
R	Hi Patrick, yes it is.
P	*Sorry about the delay, but I've only just got back rom Canada. I have been doing some filming there.*
R	We're so pleased to hear from you. We have been running the convention all day and are about to go to Porthmadog. We'll be showing episodes on the Coliseum screen, where you watched the 'rushes'.
P	*How many have you got there?*
R	About two hundred and fifty.
P	*That's good.*
R	We have TV crews, lots of journalists and there has been a great deal of media coverage.
P	*That's very good.*
R	We are going to see 'Living In Harmony' and have Frank Maher with us...
P	*I know Frank*
R	...and Ian Rakoff, whose story idea it was in part.
P	*Yes, Tomblin directed that one.*
R	And John S. Smith, who did a lot of the editing.
P	*Oh, that's good. Give them all my best wishes.*

URGENT

TO: ROGER LANGLEY

This message is addressed to the final Prisoner Convention in Portmeirion, and to all those unable to be there. Together, your persistent support over many years has, I feel sure, contributed in no small measure to the long life and continuing interest in the Series.

Who knows? You may be at Portmeirion again. You'll certainly see it once more when the movie, now in preparation, comes to the big screen.

My profound thanks to you all.

Bon voyage. And –

"BE SEEING YOU"

Patrick

Left: Telephone call from McGoohan to the writer during the 1998 *Prisoner* convention. Above: Message from McGoohan to the *Prisoner* convention, 1998

been involved in real estate. I'm not really very interested in a career. After *The Prisoner*, I even stopped acting for several years. I'd never particularly been a success. I just didn't want to follow that career any more. I wanted to do something else. I wrote some poems, did some sculpture and a few other things that interested me." Katelan elicited from the actor that he was writing a book: "It's almost finished, but I put it aside and I don't want to speak of it. I'm not even sure that I want to release it at all. I don't want to talk about my poems either. My family, when I'm dead, if my children want to publish them, they're welcome to do so." The interviewer asked what was McGoohan's 'official occupation.' The actor responded, "To live one day at a time. It's the first time anyone's asked me that question. So it's the first time I've given that answer. You get up in the morning and you ask yourself, 'now what.' I don't want every day to be the same as every other."

Asked about his nationality, McGoohan replied, "American." The conversation moved to the topic of religion and the actor's spiritual convictions. "I believe in an all-powerful being who transcends me and who has made all the things that surround us. I believe in the principle of decency, to behave well towards others and to be charitable." When Hollywood was mentioned, McGoohan enthused about his acting career. "When you face a camera, you're someone else." The actor again spoke about the planned film version of *The Prisoner*, for which he was writing the script. He confirmed that a contract had been signed and that PolyGram had invested a huge amount of money, ready for the movie to be made and released in 1997. McGoohan stated, "I get up very early, around 3:00 a.m. and I work on it for seven hours. The film will be shot in Portmeirion in the beginning and the end. There will be Rover balloons too. It's a film that will be faithful to the series. I will be executive producer and the budget is around $65 million." The interviewer put to McGoohan a rumour that Kevin Costner had been cast in the *Prisoner* movie lead role. The actor was not enamoured with the idea and remarked, "He won't be doing the film. Otherwise, I won't do it." The actor's requirement was that the person chosen should have "fire in the belly." McGoohan gave a strong impression of being very busy and heavily committed.

The actor next spoke of his cinematic delights. "Two of my favourite movies were filmed

The writer (right) with Lord Dafydd Elis Thomas at the Prisoner Shop opening, June 1999.

by Vittorio De Sica, *The Bicycle Thief* (1948) and *Miracle at Milan* (1951). I'd give my right arm to work with Kazan, *On the Waterfront* (1954), *Viva Zapata* (1952). But alas I have never met Mr. Kazan. If I'd met a director of his calibre sooner, I would be far more interested in the acting profession." McGoohan also reflected on his own early film assignments: "The first time I found myself on a film set was for *The Dam Busters*. I had exactly one day's filming and perhaps five lines. My early films constituted a rather poor introduction to the film world. In *The Dark Avenger* Errol Flynn was truly very near to the end. In *I am a Camera* I played a Swedish masseur who smoked. In *Zarak* there were certain people who behaved like stars and I don't like that. James Stewart is a magnificent example of the way to behave. I remember him doing a film at MGM studios at the same time that I was making *The Prisoner*. Jimmy Stewart was a gentleman; decency itself."

The star was certainly giving a candid account of his life and its different twists and turns. He even disclosed that he had now thrown himself into the property business: "I buy houses, I do them up and I sell them again." Wife Joan was a successful realtor, but it was always stated that her sales were at the expensive end of the market and it seemed a little incongruous to hear that her actor husband was turning his hand to property renovation and resale. The actor talked about his long marriage, "as though it was yesterday," adding, "(Joan) makes me laugh, she makes fun of me, and she doesn't let anything happen to me."[24] Somehow it seems that the actor has had in recent years an empathy with France. He did a telephone interview with one Gallic writer, wrote a personal note of thanks to another French book compiler, who had inserted a praising entry for *The Prisoner* and gave an interview for another tome published in that country. Ironically, France is one place where McGoohan appears never to have worked.[xxi]

In his next movie, *The Phantom*, the actor played the ghost of the main 'comic hero' character's father. McGoohan could be seen only by his 'son' and appeared only briefly.[xxii] One unimpressed reviewer commented, "I recommend this film only if you need a nap."[25] However, perhaps a less hasty appraisal of McGoohan's contribution was more appropriate. The actor set the tone for what many regarded as a faithful film version of the original, classic comic strip. Presented in the style of a period movie serial, McGoohan's prologue was delivered with a New York accent: "It all began a very long time ago … (a) small boy watched helplessly as his father was killed by pirates … He jumped overboard and was washed ashore on a mysterious jungle island … (whose) tribesmen presented the boy with a ring of great significance. Destined to avenge his father's death by fighting piracy, greed and cruelty in all their forms … he became the Phantom."[26] So began the legend: in every generation, each first-born male child succeeds his father as the next Phantom, creating a myth of immortality. McGoohan played the 'retired' twentieth Phantom, his son Kit Walker (Billy Zane) being the successor. In the movie, Kit has to prevent a rich madman from obtaining three magic skulls, which would unlock the secret to gaining 'ultimate power.' McGoohan, as his son's mentor, balanced the film's paranormal elements with a tart humour.

New York Times review: "The first superhero ever, created by Lee Falk in 1936, gets another shot at movie stardom 60 years after achieving fame in comics and serials. Billy Zane stars as Kit Walker, who discovers that he's the 21st in a line of purple-clad African superheroes known as 'The Phantom' or, to superstitious Bengalla Island natives, 'the Ghost Who Walks.' Xander Drax (Treat Williams), a slimy industrialist, is plotting to take over the world by uniting the three long lost magical Skulls of Touganda. Kit travels to New York, where he finds allies in crusading newspaper publisher Dave (Bill Smitrovich) and his niece, Diana (Kristy Swanson), who's also Kit's ex-girlfriend. Kit and Diana tackle Drax's forces, including the conflicted Sala (Catherine Zeta-Jones), in a quest for the Skulls that brings both sides back to Bengalla for a showdown." (Karl Williams, All Movie Guide)

McGoohan's next appearance was in *A Time to Kill* (1996), the film becoming – like *Braveheart* – another commercial success. The screenplay presented the actor in the role of Judge Omar Noose, in the adaptation of John Grisham's legal thriller novel. The judge McGoohan portrays is trying a black man accused of killing the white murderers of his daughter. The actor played perfectly the judicial role, speaking with a drawl and only giving latitude to the accused's defence attorney if the rules forced him to do so. However, one critic underrated McGoohan's judicial performance, saying that his voice, "cannot be plausibly disguised as Southern, and he appears to phone in his performance."[27]

New York Times review: "Carl Lee Hailey (Samuel L. Jackson) takes the law into his own hands after the legal system fails to adequately punish the men who brutally raped and beat his daughter, leaving her for dead. Normally, a distraught father could count on some

---

[xxi] Apart from the Paris business meeting with the makers of the TV documentary *Six into One: The Prisoner File* (1983) – see page 230.
[xxii] One source rated his part as "blink and miss."

judicial sympathy in those circumstances. Unfortunately, Carl and his daughter are black, and the assailants are white, and all the events take place in the South. Indeed, so inflammatory is the situation, that the local KKK (led by Kiefer Sutherland) becomes popular again. When Hailey chooses novice lawyer Jake Brigance (Matthew McConaughey) to handle his defense, it begins to look like a certainty that Carl will hang, and Jake's career (and perhaps his life) will come to a premature end. Despite the efforts of the NAACP[xxiii] and local black leaders to persuade Carl to choose some of their high-powered legal help, he remains loyal to Jake, who had helped his brother with a legal problem before the story begins. Jake eventually takes this case seriously enough to seek help from his old law-school professor (Donald Sutherland). When death threats force his family to leave town, Jake even accepts the help of pushy young know-it-all lawyer Ellen Roark (Sandra Bullock)." (Clarke Fountain, All Movie Guide)

On 10th July, 1996, McGoohan gave a radio interview to the BBC World Service for their programme *Outlook,* speaking from his home in California. The six minute spot could be heard across the globe and was repeated the following day on BBC Radio 4. McGoohan was asked if he felt that he was part of an alternative culture. "Never entered my mind. I'm an Irish peasant." His opinion was also sought about *The Prisoner* having become such a cult, with people even studying the show for a degree course. The actor reasoned, "Because I got away with murder really; because I left it a mystery, and mysteries and myths are always fascinating. My intention was that each beholder, each viewer (should) put his own interpretation on it." The star was questioned about the final episode and he divulged, "I directed and wrote and edited it and I finished with it then, because it's too late to do anything more about it, for better or worse, it's done." Once more, McGoohan declared that he was about to return to Portmeirion, where he would be shooting for a month, to make the forthcoming *Prisoner* movie. Asked if he would like to see Mel Gibson playing the lead role of Number Six, McGoohan enthusiastically affirmed this.[28]

There was more news of the *Prisoner* movie project in 1996, this time directly from McGoohan. He sent a fax to the managing director of Portmeirion, Robin Llywelyn, grandson of Clough Williams-Ellis, the architect who created Portmeirion: "I vividly remember your grandfather and what a wonderful character he was, a visionary, and his alarm at the first day of (*Prisoner*) shooting, with helicopters buzzing around and his wanting us to get out of there and leave his idyll in peace, and how I had to persuade him that his dream might somehow be aligned with my dream and how in the end we came together. I hope to good effect." The view of Williams-Ellis as to the original use of the resort had been: "Patrick McGoohan's ingenious and indeed mysterious television series ... stands alone for its revealing presentation of the place. When seen in colour at the local cinema,[xxiv] a performance he kindly arranged, Portmeirion seemed to me ... to steal the show from its human cast."[29] Thirty years on, McGoohan was now approaching the grandson: "As you may have heard, a movie of The Prisoner is in the works. I wrote the script (and) most of it, with your permission, will be filmed in 'The Village.' I can assure you that the fabric and spirit of the place will be preserved for the world to see." Sadly, as later became known, the film crews never arrived and the plans withered on the vine.

[xxiii] National Association for the Advancement of Colored People.
[xxiv] Each day's filming results were viewed as "rushes" at the Coliseum cinema in nearby Porthmadog (also known as Portmadoc).

Dear Roger,

The Prisoner in Portmeirion is a handsome work and much appreciated. Maybe I'll be seeing the place again one of these days. It sort of haunts me.

Currently preparing to direct a piece I wrote for one of the Networks.

Best regards to you and Karen.

Left: The cover of the writer's book, *The Prisoner in Portmeirion*, produced for the Portmeirion shop 1999. Above: Message from McGoohan about the book *The Prisoner in Portmeirion*

In 1997, McGoohan was interviewed once more by Alain Carrazé,[xxv] – by telephone from France – for the TV cable channel Canal Jimmy. The actor explained the basis for *The Prisoner*: "The purpose of the series was to explore certain areas which we are more into now than we were into then. There are more conflicts, more dissensions and more problems with bureaucracy and the overpowering death of the individual, if I may put it like that. The way I designed it was that there wasn't really a proper ending to it in the sense that one normally handles a television series. I left it much in the air, so that everyone who beholds it or sees it has their own interpretation of it. The greatest compliment that I could possibly receive is for people to debate the meaning of it and I think that is probably why it has lasted so long."[30]

Also in 1997, McGoohan telephoned this writer to say that he had been in Africa for the past two months and had only just got back. He was calling to express his disappointment at being unable to be present at the second of the London *Prisoner* anniversary events.[xxvi] However, he did endorse the occasion and expressed his good wishes for the day to be enjoyed by his attending fellow actors, production team members and of course the fans.

McGoohan's next movie, *Hysteria* (1998),[xxvii] saw the actor with top billing. He played Dr. Harvey Langston, a doctor running an institution for patients receiving psychotherapy. Shot in Montreal, the screenplay by the film's director Rene Daalder, was in the form of a dark, psychological thriller. The actor's comment on his part was a modest quip. "I run a lunatic asylum, so there is absolutely no acting required."[31] The movie contained scenes – although McGoohan was not actually in them – of nudity, sex and profanity, with one section leaning more towards 'sex romp' than medical drama.

New York Times review: "Dutch cult filmmaker Rene Daalder directed this surreal tale of thought-control experiments on the inmates of an insane asylum. Like his other films,

[xxv] See reference to a previous McGoohan interview by Carrazé, page 241.
[xxvi] See coverage earlier in this book.
[xxvii] The movie was nominated in 1998 for the Fantasporto International Fantasy Film Award as Best Film (Fantasporto is the Festival Internacional de Cinema do Porto, Portugal).

Hysteria is a rich and thematically dense sociopolitical allegory, but this time around the concept is overwhelmed by a particularly risible execution. Patrick McGoohan stars as Dr. Harvey Langston, a mad genius who spouts twisted philosophical nonsense while conducting experiments in universal consciousness and group thought. His latest guinea pig is Veronica (Emmanuelle Vaugier), who hallucinates ants all over her body and attempts to stab her doctor (Michael Maloney) in the eye with a corkscrew. Langston implants a computer chip in Veronica's head, and she enters the group consciousness of a contrived assembly of patients including a mannish Tourette's sufferer who speaks in rhyme, a musician who has separate identities in each of his arms, and Amanda Plummer as a wheelchair-bound dancer. Plummer has the film's most memorable scene, spinning about in her chair as the asylum's inmates copulate in every possible combination for the orgiastic finale. Whether the entire escapade is a dangerous cult or a radical new model for a communal civilization is open to interpretation, but most of the time the events onscreen are too laughable for it to really matter. Daalder's unique vision walks a very thin line, and he is capable of taking outrageous concepts and making them believable, but this time he misses the mark by a mile. Nevertheless, McGoohan does his best and the film is still worth watching, for even if it is a failure (and it is), it's at least an interesting one." (Robert Firsching, All Movie Guide)

As the nineties were closing, McGoohan returned to television work, becoming reconnected with the *Columbo* TV mysteries. By now, the franchise was being produced as one-off specials. Both in 1998 and 1999 McGoohan was involved with separate episodes, although in the case of the latter story, only as director and writer. Catherine McGoohan appeared in the first of the two episodes, with younger sister Anne being seen in the other. In the 1998 TV special, *Ashes to Ashes*, their father (who also directed the black comedy drama) played a mortician in charge of a funeral parlour. His cremation furnace comes in useful when a lady Hollywood gossip reporter has to be removed and her remains disposed of. McGoohan was also credited as co-executive producer and he clearly had fun with the script and the wicked character he was playing. One line of dialogue, "It's your funeral," probably struck a chord with those who remembered a *Prisoner* episode of that title. This latest appearance by McGoohan was a treat for his fans and the actor gave a stylish and humorous dark performance.

The actor's 1999 *Columbo* episode was entitled *Murder with Too Many Notes*, co-written and directed by McGoohan. This was another TV special, this time to mark the twenty fifth anniversary of the series. The plot involved a Hollywood film composer and conductor murdering a musician, of whom he is jealous.[xxviii] Anne McGoohan took the part of a witness going to a concert, thereby placing her near the murder scene at a crucial time.[xxix] The script was co-written by her father and he directed the episode. While it was good to see her father's name in the credits, *Columbo* episodes were the richer when he starred in them.

In fact, an even lesser amount of McGoohan was about to be seen – or more particularly heard, in a 1999 episode of the cartoon series *The Simpsons*. The vocal skills of the actor were employed for the voice of Number Six in a *Prisoner*-related episode entitled *The*

[xxviii] One of the characters is named "Tomblin," being the surname of McGoohan's former fellow company director and producer of *The Prisoner*.
[xxix] Anne McGoohan was also assistant script supervisor on the 1998 film of *The Man in the Iron Mask*, her father having appeared in the 1976 version.

Computer Wore Menace Shoes. Here, McGoohan was providing his Number Six character's voice for the first time in over thirty years. His animated appearance was to inform Homer Simpson about a self-built escape raft, which Homer promptly hijacks. The raft idea was used in a *Prisoner* episode, *Many Happy Returns*. *Simpsons* executive producer Mike Scully recalled McGoohan's involvement: "*Simpsons* writer George Meyer and I are huge *Prisoner* fans, so when we were fleshing out the storyline of the episode with John Swartzwelder, who wrote the script, and the rest of the staff, we started talking about a third act where Homer mysteriously wakes up on this bizarre island patterned after the one in *The Prisoner*. It gave us a great excuse to spend a day watching old episodes of the series instead of

McGoohan in *The Simpsons* episode *The Computer Wore Menace Shoes*. *The Simpsons* TM and © 1999 Twentieth Century Fox Film Corporation. All Rights Reserved.

actually working. The show was so stylistic and unlike anything else on television at the time. As a ten-year-old, I didn't understand a lot of it, but couldn't stop watching at the same time. It was an incredibly cool, imaginative show and we had heard that Patrick McGoohan was heavily involved in all aspects. We tried to recreate some of the show's look (clothes, oddly-shaped furniture, etc.) and made a special point to include Homer being repeatedly poisoned with various gasses (a staple of *The Prisoner*) and, our personal favorite, a dish of ice cream filled with syringes. While working on the story and pitching jokes, we talked about how great it would be to actually get Patrick in the episode. The last time we had seen him on screen was in *Braveheart* and he was terrific, so we decided to give it a shot. Fortunately, he said yes. Even though we've had lots of guest stars on the show, we never take it for granted because the pay is basically union scale plus a *Simpsons* t-shirt. Patrick couldn't have been nicer to work with and made absolutely no script demands (our favorite kind of guest star) and did a wonderful job. He was a total pro and we were thrilled and honored to have him be part of *The Simpsons*."[32]

One other event from 1999 can be mentioned: Carlton International Media[xxx] acquired TV rights to *The Prisoner*.[xxxi] These were previously held by PolyGram, the company which had purchased, some years earlier, the rights from the original company, ITC. Scripting rights for a big screen version had already passed through different hands during the mid-nineties and having new owners of *The Prisoner* might now impact further upon any movie remake, or TV sequel. There was still active talk about a cinema film and McGoohan was always described as being closely involved with each new proposed production. In the same year, a memorial to *The Prisoner* series was opened, endorsed by Carlton and the *Prisoner* Appreciation Society. A new, well-equipped souvenir shop was located in the Portmeirion

---

[xxx] Carlton would subsequently pass the rights over to Granada Ventures in 2004 following the merger of the two companies.
[xxxi] Hundreds of other shows, series and films were also bought, amounting to "thousands of hours" on screen.

building which had served as the home of McGoohan's Number Six character in his cult TV series.[xxxii] A special champagne ceremony took place, with some of the 'extras' from the sixties series in attendance and Lord Dafydd Elis Thomas of the Welsh National Assembly officially cutting the tape.[xxxiii]

[1] New York Post, 8th February, 1990, David Bianculli
[2] *Just One More Thing: Stories from my Life*, Peter Falk, Carroll & Graf, 2006 US
[3] Ibid
[4] Ibid
[5] TV Guide, 26th January, 1991
[6] Auto Classic 26th September, 1990 Julian McNamara
[7] Simon Bates Show, BBC Radio One, 2nd February, 1991
[8] Primetime Magazine, winter, 1990, Howard Foy
[9] Email to Bruce Clark, March, 2006
[10] Toronto Star, 18th October,1992, Greg Quill
[11] National Enquirer, March, 1992
[12] Telephone conversation with the writer, October 1992
[13] Ibid
[14] *Cult TV*, Jon E. Lewis and Penny Stempel; Pavilion Books, 1993
[15] Telephone call to the writer, c. 1994
[16] The Persuader – The TV Times of Lord Lew Grade, ATV Night, 27th August, 1994
[17] Source not verified
[18] The Guardian,1995, details unknown
[19] Source not verified
[20] Ibid
[21] In the Village Magazine, Six of One, The Prisoner Appreciation Society, April, 1996, Leslie Glen
[22] TV Week, 21st October, 1995, Jane Oddy
[23] Ibid
[24] Premiere Magazine, October 1995, Jean Yves Katelan (translations Rosemary Camilleri and Jane Rawson)
[25] Source not verified
[26] Paramount Pictures, 1996
[27] Source not verified
[28] BBC World Service *Outlook*, 10th July, 1996, Barbara Myers
[29] *Portmeirion, the Place and its Meaning*
[30] Canal Jimmy, Alain Carrazé, 1997
[31] Source not verified
[32] Interview with the writer, 2006

[xxxii] This was the site of an earlier *Prisoner* information centre and memorabilia store, operated for many years by Max Hora, a member of Six of One.
[xxxiii] This writer's book *The Prisoner in Portmeirion* was also officially launched from the shop by the resort's managing director, Robin Llywelyn, who announced, "The book is by far the best ever produced, in my opinion, on *The Prisoner*."

CHAPTER TWELVE
Be Seeing You

"This is definitely not the end. The sky's the limit."
The L.A. Tape (1983)

As the twenty first century dawned, the Internet became a lively source for stories about a *Prisoner* movie sequel, with the burgeoning number of fan websites increasing focus on McGoohan generally. Hundreds of 'cyber' pages, dedicated to the actor's many films and TV appearances, were attracting vast numbers of visitor 'hits.'[i] Of course, being first with the news is always an essential goal within the media, but the Internet can also be a gossipy medium and there is less need for verification, meaning that much of what is posted is not always reliable. Online 'spokespersons' claimed to have seen McGoohan's new *Prisoner* movie script and their reports varied from the actor having delivered his screenplay to the film studio, to his only being brought on board as consultant. On one McGoohan website, a posted copy of an email claimed to be from a Universal Studios employee, purportedly giving details of a conversation with the actor. McGoohan promptly required a rebuttal statement to be displayed prominently on the website: "I was not aware that (person referred to) would write … about our recent meeting and place it on the Internet. It was inappropriate to do so and there are a number of inaccuracies in it. I wish to make the following corrections: 1. PolyGram is not giving **me** $75 million for production of *The Prisoner*. 2. I am **not** directing it. His assumption is wrong. 3. I did not say that PolyGram would "mess" with it. I said re-writes are to be expected. 4. The *Columbo* movie was not "quite behind in production." Allowing for rain on location, the show came in at 6 hours 57 seconds **under** the scheduled time. 5. I did not "re-write the whole script." I re-wrote parts of it. 6. The 'quite attractive, blonde young woman' as my personal assistant is my daughter Anne. Plus, she is **very** attractive! I exhort (name of person) to exercise precision, restraint

---

[i] Interestingly, a Google search on the actor's name produces under half a million entries, while entering "The Prisoner" brings forth nearly twenty million results.

March 6, 2003

Dear Roger and Karen,

Thank you for the generous birthday greetings and gifts.

All much appreciated.

Patrick

Message from McGoohan to the writer 2003

and discretion in the future. This is all I have to say about the matter."[ii]

At this time, McGoohan made requests for the removal of other websites. One which was dedicated to the actor was taken down and further Internet commentary about McGoohan disappeared. One person stated that he had been in discussion with the actor who was reportedly recovering from a further medical operation. McGoohan was quoted as saying that his acting days were over, but that he was still writing and creating screenplays.[iii] Of course, Internet news reports about the actor, or purported relayed comments from him, are no substitute for his real-life appearances and communications. It was therefore not surprising that excitement about McGoohan increased, when it was announced that he would be attending a cult TV conference in Torquay, in 2000. However, just before the event date, it was stated that actor had recently cancelled his visit. Given that the actor's name had been billed for several months and that many fans had bought tickets on the strength of his appearance, it was sad for them to absorb the negative news.

In September, 2002, the Libertarian Futurist Society[iv] announced on the Internet their annual winners of the Prometheus Award. McGoohan won Best Classic Fiction for his *Prisoner* TV series. The cult series was the first winner in the Hall of Fame section that was not a novel, a short story or a collection. According to the Society, McGoohan's series was "one of television's best ever classics,"[1] exploring many themes surrounding individual rebellion in surveillance societies. Away from the Internet, McGoohan's name was next linked to two more film productions. It was reported that he had been offered the roles of Gandalf in *The Lord of the Rings* (2001 onwards) and Dumbledore in a *Harry Potter* film (2001 onwards), although it was said that the actor had declined, on health grounds.[v] However, he did complete a recording in 2001 for the Walt Disney animated movie *Treasure Planet* (2002).[vi] The actor provided the voice of the pirate character Billy Bones, McGoohan's gravelly utterances being matched to the animated features of the ugly buccaneer. The *Treasure Planet* venture meant that the actor had now worked for the Disney studios on four separate occasions.[vii]

New York Times review: "Not even the high concept of transplanting Robert Louis Stevenson's beloved adventure story to outer space can generate much in the way of novelty or fun. In spite of the crowded imagery, the throbbing sea-chantey-on-steroids score and the presence of every Disney cliché from the past 40 years (absent father, lectures on self-esteem, not one but two neurotic chatterbox sidekicks), *Treasure Planet* is remarkably uneventful, even boring." (A. O. Scott)

[ii] The emphases here are McGoohan's

[iii] It is not suggested by this writer that the information is correct or not, or that the contacts did occur or not.

[iv] The society was set up in 1982 and its Hall of Fame was established in the following year, focussing on classic fiction, mainly involving novels, novellas, short stories, poems and plays.

[v] The Dumbledore part was taken by Richard Harris (with whom McGoohan appeared fifty years earlier in *Rest in Violence*) and later Michael Gambon, while the Gandalf role was filled by Sir Ian McKellen.

[vi] The film was nominated for an Academy Award as Best Animated Feature.

[vii] The others being *Dr. Syn, Alias the Scarecrow, The Three Lives of Thomasina* and *Baby: Secret of the Lost Legend*.

 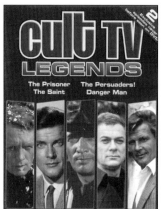 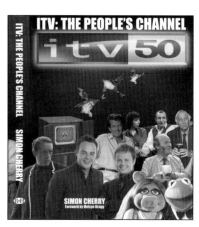

Left: New DVD for the film *Nobody's The Greatest*. Centre: *Cult TV Legends* compilation DVD including *The Prisoner* and *Danger Man*. Right: Book celebrating 50 years of ITV, featuring *The Prisoner* and with McGoohan on cover

In 2002, a thirty fifth anniversary *Prisoner* DVD was issued by Carlton. This contained, for the first time, the original edit of the opening episode *Arrival*, produced from the only taped source available, provided by this writer.[viii] Gradually, whole DVD sets of *The Prisoner* were becoming available, not only in the UK and North America, but also in France, Italy, Japan and Australia.[ix] From the end of the previous year, a limited edition set of *Prisoner* trading cards began appearing in stages and McGoohan even agreed to autograph a number of them. Later, he personally added to the growing number of collectibles, by signing photographs from his various cinema and TV appearances, to be sold on Internet auction pages. 2002 also brought renewed talk about a *Prisoner* movie, this time with Simon West[x] being named as director. On the Internet, questions were posted, asking if anybody 'out there' had more details, such enquiries always being followed by a host of answers from self-proclaimed 'reliable sources.' However, by 2003 there were no definite signs of a big screen *Prisoner* production and the story eventually went cold once more. There was also no mention of the project by McGoohan, when he sent a letter to this writer in 2003, to provide his new address. The recipient's growing concern was that whoever in the end might make a *Prisoner* sequel, the actor's age would prevent him from becoming actively involved. For now, the McGoohans were moving from their present home, where they had lived for many years, although they would be remaining within the Pacific Palisades locality.

Before moving on once more from the topic of a *Prisoner* remake, it can be observed that this same subject has been the source of much lively discussion over many years.[xi] The disagreements McGoohan had a few years back with then head of PolyGram, Michael Kuhn, the comments he himself put on the Internet, the reported rejection of his own script and the eventual news that he was no longer connected to the project at all, were all stories

---

[viii] The tape was a copy, obtained from the *Prisoner* appreciation society's US co-ordinator, Bruce Clark, he having sent the original to McGoohan.

[ix] There have been sets of CDs, with music and dialogue from the series, posters, 'moving image' pens, computer mouse mats, mugs and many other products. Even digital 'e-books' of *Prisoner* novels can be found on the Internet.

[x] In 1982, West was assistant director of the pop song video "I Helped Patrick McGoohan Escape," – see page 215.

[xi] New plans for a TV mini-series were announced at the end of 2005 – see page 269 and as to the remake history, see footnote to page 273.

which were spread around the press and the Internet, as well as a few other tales. During recent years, rumours have abounded that filming would start soon on a *Prisoner* "go project." Budget figures in the range of fifty to a hundred million dollars were quoted, but at no time have any filming dates, or schedules, ever mentioned, nor have any actor signings been announced. There being no positive outcomes in all these cases, this book has omitted lengthy excursions into the past history of sequels to the original series, to avoid discussing projects which never came to fruition. This writer has details of previous *Prisoner* sequel plans and even copies of prospective scripts. However, fascinating though these projects might be, fortunately, or unfortunately, they have so far come to nothing.[xii]

Around the time of McGoohan's seventy fifth birthday, a fellow Californian reported several conversations he said had taken place with McGoohan, as well as discussions about *The Prisoner*. He recalled how he had given the actor a printout from an Internet chat page and how McGoohan was amazed at the amount of interest being expressed in the series. The actor apparently thought it was strange for people to spend so much time on something which was, in his words, "just a TV show." The commentator felt that McGoohan had a kind of appalled fascination for the success of the show. Even at that time, the actor was said to be working upon screenplays.[xiii] McGoohan also sent a letter of thanks to this writer for his "generous (seventy fifth) birthday greetings and gifts." The message from him was warm in tone, concluding, "All much appreciated, Patrick."[2]

At the end of 2004, the actor's name was being linked to another new film. Although at the time of this biography the movie and McGoohan's role in it remain unconfirmed, the details which were announced on the Internet are included here, verbatim, for completeness: "Dean Haglund (Langly from *X Files* and *The Lone Gunmen*) plans to begin work for a movie he has co-written, which will star Patrick McGoohan. It's about Dr. Royal Rife, who invented a machine designed to kill disease organisms with electronic frequencies. If you've never heard of Rife, conspiracy buffs will tell you it's because drug companies silenced him. Set in 1970s Southern California, *Illumination* is a fictional medical suspense drama following the path of 26-year-old medical student Seamus McMillan as he pieces together a decades old mystery surrounding the life work of Royal Raymond Rife. Why was a dinner hosted in 1931 to celebrate 'The End of All Diseases'? Why has all evidence of this event been wiped clean? What has happened to the participants of this dinner? If an end to disease has been discovered, why is Seamus' first love Kate dying from terminal cancer? The search for these answers leads Seamus into a world of danger, intrigue, conspiracy theories and medical mavericks."

Co-writer Phil Leirness added: "My writing and producing partner on the film is Dean Haglund, who acted in my most recent film, *Spectres*. While we were in the midst of our first draft of the screenplay, I realised I was writing the role of Royal Raymond Rife for Patrick McGoohan. Patrick has always been my favourite actor and his work has been both inspirational and influential in my development as an artist and as an individual. He read that first draft and has been very supportive and encouraging during our rewrites and during our efforts to bring this story to the screen. I'm thrilled, for I truly can't imagine anyone else playing the role ... truly a role worthy of (McGoohan's) gifts as a performer."

[xii] Even as this book went to print, there were continuing reports of remake plans.
[xiii] Apart from TV series covered in this book, no other TV or film writing by McGoohan has become known to the writer.

Leirness continued: "In addition to his willingness to bring Royal Raymond Rife to life, Patrick was kind enough to provide me with an introduction to the great character actor Aubrey Morris.[xiv] He has always been one of my favourites and I wrote a delightful, poignant role for him in *Illumination*, which I am overjoyed to report he has accepted. The story involves attempts to track down the infamous doctor (Rife), who claimed to have invented a machine that could cure cancer back in the 1930s. The quest leads into a strange world of cover-up, deception and a race against time to save the life of a woman. In the story, when Rife refuses to bow to pressure, his lab is burnt down twice, his assistant poisoned, and a fellow doctor he worked with is given 500,000 dollars in the middle of the depression to go live in Mexico. Dr. Rife is sued for the rest of his life till 1971."[3]

In 2005, the UK's first commercial channel, ITV, now renamed ITV1, celebrated fifty years of broadcasting.[xv] In a series of advertisements for a marathon run-through of old shows, lasting over three hours, McGoohan's cult series *The Prisoner* was to the fore. To promote the celebration, ITV1 had the actor's voice barking "Who is Number One?" alluding to the top ITV show for which viewers could ultimately vote, via the corporate website. This would choose the best programme from the past half century and the position taken by *The Prisoner* was a creditable thirtieth. In a much longer advertisement for ITV's golden anniversary, a celebrity cocktail party had been created with the use of computer graphics, grouping actors and stars, past and present, mingling and talking to each other. It was incongruous to see McGoohan in his guise as Number Six, seated at a table, complete with his piped blazer, looking as much out of place amongst the VIPs as he did in his fantasy prison, "The Village," four decades earlier. The cult series itself was remembered with the usual mixture of affection and puzzlement, with screen personalities giving their views and recollections. To coincide with ITV's fiftieth anniversary celebrations, a multi-disc *ITC 50* DVD set, with *Prisoner* and *Danger Man* episodes, plus shows from the same stable, was released.

A few days earlier, the main ITV daytime show, *This Morning*, had been transmitted live from Portmeirion, with members of the *Prisoner* Appreciation Society creating once more in the North Wales open air a human chess game, based on the episode *Checkmate*, complete with Mini Moke buggy and uniformed and crash helmeted 'security guards.' It was clear from these proceedings how the series endures and how McGoohan's influence (although the suggestion would be discounted by him) has travelled the world as much as he has, touching many avid followers of the man and his iconic screen character, Number Six. Also in 2005, an official plaque, to commemorate the 1966 Portmeirion filming of *The Prisoner*, was unveiled at the resort. The actress performing the ceremony was Fenella Fielding,[xvi] who provided in the TV series (but was never seen on screen) the syrupy voice of the Village. A picture of McGoohan was engraved above an inscription, devised by this writer, reading: "1967-68, *The Prisoner* classic TV series stars Patrick McGoohan as a man who resigns from his top secret job and is held captive in 'the village,' where he is known only as 'No. 6.' Exterior scenes were filmed in Portmeirion and the 17 episodes retain cult status."

In November, 2005, the satellite TV channel Sky One unveiled its plans for a new *Prisoner* mini-series, in collaboration with Granada Ventures, the company which acquired

---

[xiv] Morris appeared alongside McGoohan in the *Prisoner* episode *Dance of the Dead* and also the *Columbo* story *Ashes to Ashes* in 1998.
[xv] As to the start of ITV, see page 53 and also footnote on that page.
[xvi] She also appeared with McGoohan in the *Danger Man* episode *An Affair of State*.

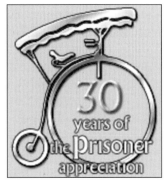  

Above Left: *Prisoner* society logo celebrating Six of One's 30th birthday, 2007. Above Right: 2006 release of The Times' CD, *I Helped Patrick McGoohan Escape*. Right: ITC 50 DVD featuring *The Prisoner* and *Danger Man*

rights to *The Prisoner* from previous holders Carlton. Media correspondent Hugh Davies commented, "It is hoped that McGoohan, 78, now living in California, will make an appearance in one of the first six hour-long episodes."[4] Owen Gibson in *The Guardian* commented, "The 1967 *Prisoner* original still has a large cult following, with many fans continuing to decode the opaque meaning of the 17 original shows online and the programme cited as a key influence by a string of today's writers and producers."[5] Sky's director of programmes Richard Woolfe described the project as a "thrilling reinvention" of The Prisoner, adding that the mini-series would be "our biggest drama commission ever and every penny will be evident on screen. We want to capture the imagination of a new generation of viewers." Writer Bill Gallagher was to handle the script, which would reflect the original, but with a modern take. However, there was to be no filming in Portmeirion and the mini-series was described as more of an "ultimate conspiracy thriller," than the sixties fantasy pyscho-drama, according to executive producer Damien Timmer. "The new series will entrap you from the opening scene. We hope it will tap into this iconic show's existing cult following, whilst creating a whole new generation of fans." The new production envisaged six to eight episodes, costing one million pounds each, in contrast to the sixties' stories individual budgets, of less than a tenth of that sum. Meanwhile, the working title for a proposed TV *Prisoner* sequel was to be *Number 6* and a broadcast date in 2007 was hoped for.[xvii] There was also talk of a feature-length production, with the Universal studio being mentioned. Movie director Christopher Nolan[xviii] was named by 'inside sources' as taking on the project.

In Portmeirion – the original filming location for the sixties cult show – managing director Robin Llywelyn launched an online poll on the hotel's website. This invited visitors to express their choice for an actor to take the new lead role. "We have already had requests from people keen to see Patrick McGoohan return to play the role," commented Llywelyn.[6] However, those nominating McGoohan were unlikely to see their wish fulfilled, given that the actor would be twice the age he was at the time at the time of *The Prisoner*. The resort continues to be referenced together with McGoohan's cult series; one reviewer covered the location for an article forty years on: "Today, Portmeirion … has changed little since *The Prisoner* was filmed there (though the bouncing white spheres – actually weather balloons – have gone). Now, daytrippers come to wander round the Disney-esque collection of buildings (and) for fans of *The Prisoner* still watching repeats on satellite TV, there's an annual convention."[7] Robin Llywelyn appeared on a German television programme about Portmeirion, saying, "Thirty million people who watched *The Prisoner* had no idea where (Number Six) was. The number of visitors to the village doubled from fifty thousand to one hundred thousand."[8]

Another 2007 proposal, involving McGoohan, needs briefly to be inserted here. During the summer, US producer and director Andre Perkowski announced his plans for a new black and white feature film adaptation of Orson Welles' 1955 stage play, *Moby Dick*, plus an accompanying documentary. McGoohan's roles had of course drawn excellent reviews half a century earlier, but as Perkowski recalled, "Welles always mentioned how he wished he (had) cast McGoohan as the lead." Using authentic film stocks and antique cameras, the new producer now hoped for "spectacular results." This writer contacted McGoohan on his behalf and it was not long before the actor responded with a welcome contact message, left on Perkowski's voicemail."[xix] At the same time, a new ITV programme[xx] was in production, highlighting the "key moments" in *The Prisoner* and the impact of its fantasy location, Portmeirion.[xxi]

McGoohan will always primarily be thought of as "Number Six," but, additionally, the label of 'the man who turned down James Bond' will remain a hard one to cast off, as the 'Saint Patrick' tag still sticks. When the twenty first James Bond movie *Casino Royale* had its premiere at the end of 2006, the media was quick to revive old stories about McGoohan rejecting the super-spy role in the sixties, as well as the lead in the TV series *The Saint*: "As history relates, the Bond producers even considered an American actor – albeit long based in the UK – Patrick McGoohan. However, ITV's own Danger Man famously spurned both 007 and Simon Templar on the grounds that both characters were 'immoral cads.'"[9]

In the United States, a special DVD[xxii] presentation of the entire *Prisoner* series was launched, prompting a comment from one online reviewer: "Generally speaking, I find it ridiculous to spend $140 on a television series, especially one that totals 17 hours. But I would make an exception for *The Prisoner Complete Series Megaset* … the brilliant British series that first ran in 1967. Patrick McGoohan … produced, wrote and directed much of the series – and took the brunt of the audiences' howls of anger at the gloriously indecipherable finale."[10] In addition, more of the actor's *Columbo* appearances were released and *The Prisoner* was issued on DVD in Germany – for the first time in that country – along with the initial thirty nine *Danger Man* episodes.[xxiii] In France, the 2006 Annual Festival of British Films was held at Dinard and for only the third time in the festival's history a television series was featured, *The Prisoner* being chosen to honour the series' fortieth

---

[xix] Unfortunately, at the time of this book going to print, it has not been possible to include further details, although the writer is maintaining contact with Andre Perkowski.
[xx] Tiger Aspect Productions was the company involved.
[xxi] Filming at the resort included "Rover" balloons and an interview with Max Hora, from the Appreciation Society.
[xxii] The "Megaset" included a lengthy series guide booklet and map of "The Village," devised by this writer.
[xxiii] What is astonishing is that despite numerous *Prisoner* and *Danger Man* video and DVD releases across twenty years, McGoohan has either never agreed, or has never been asked, to provide any screen commentaries, or new features as 'extras.' This was not remedied with 2007 British DVD sets of *Danger* Man, or *The Prisoner*.

filming anniversary.^{xxiv} As was said earlier in this book, the cult show was destined to become, for McGoohan, as much of a curse as it was a blessing. Across four decades, his sixties TV roles are what people and the media remember most.

Over Christmas 2006,^{xxv} BBC Radio 2 presented a two hour, two part tribute to the late Lord Grade. McGoohan participated and his interview segments – covered in earlier chapters of this book – were prefaced by remarks from presenter Sir Roger Moore. McGoohan recalled his dealings with Grade, obtaining him tickets for *Brand*, signing up for *Danger Man* and moving on to *The Prisoner*, as well as selling the series to CBS. The radio feature was one of only a handful over many years to include live interview comments from McGoohan. Probably the subject of the programme, Lew Grade, was the reason behind the actor's involvement. He had taken part in a television documentary about Grade over a decade earlier. His respect for the TV mogul had not dimmed, with McGoohan cheerfully offering his recollections and joking good naturedly about the interaction between the two men. "He showed me the board room once and this was at quarter to six in the morning, and he says, 'Let me show you something … This is where the board sits' and he showed me all the chairs and then said 'They do what I tell 'em. There's only one chair that matters and that's the one.' And that's Lew, he did, he ran it, he ran the show."[11]

Also in December, 2006, a year after the initial *Prisoner* remake announcement, the US channel AMC^{xxvi} informed American audiences of its plans for several new episodes, in collaboration with UK's Sky One and Granada International. A press release declared: "Through the work of Patrick McGoohan, who created, produced, wrote, directed and starred in the title role, the series became one of television's most acclaimed and influential programs. *The Prisoner* redefined what was possible in the Sci-Fi/Thriller category and remains on of the most iconic classics of our time. AMC's new series will stay true to the conceptual and visual brilliance of the original and will provide a new generation with an understanding and appreciation of Patrick McGoohan's work." Theirs would be the second adaptation in the offing, as Universal Pictures still had Chris Nolan set to helm the movie version, which Janet and David Peoples were scripting. Meanwhile, the TV series was now said to be produced by Michelle Buck and Damien Timmer. AMC executives revealed that the TV version would again involve themes of paranoia and deal with socio-political issues. However, the new show would not be a replica of the original and "(not) just a re-creation," said Rob Sorcher, an executive in programming and production. "What we're doing is an entirely new reinterpretation that stays true to the components of the McGoohan (series') vision." The 'remake' would once more revolve around a man who awakes in a place called 'The Village,' with no memory of how he arrived, confirmed Sorcher. Although the proposed new one hour series, did not yet have a lead or cast, Sorcher was confident: "This show made an explosion in the genre 40 years ago; to this day, it's loved by so many. This is an opportunity to remake a classic and reinterpret it, and it also gives us a built-in fan base."

As the year drew to a close, US news about the proposed *Prisoner* remake continued to hail the project, mentioning McGoohan not so much in a current vein, but referencing him with the sixties' original. Only time will tell whether these much-vaunted big or small screen sequels will include any appearance or participation, on the part of the actor. One

^{xxiv} Three episodes were screened: *Arrival, A. B. and C.* and *Fall Out*.
^{xxv} McGoohan and this writer again exchanged seasonal greetings cards.
^{xxvi} AMC – American Movie Classics – is a US cable television network primarily airing movies, with the slogan "TV for Movie People."

Left: *Best of British* DVD including *The Quare Fellow*. Centre: New DVD of the movie *All Night Long*
Right: New DVD of the movie *Hell Drivers*

report at the end of 2006 promised, "McGoohan and his family will be involved in the revival, and there could even be a role for the original star."xxvii 12 Alongside any new *Prisoner* version which might emerge, future generations will continue to explore the original and admire it as television's first classic and masterpiece of the medium. The popularity of the series, together with McGoohan's other works, has been a source of gratification for the actor, along with the knowledge that his treasury of cinema and television appearances will always enjoy renewed screenings or releases.xxviii Whether he would agree with many of the interpretations of the series is open to debate.

McGoohan's career has embraced stage, cinema and television productions and from his first amateur engagements in the mid-forties, up to the time of this book, over six decades have been covered. The actor's viewing public – the 'digital audience' of today – is fortunately able to access much of his filmed work and studies of him. For example, nowadays *The Prisoner* has moved well and truly onto the Internet, with World Wide Web phenomena like MySpace and YouTube. There is ever more material from the series on view, to be heard, or read about as pages, or personal blogs. Clips from McGoohan's past

xxvii History of *Prisoner* planned sequels: in the mid-eighties an American version of *The Prisoner* was planned for CBS-TV. The concept was to explore what happened to McGoohan's Number Six character from the original series, after the final episode. The actor was said not to be involved and by early 1987, nothing more was heard of the project. However, later that year, Leland Rogers, brother of singer Kenny, was exploring the possibility of a full length movie. By 1988, he was reportedly in talks with ITC, New York. A screenplay by Roderick Taylor – originally written for CBS, entitled *The Edge of Within* – was rejected as 'too avant garde' for TV audiences. The central idea was to shift "The Village" to "The City," with the son of Number Six undergoing various ordeals. Directors Rocky Morton and Annabel Jankel from TV's *Max Headroom* were to helm the production. Rogers' plans came to a dead end, although he apparently retained the rights to Taylor's TV script. In the early nineties, a *Prisoner* movie was again mooted, this time as a full Hollywood production, following the success of *The Fugitive* (1993) remake. Kevin Costner was tipped for the lead, with Steven Spielberg's company in the frame. However, by 1996 this was said to be on indefinite hold. Discussions continued to take place regarding a Wales location, using the original Portmeirion. It was reported that McGoohan had been asked to write a script and Mel Gibson was suggested for the starring role. Jumping to 2003, Simon West, director of *Lara Croft: Tomb Raider* (2001), was widely publicised to be making a big screen *Prisoner* movie. This report gathered dust, as West went on to newer pastures and it was not until the end of 2005 that any more remake rumours emerged. Now it was the UK's Granada TV and Sky TV being billed as making a six part *Prisoner* series and there were continuing news reports throughout 2006. In the US, Universal was said to have plans to produce a simultaneous movie, with Christopher Nolan directing. At the time of this book, in 2007, no more definite news has been released as to the dual proposals.
xxviii *Prisoner* conventions in Portmeirion are already arranged for 2008 and 2009, plus also a late 2007 celebration of the fiftieth anniversary of the Lotus Seven sportscar, the vehicle McGoohan drove in *The Prisoner*.

films and TV series can be seen, while audio samples turn up in newly-mixed music. Clearly the extent of appreciation from past decades has now been widened, so that people do not have to watch a domestic screen, or listen to home speakers. They are able to carry downloaded content around with them on personal players, while material relating to McGoohan, or a series such as *The Prisoner*, is shared across the globe, instantly, with just a click. Paradoxically, today's technology has given cult shows like *The Prisoner* legs which they never had while confined to the medium of television.

In 2007, Six of One, *The Prisoner* series' official Appreciation Society, reached its thirtieth birthday. As the Society's Honorary President – the position having been held by him since 1977 – McGoohan has been as important to Six of One throughout its life, as has been his cult TV series. Member and Society organiser Larry Hall, a resident of Sheffield, has followed with interest the success of *The Prisoner* cult series and the career of McGoohan. He, with his wife Pauline, met with the actor at the 1990 Motor Show[xxix] and found him to be charming and personable, as well as retaining a keen interest in Sheffield. McGoohan was particularly interested in the steps which the city was taking to reduce pollution and to develop a recycling centre. When Hall next met with the actor, McGoohan was disappointed that this time, his wife Pauline was not present, he having enjoyed sharing Sheffield reminiscences with her. In later years, Hall would be instrumental in securing the release of an album of music from *The Prisoner*, as well as taking the series to fans around Britain, with his self-organised "road shows." Hall reflects, "I think that McGoohan was a major talent in Britain for many years and his departure was a loss to our theatre, cinema and television. It was a privilege to have spent some time with him and I found him to be a very likeable individual. I hope he is gratified that his work is still appreciated, decades on and there are very few actors or TV productions which command the amount of attention or appreciation surrounding McGoohan and his cult shows."

Elsewhere, Max Hora – another long term Six of One member and organiser – opened the very first shop devoted to the *Prisoner* series, in Portmeirion, operated by him for sixteen years, until the end of the nineties. During the running of the shop, various actors or crew members from the series visited the establishment. Producer and director David Tomblin was pleased to see a display of memorabilia and pictures adorning the walls. The premises were made even more authentic by there being a Number Two globe swivel chair, a penny farthing bicycle outside the door and a Village style sign. Hora, a life-long fan of the series and admirer of McGoohan made trips to Portmeirion as a child, later self-publishing a series of booklets about the filming of *The Prisoner* there. Max comments, "I think that McGoohan was perfect for the role of Number Six and I was delighted to run my shop within the very building which was the cottage occupied by the main character in the series. During my time there I met with many film crews who were featuring the cult show in various documentaries, or promotional videos. I was always pleasantly surprised by the large numbers of overseas fans of *The Prisoner* who came into the shop and were thrilled to see a remembrance of the series. I only wish Number Six himself had been able to come into the shop, but the star has never returned to Portmeirion." This writer was quoted on one Society website: "I have seen Six of One become, over the years, a kind of alternative university. It has as many facets as the Prisoner series itself. I have met artists, teachers,

---

philosophers, scholars, technicians; people with imagination, people who think. The society is a paradox, in that members reject the normal rules and regulations of society at large and yet join our Society. Although nobody amongst our members is the same, rarely even sharing the same views, yet as a collective, Six of One succeeds. The Society has attained its own identity, extending way beyond The Prisoner. We were fortunate to have the series as such a unique basis for an Appreciation Society." To that could be added the support of McGoohan and the resort of Portmeirion, where annual conventions are held.

As McGoohan entered his eightieth year in 2007, there came new DVD releases of more of his films: a special two disk edition of *Hell Drivers* (1957), *The Quare Fellow* (1962), *Life for Ruth* (1962) and *The Man in the Iron Mask* (1976). There were plans to celebrate the approaching fortieth anniversary of *The Prisoner*, to be marked by more official memorabilia. In France, a new DVD box set of the *Danger Man* series – *Destination Danger* – was released and the series was also revamped for a similar set in Britain.[xxx] In the autumn, the entire *Prisoner* series was due for a special release, on DVD.[xxxi] In addition, other books about the series were being published, along with a pictorial 2008 calendar and smaller items of merchandise. One recent book, reviewing *The Prisoner* 'effect,' forty years on, concluded, "the series stands in a problematical relationship to the 1960s' counterculture and the cultural ferment of its times. On one level, it seems to be the very epitome of that decade's anti-establishment, libertarian values, yet there is an underlying social and cultural conservatism which at times leads creator McGoohan to attack such values and their representatives, particularly in … the surreal final episode. Indeed the whole series seems steeped in an ambiguity of intention and motive and it is this which arguably continues to fuel its fascination for analysts and fans alike all around the world, since it leaves itself purposively open to all sorts of differing readings and interpretations. As such, it remains a uniquely challenging and ingenious series, dramatising the dilemmas involved in understanding and safeguarding one's individuality in a world of increasing technological surveillance, together with the corresponding dangers of political and social conformity this might bring."

The same book commented on the autobiographical aspects of McGoohan's cult series and his unexpected use of force at the end, despite a career-long rejection of screen violence: "Even the character (McGoohan) plays serves as a cipher for his own personality. While McGoohan, like Number Six, set out to criticise the world at large, he ultimately showed how easily good intentions may become corrupted." The passage was referring to *The Prisoner*'s final episode, *Fall Out*, particularly the unexpected machine gun shoot-out and the rising body count on screen: "The decision to reverse the pacifist stance of the series in its last instalment is odd indeed." The finale, it was said, could be giving a "warning against individuality on a mass scale," and observing that "the likely effect this would have on society is complete dissolution."

However, an alternative standpoint was offered: "(The conclusion) may simply have been motivated by frustration and fatigue on the part of McGoohan, rather than any attempt to capture or criticise the spirit of the age, prompted by the simple desire to end things with a bang." In this respect, it was felt that McGoohan was betraying his own principles, in order to give his audience a memorable climax, leading to the "central

[xxx] As mentioned earlier, there had also been a recent German release of *Danger Man* and *Prisoner* DVDs.
[xxxi] Issued by Network, as were the latest *Danger Man* discs.

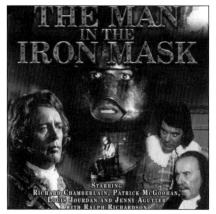  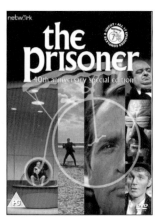

Left: New DVD of the movie *The Man in the Iron Mask*. Centre: New DVD of the movie *Life for Ruth*
Right: New 40th anniversary *Prisoner* DVD set, 2007

message" of *Fall Out*: "as moral individuals, struggling to maintain our integrity in the face of compromise and collusion, we have no greater enemy than ourselves." Interestingly, it was claimed that although Number Six found out in the end who was Number One – namely himself – he even sought to escape from this 'truth,' thereby trying to "evade the issue of his own responsibility ... to face the truth of his situation which ultimately restricts his freedom."[13]

From a different angle, another recent source advanced: "The ending of *The Prisoner* has multiple layers, meanings and aspects to it, but all of them seem to focus on the destructive, yet ultimately positive, power of rebellion, particularly when it is not isolated into the formless acts of individual youths and older men, but integrated into both the self and the society."[14]

For this biography, there remains the not inconsiderable task of summing up McGoohan's acting career and the man himself. This writer empathises with the views of those who combine the character of Number Six with that of the actor who played – and effectively created – him. However, there is a risk, when analysing *The Prisoner*'s lead figure, of creating a synthesis: an amalgamation of Number Six and McGoohan, owing to the strong personality traits present in the actor. Just as the prisoner and Number One become a mirror image of each other, it can also be argued that the same synergy is in play between the star and his screen persona; McGoohan has blurred the distinction between actor and role.

Somehow, a curious interrelation of locations, countries and nationalities have always marked McGoohan as a 'shared' commodity, in British and US appreciation circles, as well as in Europe and further afield. His dramatic training years in repertory, leading to London theatrical engagements and later appearances in British films and television, resulted in the actor becoming a household name. Looking back over the decades, the actor has said that he felt that the two things he should not have undertaken were the film *Hell Drivers* and the TV series *Danger Man*, although he once threw in the movie *Brass Target* and the US show *Rafferty*. With *Hell Drivers* he perceived that he obtained an early reputation as a villain. With his John Drake role he stated that he had felt typecast, except that he did, to his good fortune, form an association with Lew Grade. He commented ruefully about having to hear cab drivers saying to him, "What was that junk you did, *The Prisoner*?"[15]

Of his time in the USA, McGoohan has stated that his performance in the *Columbo* episode *By Dawn's Early Light* was his favourite. However, the actor has always cited his leading role in *Brand* as being the pinnacle of his career. McGoohan recalls reading his reviews, cutting out the worst ones, underlining them in red and pasting them on his dressing room mirror. He has always been able to rise above the critics' jibes. For example, at the time of the repertory stage play *Born Yesterday*ˣˣˣⁱⁱ he had to play a brawny crook, but was himself extremely skinny. One reviewer wrote, "I don't know what profession Mr. McGoohan should be in, whether it's plumbing, or construction, or banking. But it definitely shouldn't be acting."[16] That cutting promptly went up on the mirror.

McGoohan can be remembered in different ways, depending upon the point from which his career is observed. For those familiar with him from the fifties, in his repertory days, or as a rising star, his progression to television was watched with interest throughout the sixties. For the loyal British following, his removal to the United States was a loss for them and a gain for American audiences. Linking the decades there have always been bouts of renewed interest in *The Prisoner*, a series which has gained new admirers whenever it is relaunched. Curiously, the production came about halfway through McGoohan's life and has never left him since its creation. Was this the real McGoohan? Does anybody apart from his immediate family and himself know what have been, for him, his major achievements and most treasured memories? Certainly, whether the actor likes it or not, it will always be *The Prisoner* which is the primary entry in any retrospective of his television work.

As an actor McGoohan has frequently played characters in isolation, set apart from mainstream society. As an individual, he has always preferred to live for the present, than to dwell on the past. Perhaps one way to sum up the actor would be to use the views of a person with whom he did not always see eye to eye, George Markstein. When the two men parted company during production of *The Prisoner*, it might have been thought that Markstein would not have much room for praise. However, years later he described how McGoohan had contributed greatly to the project. "He was a superb actor, one of the best TV produced. He had immense ability, but he was an egomaniac – all actors are." Markstein said he felt strongly that the full potential of *The Prisoner* had not been realised and that there were certain dimensions which could have been explored further. "*The Prisoner* idea needed an actor to make it come to light and Patrick McGoohan created it on the screen, with his burning intensity and ferocity. It is really ironical that in this, of all series, the star became the ideal victim; a prisoner of his own talent and commercialism."[17]

This biography set out with the intention of avoiding McGoohan's private world. Surely, however, no work covering the man's life could avoid mentioning the formidable bond between him and his lifelong partner, Joan Drummond. Perhaps without her, McGoohan would not have had so often a port in a storm, so often a nurse when his health was poor, so often a sounding board for ideas, a dedicated partner with whom to share the glory and so often a person to give encouragement after a project failed. The ever-grateful husband says he has written hundreds of love poems to his wife and that she gave up her stage career to allow him to spend fifty years as an actor. While other show business couples' marriages have failed, the union of the McGoohans has stood the test of time. When other celebrity pairs have spoken in detail about their private lives and their

---

ˣˣˣⁱⁱ McGoohan said that he had done *Born Yesterday* four times, the first being at Sheffield. This writer has only been able to trace a later appearance in the play during the actor's time with the Midland Repertory Company.

Left: Spring 2007 McGoohan front cover of *Comics International*
Right: Summer 2007 McGoohan front cover of *Comics International*

partners, the McGoohans have exercised discretion. With the support they have given to their own family and extended family, the strength of the McGoohan clan – including its ancestors – can be perceived, a factor which caused so many bold steps to be taken in the past century.

For Patrick McGoohan the world has been a strange and changing home to him. From infant months in America, he then experienced childhood years in Ireland, over a generation in England, a couple more years in Switzerland, before returning to America and spending the next thirty plus years there, in the land of his birth.[xxxiii] During the past three decades, the actor has only infrequently set foot in Britain. There has even been talk of filming a 'biopic' about him. However, this writer feels that the venture could never do justice to the actor's colourful life. He should be remembered as a true individual, but not in the sense of being a hell-raiser, or pursuing unusual artistic goals, or even leading a lavish lifestyle. In his case, individuality comes from being a compassionate man, one who cares about the world, a person who knows about responsibility and consequences, one who strives for perfection in his work. From rangy young actor, to consummate stage performer, through the years of being a Rank pin-up, becoming a well-known TV face and later a major film star, alternatively setting up as an occasional director and writer, plus being family man and poet, these are all aspects of the man which this biography encompasses. The only part which has been omitted is a different book, one for consumption only by the actor's family and friends. It would be called "The Private Life of Patrick Joseph McGoohan."

Perhaps if the star had mixed more with those in the entertainment business, socialising and meeting contemporaries, he would have had different career choices. Possibly also there would have been more opportunities to be told – and thereby to be convinced – that his was an important screen presence. McGoohan, by avoiding 'networking' and shying away from the public glare, seems to have demonstrated a personal belief that his was just a job, one which he executed well, no more than that. Had he permitted himself to be on the receiving end of more positive input from his admirers, he might have uttered less of the self-deprecating type of statements which have been heard, or seen in print, over the years. Undoubtedly, to him, the praise and approval of his own family has been the most important factor, although one wonders whether his self-esteem could have been heightened by having more exposure among his peers and fans.

At times, the way that McGoohan has expressed his views raises the assumption that, for him, the only arbiter is himself. A fair number of his fellow actors have said how he could have been one of Britain's greatest stage and screen talents, his name sharing the reverence

---

[xxxiii] But on the opposite coast.

reserved for some of the industry's top names. Moving away from Britain at the end of the sixties was a giant step for the actor. The departure came at almost the halfway point in the actor's life; the ending of one chapter and the starting of a completely new one. What took place in England during the thirty years prior to his family's emigration, bore no relation to the next three decades in the US. Most writers have concluded that it was the perceived lack of critical success of *The Prisoner*, which had the star moving on. There was also the winding up and tax obligations in respect of Everyman Films. However, those are matters which would seem capable of being resolved. An actor moves forward to the next assignment and an arrangement is made for payment of any debts. Even in the last few years, McGoohan still refers to large sums of money being owed to him by various actors, or past colleagues. He also brings up the touchy subject of rights over *The Prisoner* and whether or not he has had a fair shake. He has always expressed great confidence ahead of a project, but has rarely heaped praise on his productions, or performances, after they have passed.

The way that McGoohan has angrily described how the press intrudes into some celebrities' lives makes one wonder whether he is speaking personally, using their experiences to reflect his own strongly held views. The actor has brushed aside reports about his ill health, or ones suggesting any other problems in his life. He has poured scorn on interviews conducted with colleagues who have known him over the years, their utterances being dismissed as rubbish, or inaccurate, or downright untrue. Here is a strong character that has always defended personal privacy to a greater degree than perhaps would any other figure in the public eye. And yet, never has any dark secret been uncovered, never have any tales of marital strife filtered through and no trace of scandal has emerged. The changes in direction taken by McGoohan, the many and varied types of part and production with which he has associated himself, almost lead to a conclusion that he has wanted to leave no trail behind, wishing always to camouflage the real personality behind the portrayal. Whatever it was that changed everything forever, over three decades ago, it is a matter of regret that the many more memorable performances which would doubtless have occurred did not breathe life.

In some ways, McGoohan is the 'prisoner' he has often alluded to, the person who does not have free choice and must exist within the constraints which are upon us all. In his case, the public glare, especially in those Mill Hill days, seemed to show a person who is not entirely confident. Often it might be thought that the strong outward personality was a cover for something less bold underneath. His having moved to pastures new meant that he never sampled the "golden age" of seventies British television. Leaving the country to pursue a new dream was possibly a form of escape. Even after his departure there must also have been US offers to star in television plays, drama series and to make guest appearances, but which were not accepted.[xxxiv]

McGoohan has always held certain men in high regard: his father, naturally, James Lodge, of the youth club, Mr. Brown (his old employer and chess-playing partner), Geoffrey Ost, in Sheffield, Orson Welles, his dresser Jimmy Millar, Sir Lew Grade and latterly Peter Falk. He also, on the other hand, seemed to be more at ease and more expansive in a number of interviews with female journalists. He has frequently been described as perfectly charming. A few published astrological studies of him have concluded that he is precisely as he is meant to be, with no aspects out of balance, or instances of his true path not being

---

[xxxiv] Some of these are referred to in the last section of Appendix One.

followed. Somehow, one feels at times that it is possible to discern the true McGoohan, to understand the life of the family man and the private person. Without delving into those personal areas, it is still possible to appreciate that here is a man who throughout his life has strived to overcome all kinds of privations, has travelled, has worked long hours and has even followed the money, whenever necessary. There were those on the set of *The Prisoner* who worked with McGoohan for only a day or so. From these persons come memories of a brusque man, difficult to work with, self-opinionated and even brutal. In contrast, amongst those who worked with him over a longer period comes nothing but admiration. If there was any truth in the McGoohans' claim that the press hounded them out of Britain, it is to the eternal shame of the British media. Whatever the catalyst for the McGoohan family exodus, Britain lost one of its best and most distinguished actors. Would there have been industry or national honours bestowed upon him?[xxxv]

As for the actor's own feelings, perhaps every time he said things like, "There is only one person to blame. People can say 'Nuts to you, Paddy boy!'"[18] there was somewhere within him an earnest plea that people would tell him how much they valued his work and appreciated his dedication. There only needed to be a different scenario at the end of the sixties for everything to have been so different. When McGoohan was making *The Prisoner*, he gave out no information and almost proudly boasted that he never gave interviews. A more constructive approach would have been to go on TV, explain what *The Prisoner* was about, laugh and join in with the critics' rebukes, or better still even to write his own book. It is the feeling of many that there is much more to McGoohan and people are convinced of this. The strength of reactions which have been witnessed so many times from the man over so many years, must leave open the possibility that he on occasions he has protested too much. One of the Village leaders, during the somewhat autobiographical *Prisoner* series, complained bitterly that McGoohan's character Number Six would never let his guard drop. These are the same signals which the actor himself has frequently given off.

Will McGoohan's predictions (even fears) that technology will take over our planet and its people prove to be true? As he said in 1967, "Only time will tell," adding that it was up to everyone to fight against bureaucracy and the powers-that-be, to avoid becoming imprisoned by any authority which is corrupt. Looking back, after four decades, it is hard to discern whether the power of *The Prisoner* series came from McGoohan driving the production and 'preaching its message,' or whether the series unexpectedly released hidden feelings within legions of fans who watched the episodes across the world. Certainly, no other television series has given rise to so much examination as has occurred within the ardent followers of *The Prisoner*'s seventeen surreal episodes. Without doubt, the cult series is the most dissected TV programme of all time. In this and many other respects, McGoohan can be said to have changed the course of television history. In 2007, the coming fortieth *Prisoner* anniversary brought back memories of the series. Channel 4's *50 Greatest TV Dramas*, in March, placed *The Prisoner* at position thirty eight. There was recognition of the series' "fan club boasting over a thousand dedicated members" and how after "four decades worth of fervent cult following ... *The Prisoner* has inspired endless analysis." In April, the series enjoyed yet another new airing, on BBC America. At the end of July, the main British TV listings magazine, Radio Times, placed *The Prisoner*

[xxxv] The former fellow director of McGoohan in their Everyman Films company, David Tomblin, received in 1994 an MBE in the Queens' birthday list, in return for his services to the film and television industry.

seventeenth in their top twenty "Greatest sci-fi shows of all time," adding, "Unusually brilliant, sometimes dreadful, this held the UK spellbound as we yearned to know who was Number One."

According to McGoohan, the simple catchphrase from *The Prisoner*, "Be seeing you," can mean several things: a greeting; a farewell on somebody's departure; a threat from someone who plans to return; a confirmation that a person is being watched, or is under surveillance. For thousands of individuals around the globe to have been so influenced over many years by an actor is a rare occurrence. Many regard the actor as their 'mentor'; this writer is aware of people in various countries basing their approach to life upon 'the rule of McGoohan.' Individuals have received the actor's *Prisoner* 'message', despite even foreign copies of episodes featuring dubbed voices, not those of the star, in languages which the actor himself could never speak. Without playing up the 'guru' aspect of McGoohan – something which he would find abhorrent – the phenomenon cannot be denied. As for the star of the cult series and – for most people – creator of it, analysing the man is a far less easy task. More preferable, to complete the picture, would be the appearance of the actor's autobiography. Or was that *The Prisoner?*

To encompass what has been said over the preceding pages, one might paraphrase the words of the old song: "I'll be looking at the moon, but I'll be seeing you."[xxxvi] In the case of this book's screen star, more appropriately the lyrics would be: "I'll be looking at McGoohan, and I'll be seeing you!"

[1] Libertarian Futurist Society Prometheus Hall of Fame Award, 2002
[2] Letter from Patrick McGoohan to the writer, 2003
[3] Internet and email reports, 2005
[4] The Telegraph, 4th May, 2006, Hugh Davies
[5] The Guardian, 4th May, 2006, Owen Gibson
[6] BBC online news, 11th May, 2006
[7] Location Location Location magazine, September, 2006, Claire Vaughan
[8] Wales – Krone, Küsten, Kauderwelsch, German TV, 24th December, 2006
[9] The Independent, 9th November, 2006, Andrew Roberts
[10] artvoice.com, M. Faust
[11] Lew Grade: The Greatest of them All, 24th and 25th December, 2006, BBC Radio 2.
[12] TV Guide online, www.tvguide.com
[13] *British Science Fiction Television*, I. B. Tauris, 2006, Sue Short; edited by John R. Cook and Peter Wright
[14] *Fall Out: The Unofficial and Unauthorised Guide to The Prisoner*, 2007, Alan Stevens and Fiona Moore
[15] Classic Images Magazine, 1987, Barbara Pruett
[16] Classic Images Magazine, 1987, Barbara Pruett
[17] Letter to Six of One, The Prisoner Appreciation Society, 1977
[18] Daily Sketch, 1st February, 1968, Fergus Cashin

[xxxvi] I'll Be Seeing You (1938), words by and © Irving Kahal, music by Sammy Fain

APPENDIX ONE

COMPLETE PATRICK MCGOOHAN SCREENOGRAPHY
OF FILMS, TELEVISION, THEATRE AND RADIO

FILM, TV, STAGE AND RADIO APPEARANCES, WITH AWARDS
(Performances, Voice, Director, Writer, Producer, Executive Producer)

The six categories used within this section are:

FILMS (including VIDEO and CABLE but not TV MOVIES, for which see TELEVISION)

TELEVISION (including TV MOVIES, but not CABLE, for which see FILMS)

THEATRE (including Repertory, West End, Broadway etc., but not TV presentations)

INTERVIEWS ON TELEVISION AND RADIO, PLUS OTHER RADIO

SCREEN AND STAGE AWARDS AND SIMILAR

OTHER FILMS, TELEVISION AND THEATRE PROJECTS (listed in some places, but which remain unconfirmed, incorrect, or were never produced, or released)

Years for cinema films appear next to titles, being the earliest date of release. Where a film was produced in Britain, or the US, there were different initial release dates. Also, some films were completed in a particular year, but were not released until much later. British and US film titles are given (sometimes these differ between the two countries) but other non-English titles are only provided for France, Germany, Italy and Spain (except where a film was originally produced elsewhere, such as Sweden).

Anomalies occur with the production and release dates of cinema and television productions. The movie Kings and Desperate Men was being filmed as early as 1978 and possibly 1977, but was not released until 1981 in North America and much later in Britain. Similarly, the film Trespasses was shot in New Zealand during 1983, but was not released for several more years (and was later given the video title Omen of Evil). With the Columbo episode Murder With Too

Many Notes, *the release date was 2001, although the episode was produced in 1999.*

Regarding television entries, sometimes the year of production given might not be the broadcast date and repeat screenings are ignored. McGoohan's 'appearances' in Prisoner video documentaries etc. are omitted, as only footage from the series was used e.g. The Prisoner Video Companion *(1990) and* Best of the Prisoner *(1990). With regard to* The Prisoner, *there were alternative pre-broadcast edit versions of the first two episodes,* Arrival *(which remained unavailable for 35 years, but was finally included on a DVD in 2002) and* The Chimes of Big Ben *(which has been released in its alternative version a few times since 1987, on video and DVD). In these, McGoohan appears in some different scenes which were deleted from the final broadcast versions.*

McGoohan was caricatured (as Number Six, from The Prisoner*) in the US cartoon series* Pinky and the Brain. *In this, the voice was provided by an impersonator, although McGoohan's own was used in the US cartoon series* The Simpsons, *listed below.*

Combined research and list © 2007 Roger Langley.

FILMS (including VIDEO and CABLE but not TV MOVIES – see TELEVISION)

Treasure Planet (2002) – (aka El Planeta del tesoro – Spain; Der Schatzplanet – Germany; Il Pianeta del tesoro – Italy; La Planète au trésor – Un nouvel univers – France). Voice over for Disney cartoon character Billy Bones. The fourth performance for Walt Disney, this time in voice only, has McGoohan speaking dialogue over animation. The film is a space-based updating of Robert Louis Stevenson's "Treasure Island," visually  impressive and fast moving. As galleons roam the heavens, pirates behave as they always do and of course a search for treasure takes centre stage. This production closed another gap in McGoohan's screen career and around this time he also provided a voice track for a TV animated offering, **The Simpsons**, in the episode *The Computer Wore Menace Shoes.*

Hysteria (1998) – Dr Harvey Langston. This limited release 'psycho thriller' movie sees McGoohan as a mad scientist, Langston, running a hospital for mentally disturbed patients. He does experiments using the mental conditions of inmates and strives to create 'group consciousness,' leading to an orgiastic finale. McGoohan puts in a spirited performance in this unbalanced study of psychological, sociological and sexual practices, but the action is far removed from his usual cinematic territory.

A Time to Kill (1996) – Judge Omar Noose (aka Die Jury – Germany; Tiempo de matar – Spain; Le Droit de tuer? – France; Il Momento di uccidere – Italy). John Grisham's tough novel about a black man's revenge for the rape of his young daughter by whites is adapted for the screen. Matthew McConaughey is a small town Southern lawyer, defending Samuel Jackson's character, who has shot those who violated his daughter. He appears before Judge Omar Noose and it  looks a certainty that the defendant will face capital punishment. Death threats are made against the family of the lawyer and he has to enlist the help of a more savvy attorney, played by Sandra Bullock. McGoohan presides over the court proceedings, appearing as a stereotypical harsh judge. The main issue, apart from obvious racial themes, is where the justice lies, if at all, in an extreme case such as this.

The Phantom (1996) – The Phantom's Father (aka Le Fantôme du Bengale – France; Das Phantom – Germany; The phantom: El héroe [or hombre] enmascarado – Spain). Based on a cartoon character created in 1936, "The Phantom" (Billy Zane) is a masked figure who watches over his native tribespeople, while enemies wish to release an ancient and deadly force of evil. The Phantom must leave his jungle lair and travel to New York, to prevent a rich madman from obtaining three magic skulls which would deliver the secret to
ultimate power. Vintage planes and automobiles, plus Art Deco production design can only do so much and the performances are less striking. McGoohan 'appears' as the Phantom's dead father. The mythology behind the movie was needed, but the storyline is not the stuff of more popular and accessible superheroes. This is the movie's strength, for fans, and weakness, for mainstream cinema goers.

Braveheart (1995) – Longshanks, King Edward I (aka Braveheart – France / Germany / Spain; Braveheart – cuore impavido – Italy). Set in the late thirteenth century, the movie tells the story of Scotland's hero William Wallace (Mel Gibson). Leading Scottish resistance forces, he struggles to free Scotland from English rule, under Edward I (McGoohan). Portrayal of the king is brutal and the ruthless monarch, known by the nickname "Longshanks," is the embodiment of evil. The movie is ambitious and passionate, but some scenes repel. Much of the
production is a vehicle for Gibson, whose character rebels when his new wife is killed by English soldiers and he is stirred into action. A revolt against the English becomes all out war, with a series of bloody battles. McGoohan was an inspired choice for the heartless king, his performance being impressive.

Trespasses (1987; filmed 1983) – Fred Wells (aka Die Antwort ist Blei – Germany; Finding Katie – USA working title; Omen of Evil – video title). McGoohan plays the sullen and possessive widower, Fred Wells, whose daughter Katie (Emma Piper) runs away from home to join a local commune. The religious Wells wants to retrieve his daughter and save her from indoctrination within the cult. The film, shot in New Zealand, has its darker moments with initiation ceremonies, while McGoohan's character becomes ever more
obsessive. Katie's loss of her virginity in a sex ritual was cut from some screenings. When the group's guru is murdered, the culprit could be McGoohan. Wells becomes unstable and is helped by his returning daughter, now pregnant. Incestuous undertones may be present in this psychological drama.

Baby: Secret of the Lost Legend (1985) – Dr Eric Kiviat (aka Dinosaur... Secret of the Lost Legend (TV title); Baby – Das Geheimnis einer verlorenen Legende – Germany; Baby, il segreto della leggenda perduta – Italy; Baby: Le secret de la légende oubliée – France). This movie sees McGoohan enjoying his third movie with the famous Disney studio. He plays a glory-seeking zoologist looking for a rumoured brontosaurus family, deep in the Congo. The father dinosaur is killed by the evil scientist and he captures the mother.
Others around him prefer to try and save the baby and rescue its mother. The action is a prolonged chase through the jungle, involving semi-clad natives, menaced by McGoohan and corrupt cops in his pay. This equally sad and saccharine movie offers older children Disney-style entertainment, with McGoohan enjoying yet

another contact with the famous studio. Some reports say that the movie falls between two stools, being not really a kids' movie, while being too childish for adults.

Scanners (1981) – Dr Paul Ruth (aka Scanners – Ihre Gedanken können töten – Germany; Telepathy 2000 – (alternative title)). David Cronenberg's sci-fi horror movie has McGoohan as Dr. Paul Ruth, whose tranquillising drug for pregnant women leads to unnatural side effects, whereby an unborn child becomes a "scanner." These extraordinary beings have ESP (extra-sensory perception) and cause 'mind-blowing' effects on a person they are 'scanning.' After commercial production of the drug takes place, a small army of

scanners is raised by an evil doctor. McGoohan's character produces a 'good' super-scanner to combat the evil ones, leading to a battle between the telepaths. The visceral, head exploding effects punctuate a plot thought by some to be slow and confusing. But the movie has attained cult status and spawned sequels.

Kings and Desperate Men (1981 Canada; 1983 US; 1984 UK; filmed from 1978, or possibly 1977) – John Kingsley (aka Kings and Desperate Men: A Hostage Incident). A precursor to "Die Hard" perhaps, "Kings" is to some extent experimental. Director Alexis Kanner (who plays the lead character Lucas Miller) adds a multi-layered soundtrack and innovative camera angles. Regarded variously as too lengthy, or over the top, the movie may have suffered from being too long in production, or left mostly in the hands of one man. However, the results are stimulating

and McGoohan, a radio talk show host, is paired once more with Kanner, last seen together in "The Prisoner." Terrorists hijack the studio and demand that a 'trial' is conducted over the airwaves. Kingsley's own family is taken hostage and during one unexpected turn of events, a judge who has also been kidnapped by the terrorists dies. Some scenes between the two main men are memorable, but Margaret Trudeau, as Kingsley's wife, reported friction on the set.

Escape from Alcatraz (1979) – Prison Warden (aka L'Évadé d'Alcatraz – France; Flucht von Alcatraz – Germany; Fuga da Alcatraz – Italy; Fuga de Alcatraz – Spain). Filmed on location at the infamous island prison, "Escape From Alcatraz" was a box-office success. Based on the true story of the only man ever to escape from the penitentiary, Frank Morris (Clint Eastwood), the 'bad guy' is the fanatical Warden

(Patrick McGoohan). He runs a harsh regime and can barely keep his rage under control when dealing with the insubordinate inmate. The superior likes to control people and events, keeping a bird in a cage as a visible reminder to himself and prisoners who come to his office. He is convinced that Eastwood is plotting an escape, but his frustration turns to anger when he is unable to discover the plan and method; he is incensed when Morris goes missing.

Brass Target (1978) – Colonel Mike McCauley, OSS. (aka La Cible étoilée – France; Obiettivo Brass – Italy; Objetivo: Patton – Spain; Verstecktes Ziel – Germany). McGoohan is OSS Colonel Mike Macauley, but dies early on in the film when he is garrotted, thus silencing his American accent. The plot of the movie involves the transporting of gold bullion which was

seized during World War II. The film also involves a plan to kill General Patton (George Kennedy). The officers in wartime Germany who stole Nazi gold (with the help of OSS officer McGoohan) become the subject of an investigation, supervised by Patton. The general is killed on the orders of his own men, and few characters remain alive for the film's ending. Reviews tend to be critical of a confusing and under-developed movie.

Silver Streak (1976) – Roger Devereau (aka El Expreso de Chicago – Spain; Trans-Amerika-Express – Germany; Transamerica Express – France; Wagons lits con omicidi – Italy). A train from Los Angeles to Chicago is carrying George Caldwell (Gene Wilder), who strikes up an acquaintanceship with Hilly Burns (Jill Clayburgh). The woman confides that her boss is about to expose a gang of art forgers. That evening, George sees Hilly's boss falling from the train, but nobody believes him. Detective

Sweet (Ned Beatty) starts to investigate, but he too is killed. Behind all this is master forger Roger Devereau (McGoohan). He hijacks the locomotive, kills the driver and jams the controls at full speed. He is shot after coming under fire with police in a helicopter and is killed in an unpleasant way by an oncoming train. The movie was chosen as the Royal Performance film in London during the Queen's Jubilee Year in 1977, at which the Queen Mother attended.

Un Genio, Due Compari E Un Pollo (1975) – Major Cabot (aka A Genius, Two Friends, and an Idiot – USA; A Genius, Two Partners and a Dupe (alternative title); Nobody ist der Größtet – Germany; Nobody's the Greatest (video title); The Genius (alternative title) Trinity Is

Back Again – USA; Un génie, deux associés, une cloche – France). Co-produced and co-directed (but uncredited) by Sergio Leone, this was his last cowboy film and one of the last 'spaghetti westerns.' McGoohan has a role as a Svengali type Major Cabot, while hammy acting and bad script lines occur around him. A good deal of buffoonery falls flat. The movie's "Nobody" alternative title was created to cash in on the earlier, successful "My Name Is Nobody" film, also starring Terence Hill (although he plays a different character in the subsequent production). Some sources claim that McGoohan's screen voice is his own, but this does not seem to be borne out by what is heard on screen. However, curiously, another character in the film does have a dubbed voice which is surely McGoohan's.

Catch My Soul (1974) – Director (aka Santa Fe Satan). This film was McGoohan's only cinematic undertaking as a director and the production followed Jack Good's earlier stage version in the late sixties. There are conflicting reports about McGoohan having directed the first cut, but wanting his name removed from the film when Jack

Good added footage of a religious nature, something with which McGoohan did not agree. The musical is a rock opera version of "Othello," the second time McGoohan was involved with a screen adaptation of the Shakespearian play, the earlier one being the movie "All Night Long." Set in the American South West, Othello (Ritchie Havens) is an evangelist who wanders into a commune headed by Iago (Lance LeGault). He weds Desdemona, but murder and tragedy follow.

Mary, Queen of Scots (1971) – James Stuart (aka Marie Stuart, reine d'Écosse – France; María, reina de Escocia – Spain; Maria Stuarda regina di Scozia – Italy; Maria Stuart, Königin von Schottland – Germany). Queen Mary (Vanessa Redgrave) seeks to claim the Scottish crown. Her half brother, James Stuart, the Earl of Moray (McGoohan, adopting a Scottish accent) wants her merely to remain powerless, although other Scottish lords want her killed. Naturally, Elizabeth I (Glenda Jackson) also favours the second option and so
proof is obtained of Mary's complicity in a French plot leading to her being placed on trial and executed. The screenplay ignores the historical facts that Elizabeth and Mary never met and the latter's captivity was endured for nearly two decades. The movie offers beautiful scenery, sumptuous costumes and a top cast.

Documentaries – (1971/2) – see main text regarding partnership with Kenneth Griffith.

Shooting The Moonshine War (1970) – a seven minute promotional film showing location work in an unidentified rural setting, beginning with the arrival of MGM equipment trucks. The narrator, who describes himself as one of the local residents, provides a commentary as two car chases are filmed. The film's director and five main actors – including McGoohan – participated.

The Moonshine War (1970) – Federal Prohibition Agent Frank Long (aka The Whiskey War (alternative title); Whisky brutal, or Der Whisky Krieg – Germany; I Contrabbandieri degli anni ruggenti – Italy; La Guerre des bootleggers – France; El Infierno del Whisky – Spain). In this comedy drama set during the US thirties era, a federal prohibition agent Frank Long (McGoohan) has to find illicit stills and confiscate 'moonshine' whisky. However, the corrupt Long sells seized liquor in another state and he is eventually sacked.
A showdown occurs at the end of the movie with explosive results. McGoohan adopts a growling accent in this caper, adapted by Elmore Leonard from his own novel. The direction is along "Bonnie and Clyde" lines, but there is some lively dialogue.

The Man Who Makes the Difference (1968) – promotional short film featuring the work of John M. Stevens and his work on second unit cinematography, including Ice Station Zebra. McGoohan appears very briefly.

Ice Station Zebra (1968) – David Jones (aka Base artica Zebra – Italy; Destination: Zebra, station polaire – France; Eisstation Zebra – Germany; Estación polar Cebra – Spain). Famed as Howard Hughes' favourite movie, and directed by John Sturges ("The Great Escape," "The Eagle Has Landed" and "The Magnificent Seven") this movie was originally presented in Cinerama. A top notch cast heads the action based on an Alistair MacLean novel about a race between Russia and the United States to recover a
satellite at the North Pole. This leads to plots and counter-plots to prevent recovery of the device. Rock Hudson's nuclear powered submarine goes under the ice-cap with secret agent McGoohan on board and a Russian man, plus a fiercely military minded American soldier. The US contingent has to fight off the opposing Russian force at the Pole as well as dealing with sabotage attempts aboard. McGoohan made this movie during his work on the British TV series "The Prisoner," leading to an episode being filmed without him, using a 'substitute' character.

Red Reflections (1966) – Voice only on part of a short film made by "The Prisoner" music editor Eric Mival, which was unreleased.

Koroshi (1966) – John Drake (aka Danger Man – Das Syndikat der Grausamen – Germany; Danger Man: Koroshi (UK series title); Dick Carter, lo sbirro – Italy); feature length combined Danger Man episodes "Koroshi" and "Shinda Shima" for cinema presentation (also on TV).

Dr. Syn, Alias the Scarecrow (1963 – Reverend Dr Christopher Syn (aka The Scarecrow of Romney Marsh; Le Justicier aux Deux Visages – France; L'Inafferrabile Primula Nera – Italy; La mascára del Dr. Syn – Spain) (also shown in US as a three part TV serial + extra scenes as part of The World of Walt Disney; aka L'Épouvantail – France). In this Disney colourful drama,

McGoohan appears as Dr Christopher Syn, the vicar of Dymchurch, in late eighteenth century England. However, he leads a double life and dons a scarecrow disguise to enable himself and local folk to commit smuggling raids around the Kent coast, to remedy their poverty. He also saves two men who have been 'press ganged' and even one of his local flock who has been convicted in court for smuggling. The original TV title was "The Scarecrow of Romney Marsh," based on the Dr Syn novels written by Russell Thorndike (brother of actress Dame Sybil Thorndike), in which the main character was not a vicar, but a pirate.

The Three Lives of Thomasina (1963 – Veterinary Surgeon Andrew Macdhui MR.CVS (aka Les Trois Vies de Thomasina – France; Die Drei Leben des Thomasina – Germany). In this Walt Disney movie, the action is set in the early twentieth century, in a small Scottish village. Thomasina is a cat, which 'dies' at the hands of a little girl's widowed veterinarian father. However, the animal is nursed back to life by a local woman, thought by some to be a

'witch.' The little girl who previously owned the cat discovers that her pet is still alive, living with the woman, and she tries to get her back. Her father develops a friendship with the woman, leading to a happy ending with a wedding and the daughter, plus cat, as 'bridesmaids.'

The Quare Fellow (1962) – Warder Thomas Crimmin (aka Queens of Hearts (alternative title); Der Todeskandidat – Germany; La Valigia del boia – Italy). Brendan Behan's play about a condemned man is transferred to a grim screenplay. McGoohan, as a Dublin death-row prison guard, harbours a growing empathy with two prisoners. Fresh from training college, he has strong views on capital punishment.

Two inmates are awaiting execution of their death sentences and one is reprieved while the other is not. As McGoohan gets to know the condemned man, his belief in capital punishment is shaken and the warders are seen as much prisoners of the system as the inmates.

Life for Ruth (1962) – Dr James 'Jim' Brown (aka Condemned to Live, sometimes shown as Condemned to Life; Accusé, levez-vous – France; Brennende Schuld – Germany; Delitto di coscienza – Italy; Leben für Ruth –

Germany; Vida para Ruth – Spain; Walk in the Shadow – USA) (also listed in one source only as No Life for Ruth). Filmed in the north of England, the story presents a father (Michael Craig) placing his daughter's life in God's hands, instead of heeding the advice of surgeons. Eight year old Ruth dies because there can be no blood transfusion and a court case ensues. A failed

prosecution of the father at least leads to his being saved from a would-be suicide attempt. McGoohan, as Dr Brown, comes to see both sides of the argument in this drama, where religion and medical ethics are in conflict.

All Night Long (1961) – Johnny Cousin (aka Tout aux Long de la Nuit – France; Die Heiße Nacht – Germany; Noche de pesadilla – Spain). The "Othello" borrowed plot is one of jealousy and scheming amongst jazz musicians at a wedding anniversary party. The celebration is being held in a London warehouse, giving a

backdrop of a jam session with musicians like Dave Brubeck, Johnny Dankworth and Tubby Hayes. A woman in the band of Johnny Cousin (McGoohan) wants to retire to concentrate upon her marriage. Cousin doctors a tape recording to try and break up the marriage, but the scheme misfires and his own marriage and career are ruined. McGoohan sports an American accent and at the end is alone with his drum-kit in the empty warehouse. The actor practised drumming in advance of the movie, in order to give an authentic portrayal. This was the first of two screen "Othello" adaptations involving McGoohan, the other being the movie "Catch My Soul."

Two Living, One Dead (1961) – Erik Berger (aka Asalto a mano armada – Spain; Två levande och en död – Sweden). In this Anthony Asquith directed drama, McGoohan plays a dour Swedish postal clerk, Erik Berger. During an armed raid on his post office, his character is unharmed because he hands over money, thereby avoiding getting shot like some of his colleagues. As a result, Berger is branded a coward. He is passed over for promotion and the job is given to one of the hero workers. McGoohan's relationship with his wife (Virginia McKenna) deteriorates and his son suffers at school because his father is a coward. Later, a stranger tells Berger that he and his

brother were the robbers and he wants to make amends for ruining McGoohan's life. Berger stages a mock hold-up to restore the community's faith in him and enable him to return home to live a normal life once more. This curious tale was shot in Scandinavia and afforded McGoohan a break from filming the first "Danger Man" series.

Nor the Moon by Night (1958) – Game Warden Andrew Miller (aka Rencontre au Kenya – France; Elephant Gun –USA; Gnadenloser Dschungel – Germany; El Valle de las mil colinas – Spain; La Valle delle mille colline – Italy; Velaba ruft – Germany). Shot on location in Africa, this fourth and last film for McGoohan with Rank (made before terminating the agreement by mutual consent) sees him as a game warden. He is joined by his girlfriend on the African reserve which he runs.

There is a threat of illegal poaching and rivalry develops between Miller and his brother over the woman. A nasty incident with a lion provides the finale, but during the movie McGoohan is seen delivering a rare screen kiss with actress Anna Gaylor.

The Gypsy and the Gentleman (1957) – Jess (aka Gipsy (alternative title); Dämon Weib – Germany; La Zingara rossa, Italy). Directed by Joseph Losey, this uneven Regency melodrama, involves an aristocrat falling in love with a gypsy girl who marries him, but installs her gypsy lover Jess (McGoohan) as horse-master. In a final scene, coaches collide on a bridge with occupants thrown into a river, drowning the ill-fated married couple. Greek actress Melina Mercouri made her English

film debut, playing the tempestuous gypsy girl Belle and McGoohan notched up his third movie with Rank.

Hell Drivers (1957) – G. 'Red' Redman (aka Duell am Steuer – Germany; Hard Drivers (alternative title); I Piloti dell'inferno – Italy; Ruta infernal –Spain; Train d'enfer – France). In this action-packed truck-driving thriller, Stanley Baker takes a job hauling ballast and finds that to make real money he must emulate his foreman, "Red" Redman, who is an Irish bully. The rivalry between the drivers causes friction and accidents. Baker finds that the company is being run in a corrupt way by the manager (William Hartnell) and the action

ends in a climactic race between trucks driven by Baker and McGoohan (in his second film with Rank). Fist fights, dangerous road antics and heavy drinking make for some lively scenes.

High Tide at Noon (1957) – Simon Breck (aka Alta marea a mezzogiorno – Italy). On a remote, rugged Nova Scotia island a woman in a small fishing community attracts the interest of Simon Breck (McGoohan), a member of a 'black sheep' family. There is rivalry between him and a handsome stranger. The woman weds the other man but after a gambling session with Breck, the house is lost and later the husband is drowned, leading to Breck wanting to call in the debt and claim the woman. This was McGoohan's first film under his contract with the Rank Organisation. The movie's director, Philip

Leacock, would later helm the McGoohan TV film, "Three Sovereigns for Sarah."

Zarak (1956) – Indian Army Adjutant Moor Larkin (aka Zarak Khan – Germany; Zarak le valeureux – France). Pillaging, plundering and passion abound in this gung-ho Cinemascope adventure, filmed in Morocco. A small bandit army terrorises the North West Indian frontier and a British major (Michael Wilding) is assigned to capture the chieftain Zarak Khan (Victor Mature) and his men. He succeeds, but the bandit escapes and his raiders then attack the British garrison, with much slaughter. Zarak joins forces with an Afghan ruler and captures the English commander. Out of respect, Zarak prevents the proposed execution,

enabling an English rescue party to save the intended victim, but in so doing the bandit sacrifices his own life. McGoohan plays a very British adjutant and Anita Ekberg provides the glamour.

The Dark Avenger (1955) – uncredited, played Sir Oswald (aka Der Schwarze Prinz – Germany; The Black

Prince – UK working title; The Warriors USA; L'Armure Noir – France). A mature Errol Flynn (his last film) is the Black Prince in a movie set in France during the Hundred Years War. Edward III has left his son to rule Aquitaine and the prince organises a jousting tournament to release French-held prisoners. Peter Finch plays a villainous Count. There is a final rousing castle siege, utilising the MGM Borehamwood studio "Ivanhoe" movie set. "The Dark Avenger" was the European title, referring to Flynn's swashbuckling character, while in America the movie was called "The Warriors."

I am a Camera (1955) – Swedish water therapist (aka Une Fille Comme Ça! – Je Suis un Camera – France; La Donna è un male necessario – Italy; Sóc una càmera – Spain (Catalan title); Soy una cámara – Spain). In Berlin in the thirties the decadent but often opulent lifestyle of the rich is documented. McGoohan appears briefly, giving some very precise orders for the creation of therapeutic hot and cold baths. Julie Harris repeats her stage role as Sally Bowles, befriending a writer, played by Lawrence Harvey. Filmed in England,

the production (later to become the musical hit "Cabaret") is indifferent, against a pre-Nazi Germany backdrop, avoiding head-on treatment of subsidiary subjects such as homosexuality, abortion and anti-Semitism.

Passage Home (1955) – Merchant Seaman McIsaacs (aka Il Cargo della violenza – Italy; Eine Frau kommt an Bord – Germany; Viaje de vuelta – Spain). In the early thirties, a run-down merchant ship has to take on board a stranded British woman as a passenger, for the return journey from South America. The presence of the woman on board causes rivalry between the captain (Peter Finch) and his first mate (Anthony Steel), with conditions made worse by disharmony amongst the

crew, bad food and a dangerous storm. Virtuous Steel struggles to protect the woman from the advances of Finch. McGoohan's early role is as one of the ship's crew.

The Dam Busters (1954) – uncredited, played RAF guard (aka Les Briseurs de barrages – France; I Guastatori delle dighe – Italy; Mai '43 – Die Zerstörung der Talsperren – Germany; Mai 1943 – Die Zerstörung der Talsperren – Germany; The Dambusters – USA alternative spelling). This British film tells the story of the Barnes Wallis "Bouncing Bomb," used in World War II. Much of the film covers creation of the weapons and pilot training in low level bombers. The aircraft must later drop skimming bombs precisely

into reservoirs in the Ruhr valley, to destroy the dam and cause catastrophic flooding. McGoohan's appearance, as a guard outside a briefing room, involves only a couple of spoken lines. However, while "Passage Home" was his first credited appearance, "The Dam Busters" was his first true role with dialogue.

TELEVISION (including TV MOVIES, but not CABLE – see FILMS)

Not included below are TV interview appearances – see separate section in this appendixand page 307 for TV photo roles.

The Simpsons (1999) – Voice of Number Six in episode "The Computer Wore Menace Shoes."

Columbo (1999) – Director + Writer of episode "Murder with Too Many Notes," with daughter Anne also appearing. See Appendix Two for list of episodes and short synopses.

Columbo (1998) – Eric Prince + Director + Co-Executive Producer of episode "Ashes to Ashes," with daughter Catherine also appearing. See Appendix Two for list of episodes and short synopses.

The Best of Friends (1991) – George Bernard Shaw (also shown in USA as a Mobil-sponsored "Masterpiece Theatre" presentation)

Columbo (1989) – Attorney Oscar Finch + Director of episode "Agenda for Murder" and reportedly McGoohan also did some writing on this episode. McGoohan won an Emmy for his performance in this episode. See Appendix Two for list of episodes and short synopses.

Murder, She Wrote (1987) – Attorney Oliver Quayle in episode "Witness for the Defense."

Of Pure Blood (1986) – Dr Felix Neumann (aka The Nazis: Of Pure Blood; Au Nom de la Race – France; D'un sang trop pur – France; Bluterbe – Germany (video title); La Stirpe del sangue – Italy) – CBS Sunday Movie. Lee Remick plays Alicia Browning, a New York casting agent who learns of the death of her son in Germany and that she has a grandson. She discovers that there was a wartime Himmler programme to breed pure Aryans. McGoohan, as Remick's uncle, is uncharacteristic and disconcerting, with his German accent and elderly makeup. Alicia realises that her real father was a war criminal and, four decades on, she has stumbled upon a covert Nazi organization which intends to create a new master race. Fortunately, McGoohan is able to protect his niece and great grandchild.

Three Sovereigns for Sarah (1984) – Chief Magistrate – PBS American Playhouse. Director of this television drama was Philip Leacock, who previously directed McGoohan in the 1957 movie "High Tide at Noon." McGoohan plays a British magistrate sent to New England to apply the rule of law, after colonists have developed their own ways of handling the Salem witch trials. The setting is the story of Sarah Cloyce (Vanessa Redgrave), an accused woman who survives the ordeal, although her sisters were tortured, found guilty and burned. Sarah proves that her family is innocent of the charges, in this lengthy drama.

Jamaica Inn (1982) – Joss Merlyn (aka L'Auberge de la Jamaïque – France). In this television film, Mary Yellan (Jane Seymour), her father having been killed by a notorious ship-wrecking gang, goes to live on the Cornish moors with her aunt (Billie Whitelaw) and wicked uncle Joss Merlyn, (McGoohan), the landlord of Jamaica Inn. She finds that he is up to villainy with local men, who draw ships onto the Cornish rocks and plunder the wrecks. The teleplay

by Derek Marlowe, from the Daphne du Maurier novel, presents McGoohan as a drunk and drooling Joss Merlyn, in a lengthy tale, filmed decades earlier by Alfred Hitchcock. "Prisoner" director Peter Graham Scott produced the 1982 version.

The Hard Way (1979) – John Connor (aka Le Dernier contrat – France; Der bittere Weg – Germany; Der Profi-Killer – German video title). This brooding ITC production for television involves Irish hit-man, John Connor (McGoohan), being made to undertake one last assassination. He wants to retire but is forced to take a final job as his employer threatens to harm Connor's family. When the moment comes to perform the contracted assassination, Connor double-crosses his employer. The film's climax involves a trap laid by the employer in an old disused country house. A dramatic showdown (with Lee Van Cleef) provides the film's finale.

Rafferty (1977) – Dr. Sid Rafferty (pilot + 12 x 50 minute episodes) (+ Director on episode "The Wild Child" – Internet sources wrongly refer to "The Outcast," but no such "Rafferty" story exists, although the title was used for episodes of "The Adventures of Sir Lancelot," in which McGoohan appeared and "Assignment Foreign Legion," although he was not in the episode of that title, but was in another, "The Coward.") The series was listed in one 1977 source as "A Man Called Rafferty," possibly relating to the pilot. See Appendix Two for list of episodes and short synopses.

Columbo (1976) – Director of episode "Last Salute to the Commodore" and reportedly, McGoohan also altered the script and added a character. See Appendix Two for list of episodes and short synopses.

The Man in the Iron Mask (1976) – Nicholas Fouquet (aka L'Homme au masque de fer – France; Der Mann mit der eisernen Maske – Germany; L'Uomo dalla maschera di ferro – Italy). Made for television in 1976 and directed by Mike Newell ("Harry Potter and the Goblet of Fire," "Four Weddings and a Funeral," "Donnie Brasco"), this UK production tells the Alexandre Dumas historical story of Louis XIV of France. McGoohan, as the unscrupulous Minister of Finance, orders the king's twin Philippe to be thrown into the Bastille, away from the sight and knowledge of the public. The sadistic and scheming Fouquet oversees the applying of the metal face mask to Phillipe (both twins being played by Richard Chamberlain). D'Artagnan and the Musketeers devise a plan to rescue Philippe and restore him to his rightful position as king of France. Fouqet later seals his own fate by mistakenly dubbing Louis the pretender. The movie includes a thrilling cliff top sword fight with McGoohan doing his own risky stunt work.

Columbo (1975) – Nelson Brenner + Director in episode "Identity Crisis" and reportedly McGoohan also did some rewriting of this episode. See Appendix Two for list of episodes and short synopses.

Columbo (1974) – Colonel Lyle C. Rumford in episode "By Dawn's Early Light." McGoohan won an Emmy for his performance in this episode. See Appendix Two for list of episodes and short synopses.

Journey into Darkness (1968) – hosted a compilation of two episodes "The New People" + "Paper Dolls" which were shown as separate episodes in the "Journey to the Unknown" series, without McGoohan. See page 181 for more details.

The Prisoner (1966-7) – Number Six + other uncredited parts e.g. as his 'double,' or imaginary figures (17 x 50 minute episodes) (Executive Producer of series + Director + Writer (as Paddy Fitz) on episode "Free for All" + Director on episode "Many Happy Returns" (as Joseph Serf) + Director on episode "A Change of Mind" (as Joseph Serf) + Director + Writer on episode "Once upon a Time" + Director + Writer on episode "Fall Out") (aka Le Prisonnier – France; Nummer 6 – Germany; Il Prigioniero – Italy; El Prisionero – Spain). See Appendix Two for list of episodes and short synopses.

Koroshi (1966) – feature length combined Danger Man episodes "Koroshi" and "Shinda Shima" – see entry in films (also shown on TV).

Danger Man (1966) – John Drake (final fourth series of 2 x 50 min episodes) (aka Secret Agent; aka Destination Danger – France; aka Geheimauftrag für John Drake – Germany). (the US Secret Agent episodes featured a different opening from UK ones). See Appendix Two for list of episodes and short synopses.

Danger Man (1965) – John Drake (third series of 13 x 50 min episodes) (aka Secret Agent; aka Destination Danger – France; aka Geheimauftrag für John Drake – Germany). (+ Director on episodes "To Our Best Friend" and "The Paper Chase"). See Appendix Two for list of episodes and short synopses.

Danger Man (1964) – John Drake (second series of 32 x 50 min episodes) (aka Secret Agent; aka Destination Danger– France; aka Geheimauftrag für John Drake – Germany). See Appendix Two for list of episodes and short synopses.

The Scarecrow of Romney Marsh (1964) – see Dr. Syn, Alias the Scarecrow in films list.

The Prisoner (1963) – The Interrogator (BBC play).

Shadow of a Pale Horse (1962) –The Prosecutor (Play Of The Week).

Serjeant Musgrave's Dance (1961) – Serjeant Musgrave (Play Of The Week).

The Man out There (1961) – Nicholai Soloviov (Armchair Theatre).

Danger Man (1959/60/61) – John Drake (first series of 39 x 25 min episodes) (aka Geheimauftrag für John Drake – Germany) (+ Director on episode "Vacation"). See Appendix Two for list of episodes and short synopses.

Brand (11th August, 1959) BBC live telecast – see theatrical listings.

The Iron Harp (1959) – ? (CBC production in Canada).

A Dead Secret (1959) – Frederick S. Dyson (Play of the Week).

The Big Knife (1958) – Charlie Castle (Play of the Week).

The Greatest Man in the World (1958) – Jack 'Pal' Smurch (Armchair Theatre).

Rest in Violence (1958) – Matthew "Mat" Galvin (Play of the Week).

This Day in Fear (1958) – James Coogan (Television Playwright).

Disturbance (1958) – Flint.

All My Sons (1958) – Chris Keller.

Rendezvous (1957) – Priest in episode "The Hanging of Alfred Wadham" + Stoner in episode "The Executioner."

Assignment Foreign Legion (1957) – Captain Valadon in episode "The Coward."

The Adventures of Aggie also known as Aggie (1956) – Jocko in episode "Cock and Bull" + Migual in episode "Spanish Sauce."

The Makepeace Story (1956) – Seth Makepeace in episode "Ruthless Destiny" (cycle of 4 plays as part of Sunday Night Theatre) (in some sources referred to as The Makepeace Saga).

The Adventures of Sir Lancelot (1956) – Sir Glavin in episode "The Outcast."

Terminus (1955) – James Hartley in the story "Margin for Error."

You Are There (1954) – Charles Stewart Parnell – in episode "The Fall of Parnell" (also one source mentions

McGoohan being in an episode relating to the Charge of the Light Brigade, which is unconfirmed).
The Vise (1954/5/6 – but see main text as to dates) – Tony Mason in episode "A Gift from Heaven" + Tom Vance in episode "Blood in the Sky."

THEATRE
(Repertory, London, Provinces, Broadway etc., but not TV plays)

Regarding McGoohan's London West End stage debut – Hobson's Choice, 1952, see Chapter Two – there are two other candidates for this, according to different sources. The latest relates to Henry V, 1953, while the earliest relates to The Brontes, although this was part of the play's 1948 tour. An incorrect 1952 listing for The Brontes is also given in some places. It is also worth mentioning here that in the main, only one listing is given for each performance of a repertory production, instead of showing all venues during tours. Sheffield Playhouse presentations were mainly fortnightly, but where a longer gap exists, some plays continued for three or even four weeks. A few plays are shown in italics, indicating that it is unconfirmed as to whether McGoohan appeared in the play, or whether it was actually presented during his Sheffield rep days. One or two other italicised entries denote plays where McGoohan was billed, but did not appear, or he reportedly pulled out. The most reliable sources, or those mostly referring to a particular year are used below. It can also be mentioned here that in the list of plays which follows, McGoohan's involvement in a non-acting capacity is also shown e.g. Assistant Stage Manager. Additionally, his earlier appearances in local and youth club productions are given, to provide a complete picture. Finally, also included are plays in which Joan Drummond appeared, sometimes in the company of her husband in the same play. She also appeared in the long-running production of The Mousetrap, at the Ambassadors Theatre, London, in the 1956/7, 1957/8 and 1958/9 seasons.

1994

A Christmas Carol (1994) – Birmingham Theater, MI – *advertised with McGoohan starring, but no performances known of, except for possibly a couple of shows without McGoohan.*

1985

Pack of Lies (1985) – Stewart – Royale Theatre, New York. There were a hundred and twenty performances, from 11th February to 25th May, 1985. McGoohan was nominated for the Drama Desk Award for an Outstanding Actor in a Play.
Pack of Lies (1985) – Stewart – the Wilbur Theater, Boston. This was the play's brief January opening.
The Master Builder (c. 1985) – ? – *a semi-professional production in Los Angeles (so it was claimed in 1989 by Michael Meyer, translator of the 1959 Brand in which McGoohan appeared). No other details have been found relating to this.*

1983

Moby Dick (1983) – *Captain Ahab – The Royal Exchange Theatre, Manchester – McGoohan withdrew – see page 228.*

1959

Brand (8th April 1959) – Brand – Lyric Opera House, later known as Lyric Theatre, Hammersmith, The 59 Theatre Company. The play (also transmitted by BBC TV as a live telecast on 11th August) won the McGoohan the London Drama Critics Award for Best British Theatre Actor.
Danton's Death (27th January 1959) – St Just – Lyric Opera House, later known as the Lyric Theatre, Hammersmith, The 59 Theatre Company (also transmitted on TV but after McGoohan had left the cast).

1956

Ring for Catty (14th February 1956) – Leonard White – Lyric Theatre, London (with Joan Drummond as Madge Williams) A revised, more serious version of Time On Their Hands, (see 1954 below).

1955

Moby Dick (16th June 1955) – A Serious Actor + afterwards Starbuck – the Duke of York's Theatre, London, being an Orson Welles production (the title became Moby Dick – Rehearsed when the play was later published). See also the footnote regarding the filming of Moby Dick, in the main text where the play is covered and reference to the play in the television listings for 1955.
Serious Charge (17th February 1955) – Rev Howard Phillips – the Garrick Theatre, London.

1954

Babes in Toyland (1954) – ? – *possibly a London pantomime.*
Aren't People Wonderful (November 1954) – Colin Brown – the Embassy Theatre, London.
Grace and Favour – (27th July to 1st August 1954) – producer – Q Theatre, London.
Time on Their Hands (July 1954) – Leonard White (see also Ring For Catty, 1956) – Q Theatre, London.
Spring Model (June 1954) – Roy Mawson – Q Theatre, London (one source states that McGoohan played Alex Atkinson; see also Windsor Repertory Company, 1953)
Burning Bright (May 1954) – Jack Connolly – listed elsewhere as Jock Connelly – Q Theatre, London.
The Male Animal (22 February 1954) – Tommy Turner – Windsor Repertory Company, Theatre Royal, Windsor
The River Line (8 February 1954) – Philip Sturgess – Windsor Repertory Company, Theatre Royal, Windsor

1953

Old Bailey (10th November 1953) – Robert Bailey II – the Theatre Royal, Bristol, with Old Vic Company.
Antony and Cleopatra (20th October 1953) – Pompey – the Theatre Royal, Bristol, with Old Vic Company *(plus a lesser role as a schoolmaster)*
The Cherry Orchard (29th September 1953) – Peter Trofimov, Student – the Theatre Royal, Bristol, with Bristol Old Vic Company (see also Sheffield Playhouse, 1948).
The Castiglioni Brothers (7th September 1953) – Camillo Castiglioni – the Theatre Royal, Bristol, with Bristol Old Vic Company.
Henry V (23rd June 1953) – Chorus + MacMorris + Montjoy – the Theatre Royal, Bristol, with Bristol Old Vic Company (the play transferred to the Old Vic Theatre, London on 30th June 1953).
Spring Model (27 April 1953) – Roy Mawson – Windsor Repertory Company, Theatre Royal, Windsor (see also Q Theatre, 1954)
Wishing Well (13 April 1953) – John Pugh – Windsor Repertory Company, Theatre Royal, Windsor
Born Yesterday (February 1953) – Harry Brock – The Midland Theatre Company, College Theatre, Coventry (also seen at Co-operative Hall, Nuneaton, the Arts Centre, Netherton and Stanford Hall, Loughborough; see also Sheffield Playhouse, 1950)

1952

Between 1952 and 1954 McGoohan appeared at other theatres. One source states that the actor appeared in up to twenty seven brief productions, over twenty of which are listed in this theatre section. Performances at the Bristol Old Vic (above) took place during two seasons, although one source mentions that McGoohan spent three seasons there. Also, added here, immediately below, is an uncertain double reference to King Lear, *which is unconfirmed.*

King Lear (1952) – *King Lear* – *the Theatre Royal, Bristol, with The Old Vic company (one source refers to this, but the play was only at Bristol in earlier and later years).*

King Lear (1952) – *King Lear* – *The Playhouse, Sheffield Repertory Theatre (see main text comment of director Peter Graham Scott, at the time of the film Jamaica Inn).*

Private Lives (8th December 1952) – Elyot Chase – The Midland Theatre Company, College Theatre, Coventry (also seen at Co-operative Hall, Nuneaton, the Arts Centre, Netherton and Stanford Hall, Loughborough).

Caroline (17th November 1952) – Robert Oldham – The Midland Theatre Company, College Theatre, Coventry.

The Cocktail Party (27th October 1952) – ? – The Midland Theatre Company, College Theatre, Coventry (see also Sheffield 1952 entry below).

Deep Are the Roots (6th October 1952) – Sheriff Serkin – The Midland Theatre Company, College Theatre, Coventry (also seen at Co-operative Hall, Nuneaton, the Arts Centre, Netherton and Stanford Hall, Loughborough).

Hobson's Choice (15th September 1952 – see also London below and 1949) – The Midland Theatre Company, College Theatre, Coventry.

A Priest in the Family (25 August 1952) – Rory Murphy – Windsor Repertory Company, Theatre Royal, Windsor

Hobson's Choice (June 1952) – Albert Prosser – the Arts Theatre Club, London (see also September, 1952 and 1949).

Cupid and Psyche (21st April 1952) – Mac – Royal Court Theatre, Liverpool. *(This production was on tour in Edinburgh from 31st March 1952 and Glasgow, but the Playhouse Theatre history does not list the play as having been performed at Sheffield. The play was also to have visited London, but this eventually did not happen).*

Mrs Dane's Defence (31st March 1952) – ? – *The Playhouse, Sheffield Repertory Theatre*

By Candlelight (17th March 1952) – ? – *The Playhouse, Sheffield Repertory Theatre*

September Tide (3rd March 1952) – ? – *The Playhouse, Sheffield Repertory Theatre*

The Cocktail Party (18th February 1952) – ? – *The Playhouse, Sheffield Repertory Theatre*
(see also Midland Theatre Company, 1953).

For completeness, the last four Sheffield plays above are included, prior to McGoohan appearing in Liverpool, but his involvement in them is unconfirmed.

Who Goes There (4th February 1952) – Guardsman Arthur Chrisp – The Playhouse, Sheffield Repertory Theatre.

The Taming of the Shrew (21st January 1952) – Petruchio – The Playhouse, Sheffield Repertory Theatre.

1951
The Princess and the Swineherd (22nd December 1951) – Prince Dominic (Joan Drummond in role of Princess Clair-de-Lune) - The Playhouse, Sheffield Repertory Theatre.

Return to Tyassie (3rd December 1951) – (Joan Drummond in role of Susan Hubbard) – The Playhouse, Sheffield Repertory Theatre.

Treasure Hunt (19th November 1951)   William Burke (Joan Drummond in role of Veronica Howard) – The Playhouse, Sheffield Repertory Theatre.

Crime Passionnel (5th November 1951) – Georges – The Playhouse, Sheffield Repertory Theatre.

The Little Foxes (22nd October 1951) – Oscar Hubbard (Joan Drummond in role of Alexandra Giddens) – The Playhouse, Sheffield Repertory Theatre.

Man and Superman (8th October 1951) – John Tanner – The Playhouse, Sheffield Repertory Theatre.

Mr. Gillie (24th September 1951) – Dr Watson (Joan Drummond in role of Nelly) – The Playhouse, Sheffield Repertory Theatre.

The Holly and the Ivy (10th September 1951) – David Patterson – The Playhouse, Sheffield Repertory Theatre.

The Happiest Days of Your Life (27th August 1951) – Rainbow (Joan Drummond in role of Barbara Cahoun) – The Playhouse, Sheffield Repertory Theatre.

A Lady Mislaid (16th July 1951) – (Joan Drummond in role of Jennifer Williams) – The Playhouse, Sheffield Repertory Theatre.

Saint Joan (2nd July 1951) – Dunois (Joan Drummond in role of Joan)– The Playhouse, Sheffield Repertory Theatre.

Captain Carvallo (18th June 1951) – (Joan Drummond in role of Anni) – The Playhouse, Sheffield Repertory Theatre.

Milestones (5th June 1951) – John Rhead (Joan Drummond in role of Nancy Sibley)– The Playhouse, Sheffield Repertory Theatre.

The Rivals (28th May 1951) – Sir Lucius O'Trigger (Joan Drummond in role of Lucy) – The Theatre Royal, Bath.

The Rivals (14th May 1951) – Sir Lucius O'Trigger (Joan Drummond in role of Lucy) – The Playhouse, Sheffield Repertory Theatre.

Castle in the Air (30th April 1951) – ? – The Playhouse, Sheffield Repertory Theatre.

Home at Seven (16th April 1951) – Inspector Hemingway (Joan Drummond in role of Peggy Dobson) – The Playhouse, Sheffield Repertory Theatre.

The Heiress (2nd April 1951) – (Joan Drummond in role of Maria) – The Playhouse, Sheffield Repertory Theatre.

Vanity Fair (19th March 1951) – Captain Dobbin (Joan Drummond in role of Becky Sharp) – The Playhouse, Sheffield Repertory Theatre.

Venus Observed (5th March 1951) – Dominic (Joan Drummond in role of Perpetua) – The Playhouse, Sheffield Repertory Theatre.

Wilderness of Monkeys (19th February 1951) – Roger Payne – The Playhouse, Sheffield Repertory Theatre.

Hamlet (22nd January 1951) – Laertes – The Playhouse, Sheffield Repertory Theatre.

1950

The Silver Curlew (26th December 1950) – Sid (Joan Drummond in role of Poll) – The Playhouse, Sheffield Repertory Theatre.

The Family Honour (4th December 1950) – Larry (Joan Drummond in role of Bridget) – The Playhouse, Sheffield Repertory Theatre.

Bonaventure (20th November 1950) – Willy Pentridge (Joan Drummond in role of Nurse Phillips) – The Playhouse, Sheffield Repertory Theatre.

The Philadelphia Story (6th November 1950) – Macauley (Mike) Connor (Joan Drummond in role of Dinah Lord) – The Playhouse, Sheffield Repertory Theatre.

The Workhouse Ward (23rd October 1950) – Antigone – First Guard – The Playhouse, Sheffield Repertory Theatre. The play was preceded by another play, The Rising Of The Moon – Policeman B.

The Foolish Gentlewoman (9th October 1950) – (Joan Drummond in role of Jacqueline Brown) – The Playhouse, Sheffield Repertory Theatre.

Summer Day's Dream (25th September 1950) – Christopher Dawlish (Joan Drummond in role of Rosalie Dawlish) – The Playhouse, Sheffield Repertory Theatre.

Young Wives' Tale (11th September 1950) – (Joan Drummond in role of Eve Lester) – The Playhouse, Sheffield Repertory Theatre.

Born Yesterday (24th July 1950) – Paul Verrall – The Playhouse, Sheffield Repertory Theatre (see also The Midland Theatre Company, 1953)

The Lady's Not for Burning (10th July 1950) – Humphrey Devise (Joan Drummond in role of Alizon Eliot)– The Playhouse, Sheffield Repertory Theatre.

Before the Party (26th June 1950) – (Joan Drummond in role of Susan Skinner) – The Playhouse, Sheffield Repertory Theatre.

Edward, My Son (12th June 1950) – Cunningham + Mr. Prothero (Joan Drummond in role of Betty Fowler) – The Playhouse, Sheffield Repertory Theatre.

Top Secret (29th May 1950) – Peter Crabbe (Joan Drummond in role of Patricia Winter) – The Playhouse, Sheffield Repertory Theatre.

Love in Albania (15th May 1950) – ? – The Playhouse, Sheffield Repertory Theatre.

Miss Mabel (1st May 1950) – Peter Barlow (Joan Drummond in role of maid at Miss Mabel's house) – The Playhouse, Sheffield Repertory Theatre.

Ann Veronica (17th April 1950) – Policeman (Joan Drummond in role of Landlady + Kitty Brett) – The Playhouse, Sheffield Repertory Theatre.

Little Lambs Eat Ivy (3rd April 1950) – Clifford Magill (Joan Drummond in role of Biccy) – The Playhouse, Sheffield Repertory Theatre.

The Gioconda Smile (20th March 1950) – First Warder (Joan Drummond in role of Doris Mead) – The Playhouse, Sheffield Repertory Theatre.

The Human Touch (6th March 1950) – Sandy (Joan Drummond in role of Lady Janet Graham) – The Playhouse, Sheffield Repertory Theatre.

The Browning Version *(1950) – ? – The Playhouse, Sheffield Repertory Theatre (one source suggests that this was performed singly in this year, but see also Playbill entry, in 1949).*

The Constant Wife (20th February 1950) – (Joan Drummond in role of Marie Louise Durham) – The Playhouse, Sheffield Repertory Theatre.

Macbeth (23rd January 1950) – Macduff (Joan Drummond in role of Fleance + Second Apparition + a gentlewoman attending on Lady Macbeth) – The Playhouse, Sheffield Repertory Theatre.

1949

Othello (1949) – although there are references to McGoohan having acted in this production (and even taking the role of Othello), the play does not appear in the Sheffield Playhouse history, which refers to Othello being produced only at the theatre in 1932 and 1955. Whilst this does not preclude McGoohan from appearing in a production elsewhere, it should be noted that this listing is for completeness and to acknowledge that reference to the play does appear in other sources.

The Rose and the Ring (26th December 1949) – Count Hedzoff (Joan Drummond in role of Princess Angelica) – The Playhouse, Sheffield Repertory Theatre.

The Chiltern Hundreds (28th November 1949) – (Joan Drummond in role of Bessie) – The Playhouse, Sheffield Repertory Theatre.

Playbill (14th November 1949) – two plays being The Browning Version – Peter Gilbert + Joan Drummond as Mrs. Gilbert, both playing newlyweds + The Harlequinade – Policeman (Joan Drummond in role of Muriel Palmer) – The Playhouse, Sheffield Repertory Theatre.

The Paragon (31st October 1949) – Delivery Man – The Playhouse, Sheffield Repertory Theatre.

Noah (17th October 1949) – Ham (Joan Drummond in role of Ada) – The Playhouse, Sheffield Repertory Theatre.

Rain on the Just (3rd October 1949) – ? – The Playhouse, Sheffield Repertory Theatre.

Shooting Star (19th September 1949) – Jack Bannerman (Joan Drummond in role of Mavis Pink) – The Playhouse, Sheffield Repertory Theatre.

The Damask Cheek (5th September 1949) – (Joan Drummond in role of Daphne Randall) – The Playhouse, Sheffield Repertory Theatre.

Hobson's Choice (25th July 1949) – Fred Beenstock + Assistant Stage Manager – The Playhouse, Sheffield Repertory Theatre (see also two entries in 1952).

The Indifferent Shepherd (11th July 1949) – Assistant Stage Manager – The Playhouse, Sheffield Repertory Theatre.

Present Laughter (27th June 1949) – Fred + Assistant Stage Manager – The Playhouse, Sheffield Repertory Theatre.

A Month in the Country (13th June 1949) – Assistant Stage Manager – The Playhouse, Sheffield Repertory Theatre.

Trouble in the House (30th May 1949) – Assistant Stage Manager – The Playhouse, Sheffield Repertory Theatre.

Better to Have Loved (16th May 1949) – Assistant Stage Manager – The Playhouse, Sheffield Repertory Theatre.

Dr. Angelus (2nd May 1949) – Dr George Johnson + Assistant Stage Manager – The Playhouse, Sheffield Repertory Theatre.

Miranda (18th April 1949) – Assistant Stage Manager – The Playhouse, Sheffield Repertory Theatre.

The Doctor's Dilemma (4th April 1949) – Redpenny + Mr. Danby + Assistant Stage Manager – The Playhouse, Sheffield Repertory Theatre.

The Linden Tree (21st March 1949) – Assistant Stage Manager – The Playhouse, Sheffield Repertory Theatre.

The Blind Goddess (7th March 1949) – Butler + Assistant Stage Manager – The Playhouse, Sheffield Repertory Theatre.

The White Sheep (21st February 1949) – Assistant Stage Manager – The Playhouse, Sheffield Repertory Theatre.

Twelfth Night (24th January 1949) – Sea Captain, friend to Viola + First Officer + Assistant Stage Manager – The Playhouse, Sheffield Repertory Theatre.

1948

Toad of Toad Hall (27th December 1948) – Chief Ferret + Gaoler + Assistant Stage Manager – The Playhouse, Sheffield Repertory Theatre.

Mr. Bolfrey (6th December 1948) – ? – The Playhouse, Sheffield Repertory Theatre (the Sheffield Theatre history lists for 6th December Mr. Bolfrey and Home and Beauty and so one listing must be an error. Therefore, for Home and Beauty the date 6th September is used here, as it appears as such in other sources. In any event, it is unconfirmed as to whether McGoohan ever appeared in Mr. Bolfrey, whatever the date).

The Far-Off Hills (22nd November 1948) – Assistant Stage Manager – The Playhouse, Sheffield Repertory Theatre.

The Cherry Orchard (8th November 1948) – A Tramp + one "Guest" in group scene + Assistant Stage Manager – Sheffield Repertory Theatre (see also Bristol Old Vic, 1953)

Fools Rush In (18th October 1948) Assistant Stage Manager – The Playhouse, Sheffield Repertory Theatre.

The Hasty Heart (4th October 1948) – Blossom – The Playhouse, Sheffield Repertory Theatre.

The Guinea Pig (20th September 1948) – ? – The Playhouse, Sheffield Repertory Theatre.

Home and Beauty (6th September 1948) – Clarence – The Playhouse, Sheffield Repertory Theatre (the Sheffield Theatre history lists for 6th December Mr. Bolfrey and Home and Beauty and so one listing must be an error. Therefore, for Home and Beauty the date 6th September is used here, as it appears as such in other sources).

You Can't Take It With You (26th July 1948) – Donald – The Playhouse, Sheffield Repertory Theatre.

Saloon Bar (12th July 1948) – Peter + one of the Four Mayfairites + A Strange Customer – The Playhouse, Sheffield Repertory Theatre.

The Winslow Boy (29th June 1948) – ? – The Playhouse, Sheffield Repertory Theatre.

The Brontes (15th June 1948) – Rev William Weightman – St James Theatre, London (see also previous listing)

The Brontes (31st May 1948) – Rev William Weightman – The Playhouse, Sheffield Repertory Theatre (presented also in London as part of a repertory festival)

For completeness, the below, initial Playhouse presentations from the start of 1948 are included, although McGoohan had only just started working at the theatre. He may have assisted with tasks relating to the plays but no appearance of his name has been found in respect of the casts. The next play above is his first known casting. Similarly, with the next listing after The Brontes, The Winslow Boy may have been presented while McGoohan was away, in London, or elsewhere, with The Brontes.

Grand National Night (10th May 1948) – ? – The Playhouse, Sheffield Repertory Theatre.
Love in Idleness (26th April 1948) – ? – The Playhouse, Sheffield Repertory Theatre.
An Inspector Calls (12th April 1948) – ? – The Playhouse, Sheffield Repertory Theatre.
Blithe Spirit (29th March 1948) – ? – The Playhouse, Sheffield Repertory Theatre.
Power Without Glory (15th March 1948) – ? – The Playhouse, Sheffield Repertory Theatre.
Lady from Edinburgh (1st March 1948) – ? – The Playhouse, Sheffield Repertory Theatre.
The Marquise (16th February 1948) – ? – The Playhouse, Sheffield Repertory Theatre.
Duet for Two Hands (2nd February 1948) – ? – The Playhouse, Sheffield Repertory Theatre.
Julius Caesar (19th January 1948) – ? – The Playhouse, Sheffield Repertory Theatre.

1946-1948
"The Curtain Club" performances
(various venues, see early text in this book)

The Taming of the Shrew (19 -21 February 1948) – Petruchio
Devon and Earth Horatio (17 August 1947) – A Visitor.
The Arrow of Rope Problem (17 August 1947) – Julian Brandon.
Problem in Porcelain (April 24-26 1947) – Julian Force.
Rope (20-22 February 1947) – Wyndham Brandon.
Musical Chairs (31st October-2nd November 1946) – McGoohan was announced as appearing in the cast but did not appear in the programme or reviews. He did not appear in the next Curtain Club production for December 1946 which was an experimental piece of theatre The Arrow of Song by T.B. Morris, boasting an exclusively female cast.

My Lady in Darkness at Rookery Nook (18 August 1946) – The Man Voulain.
Curtains for Two (18 August 1946) – First Man
Rookery Nook (16-18 May 1946) – Gerald Popkiss
The Duke in Darkness (7-9 March 1946) – Voulain

1945 -1948
Youth Club performances

Viceroy Sarah – (1948) – St. Vincent's Youth Club, Sheffield.
A Hundred Years Old – (1947) – St. Vincent's Youth Club, Sheffield.
Quality Street – (1946) – St. Vincent's Youth Club, Sheffield.
The Duke in Darkness – (c. 1945/6) – St. Thomas,' Sheffield.
Milestones – (1945) – St. Vincent's Youth Club, Sheffield.
Pride and Prejudice – (1945) – St. Vincent's Youth Club, Sheffield.
The Thread of Scarlet – (c.1945) – St. Vincent's Youth Club, Sheffield.

INTERVIEWS ON TELEVISION AND RADIO, PLUS OTHER RADIO

Alain Carrazé (1997) – a live telephone interview filmed for French TV with McGoohan (only his voice was heard) and included on the French "Prisoner" DVD set (2000).

BBC World Service (1996) – radio interview with McGoohan speaking from his California home for six minutes in the programme "Outlook," repeated the following day on BBC Radio 4.

The Persuader – The TV Times of Lord Lew Grade (1994) – a documentary and interview of Grade, with guest appearances including McGoohan (part of retrospective TV evening called "ATV Night").

Simon Bates Show (1990) – a Radio One McGoohan interview at time of the actor's UK Motor Show visit, to collect a replica "Prisoner" sportscar.

Radio Interview (1985) – regarding the death of Orson Welles on US National Public Radio.

The Today Show (1985) – a McGoohan TV interview at the time of his stage play "Pack of Lies" (there were also other related interviews at this time in the USA and Canada).

The L.A. Tape (1983) – McGoohan's own produced "Prisoner" interview and documentary, with additional quirky scenes, which has never been screened.

Six into One: The Prisoner File (1983; screened 1984) – a documentary about "The Prisoner," with the participation of appreciation society members, in which McGoohan was interviewed.

Greatest Hits of 1968 (1982; screened 1983) – a nostalgia show, with McGoohan interviewed by Mike Smith, with "Prisoner" appreciation society members present, using a mock-up "Village" set, (filmed while the actor was in the UK making the TV movie "Jamaica Inn").

Prisoner Appreciation Society interview (1979) – recorded while McGoohan was in Ireland filming "The Hard Way" (later distributed as an audio tape cassette and subsequently sold as a compact disc, against McGoohan's wishes – see page 218.)

Warner Troyer (March, 1977) – TV Ontario, a public television network TV interview with McGoohan, mainly regarding "The Prisoner."

Farewell Companions (23rd March, 1956) – BBC Radio – on the life of the Irish rebel Robert Emmet (recorded 11th August 1955 – see main text for brief details).

Saturday Night Theatre (early 1950s) – Sheffield Playhouse productions broadcast as excerpts, with McGoohan's voice being heard (unconfirmed, but reported by sources).

SCREEN AND STAGE AWARDS AND SIMILAR

This loose grouping of awards, presentations and premiere screenings includes productions with which McGoohan was involved (shown in italics if he did not receive an award personally., Not all of the productions upon which the actor worked are listed, but some significant ones are included.

Best Classic Fiction (September 2002) category of the Libertarian Futurist Society's Prometheus Awards – Patrick McGoohan won for his "Prisoner" TV series.

Academy Award (1995) for the film "Braveheart" for Best Picture and Best Director for Mel Gibson.

Award (1993) jointly given by ITC and Six of One, "The Prisoner" Appreciation Society, in London being a silver plaque with penny farthing bicycle design plus inscription relating to the excellence and longevity of the series.

Emmy (1990) for Outstanding Guest Actor in a Drama Series as Oscar Finch in "Columbo" episode "Agenda For Murder."

Motor Show (1990) – National Exhibition Centre, Birmingham – McGoohan attended to collect a replica "Prisoner" sports car, awarded to him by Caterham Cars. Each model had a facsimile signed plaque and McGoohan's limited edition car was number 6.

"A Pack of Lies," nominated for the Drama Desk Award for an Outstanding Actor in a Play.

New York Television Festival (1983) Drama Award for the film "Jamaica Inn."

Royal Premiere (1976) of "Silver Streak" at Odeon Cinema, London, with Queen Elizabeth, the Queen Mother, attended by McGoohan and other stars of the film.

Emmy (1975) for Outstanding Single Performance by a Supporting Actor in a Comedy or Drama Series as Colonel Lyle C. Rumford in the Columbo episode "By Dawn's Early Light."

Mary Queens of Scots (1971) – nominated for five Academy Awards.

Fall Out (1969) – nominated for the science fiction Hugo award for Dramatic Presentation – the eligibility year being 1968.

Danger Man award (1967) for The Best Produced TV Programme from the Hollywood Screen Producers Guild (this was before "The Prisoner" had aired).

Award (1962) for Best Film of 1962 for "The Quare Fellow" from the British Producers' Association.

Award (1959) for Best British Theatre Actor as Brand from the London Drama Critics.

Award (1959) for Television Actor Of the Year as Jack 'Pal' Smurch in "The Greatest Man In The World" from The Guild Of Television Producers and Directors.

Cannes Film Festival (1957) McGoohan took part in the Parade of Stars.

Beau Brummel Award (?year) as best-dressed man in Britain (unconfirmed).

Personality of the Year Award (?year) as the most popular actor (unconfirmed).

OTHER FILMS, TELEVISION AND THEATRE PROJECTS
(listed in some places, but which remain unconfirmed, incorrect, or were never produced, or released)

Unconfirmed stage entries are in italics in the theatrical listings, elsewhere in this appendix. The listings below are brief, as they are more fully covered in the main text and can simply be found using this book's index. There were also documentary projects, around 1970, upon which McGoohan worked with actor and colleague Kenneth Griffith, covered in this book's main text. Also listed below are planned remakes of, or sequels to, The Prisoner, as McGoohan's involvement was often announced and the actor said he had written at least one script. He also reportedly turned down offered roles such as James Bond, or The Saint, but no scripts were considered. In addition, the actor referred in interviews to screenplays, scripts, or novels, written, or being written, by him: Escape, Century 22, Oasis, Prisoners, Stop and a sequel to The Prisoner. Finally, of course McGoohan appeared in a number of trailers, made for the movies in which he appeared over many years. There were also trailers produced for The Prisoner, being generic ones for the series, plus individual ones for episodes, although these were not screened in Britain (but found their way onto DVDs).

Moby Dick Rehearsed (2007) – new proposed film, possibly involving McGoohan.
The Prisoner remake/sequel (2006/7) – planned movie, Christopher Nolan directing.
The Prisoner remake/sequel (2005/6/7) – planned mini-series.
Illumination (2004 onwards) – see main text.
The Prisoner remake/sequel (2003) – planned movie, Simon West directing.
Harry Potter films (2001 onwards) – reportedly offered role of Dumbledore.
Lord of the Rings (2001) – reportedly offered a role.
Mission Impossible II (2000) – reportedly offered a role.
Bedlam (1996) – possibly "Hysteria," the same year.
The Prisoner remake/sequel (later 1990s) – planned movie, Mel Gibson named.

The Prisoner remake/sequel (1993) – planned movie, with Steven Spielberg's name linked.

Babylon 5 (1990s) – script offered to McGoohan.

The Prisoner remake/sequel (1987) – Leland Rogers' "The Edge of Within" script, in collaboration with ITC.

The Prisoner remake/sequel (1980s) – CBS-TV production planned.

The L.A. Tape (1983) – McGoohan's own film, which remains unscreened.

The Last Enemy (1980s) – work reportedly started on this drama.

Flash Gordon (1980) – a role reportedly offered to McGoohan.

Superman (1978) – Jor-El role reportedly offered to McGoohan.

Dune (late 1970s) – a movie did appear later, in 1984.

Unknown title (late 1970s) – proposed film of a man building a log cabin between Manhattan skyscrapers.

Twinkle, Twinkle, "Killer" Kane (1970s) – became the movie "The Ninth Configuration" (1980).

'Chickens' (c. 1979) – McGoohan planned a 150mm high speed camera filming of thousands of chickens hatching and river trout on his Montana land.

Documentaries (1979) – In a report at the time it was said that McGoohan often joined partners in a small film company to make documentaries.

Rafferty (1977) – series episode "The Outcast," listed by some sources as directed by McGoohan, but there is no story of this title.

Trilogy of Terror (1975) – 1975 US TV movie, confused with Journey into Darkness (1968).

Porgi l'altra guancia (1974); aka Turn the Other Cheek, which may have been confused with Un Genio, Due Compari E Un Pollo (1975).

Healing Hands (1972) – chiropractic movie not produced.

Isabella of Spain (1971); aka Isabel de España – McGoohan's supposed part being Archbishop of Toledo and with Glenda Jackson in the lead role.

Vagabond (c. 1970) – see main text.

When Trumpets Call (c. 1970) – see main text

Mercenary movie (c. 1970) – see main text – possibly to be called The Soldier.

Black Jack (c.1970) – see main text

Brand (c.1970) – planned movie by McGoohan, with proposed Norwegian locations.

Tai Pan (c. 1970) – no film of this title was produced until 1986 (but a TV movie with Richard Chamberlain apparently was made).

Kelly's Heroes (1970) – McGoohan was reportedly offered a role.

Butch Cassidy and the Sundance Kid (1969) – McGoohan was reportedly offered the role taken by Robert Redford.

William the Conqueror (c. 1968) – McGoohan was reportedly asked to direct this movie, but no record of a completed film can be found.

Prudence and the Pill (1968) – McGoohan turned down the offer of a role.

The Prisoner Press Conference (1967) – the event was apparently filmed, but no footage has been screened or found.

The Prisoner (1967/8) – the pilot episode's working title was "The Arrival", said to be originally up to ninety minutes. Several other scripts, ideas, or proposals, were not taken further (see also Chapter Five):

"The Outsider" by Morris Farhi – Number Six discovers a crashed plane and locates the pilot. Concealing the man, the prisoner endeavours to convince the Village that the pilot died, leaving Number Six free to form an escape plan. The missing plane and the man lead to a search and rescue operation and the prisoner tries to make contact with those looking for the pilot. Eventually, despite an apparent escape, Number Six finds himself back in the Village and the pilot turns out to have been an agent of Number Two, engaging in an exercise simply to break the will of the principal inmate.

"Don't Get Yourself Killed" by Gerald Kelsey – in a plot similar to that used in "The General" the Villagers are undergoing education sessions. Meanwhile Number Six meets with members of an escape committee, but finds to his surprise that one of their achievements has been to locate a reserve of gold. With some double dealing and a botched escape attempt, the twist in the tail is that the haul was only worthless "Fool's Gold".

"Ticket to Eternity" by Eric Mival (music editor) – an attempt is made to persuade Number Six that he has travelled back in time and found a disused and ruined Village. A diary purporting to be his suggests that the prisoner accepted an offer of 'eternal life' and a chance to meet Number One. Number Six is expected to reveal his resignation secret, if he believes what happened 'in the past'. Naturally our hero becomes suspicious and discovers the ruse.

"Friend or Foe" by Eric Mival – a black activist with whom Number Six forms an alliance is killed by the Village guardian. When the deceased appears to return, claiming that he staged his own death, an escape takes place, with the resurrected inmate and Number Six reaching London. Later the main character pulls off a mask from the face of the returning friend, revealing him to be fake – and white, to boot. Strangely, a similar ending was employed by McGoohan in the final episode "Fall Out", in which a mask is removed from a mystery figure, revealing the true identity of Number One.

(Contributor unknown) – during a visit by a travelling circus, Number Six disappears from inside a magician's box.

(Contributor unknown) – a mystery prisoner turns out to be the late President Kennedy, still alive.

Tales of the Vikings (1960) (aka The Vikings) – some Internet sources place McGoohan in the cast.

The Flying Carpet (1960) – listed by a source as narrated by McGoohan.

Terminus Number One (1959) – confused with Terminus (1955)

Rendezvous (1957) – a possible third appearance, in addition to two known ones.

The Little World (1957) – McGoohan is not listed as appearing in this BBC play.

The Third Miracle (1957) – McGoohan is not listed as appearing in this BBC play.

The Vise (1954/5/6) – a possible third appearance, in addition to two known ones.

Moby Dick (1955) – sixteen millimetre film by Orson Welles, or a television production.

The Whiteoak Chronicles (1954) – BBC presentation, listed by some sources as involving McGoohan.

TV PHOTO ROLES – in order of appearance on pages 293 - 295

Oliver Quayle, Oscar Finch, Eric Prince, George Bernard Shaw, Dr. Felix Neumann, Chief Magistrate, Joss Merlyn, John Connor, Dr. Sid Rafferty, Nicholas Fouquet, Nelson Brenner, Col. Lyle C. Rumford, Host of *Journey into Darkness*, The Interrogator (1963 play *The Prisoner*), Serjeant Musgrave, Nicolai Soloviov, Pastor Brand, Jack 'Pal' Smurch, James Coogan

APPENDIX TWO

EPISODE GUIDES TO RAFFERTY, COLUMBO, THE PRISONER AND DANGER MAN, WITH ORIGINAL UK AND US BROADCAST DATES

RAFFERTY – pilot + 12 x 50 minute episodes
US broadcast dates: 5th September, 1977 to 28th November 1977

Pilot:

Ex-Army doctor Sidney Rafferty, a widower, witnesses a stabbing on a bus and orders the driver straight to the hospital. Later, back at his surgery, he tends to a full waiting room of patients. At the end of the day, Rafferty is back in his single person's apartment, after a day of drama.

Episode 1: Brothers and Sons

Rafferty seeks a missing mother, who has left her children behind. His mission is as social as it is medical, to reunite the offspring with their parents.

Episode 2: A Point of View

A woman is violated in the hospital underground car park. Herself a doctor, she wants to keep her traumatic experience a secret. Meanwhile, after Rafferty has helped a young blind woman, he establishes that the other doctor's attacker was one of her psychiatric patients.

Episode 3: The Narrow Thread

A multi-plot episode has a pregnant air hostess, a young deaf boy and an elderly man confined to a wheelchair. Rafferty helps these patients and their stories provide the background.

Episode 4: The Cutting Edge

A virtuoso violinist has a problem with his hand, as does a post-operative girl who has been given cocaine. Rafferty has to perform surgery, help a nurse who has a problem and keep at bay a female lawyer who is bringing a lawsuit against him and the hospital.

Episode 5: Death out of a Blue Sky

A light aircraft crash kills an experienced pilot and Rafferty talks to some old folk's home residents who witnessed the incident. The doctor has to help decide where the pilot committed suicide or not.

Episode 6: The Price of Pain

A driver overtakes Rafferty's car and causes a crash down a hillside. The doctor goes to the aid of an unconscious young woman where elsewhere a young woman, clothes torn, is found in distress in a wooded area.

Rafferty deals with a police investigation, news reporters and his own secretary wanting to wine and dine him.

Episode 7: Walking Wounded

A skyborne hang glider has an accident and a veteran cop is suffering from back pain. Rafferty also deals with an anorexia case by removing the girl's privileges unless she eats.

Episode 8: The Burning Man

In a forest fire, a man is severely ill and has to deal with some tricky situations involving a Native American reservation, with inadequate resources.

Episode 9: The Wild Child (Director: Patrick McGoohan)

In an episode directed by McGoohan, Rafferty is on a bus which knocks over a young girl. Staying with his patient he has to remain in a small town and finds that he is for various reasons unable to leave. Hereditary illness, religious practices and a closed community are amongst his problems.

Episode 10: The Epidemic

A polio epidemic requires Rafferty to formulate a disaster plan. A local burger van is responsible for an outbreak of botulism and Rafferty is as much medical detective as he is doctor.

Episode 11: Will to Live

Rafferty goes to the aid of his secretary who is dying but he favours a homeopathic/holistic approach. He takes her home, stops her medication and she regains her health.

Episode 12: No Yesterday and No Tomorrow

A driver causes a crash and is found collapsed at the steering wheel. McGoohan is mainly absent from the story, while his surgery partner deals with the medical problems of the day. The injured driver is a fugitive from gangsters and has to be protected at the hospital.

COLUMBO – various seasons from 1968 pilot to 2003

By Dawn's Early Light (episode 28 in the 4th season, 1974/75; US broadcast date 27th October, 1974)

McGoohan played (and won an Emmy for his role) Colonel Lyle C. Rumford, the proud commandant of a military academy. He is incensed that the owner of the property wants to turn it into a college and plans a murder with a backfiring cannon.

Identity Crisis (episode 34 in the 5th season, 1975/76; directed by McGoohan; US broadcast date 2nd November, 1975)

McGoohan plays Nelson Brenner, a wily secret agent working for a covert government organisation.

Last Salute to the Commodore (episode 37 in the 5th season,1975/6; directed by McGoohan; US broadcast date 2nd May, 1976)

The Commodore vanishes at sea at the hands of a greedy family member. This was the first Columbo 'whodunnit'" where the murderer is revealed at the end of the episode, although McGoohan does not appear.

Agenda for Murder (episode 50 in the 9th season, 1990; directed by McGoohan; US broadcast date 10th February, 1990)

McGoohan plays Oscar Finch (and won an Emmy for his role), a lawyer who uses illegal and underhand methods to get his clients acquitted. Finch dispatches a fellow conspirator to make it look like a suicide.

Ashes to Ashes (TV special; directed by McGoohan; US broadcast date 8th October, 1998)

McGoohan appears as Eric Prince (his daughter Catherine also appears in the episode). A Hollywood gossip reporter has disappeared and mortician McGoohan puts to good use his cremation furnace.

Murder with Too Many Notes (TV special marking the series' 25th anniversary; directed by McGoohan, who also co-wrote the teleplay; US broadcast date 12th March, 2001)

A Hollywood film composer and conductor murders a musician of whom he is jealous. (McGoohan does not appear, but his daughter Anne is seen in the episode).

THE PRISONER – 17 x 50 minute episodes
UK broadcast dates: 29th September, 1967 to 1st February, 1968

1. Arrival
After resigning from a top level position, a man returns to his London home to pack for a holiday. He is gassed and wakes up in an unusual village, from which there is no escape. Strange characters, with numbers instead of names want to find out why he resigned.

2. The Chimes of Big Ben
The man is now referred to as Number Six and finds he has a new next-door neighbour, Nadia. She tells him that the Village is situated on the Baltic and they plan an escape.

3. A. B. and C. (original working titles: 1, 2 and 3, or Play in three Acts)
The Village leader, Number Two, uses a new wonder drug to tap into Number Six's dreams. The purpose of the exercise is to see to whom Number Six was selling out. The unconscious man is able to fight back, from within his own slumber.

4. Free for All (Writer – as Paddy Fitz – and Director: Patrick McGoohan)
It is election time in the Village and a new Number Two needs to be elected. Number Six is persuaded to stand. He runs his election campaign hoping to discover who is the entity behind the Village, Number One.

5. The Schizoid Man
Number Six awakes in a different Village apartment, with a new appearance and unfamiliar habits. He is referred to as Number Twelve and an identical double is used to impersonate him.

6. The General
"Speedlearn" is a subliminal process for educating the population of the Village, developed by a Professor with the aid of an unseen "General." Number Six intends to destroy the "General," to prevent a false learning process being used on citizens.

7. Many Happy Returns (Director: Patrick McGoohan – as Joseph Serf)
Number Six finds the Village deserted and realises that he has an opportunity to escape. He builds a raft and sets sail, eventually reaching a coast somewhere. He discovers that the place is known to him, but will he end up in the Village once more?

8. Dance of the Dead
Number Six finds a dead man washed up on the Village beach. He later sets it afloat with a rescue note, although he is spotted doing this. Later he has to stand trial, in front of carnival characters.

9. Checkmate (original title: The Queen's Pawn)
Number Six takes the position of Queen's Pawn in a human game of chess. Number Two brainwashes the Queen to fall in love with Number Six and track's the prisoner's movements with a transmitter in her locket. Number Six plans an escape by sea, but misjudges those who are helping him.

10. Hammer into Anvil
When a young woman is driven to suicide by Number Two, Number Six avenges her death by making Number Two believe that he is an agent sent to report on the Village leader's instability.

11. It's Your Funeral
The Prisoner learns of an assassination plot and warns Number Two. However, the intended target is not who Number Six first thought was going to be killed and there is a secondary plan which will discredit the Prisoner.

12. A Change of Mind (Director: Patrick McGoohan – as Joseph Serf)
Number Six is declared "Unmutual" by the Village and must undergo "Instant Social Conversion." He manages to get the Village doctor on his side and with her help he has a counter plan.

13. Do Not Forsake Me Oh My Darling (original title: Face Unknown)

Number Six's mind is transformed into another man, who is sent back to the Prisoner's London home. From here, his mission is to locate a Professor Seltzman, who can undo the mind swap.

14. Living in Harmony

Number Six finds himself in a western town called "Harmony." As the Sheriff, he refuses to use a gun until a killing forces him to carry one. The fantasy is revealed after some dramatic events.

15. The Girl Who Was Death

A spoof spy story presents Number Six being pursued by a woman in white. She is the daughter of a crazed scientist who wants to destroy London.

16. Once upon a Time (Writer and Director: Patrick McGoohan; original title Degree Absolute)

 Number Two decides the only way to obtain information from Number Six is by "Degree Absolute." Who out of the two will survive this ultimate test and finally meet Number One?

17. Fall Out (Writer and Director: Patrick McGoohan)

An underground assembly puts on trial some rebellious Village characters and also salutes the former Number Six, who has emerged victorious from his most recent ordeal. Soon he will be back in London, but will he be free of the Village?

*There were two early edits of the first two episodes, which came to be known years later as The 'alternative' Arrival and The Chimes of Big Ben (see descriptions in the main text).

DANGER MAN – fourth series of 2 x 50 min episodes
UK broadcast dates: 5th January, 1968 to 12th January, 1968

1. Koroshi

A young Japanese woman dies by inhaling gas from an artificial flower before she can report the existence of a Japanese death cult to her British contact. Drake infiltrates the cult as a journalist reporting on a floral festival.

2. Shinda Shima

Drake gets inside the cult's headquarters posing as an electronics expert.

(Note: the two episodes were later combined as a 'feature length movie,' called Koroshi).

DANGER MAN – third series of 13 x 50 min episodes
UK broadcast dates: 9th December 1965 to 7th April 1966

1. To Our Best Friend (Director: Patrick McGoohan)

Drake heads to Baghdad to clear the name of a spy suspected of leaking secrets.

2. The Man on the Beach

A murdered contact complicates Drake's mission in Jamaica.

3. Say It with Flowers

 In Switzerland Drake must determine if an enemy agent is really dead.

4. The Man Who Wouldn't Talk

Drake must free a captured British spymaster before he sells his secrets.

5. Someone Is Liable to Get Hurt

A mysterious woman, an ancient prison cell and a gun-runner – a recipe for disaster.

6. Dangerous Secret

Drake must clean up after the government bungles an attempt to silence a young scientist.

7. I Can Only Offer You Sherry

Drake investigates an unlikely spy.

8. The Hunting Party

A security leak points to a wealthy lord.

9. Two Birds with One Bullet

A political party plans to assassinate their own candidate.

10. I Am Afraid You Have the Wrong Number

Drake pursues a rogue agent.

11. The Man with the Foot

Drake drives to Spain for a well-earned holiday. But instead of sun and relaxation, he is greeted by miserable weather and a determined enemy agent.

12. The Paper Chase (Director: Patrick McGoohan)

Secret documents fall into the wrong hands.

13. Not So Jolly Roger

Drake works as a disc jockey at a pirate radio station.

DANGER MAN – second series of 32 x 50 min episodes
UK broadcast dates: 13th October 1964 to 2nd December, 1965

1. Yesterday's Enemies

Drake travels to Beirut to untangle a web of Middle Eastern espionage

2. The Professionals

Drake is targeted by a Czech spymaster who uses a beautiful young woman to ensnare his enemies.

3. Colony Three

Posing as a clerk, Drake infiltrates a strange spy school in this very 'prisoneresque' episode of Danger Man.

4. The Galloping Major

Sent to Africa to monitor an election, Drake discovers a danger far more devious than ballot-stuffing.

5. Fair Exchange

John Drake must follow an avenging agent, bent on murderous revenge.

6. Fish on the Hook

In Egypt, Drake must uncover the identity of, and save, the mastermind behind the Controller – or the entire Middle Eastern British spy network will be compromised.

7. The Colonel's Daughter

The death of a butterfly collector's assistant in India opens an unlikely investigation.

8. The Battle of the Cameras

Agent John Drake becomes a gambler in the South of France to infiltrate the mysterious world of international secrets for sale.

9. No Marks for Servility

In a Roman villa, Drake becomes an unwilling manservant to an unscrupulous extortionist.

10. A Man to be Trusted

Drake is sent to the Caribbean to investigate a murder and see if the local intelligence contact can be relied on.

11. Don't Nail Him Yet

Drake poses as a put-upon schoolteacher to win the confidence of a suspected spy.

12. A Date with Doris

Drake flies into Havana using the cover of a journalist, there to interview one of the heroes of the revolution, Joaquin Paratore. His real purpose is to rescue another agent posing as a journalist who has been framed for the murder of a famous actress.

13. That's Two of Us Sorry
Fingerprints left at the scene of a robbery in Scotland appear to belong to an agent whose been dead twenty years.

14. Such Men Are Dangerous
Posing as an ex-convict, Drake is recruited by an ultra-right wing organisation that trains assassins to eliminate world leaders.

15. Whatever Happened to George Foster?
Drake must stop a wealthy British industrialist who is subverting a small nation to his own ends.

16. A Room in the Basement
Embassy walls and diplomatic immunity hide the kidnapped colleague of agent John Drake. Drake comes to the rescue when the man's wife approaches him for help.

17. The Affair at Castelevara
Drake and his American counterparts have competing plans to prevent the execution of a former Central American Revolutionary.

18. The Ubiquitous Mr. Lovegrove
After a car crash, Drake finds himself enmeshed in a strange plot surrounding a casino.

19. It's Up to the Lady
Drake follows a couple on the run to Greece to prevent them from defecting.

20. Have a Glass of Wine
In France's wine country, Drake, a Russian agent and a local spy compete for control of a woman bearing military secrets.

21. The Mirror's New
A British diplomat in Paris goes missing for a day, but can't seem to remember what happened.

22. Parallel Lines Sometimes Meet
Drake trails two scientists to the West Indies.

23. You Are Not in Any Trouble, Are You?
To topple an Italian murder-for-hire ring, Drake puts out a hit on himself.

24. The Black Book
Drake goes undercover to discover who is blackmailing a general's brother.

25. A Very Dangerous Game
Disguised as a defecting music teacher, Drake infiltrates a spy ring in Hong Kong, and is requested by the Chinese to spy on British Intelligence.

26. Sting in the Tail
Drake tries to get at an assassin by tailing the killer's mistress.

27. English Lady Takes Lodgers
Investigating a security link in Spain, Drake finds himself enmeshed in a murderous scheme.

28. Loyalty Always Pays
Did an African defence minister strike a secret deal with the Chinese?

29. The Mercenaries
Drake interferes in a plot to take over an African republic.

30. Judgement Day
Drake finds himself at the mercy of a band of Israeli renegades.

31. The Outcast
Was the murdered girlfriend of a missing sailor selling coded secrets?

32. Are You Going to Be More Permanent?
Who is responsible for the disappearance of agents in Vienna?

DANGER MAN – first series of 39 x 25 min episodes
UK broadcast dates: 11th September, 1960 to 20th January, 1962

1. View from the Villa
John Drake is assigned to investigate the murder of a banker, Frank Delroy. The trail leads Drake to the home of Delroy's lady friend, a small seaside resort, where he recovers five million dollars and solves the murder of Delroy.

2. Time to Kill
John Drake flies to Paris, where his assignment is to find an international killer. He refuses to assassinate the man, but undertakes to retrieve him. The task becomes more difficult when Drake finds himself handcuffed to a young woman, Lisa Orin.

3. Josetta
A blind young woman, Josetta, is the only one who can identify her brother's killer. John Drake has the task of helping her to find and identify the killer.

4. The Blue Veil
John Drake flies to the Arabian desert to investigate stories of slavery and finds himself befriending a Muslim lad and helping a stranded showgirl who believes Drake to be a slave broker.

5. The Lovers
At the request of an old enemy, Drake takes charge of security as the President of Boravia and his wife visit London.

6. The Girl in Pink Pyjamas
When a dazed girl is found wandering along a country lane, dressed only in her pyjamas, Drake discovers a plot to assassinate a Balkan President.

7. Position of Trust
When Drake is shown a photograph of a young girl who is the victim of drugs, he sets out for the Middle East to break up the ring supplying opium. He is aided by an American agent, Sandi Lewis. Together they trace the source of the drugs, with the help of a courageous little man.

8. The Lonely Chair
When the daughter of a wealthy industrialist is kidnapped, Drake impersonates her crippled father in an attempt to save her without having to hand over crucial designs.

9. The Sanctuary
John Drake has to impersonate a prisoner who has just been released after serving a sentence for bombings. His assignment is to infiltrate a group of IRA commandos.

10. An Affair of State
Drake flies to a small Caribbean State to investigate the apparent suicide of an American economics expert, he uncovers a plot to obtain large sums of money, and in return he nearly loses his life.

11. The Key
When someone is leaking information from the American Embassy in Vienna, Drake is called in to investigate when the finger of guilt points to the Ambassador.

12. The Sisters
When a young, beautiful refugee pleads for political asylum, Drake is called in to investigate by his superior, Hardy. When the girl's sister arrives, Drake has a double problem to solve.

13. The Prisoner
Drake's assignment is to find a double for James Carpenter, an American who is confined to the US Embassy in a Caribbean city. Finding the double is only half of the problem. Substituting him under the eyes of the police is the other.

14. The Traitor

Drake travels to Kashmir in Northern India to seek out Noel Goddard, a former executive in the Indian Government, now a traitor. On identifying Drake, Goddard is given the message: 'John Drake. NATO agent. Eliminate.'

15. Colonel Rodriguez

John Drake flies to the Caribbean to aid an American journalist who had been arrested on a spy charge, but before he can effect a rescue is accused of the murder of a young nightclub singer.

16. The Island

John Drake is flying back to the mainland with two prisoners, when his plane crashes in the sea, near a tiny island. On reaching the island Drake finds himself a wanted man as the island's hermit owner believes Drake is an escaped prisoner.

17. Find and Return

Hardy assigns Drake to fly to the Middle East to find Vanessa Stewart, a beautiful girl wanted for espionage. Posing as a Baltic agent, Drake persuades her to accompany him before the British find her. A subplot comments drily on the ethics of espionage.

18. The Girl Who Liked GI's

Drake is assigned to investigate the murder of a young G.I. in Munich. He was last seen in the company of a young German girl, Vicki. Was she involved in the plot? Drake, posing as an American soldier, must find the answer.

19. Name, Date and Place

When several prominent people are killed, there appears to be no connection. But John Drake's investigations uncover a murder ring, which he hires to kill himself.

20. Vacation (Director: Patrick McGoohan)

While vacationing on the Riviera, John Drake recognises a professional assassin. He succeeds in replacing the killer and undertakes an assignment working in the dark, as he has no idea who his victim is.

21. The Conspirators

John Drake's assignment takes him to a small island off the coast of Brittany. He must protect Lady Lindsay, widow of a British diplomat, and her two young sons, from two killers.

22. The Honeymooners

When a Chinese businessman is murdered, a young couple on honeymoon become the prime suspects. John Drake flies out to the Far East to assist them, and finds himself in a dangerous situation.

23. The Gallows Tree

John Drake travels to the Scottish Highlands when the fingerprints of a stolen car belong to a master spy believed to have been killed ten years earlier.

24. The Relaxed Informer

Drake's latest case is to unravel a security leak. The suspect is Ruth Mitchell, an interpreter; but as Drake later discovers, she has been unwittingly made to reveal vital secrets, without her knowledge.

25. The Brothers

A plane crashes off the coast of Sicily and a diplomatic satchel is taken by mountain bandits. John Drake's task is to recover the stolen property, for which he enlists the aid of one bandit's girlfriend.

26. The Journey Ends Halfway

Drake travels to China to investigate the disappearance of an eminent doctor who had been trying to escape the Communist regime.

27. Bury the Dead

NATO agent Tony Costello is killed in a car crash while investigating a case of gun running. John Drake flies to

Sicily to investigate and finds Costello's girl friend who is convinced it was murder. Before the case is solved, Drake discovers that you can bury the dead more than once.

28. Sabotage

When Paul Jason of Jason's Airlines is killed and several of his planes crash, John Drake assumes the identity of a hard drinking pilot to investigate the crash. Drake discovers a case of smuggling and finds himself in a tricky situation.

29. The Contessa

Drake has to travel to Genoa after discovery of cocaine. His mission is to await the docking of a ship which is being used in a drug smuggling operation. Drake himself is drugged at one point.

30. The Leak

Drake joins forces with a European doctor when workers at an African nuclear power plant fall ill.

31. The Trap

Drake travels to Venice to investigate the case of Beth Warren, a cipher expert at the American Embassy in London. She disappeared form her job, and rushed to Venice to be with her boyfriend when his brother was dying. But Drake discovers she is being used for the knowledge she has.

32. The Actor

Drake travels to Hong Kong to investigate the murder of a sound technician working for a radio station. He uncovers a plot where the secret information is being sent out in code over the air, transmitted as part of the station's English lessons.

33. Hired Assassin

Drake poses as a professional assassin in an attempt to prevent the assassination of a South American President. He joins a revolutionary group who are planning to kill the President.

34. The Coyannis Story

John Drake travels to a Balkan country to investigate the misappropriation of funds by a Minister. Drake uncovers the plot. Involving love, politics and revenge.

35. Find and Destroy

A miniature submarine is wrecked off the coast of a South American country. John Drake's assignment from British Intelligence is to blow her up. Disguised as a fisherman, Drake races against time to find the submarine before the agents of a foreign power can.

36. Under the Lake

When twenty five million dollars in forged currency floods the European capitals, John Drake is assigned by U.S. Intelligence to trace the source. The trail leads to an ex-Nazi General staying at a lake-side hotel in the mountains. Drake faces death before he can solve the case and uncover the secret of the lake.

37. The Nurse

Drake travels to the Arabian Desert to rescue the American Consul and his family from terrorists who have assassinated the King. On arrival Drake finds he has additional problems trying to protect a pretty Scots nurse and the baby in her care – the future king.

38. Dead Man Walks

Hardy assigns Drake to investigate when the entire research team working in tropical diseases is killed by mysterious accidents. Drake travels to India, and uncovers clues that one of the scientists may be alive.

39. Deadline

When a wave of terrorism in the African jungle is likely to lead to a mass uprising, The Danger Man takes on the disguise of a 'gun-runner' in an attempt to penetrate the extremist organisation behind it.

APPENDIX THREE

FILM AND TV PRODUCTIONS
DIRECTED BY PATRICK McGOOHAN

DANGER MAN (1960) – Vacation.

DANGER MAN (1964-66) – To Our Best Friend.

DANGER MAN (1964-66) – The Paper Chase.

THE PRISONER (1966/7) – Free For All – and written – under the pseudonym "Paddy Fitz."

THE PRISONER (1966/7) – Many Happy Returns – McGoohan removed the original director Michael Truman and also director Roy Rossotti from A Change of Mind. He then directed the stories himself, using the name Joseph Serf. As well as dismissing director Robert Asher, – although Asher's name is retained in the screen credits of It's Your Funeral – McGoohan also rejected editor Geoffrey Foot's work on Dance of the Dead, see Chapter Five.

THE PRISONER (1967) – A Change of Mind

THE PRISONER (1967) – Once Upon A Time – and written.

THE PRISONER (1967) – Fall Out – and written.

CATCH MY SOUL (1974) – Jack Good's stage musical, the only movie McGoohan directed.

COLUMBO (1975/6) – Identity Crisis.

COLUMBO (1975/6) – Last Salute to the Commodore.

RAFFERTY (1977) – The Wild Child (some sources incorrectly list The Outcast as directed by McGoohan. There is no Rafferty episode of that name, but there is one in The Adventures of Sir Lancelot (1956) and Danger Man, although neither was directed by McGoohan).

THE L.A. TAPE (1983) – McGoohan's personal film about The Prisoner.

COLUMBO (1990) – Agenda for Murder.

COLUMBO (1998) – Ashes to Ashes.

COLUMBO (1999) – Murder with Too Many Notes.

APPENDIX FOUR

ORDER OF EPISODES OF THE PRISONER

There has always been much debate about the correct screening order of episodes of *The Prisoner*. It is not the purpose of this book to discuss the arguments in favour or against any particular order. However, it is useful to present a table below showing the known order of episodes within four early categories, discussed below and entered at the head of the table's columns.

Early publicity stills were labelled with letters and numbers, for example in the case of the episode *Free for All*, P2 or E2. This denoted that it was the second episode made in Portmeirion and was also classed as the second episode. In fact, *Free for All* was being filmed alongside the first episode *Arrival*, at the start of September, 1966, but *Arrival* was still in production in Portmeirion when shooting on the episode *The Chimes of Big Ben* started in North Wales at the end of September. During the middle of that month, the episode *The Queen's Pawn* – later to become known as *Checkmate* – was being made, alongside the episode *Dance of the Dead*. In the following spring there followed some further Portmeirion shooting on *Many Happy Returns* and *Hammer into Anvil*, completing the main North Wales location work for McGoohan. The raft escape filming was done off the Abersoch coast, about twenty miles away.

It can therefore be seen that there was a shooting order of 'convenience', depending on which actors, extras or props were present and which scenes had to be filmed and thus how some scenes from later episodes came first. The pattern left on the lawn by removal of the giant *Checkmate* chessboard squares is visible as two shades of grass, when the opening sequence of *The Prisoner*, *Arrival*, is viewed. The first column of the below table shows the order in which episodes were produced back at the studio at MGM in Borehamwood, from October 1966 through to the end of 1967. The next column shows the "Catalogue" or "Warehouse" order. The adjacent column is the ITC "Story Information" book order. Considering that the photographs were for publicity purposes, as was the ITC book, it is odd that they do not adopt the same numbered order. Finally, the British 'standard' screening order appears in the end column and this, once again, is different from the other orders.

For some screenings in the UK and in some other countries, a different order of episodes was adopted, for example with *Many Happy Returns* being placed straight after *Arrival*. It can be argued that the order of episodes in the main is not vital, as they are all self-contained and it has often been said that as long as *Arrival* comes first, with *Once Upon A Time* and *Fall Out* at the other end, the episodes in the middle can be arranged to one's own preference. It must also be borne in mind that although McGoohan and others claim that the series was supposed to stop after thirteen episodes and that they were persuaded to do four more, in fact early publicity claimed that there were going to be twenty six episodes. Other ITC series at that time even used to have as many as thirty episodes in a series – some press reports claimed that *The Prisoner* originally was to have the same number – examples being *Man in a Suitcase* and *The Champions*.

Strangely, *Fall Out* was not given the number seventeen in the catalogue order but this numbering was applied to *The Girl Who Was Death*. The reason for this might be that the episode was being considered as a possible closer for the series – whether or not there was to be a later series – and *The Girl* was initially planned as a two hour 'special'. As seen in the main text of this book, scriptwriter Terence Feely recalled the idea for the two hour special, but funding became a factor and, apparently, the ATV boss Lew Grade would not finance the whole planned production. Consequently several scenes which had been prepared in outline were not filmed, including a chase round a maze.

EPISODES ORDER COMPARISON LISTS

Production order	ITC 'Catalogue' or 'Warehouse' order	ITC "Story Information"	British 'standard' screening order
Arrival location September, 1966	1	Arrival	Arrival
Free Sept, 1966	2	Returns	Chimes
Checkmate studio October, 1966		ABC	ABC
Dance	3 to 7: precise catalogue order of *Checkmate*, *Dance*, *Chimes*, *Once* and *Schizoid* is not known	Schizoid	Free
Chimes		Free	Schizoid
Once December		Check	General
Schizoid Christmas/ New Year 1967		Chimes	Returns
Funeral mid January	8	General	Dance
Change end January	9	Funeral	Checkmate
ABC February	10	Hammer	Hammer
General early March	11	Change	Funeral
Hammer	12	Dance	Change
Returns London scenes April	13	Girl	Forsake
Forsake August	No episode listed as number 14 found	Harmony	Harmony
Harmony September	15	Forsake	Girl
Girl October	*Harmony* 16 reason unknown	Once	Once
Fall up to end 1967	*Girl* 17 reason unknown	Fall	Fall

APPENDIX FIVE

QUESTIONNAIRE COMPLETED BY
PATRICK McGOOHAN EARLY 1960s

FULL LEGAL NAME: Patrick McGoohan.

PLACE OF BIRTH: New York. U.S.A.   **DATE OF BIRTH:** 19. 3. 28.

HEIGHT & WEIGHT: 6' 2"   **COLORING: HAIR:** Auburn **EYES:** Blue
13stone 7 lb (189 lbs)

MARRIED OR SINGLE: Married.   **IF MARRIED, TO WHOM:** Joan Drummond
(actress)

DO YOU HAVE ANY CHILDREN: (STATE NAMES & AGES)
Catherine, Anne, One on the way.

ARE YOU AN AMERICAN CITIZEN: (IF NOT WHAT COUNTRY)
British subject.

WHERE DID YOU ATTEND SCHOOL: (COLLEGE TOO?)
Ratcliffe College, Leicester.

MOVIES YOU'VE APPEARED IN: (PART YOU PLAYED TOO, PLEASE)
Hell Drivers
Zarak
I Am A Camera
The Gypsy and the Gentleman
High Tide At Noon
Nor The Moon By Night.

PLAYS YOU'VE APPEARED IN:
About 300
(West End) Serious Charge — Moby Dick — Orson
Welles Version — King For Cutty — Jason's
Death — Brand — Hobson's Choice.

FAVORITE ROLE TO DATE:

WHICH DO YOU PREFER—STAGE, SCREEN OR TV:
All of 'em — well mixed.

ANY PARTICULAR TYPE OF ROLE YOU'D LIKE TO PLAY:
Good ones.

IS THERE ANYBODY YOU'D LIKE TO PLAY OPPOSITE:
Good actresses. Any of 'em

WHAT WOULD YOU DO IF YOU WEREN'T AN ACTOR:
No idea

DO YOU, OR SOMEBODY ELSE KEEP A SCRAPBOOK ON YOUR CAREER:

DO YOU DANCE: (WHAT KIND.
YES COSSACK.

HAVE YOU EVER SEEN A "PLAYBACK" OR "REPEAT" OF ANY SHOWS, ETC.
YOU'VE EVER APPEARED IN: YOUR REACTION:
YES   (AM ALLOWED THIS)

HOW CAN A FAN HELP YOU THE MOST:
KEEPING OUT OF THE WAY AND
TELLING EVERYBODY ELSE

DID YOU COME FROM A LARGE FAMILY:
YES

WHAT WAS YOUR FIRST AMBITION:
TO WALK

HOW DO YOU LEARN YOUR LINES FOR PLAYS, TV, MOVIES:
SWEAT.

WHAT KIND OF A CAR DO YOU OWN: (COLOR & MAKE)
FIAT STATION WAGON

ARE YOU SUPERSTITIOUS: (ABOUT WHAT)
NO.

WHO HAS BEEN THE GREATEST INFLUENCE ON YOU:
JESUS CHRIST

FAVORITE COLORS:

WHAT CHURCH DO YOU ATTEND:
MY BUSINESS.

HOBBIES:
CHESS, WRITING, ACTING.

WHAT DO YOU LIKE TO DO IN YOUR SPARE TIME:
RELAX

IDEA OF A NICE EVENING OUT:
& STAYING AT HOME

FAVORITE RECORDS - BY WHOM:
NO FAVORITES.

FAVORITE BOOKS & AUTHORS:
READ 'EM ALL.

DO YOU PLAY MUSICAL INSTRUMENT:(WHAT,   DO YOU SING
VIOLIN ?   *WHAT ?*

FAVORITE PASTIME:
WRITING

WHAT IS YOUR WORST FAULT:
YOU TELL ME

YOUR PET PEEVE:
QUESTIONNAIRES.

TYPE OF MUSIC YOU LIKE BEST:
MIX IT

WHO IS YOUR BEST FRIEND IN SHOW BIZ:

FAVORITE TYPE OF FOOD:
EAT EM ALL.

DO YOU HAVE A FAVORITE RESTAURANT:
No.

WHAT SECTION OF THE NEWSPAPER INTERESTS YOU MOST:
EDITORIAL

HOW LONG HAVE YOU BEEN ACTING:
SINCE BIRTH LIKE EVERYONE ELSE

DO YOU THINK THERE IS ANY GOOD TO FAN CLUBS:
DEPENDS ON the fanclub.

DO YOU HAVE ONE:(IF SO, PLEASE GIVE NAME-ADDRESS ETC.)

HOW DO YOU FEEL ABOUT GETTING FAN MAIL:
TIRED.

DO YOU EVER MAKE P.A. TOURS:
Not if I CAN HELP IT.

CAN YOU APPEAR ON "LIVE" TV OTHER THAN YOUR SHOW:
YES

WHAT ROLE HAVE YOU PLAYED THAT HAS BEEN THE HARDEST CHALLENGE:
ONLY ONE LINE !! ALL OF EM

GREATEST THRILL:
LIVING.

GREATEST DISAPPOINTMENT:
LIVING WITH MYSELF.

FAVORITE SPORTS:
RUGBY, SQUASH

WHO DO YOU ENJOY SEEING IN A SHOW:
ANYONE GOOD.

WHERE DID YOU TAKE ACTING LESSONS:
NOWHERE OBNIOVSKY

HOW MANY LANGUAGES DO YOU SPEAK:
ONE BADLY

HOW DID YOU GET STARTED IN SHOW BIZ:
TEABOY IN REPERTORY COMPANY

WHAT IS YOUR FAVORITE CHARITY:
No FAVORITES.

FAVORITE SINGERS & BANDS:

WERE YOU IN THE ARMED FORCES:(WHICH ONE)
No

ARE YOU UNDER CONTRACT TO ANYBODY-FOR HOW LONG:
No

DO YOU HAVE A NICKNAME:(WHAT)
No

FUTURE PLANS:
ANYTHING THAT COMES UP

ANYTHING YOU'D LIKE TO ADD:
No

APPENDIX SIX

ABOUT THE WRITER

Roger Langley has been a principal organiser of Six of One, the appreciation society for *The Prisoner*, for thirty years. As he entered his teens, he was excited by the new UK adventure series, *Danger Man*, starring Patrick McGoohan. By 1967, and having reached the age of majority – in those days twenty one – the writer was captivated by McGoohan's later series, *The Prisoner*. At this time Langley was training as a lawyer. He specialised in criminal defence cases during almost forty years in the law. As well as being a partner in his own law firm for over two decades, Langley began editing and creating fan-based publications arising from *The Prisoner*. Novelisations, non-fiction works, reviews and guides followed, with the writer also being asked to write sleeve notes for CD and DVD sets. Additionally, Langley collaborated on various books, trading cards and *Prisoner*-based scripts, as well as doing research and assisting with publishing, having close contact with companies like ITC, PolyGram, Carlton and Granada, plus the hotel resort of Portmeirion, where *The Prisoner* was filmed. Himself a keen follower of cinema and sixties' genres, Langley sought out amateur cine filmed segments of the 1966 *Prisoner* location shoot in Portmeirion, even finding curios such as three dimensional photographic images taken at the time, to be looked at in 'stereo' in a viewer. As well as giving the occasional lecture, creating websites – including one dedicated to the history of Portmeirion – and writing fiction, the writer also conducted interviews with *Prisoner* actors and wrote humorous sketches for some of them, to be performed at conventions. Langley lives in East Anglia, with his wife Karen – whom he met at a *Prisoner* convention – and their three children. He enjoys contact with fans of the series and McGoohan from around the world and has recently assisted with *Prisoner* or *Danger Man* projects in USA, France, Italy, Germany and Australia, as well as in his home country. Langley wrote *The Prisoner in Portmeirion* (1999), *The Prisoner Series Guide* (2005) and the recent US *Prisoner DVD Megaset* booklet. He has produced maps and other publications about the series over many years and continues to provide magazines for its appreciation society.

APPENDIX SEVEN

ACKNOWLEDGEMENTS

This biography of Patrick McGoohan arose simply from the writer originally compiling a 'screenography' of his work, fifteen years ago. The resulting book just 'grew', being written during the intervening period – when time was available – with each newly found press cutting, article, or interview meaning amending and expanding the text, sometimes completely rearranging it. Even so, this biography could have been considerably longer; covering individually the actor's stage work, or more than a hundred *Danger Man* and *Prisoner* episodes or all his other screen work, could each have produced a separate book.

This study of McGoohan's achievements is, like the man, the sum of its parts. There is no bibliography within this book for one simple reason. Prior to the arrival of this biography, there were no books dedicated to the actor and so there were none which could be used as resources. However, in writing a book such as this one, where the details cover four score years, it is of course necessary to consult a variety of sources. It is fortunate that tributes to McGoohan are plentiful, in the form of numerous articles over the years, or nowadays in the form of websites and even web logs, "blogs." It is not this writer's intention simply to reproduce this material, or to plagiarise. For this reason, throughout the text and separately, journalists and other various interviewers have been named and credited wherever possible, as has the publication in which their words appeared. Thanks are expressed here to the various writers and publications referred to during the writing of this book and to other persons who lent assistance with the compiling of data from many different origins.

The writer has himself built up a collection of material and memorabilia relating to McGoohan over several decades. During this time, there has been contact with other admirers of the actor, who have generously provided items from their own collections. Other sources within *The Prisoner* appreciation society plus Internet locations added to the well-stocked information platform, from which this biography could be created. This writer thanks all the people who, over the years, have ensured that the McGoohan story – many would say legend – has been preserved.

Credit is therefore not only due to the many publications mentioned or listed in this book, but in addition, the writer acknowledges, alphabetically, Camera Obscura magazine, Classic Images magazine, the BFI and Internet Movie Database websites, plus other publications mentioned within this book, or its reference section. Also, friends, colleagues and persons whose contributions helped fill in blanks are gratefully noted here, alphabetically: Ingrid Augustin, Jacques Baudou, Alain Carrazé, Bruce Clark,[i] Matthew Courtman,

---

[i] Bruce – Six of One's North American organiser – is also credited separately below as to his exclusive photographs used in this book and is also thanked for undertaking helpful enquiries in the US, as well as being a channel of communication between the writer and American people.

Simon Coward, Billy Cutshaw, Patrick Ducher, Philippe Ferrari, Leon Finch, S.J. Gillis, Max Hora, Phil Kendrick, Patrick Kilmer and Sheila Joslin, Will Leslie, Glenies McCairns, Jeanne Moyer, Richard Myers, Hélène Oswald, Victoria Peers, Michelle Perry, Barbara Pruett, Steven Ricks, Isobel Smith, Andrew Staton, Davey Taeusch and Rae Wittrick. A few names belong to persons who were not directly contacted by the writer, but whose information, from writings, helped greatly in verifying dates or events etc. Gratitude is expressed to the senders of many other cuttings, from within the membership of Six of One, provided to the writer from around the world over many years. He regrets any omission of names, either through inadvertence, or as a result of no longer having the details.

Special thanks are also due to Antonia Coffman and Mike Scully of the Fox Film Corporation, Sue Crabtree, of the University of Kent, Moonyean Edwards, of the Theatre Royal, Windsor, Peter Falk, Jan'et, of Peter Falk's Office, Robin Llywelyn, of Portmeirion Hotel, Norman McInerney of the Irish Valuation Office, Andre Perkowski, Frank Ratcliffe, formerly of ITC/PolyGram, Sian Truszkowska, of the Ratcliffian Association, Kathy McNulty Webb, a distant McGoohan relative and Louise Weston, of the BBC Written Archive.

Warm thanks are also expressed to the people of Sheffield and environs: John Bishop, James Blake, Ron Clayton, Bill and Ted Cummings, Ann Dale, Bryan Dunstan, Martin Fenwick, Mary Fleming, Margaret Goodson, Audrey Haden, Vincent Hale, Geoff and George Hespe, James Larkin, Teresa Lodge, Vincent Maher, Duncan Miller, Kathleen Page, Christine Smith, Kevin Smith, Shelagh Turner, Ted Wainwright, Kitty Ward and Tony Womack.

Also, mention is needed regarding some photographs in this book. Several of the *Danger Man/Secret Agent* were exclusively provided by Bruce Clark, the US representative of Six of One. The four photos of repertory performances come from the Sheffield Theatre history book by T. Alec Seed, 1959. Other photos and illustrations gratefully used come from publicity material, theatrical programmes, or film and video releases etc., or are from the writer's own collection. Copyright, where applicable, remains with the original owners. As to quotations used in this book, most are specifically referenced – there are also extracts from original ITC, other production company publicity releases and material from within Six of One – or are stated to be unknown if that is the case.[ii] As a general rule, where more than one quotation appears in the book from a single source, the endnote to identify the item appears next to the last of the quotations used.

One essential acknowledgment can be recorded here, being the *Prisoner* Appreciation Society itself and its founding member, David Barrie. Without the formation of the Society – its existence spanning thirty years – there would never have been so much interest in McGoohan. As Six of One's Honorary President through three decades, the actor repaid the Society's interest in his classic television series, in the form of support for Six of One. Its thousands of members across the decades and their millions of hours of time freely given to events and publications, over the decades, have ensured that McGoohan's profile remains high.

Immeasurable thanks go to this writer's wife, Karen, who transcribed scores of dictation tapes to create the book's various drafts, dealt with myriad insertions and updates, as well as finding countless things which had been misplaced, or covered up and were thus 'lost.' Quite simply, this book could not have been completed without her invaluable assistance. Also, the writer particularly thanks Bruce Sachs, of Tomahawk Press for his essential input and improvements, as well as editing this book. And thanks to Steve Kirkham of Tree Frog for his excellent work on designing the book.

In closing, the words of many fine actors who worked with McGoohan – some of whom are no longer with us – will not be forgotten. Expressions of respect for the quality of *The Prisoner* and its star have come from the mouths of his co-actors over the years. This writer had the good fortune to meet with many of them.

[ii] In some cases where details were inadvertently not retained, the writer has not been able to locate original sources. Also, some cuttings were kindly supplied to the writer over the years with no details provided by the senders.

For more information about Patrick McGoohan and The Prisoner, Six of One – the official appreciation society since 1977 – produces mailings and holds conventions in Portmeirion.
www.sixofone.co.uk
www.sixofone.org.uk
www.portmeiricon.com
www.ThePrisonerAppreciationSociety.com

ADDITIONAL PHOTO CREDITS

Chapter 1: Photo from the play *A Hundred Years Old*, courtesy of Kitty Ward

Chapter 2: Sheffield Repertory photos from *The Sheffield Repertory Theatre: A History*, 1959, by T. Alec Seed

Chapter 3: *The Greatest Man in the World* photos from *The Armchair Theatre*, 1959, ABC Television

Chapter 4: Several *Danger Man*, or *Secret Agent*, photos courtesy of Bruce Clark

Chapter 9: Two *Hard Way* photos courtesy of Frank Ratcliffe

Chapter 10: *Jamaica Inn* signed photo courtesy of Arabella McIntyre-Brown

Chapter 11: Motor Show photo of McGoohan seated in car and wearing sunglasses courtesy of Arabella McIntyre-Brown

Four pictures first appeared in the 1988 Performing Arts Annual, published by the Library of Congress, Washington, USA

INDEX

Not listed separately within this index are: "Patrick McGoohan," *Danger Man*, or *The Prisoner*, or names of individual episodes, or their main characters – as they appear throughout this book – or Appendices, footnotes, endnotes and illustrations. Episode titles are listed, with story synopses, in Appendix One, as are non-British titles for McGoohan's films and television work. Some alternative titles for films are given, but mainly these appear in Appendix One. Journalists and their publications are generally not included, but do appear in the lists of reference sources, at the end of chapters.

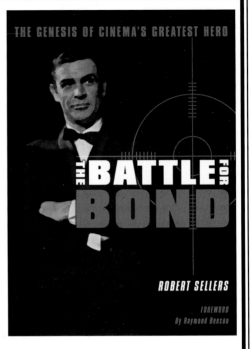